INFERNO

Dante Alighieri

INFERNO

Translated by
Stanley Lombardo

Introduction by
Steven Botterill

Notes by
Anthony Oldcorn

Hackett Publishing Company, Inc.
Indianapolis/Cambridge

For further information, please address:

Hackett Publishing Company, Inc.
P.O. Box 44937
Indianapolis, IN 46244-0937

www.hackettpublishing.com

Cover design by Brian Rak and Carrie Wagner
Interior design by Carrie Wagner
Composition by Agnew's, Inc.
Printed at Versa Press, Inc.

Library of Congress Cataloging-in-Publication Data

Dante Alighieri, 1265–1321.
  [Inferno. English & Italian]
  Inferno / Dante Alighieri ; translated by Stanley Lombardo ;
introduction by Steven Botterill ; notes by Anthony Oldcorn.
    p.   cm.
  Includes bibliographical references and index.
  ISBN 978-0-87220-917-6 (pbk.) — ISBN 978-0-87220-918-3 (cloth)
  I. Lombardo, Stanley, 1943–   II. Title.
  PQ4315.2.L64 2009
  851′.1—dc22

                                                      2008048091

The paper used in this publication meets the minimum requirements of American
National Standard for Information Sciences—Permanence of Paper for Printed
Library Materials, ANSI Z39.48–1984.

For

Brian Rak

il miglior fabbro

Contents

Introduction

"To me, the whole world is a homeland, like the sea to fish. . . ." Thus wrote Dante Alighieri, probably between 1303 and 1305, in *On Eloquence in the Vernacular* (*De vulgari eloquentia* [*DVE*]), his unfinished prose treatise on language. Like the writing for which Dante is most famous—his poetry—this statement conveys multiple meanings: on the one hand, a declaration of the boundlessness of Dante's interests, on the other, an allusion to his life in exile. It is, moreover, prophetic; the composition of the great poem in which Dante would chronicle his journey through that *other* world, the afterworld, still lay ahead of him, even if the experience that poem purports to relate was supposed to have transpired in the year 1300. Dante's cognizance of the unbounded world that was his homeland would prove to be mutual: though the *Divine Comedy* was published to immediate acclaim in his native Italy and has been read and studied ever since its first canticle, *Inferno,* first appeared in the second decade of the fourteenth century, the *Comedy* (or *Comedía,* as he titled it) has never been more widely read or more intensely studied than it is today. If Dante once claimed the whole world as his home, today the world or at least the Western world claims him as one of the brightest gems of its cultural inheritance.

Written in Italian, or to be more precise, Tuscan (since the nationalized language we know as Italian did not yet exist), the poem was the work of an extremely ambitious poet who was also a keen observer of the variability of ordinary European languages across time and space, an arbiter of their uses and prospects, and—significantly—a politician forced into exile from his native Florence. As ambitious as Dante was, however, his ambitions were focused not solely on his own destiny and that of his poem, but also on the particular kind of language in which it was written. Dante's Tuscan was a vernacular, or a natural, historically variable language—the ordinary, everyday kind of language that we learn, as he put it, "from nurses and those who bring us up" (*DVE* I.i)—a kind of language he thought nobler than what he saw as artificial, grammar-based, unchanging languages like Latin. Dante, moreover, saw the vernacular as capable of great eloquence, and—in what he called its most exalted, or "illustrious," form—as even having the potential to offer a kind of redemption of the fractious political order he knew so well. Though not always in the precise ways he might have hoped, Dante's ambitions proved well founded. The histories of the *Comedy* and of modern European languages—or at least the Italian one that the *Comedy* would in fact do much toward calling into being—are so intimately connected that it can be difficult to imagine one without the other.

So immediately successful and widely disseminated was Dante's poem in his native Italy that more than eight hundred handwritten manuscripts survive from the fourteenth century alone. In England, Chaucer initiated the *Comedy*'s reception, responding to its themes and drawing on its techniques in some of his own poems, themselves written, like the *Comedy,* in a rapidly mutating vernacular whose development they would influence. But the remarkable success of the *Comedy* in the fourteenth century gave way to relative neglect in the early modern era, by which time various philosophical and theological underpinnings of the *Comedy* came to seem as outmoded as the Aristotelian and scholastic ideas in which many of them had their roots. To others, neo-Latin seemed a more promising and elegant vehicle for literary expression than the vernacular and sometime coarse language of the *Comedy.* The poem's moment seemed to have passed.

Romantic nostalgia for things medieval, Gothic tastes for the *Inferno*'s hair-raising narrative, and nationalism coincided with a reversal of these fortunes. In nineteenth-century Italy, the *Comedy* came to be recognized as a national epic, the source of an entire literary tradition and, in many ways, of the very language in which that tradition finds expression. It became an object of fascination for English-speaking readers in the late eighteenth to early nineteenth century, with the appearance of a stream of translations that has continued to this day and whose surge in recent years has made it a commercial and linguistic as well as a literary phenomenon. Nor were English-speaking writers immune to its charms; the *Comedy* served as a master text on both sides of the Atlantic for such nineteenth-century authors as Tennyson, George Eliot, and Longfellow before becoming, in the twentieth century, the incongruous touchstone of Modernism in the hands of Pound, T. S. Eliot, Joyce, and others.

And the Italian and English linguistic communities are far from the only ones on which the poem has left its mark. It has, for example, served as a model for many Russian writers, including Gogol, Mandelstam, and Solzhenitsyn, and has been translated—mostly in the past few decades—into scores of other languages, including Mongolian and Welsh. Visual artists too have taken inspiration from it: Botticelli, Blake, Delacroix, Doré, and Amos Nattini among many others have depicted its scenes, and filmmakers and graphic novelists have drawn on or adapted it, from Fellini, Pasolini, and Peter Greenaway to the comic book and animated versions of the *Comedy* by Sandow Birk, which are set in the cities of a postapocalyptic but eerily familiar North America. A poet once seen as a vulgar apologist for an obsolete worldview has today successfully ridden so many successive and far-reaching waves of literary, linguistic, and art history as to have become—in a vernacular phrase whose coinage and application to Dante would not have surprised him—a global icon.

Dante and Our Life of Mind and Body

Yet despite its worldwide celebrity and universally acknowledged cultural significance, Dante's masterpiece is, all too often, still not *known*. To be sure, the *Comedy* places considerable demands on its audience despite having been written in the vernacular for a wide, general audience rather than in Latin—a literary language that by the fourteenth century was known only to scholars and clerics. Any reader[1] of the poem must have some familiarity with, among other things, the basics of Christian theology, the Christian and Hebrew

---

1. Here and in what follows, "reader" and "listener" (as well as variations on these terms) are used interchangeably. Low literacy rates in the fourteenth century ensured that the majority of the *Comedy*'s early audience consisted of listeners to a poem either read aloud by someone who was literate or recited wholly or in part from memory.

scriptures, classical mythology, classical and medieval philosophical thought, and the politics of Dante's day—or at least have ready access to such basics by way of commentary or footnotes provided by scholars. But in the end, the audience that Dante most desires and that the *Inferno* most fundamentally assumes is one of intelligent human beings interested in what it means to be human.

The *Inferno,* like the *Comedy* as a whole, has its seed in Dante's thinking about the human condition, a subject with which he was clearly at grips in the *De vulgari eloquentia,* begun a few years before he began the *Inferno.* For the author of the *De vulgari eloquentia,* the human being is uniquely situated in the universe, at the nexus of body and soul, physical and spiritual, material and immaterial. Neither pure matter like nonrational animals nor pure spirit like angels, human beings alone are created in the image of God, the God who became incarnate in Jesus Christ and continues to sustain His creation in existence through the activity of the divine mind. With this uniqueness comes unique responsibility. As rational animals, members of the human race are not called upon to follow natural instinct as nonrational animals are; rather, they are led by reason, which takes diverse forms in different individuals—to the extent that each individual is nearly a species unto him- or herself.

Such diversity precludes the possibility that one might know the actions and feelings of another simply by knowing one's own actions and feelings, as Dante claims nonrational animals do with other members of their own species—and are able to do because nonrational animals of the same species are identical with respect to action and feeling. (For Dante, interspecies understanding between nonrational animals seems to be a theoretical impossibility, and at any rate, would serve no communal purpose.) Human knowledge of the inner lives of others requires something more: speech.

Speech is a signal based on reason (that is, instilled with meaning) and mediated through sense perception (since humans, unlike angels, cannot know the thoughts of others through sheer intellection) that allows us "to expound to others the concepts formed in our minds" (*DVE* I.ii). If this signal were purely rational, notes Dante, "it could not make its journey; if purely perceptible, it would neither derive anything from reason nor deliver anything to it" (*DVE* I.iii). Like the plot of the *Divine Comedy,* the rational-perceptible compound that is speech thus involves a kind of journey—in this instance, one that is a precondition for the possibility of understanding between human beings and, by implication, for human community itself.

For Dante, the faculty of reason is subject to abuse, as it was when humans in their pride tried to build the Tower of Babel, or the Tower of Confusion, and were punished with the *confusio linguarum* ("confusion of languages"), the creation of the multiple languages from which the vernaculars we now speak have descended:

> And the earth was of one tongue, and of the same speech. . . . And they said: Come, let us make a city and a tower, the top whereof may reach to heaven: and let us make our name famous before we be scattered abroad into all lands. And the Lord came down to see the city and the tower, which the children of Adam were building.
>
> And he said: Behold, it is one people, and all have one tongue: and they have begun to do this, neither will they leave off from their designs, till they accomplish them in deed. Come ye, therefore, let us go down, and there confound their tongue, that they may not understand one another's speech. And so the Lord scattered them from that place into all lands, and they ceased to build the city. And therefore the name thereof was called *Babel,* because there the language of the whole earth was confounded: and from thence the Lord scattered them abroad upon the face of all countries. (Gen. 11:1, 4–9)

By means of a kind of punishment especially suited to the sin, or *contrapasso* (a model that Dante will follow repeatedly in the *Inferno*), what is, on Dante's reading, the abuse of the faculty of reason exemplified by the building of the Tower of Babel was punished with a blow to a crucial component of that faculty—the intelligibility of speech itself—a blow that, were it not limited or mitigated, would have left each human stranded in his or her own world.

But reason can also be used properly, e.g., to rejoice in God, as it was when Adam spoke the first word, the name of God: "If, since the disaster that befell the human race, the speech of every one of us has begun with 'woe!,' it is reasonable that he who existed before should have begun with a cry of joy; and, since there is no joy outside God, but all joys are in God, and since God Himself is joy itself, it follows that the first man to speak should first and before all have said 'God'" (*DVE* I.iv). The duty to use rational thought not only to convey but also to respond to meaning as the basis of a rightly ordered life—as Adam responded to the presence of God—is fundamental to Dante's conception of human life. It is in turn fundamental to the demands he places upon readers of the *Comedy,* a poem as intellectually, morally, and politically profound as it is rich in image and sound.

It soon becomes clear to any reader of the *Inferno,* for example, that this is no ordinary story but one whose depths are often merely suggested by its surface. The poem begins in what appears to be a recognizable, even banal set of circumstances, especially for a medieval audience: the narrator tells that he once found himself lost in a dark wood, that at dawn he made his way out and began climbing a hill, only to be menaced by wild animals from which he was saved by the intervention of a stranger. But well before the appearance of this stranger, it becomes clear that none of these things is exactly, or only, what it seems: the traveler is journeying not only through a wood but through life, "our life" (I.1); the animals are unusually fierce and colorful, and some belong to species not commonly found in the woodlands of medieval Tuscany; the stranger turns out first to be the soul of a man long dead and then to be not just any random revenant but none other than the great Roman poet Virgil. By the middle of the first canto of the *Inferno,* then, barely three score lines of verse into our reading, we already know that the story we are to be told will be, in an important sense, fantastic; that it will point to understandings beyond the literal level of its narrative (that "dark wood" of the second line of the poem, for example, though intelligible enough on a literal level, is surely too rich in its suggestiveness to be interpreted on a literal level alone); and that it will take place not in the world we know from our own tangible experience but in the one we might hypothesize, or even believe in, as awaiting us after death. The traveler's journey, we now realize, will take him—and us—not only through this life of ours but also through the life to come.

Questioning *Inferno*

The skillfully orchestrated atmosphere of mystery with which the *Inferno* opens is, in part but crucially, a straightforward narrative device aimed at capturing the interest of readers and ensuring that they continue to pay attention to find out what happens next. Canto I deliberately puzzles the reader in order to create suspense: Where are we? Who is telling us this story? What is going on here? Why is this happening? What does it all *mean?* The reader's experience of the *Inferno* thus begins in questions, questions to which the answers do not always become apparent right away—often, indeed, not until much more of the text, of the *Inferno* alone or even of the other two parts of the *Comedy,* has finally been digested. (Many clues laid down in the *Inferno* are not resolved—if they ever are—until the *Paradiso,* the third and final canticle; the *Comedy* is carefully structured so as, ideally, to keep us reading beyond the end of its first and most immediately attractive section.) Dante, indeed, seems in some ways more interested in questions than in answers. Contrary to the popular (mis)conception of him as narrowly judgmental, didactic, and dogmatic, his approach from the very beginning is to put things before his readers and invite them to sort them out for themselves.

Everyone may "know," for example, that the three beasts of Canto I represent Lust, Pride, and Avarice—or something else—but the poem itself nowhere says so. Rather, it presents us with compelling plot and captivating images, makes clear that it encourages a reading that penetrates beneath the surface (most explicitly in the several interventions in authorial voice that have collectively become known as "Dante's addresses to the reader"), and goes on to charge us with the duty of using our divinely bestowed powers of reasoning to work out a satisfactory interpretation. This approach remains constant throughout the narrative of the *Inferno.* Readers follow along in the company of the protagonist and his guide Virgil, partake in the encounters with men, women, and demons that the narrative recounts, and learn from those encounters—or not, or not yet—just as the protagonist does, in accordance with their own abilities and their gradually developing understanding. As author, Dante is of course pulling all the strings; but that does not make us—or even his characters—his puppets. If anything, he so arranges matters as to call into question many of the most important things that his own text asserts, at least to the extent of requiring readers to think about them actively rather than to accept them passively, on the text's own authority, like so many baby cuckoos in the authorial nest.

The most striking example of this, I repeat, constant approach is perhaps found in the sequence of cantos that follow the dramatic episode at the beginning of Canto III in which the protagonist and Virgil find themselves at the Gate of Hell, above which is written a series of propositional statements and a final warning:

> THROUGH ME IS THE WAY TO THE CITY OF WOE.
>   THROUGH ME IS THE WAY TO SORROW ETERNAL.
>   THROUGH ME IS THE WAY TO THE LOST BELOW.
> JUSTICE MOVED MY ARCHITECT SUPERNAL.
>   I WAS CONSTRUCTED BY DIVINE POWER,
>   SUPREME WISDOM, AND LOVE PRIMORDIAL.
> BEFORE ME NO CREATED THINGS WERE
>   SAVE THOSE ETERNAL, AND ETERNAL I ABIDE.
>   ABANDON ALL HOPE, YOU WHO ENTER.
>
> (III.1–9)

The imperative—"Abandon all hope, you who enter"—has become probably the most famous single line in the whole Dantean corpus. The propositions are less renowned but equally characteristic of the fundamentals of Dante's project. This gate, the hammering verses tell us, is the way to eternal suffering; and it was made, for all eternity, by divine power, the supreme wisdom, and primordial love, all motivated by justice.

To dip into the poisoned well of marketing jargon, this is Hell's mission statement, the clearest and most economical expression of its purpose and the circumstances of its creation. The inscription carries, within the terms of Dante's narrative at least, absolute authority. And yet much of what immediately follows in that narrative seems expressly designed to cast doubt upon its validity. No sooner have the protagonist and Virgil passed through the gate than they meet a group of sinners whose fate seems at odds with the sense of finality and order suggested by the inscription. The so-called "neutrals" of Canto III are specifically designated as belonging really neither to Hell nor to Heaven, because their moral cowardice (in failing to choose either good or evil) is so repugnant that neither arm of the postmortem universe's judicial system wants anything to do with them. Their anomalous position in the hereafter betrays itself in fact as less a consequence of "justice" than of historical contingencies within the judicial system itself.

As Virgil and the protagonist advance, they (and we) meet another group of souls who, we are told, did not sin at all—except that they were never baptized (a prerequisite for salvation, even for infants) and did not worship the Christian God, a deity whose existence some of them, at least, never had the opportunity to learn about because they were born and lived their otherwise virtuous lives outside the chronological, cultural, and/or geographical remit of Christianity. Yet divine power, wisdom, and love, inspired by justice, have combined to damn them for all eternity. Where exactly, says a voice in at least some readers' heads, is the justice in that? What kind of power could enforce such a justice, what kind of wisdom could find it prudent, what kind of love could allow it? To return to the case of the "neutrals," what does it say not only about the Supernal Architect but also about His creation when the vestibule of what is surely one of His most intricately designed structures is populated with souls of a kind that cannot be accommodated within the structure proper? And consider Francesca da Rimini (Canto V), perhaps the most notorious, and certainly the most discussed, case of moral ambiguity in all the *Inferno:* if her plight reflects only the majestic workings of infallible divine justice, in which the believing Christian, surely, is meant only to rejoice, how can she present such a powerful case in her own defense that the poem's protagonist is moved to tears of pity for her and finally faints dead away?

Less important than the exact formulation of such questions— or even the fact that they, and others like them, often turn out to have no single satisfactory or authoritative answer—is the fact that they can be posed at all. They are, indeed, designed to be posed by the structure of the *Inferno* itself. From the outset of its narrative (after Cantos I and II have set the scene and explained the "backstory" that accounts for Virgil and the protagonist's presence on it), the *Inferno* makes clear that the story it tells is intended to be subjected to questioning. Its characters—especially the protagonist—frequently ask questions along the way, and they receive variably reliable and informative answers. Questions taking the form of objections may be temporarily silenced, as are those of the ferry pilot Charon by Virgil in III.96—"question us no more"—yet the objections keep coming. In Canto V, Minos, judge of the Underworld, picks up where Charon left off, and it appears in Canto VII that Plutus, for all of his cackling, does the same on behalf of Minos. A reader is expected to be no less on guard. Simply to accept the provocatively unjust-seeming damnation of the virtuous pagans, lazily to condemn Francesca in spite of the rhetorical force with which she defends herself, is too easy—is, indeed, an abdication, from Dante's point of view, of the reader's human responsibility to try to see why things are as they are.

Not that the damnation of the virtuous pagans is *actually* unjust, or that Francesca's self-defense is actually valid; that could indeed never be. For Dante the convinced but relentlessly inquiring Christian believer, the propositions over the Gate of Hell are, in the final analysis, true, and in God's universe they could never be otherwise. They may be, as the protagonist complains, "hard" (III.12)—difficult to comprehend, painful in their application, and subversive of our assumptions about the way things are and the way things should be. But they remain open to scrutiny and, by implication, to questioning. Like foot traffic on the Ponte Sant' Angelo in the Jubilee year of 1300 (XVIII.28–33), however, questions between the reader and the text of the *Inferno* run in both directions, and we may find ourselves answering in ways that we could not have predicted any number of questions posed by the text to *us*. In urging us to think about ultimate truth, the *Inferno* aims to activate within us the principles of upright living—virtue, in a word—that should motivate every moment of our lives in this world, so that the understanding

of Hell we may acquire in this life will never be translated into ac-
tual experience after death.

Because—for all that the narrative of the *Inferno* is set in the next
world—the poem is very much about this one. Yes, it offers a rep-
resentation of how Hell literally and actually is, and there seems to
be no reason to doubt that Dante believed this representation to be,
in some sense, a true one (though exactly in *what* sense is a question
that has generated some of the most intelligent and provocative
Dante scholarship of the past several years). But because, as we have
seen, the literal level of the *Inferno's* narrative and imagery consis-
tently and designedly directs attention beyond itself to ways of read-
ing that find meaning beneath the surface level of the literal, it
becomes easier to see that the poem's representation of an actually
existing Hell is not the sole purpose for which it is called into being.
Instead, that representation itself becomes—or at least *can* become—
a starting point for thinking about a subject by no means uncon-
nected to the soul's eternal destiny but inevitably, for most of us,
somewhat closer to home: the life of this world rather than the next.

(Auto)Biography in Hell

Like most narratives created by human beings, the *Inferno* tells the
story of one of our own—a fellow human being—placed in a par-
ticular set of (perhaps extraordinary) circumstances and responding
to them in accordance with a particular set of (perhaps not so ex-
traordinary) human capacities. In fact it tells many such stories, if
the whole panoply of characters who populate Dante's Hell is taken
into account, all of them present there as embodiments of their own
individual experience, whether this be articulated through the
lengthy self-regarding speeches of a Brunetto Latini (Canto XV) or
an Ugolino (Cantos XXXII–XXXIII) or through a single dismis-
sive epithet applied to them by the narrator. And because the *Inferno*
is also a tale of the afterlife, and therefore, in one sense, of the fan-
tastic, it includes the stories of many beings who are not human at
all, from the Gate of Hell itself, to the variously hybrid monsters
who staff the structure of Hell, to the heavenly emissary who comes
to rescue Virgil and the protagonist from their perplexity before

the gates of Dis in Canto IX. But at its core is the narrated experience of a single, human character, whom until now I have been calling "the protagonist." His identity, his very name, takes second place, as that drama unfolds, to his dramatic function (the name itself is only revealed, in a moment of high emotional excitement, in the great scene of recognition and purification at the very end of the *Purgatorio*).

Throughout the *Inferno,* our hero remains, strictly speaking, anonymous; and yet, of course, we somehow "know" that his name is Dante. We garner enough details along the way (especially—and this is a not insignificant point about the way we read Dante today—if we read the footnotes) to deduce that the character who says "I" in the course of the infernal journey—both in the real time of events happening in the plot and in the retrospective recollection entrusted to the narrator, the protagonist's older and wiser self who has completed the journey through all three realms of the afterlife—has a personal history and a set of experiences that are in every way compatible with what we know of those of Dante Alighieri of Florence, born there in the spring of 1265 and therefore exactly "midway through the journey of our life"—halfway through the canonical seventy-year life span—when the protagonist of the *Inferno* sets out on his journey in the spring of 1300.

Not only does Dante, as both protagonist and narrator, tell us what happened to him in Hell; his tale harks constantly back to what happened to him on Earth. Likewise, all the characters he encounters along his way, from the most prominent to the most insignificant, are seen not only in the lurid light of their current, infernal circumstances but also in that other light—however they may try, usually in vain, to give it a warm nostalgic glow—of the lives, the choices, the deeds that brought them to this pass. The present tense of the *Inferno* depends for its meaning on the past tense of life on Earth. The very fact that earthly life is now so irredeemably past, that the endless appalling present of Hell is all that there now is or will ever be, is the characters' tragedy—or would be if the reader were not called upon, as suggested above, to work out why their fate is just and therefore not tragic.

As the only character in the *Inferno* who is still in a position to learn, grow, and change, Dante the protagonist, endowed as he is with his own personal history but learning now to view it against the background of history as a seamless and providentially ordered unity, comes to stand for his readers. He is then, among other things, a stand-in for those who are still alive and therefore capable of change, of contemplating the possible future outcomes of their own lives by reflecting on the fates of the dead, themselves so numerous that he "had not thought death had undone so many" (III.57). (Auto)biography and its readership thus become the means by which human history is introduced into the eternity of Hell, and the timeless truth of what Hell is manages to throw revealing—and warning—light on what life on Earth still can, and cannot, be.

Instances of autobiography in the *Inferno* are numerous and varied in both tone and substance; indeed, it could be said that every time the inhabitants of Hell open their mouths—or try to—they add another page to the narrative of their lives, and afterlives. Some individual stories are brief but unforgettable, like the sting-in-the-tail confession made by the nameless suicide of Canto XIII:

> I was from the city that changed her first patron
> > for the Baptist, for which the one who gave place
> Will plague her forever with his wars.
> > And if at the Arno's bridge there was no trace
> > > or fading semblance of that ancient god, Mars,
> Those citizens who built her up again
> > when Attila made ashes of what used to be
> > > would have performed their labor all in vain.
> I turned my house into my gallows tree.
>
> (XIII.143–51)

Other stories are extensive, elaborate, even occasionally poignant self-revelations, carefully shaped by their speakers to convey the best possible impression of their own past achievements and present situation. But, usually, at the same time, they are crafted by their author so as to present lastingly powerful images of the human capacity for self-deception about our own actions and motivation and of the profound and painful moral ambiguity at the heart of every aspect of human behavior. The principal autobiographical narrators of the *Inferno* are Francesca (Canto V), Farinata (X), Piero della Vigna (XIII), Brunetto Latini (XV), Ulysses (XXVI), and Ugolino (XXXII–XXXIII), a group sometimes known, because of the ethical paradoxes on the basis of which every one of their self-portraits is constructed, as "Dante's noble sinners." Telling the truth—but telling it slant, and often unawares—they use all the rhetorical skill at their (or their author's) command as they create their own versions of events, deliver their own speeches for the defense, and present the proof of their own innocence. But all the time the context in which they speak—the depths of a Hell ordained by infallible divine justice—contradicts them unanswerably.

The poem's protagonist may faint for grief before Francesca, pay fulsome tribute to Brunetto, and display at least a political sympathy for Ugolino or Farinata. But we are called upon to listen more carefully than he does, to hear the truth that lies behind the words, to understand why whatever nobility these sinners may have possessed was never enough—however much they want us to think otherwise—to save them from damnation.

Consider, above all, Ulysses. His great autobiographical speech in Canto XXVI is deliberately highlighted as a rhetorical set piece by many features of the text (including Virgil's reverent introduction of the speaker, the way in which Dante is prevented from even speaking to him, much less interrupting or asking questions, and his immediate departure from the narrative scene the moment his story is told). Its content has always been recognized by readers as an exciting traveler's tale culminating in an astonishingly powerful statement of humanity's fundamental aspirations to knowledge and understanding, aspirations that the author of the *Comedy* clearly shared and that his poem is, to an extent, designed to impart to its readers:

> When I left
> Circe, who had held me back
> a year or more on her isle near Gaeta,
> before Aeneas gave it that name,

Neither the sweet thought of my son, nor reverence
    for my old father, not the love I owed
        Penelope and that would have made her glad
Could overcome my burning desire
    for experience of the wide world above
        and of men's vices and their valor.
I put forth on the deep, open sea
    with one ship only, and a skeleton crew
        of companions who had not deserted me.
I went up one coast, then another, as far as Spain,
    as far as Morocco; I saw Sardinia
        and the other islands lapped by the waves.
My crew and I were old and slow
    when we pulled into the narrow straits
        where Hercules had set up his pillars
To mark where men should not pass beyond.
    I had left Seville on the starboard side
        and off the port left Ceuta behind.
"Brothers," I said, "who through a hundred
    thousand perils have reached the West,
        do not deny to the last glimmering hour
Of consciousness that remains to us
    experience of the unpeopled world
        that lies beyond the setting sun.
Consider the seed from which you were born!
    You were not made to live like brute animals
        but to live in pursuit of virtue and knowledge!"
This little speech steeled my crew's hearts
    and made them so eager for the voyage ahead
        I could hardly have restrained them afterward.
We swung the stern toward the morning light
    and made our oars wings for our last, mad run,
        the ship's left side always gaining on the right.
All of the stars around the opposite pole
    now shone in the night, while our own was so low
        it did not rise above the ocean's roll.
Five times had we seen it wax and wane,

the light on the underside of the moon,
   since we began our journey on the main,
And then a mountain loomed in the sky,
   still dim and distant, but it seemed to me
   I had never seen any mountain so high.
We shouted for joy, but our joy now
   turned into grief, for a whirlwind roared
      out of the new land and struck the ship's prow.
Three times it spun her around in the water,
   and the fourth time around, up the stern rose
   and the prow plunged down, as pleased Another,
Until above us we felt the waters close.

(XXVI.90–142)

Yet for all of its inspiring rhetoric and narrative appeal, Ulysses' speech is rotten at its core. As the speech unfolds and as it is implicitly commented upon in both the canto that directly follows it and at the beginning of the *Purgatorio* (where the mountain of lines 133–35 will again come into view—only now revealed as the island mountain of Purgatory itself), the speech reveals itself as an account of a series of wicked acts and, for anyone who might listen to it carelessly, even as potentially corrupting. For "at that stage of life when it befits a man / to lower his sails and coil up his ropes" (XXVII.80–81), Ulysses in fact disregarded his obligations to home and family, behaved in a manner inappropriate to his (old) age, transgressed a boundary fixed by the deities of his own religious culture, surrendered to an illegitimate desire to know things he (by divine will) was never meant to know, and, worst of all, used the linguistic skill and crafty wiles for which he had always been famous to persuade others to join him on his illicit and foredoomed voyage beyond the limits of the permissible to destruction. (The self-exculpating false modesty of XXVI.121–23 alone—"This little speech steeled my crew's hearts / and made them so eager for the voyage ahead / I could hardly have restrained them afterward"— should be enough to give any listener pause.)

Ulysses' self-presentation as a dauntless hero of the human spirit— plausible enough when lines 118–20 are quoted, as they often are, out of context ("Consider the seed from which you were born! / You were not made to live like brute animals / but to live in pursuit of virtue and knowledge!")—crumbles to dust when his words are heard in their infernal setting. And we are left, as we always are when the denizens of Dante's Hell claim to be telling us the truth about themselves, with something much more complex, more challenging, and in the end more compelling than the story that the character thought he (or she) was telling us.

For it should not be forgotten that Dante, as author, clearly does resonate to Ulysses' challenge (as would, centuries later, Primo Levi—in the unimaginably horrible circumstances in which he depicts himself, in *If This Is a Man*, struggling to recite the Ulysses canto in Auschwitz),[2] and that those lines about the essentially human yearning for knowledge and virtue do still encapsulate an idea of inescapable centrality to Dante, one that the whole *Comedy* sometimes seems to have been conceived and written to illustrate. Indeed, so central is the yearning for knowledge and virtue to Dante that the autobiography of Dante (himself an intellectual and poetic voyager into the unknown whose voyage is sanctioned by God) will come to supplant that of Ulysses (a voyager who was bold but misguided precisely in that he exceeded divinely imposed natural limits without divine sanction), as the supreme instance of what human intellect, art, and, crucially, virtue are capable of doing in the world. Ulysses' story, in short, is Dante's own; but if Dante is to be believed, it is Dante alone who can tell it with a happy ending.

Dante the Politician, Dante the Poet

Two aspects of the historical Dante's own biography have particular pertinence for the projection of that biography onto the protagonist of the *Inferno*: politics and poetry. The *Inferno* is saturated with politics—specifically with the politics of factional division, personal rivalry, and vicious internecine struggle within the city-state that Dante himself knew all too well during his career as an ambitious

---

2. See Primo Levi, *If This Is a Man,* translated by Stuart Woolf. New York: Orion Press, 1959; Italian title *Se questo è un uomo,* Turin: Da Silva, 1947.

aspirant to political glory in Florence in the 1280s and 1290s. The humiliating destruction of that career by the events of 1300–1301, when the governing party to which Dante belonged was violently overthrown by the conjoined machinations of its own internal opponents and the Papacy—and Dante forced into permanent exile— was probably the single most potent inspiration for the *Comedy* itself. It is not hard to see the whole series of writings that Dante undertook from about 1302 onward (*De vulgari eloquentia, Convivio,* the *Inferno,* and in due course the rest of the *Comedy*) as successive attempts, in different genres, to arrive at an intellectually and emotionally satisfying understanding of the issues—political, social, philosophical, even linguistic—raised by this cataclysm.

So throughout the *Inferno* appear characters from the recent political past of Florence and other Italian city-states, there to be held up for varying degrees of denunciation (and sometimes—Farinata in Canto X is the obvious and most powerful example—for a much more complex reevaluation of their real but morally complicated qualities). Throughout the *Inferno* the cities of medieval Italy are decried, one by one and often with linguistically appropriate slang terms of abuse, for their ethical and social failings at both the communal and the individual level. Throughout the *Inferno* Florence itself serves as the key example of a community destroyed by its own arrogance and corruption, indeed a Hell on Earth (just as Hell itself is a city that not only morally but even architecturally resembles Florence, with its walls, its gates, its towers, its pseudobaptismal fonts for condemned simoniacs that look like the real ones in the Florentine Baptistery of San Giovanni (XIX.16–21).

Here, of course, Dante is settling scores; the *Inferno* is, among much else, a prolonged howl of anguish and execration directed by its psychologically wounded author at the city and the men (chief among them Pope Boniface VIII) whom he blamed for the loss of all that he held dear. But there is more to it than that. The destruction of community that Dante experienced in Florence and that he depicts in Hell goes far beyond the personal suffering of a single individual, even when that individual is Dante Alighieri; it strikes at the very roots of what human beings, living in a divinely created and regulated universe, are meant to do and to be. The bonds of community, those shared social and moral values expressed and communicated in a shared vernacular language that were so deliberately and maliciously rent asunder in Florence—and that are utterly absent from Dante's Hell—are seen by Dante (once again from the *De vulgari eloquentia* onward) as a necessary part of God's plan for human happiness, neglected or damaged by human beings only at their mortal peril. Hell is the final destination of those who opt out of God's plan; and Hell as portrayed by Dante, with its innumerable images of sinners who cannot establish connections with other human beings because they cannot speak without lying, or cannot speak clearly, or cannot speak at all, becomes a kind of ghastly parody of Florence, the city where there was no community because no one's word could be trusted, no one spoke as or when they should have, no one spoke the truth. Dante's own experience of politics in the narrow sense undoubtedly stands at the heart of his articulation—which extends throughout the whole *Comedy,* and in ways that go far beyond the concentration on civic community and Florence that dominates the *Inferno*—of a vision of politics in the broadest possible sense, as the whole amalgam of values, practices, relationships, and capacities that enable human beings to form social units and thereby to overcome the ethical danger of solipsism by establishing viable and morally upright communities. This is where the inhabitants of Dante's Florence failed, and thus it is what the denizens of his Hell are likewise shown as failing to do; the Inferno is the realm of selfish individualism run rampant, the negation of community erected into a system of eternal punishment, a place, in short, where the concealed corruption at the moral heart of human politics is laid bare.

But the young Dante was not only a politician; he was also a poet. The vital importance of that vocation for him is yet another of the many features of the *Inferno* that are adumbrated in the *De vulgari eloquentia,* in which poets—Dante himself prominent among them— are charged with the reform of the Italian vernacular through the development of a newly charged poetic diction that will serve as the basis for the creation of not just cultural but even political unity throughout the Italian peninsula. Poets and their poetry are equally prominent in the *Inferno,* for good and ill. Most obviously, Dante's guide on his journey is a poet, Virgil, and is hailed as such from the first moment of his entry into the narrative (I.73–87). The presence of Virgil's most significant work, the *Aeneid*, is detectable on almost every page of the *Inferno*. This is especially so in the first few cantos, where not only are situations and imagery repeatedly owed to it but several passages are translated or adapted wholesale in an obvious act of homage at the intertextual level analogous to the overt tribute paid by the protagonist to Virgil at the time of their first meeting. (The *Aeneid,* indeed, can reasonably be seen as standing alongside the Bible as one of the two great predecessor texts on which the entire conception and achievement of the *Comedy* rest; and in the case of the *Inferno* at least, it should not be unthinkable to suggest that the *Aeneid* is the more important.)

And alongside the master poet Virgil appear many others, from his colleagues in the classical pantheon who form the reception committee that greets the travelers in Limbo to characters whose historical activity as poets clearly informs their representation as damned sinners (Piero della Vigna in Canto XIII and Brunetto Latini in Canto XV). Furthermore, traces of the work of many poets not actually present in the narrative are, of course, made clearly and constantly visible through allusion and other forms of reference. Even a hapless consumer of poetic production like Francesca da Rimini (Canto V) is shown as having learned enough about the art to reproduce its language—or its clichés—and to absorb its (questionable) morality. (In Francesca's case, the most blameworthy poet—the one who served best as the corrupting go-between for her and her lover—may well have been the author of the *Vita nuova* [*New Life*], a late thirteenth-century collection of lyric poems whose adjoining commentary stated unequivocally that a vernacular poet's only proper subject is love; its author was Dante himself.)

Poetry matters to Dante because it is the supreme instance of linguistic usage—the kind of language that, at its best, most effectively combines the communication of ideas with beauty—and because language itself is the supreme product of a uniquely human attribute, the possession both of a mind with which to think and of a body that can be used to express and communicate the nature of that thinking. For Dante, as we have seen, human beings are defined as the creatures who use language (as the *De vulgari eloquentia* explains, neither animals nor angels have or need it). And the human beings who use language the best—poets—are therefore, in some sense, the best human beings. But in what sense? Poets, after all, are obviously capable of sinning—as the presence in Hell of Piero della Vigna (Canto XIII), Brunetto Latini (XV), and Bertran de Born (XXVII) attests. The exploration of that question will turn out to be, along with the political theme mentioned above, one of the two main thematic threads that run through the whole of the *Inferno.*

The Limits of Poetry

The main vehicle for thematic treatment of poetry in the *Inferno* is the character Virgil. Introduced into the narrative (as noted above) precisely as a poet, and especially as the author of the *Aeneid,* he goes on to fulfill many other roles in the course of his journey with Dante—guide, philosopher, teacher, friend, mother figure, and (eventually in the *Purgatorio*) father figure—but all of them are centrally informed by his stature as poet. That, indeed, is the explanation given in Canto II for his being present in the narrative at all: there he explains that Dante's beloved Beatrice commissioned him to go to the errant Dante's aid armed with his poetic eloquence, his "beautiful words" (*parola ornata*). Those words—synecdoche, surely, for poetry itself—serve Dante well on many occasions in the *Inferno,* telling him things he needs to know, warning him away from things he must avoid, persuading opponents of his journey to withdraw their opposition.

In practice, Virgil's speech is often beautiful—just as poetry, for the Dante of the *De vulgari eloquentia,* is meant to be. And in its persuasiveness it is often powerful. "What greater power could there be," says the *De vulgari eloquentia* (I.xvii), "than that which can melt the hearts of human beings, so as to make the unwilling willing and the willing unwilling?" But it is not infallible. Outside the gates of the City of Dis, in Canto VIII, Virgil attempts to do what he has done successfully before (and will do again): to cajole the demonic inhabitants of the city into allowing him and Dante entry within their walls. He fails. After brief negotiations they mockingly slam the city gates in his face, and a humiliated and reluctant Virgil returns to Dante's side with—a wonderful touch of psychological realism— "deliberate steps" (VIII.117).

What we are being shown here is the fallibility and, by extension, the moral danger, not just of speech but of poetry. Virgil, the eloquent deployer of words—the poet—does not, in fact, possess a word that is equal to all occasions. (Indeed, he will be heard later on in the *Inferno* saying things that are not only inapt but also downright wrong.) In this instance, he compounds his failure to convince the demons with an act of linguistic carelessness that not only creates a misleading impression of the truth but also needlessly frightens Dante, who has mistaken the impression itself for the truth.

> "We still ought to win this fight," he began,
>   "unless—but so great a Lady offered us help!
>   Ah, it is taking so long for someone to come."
> I was well aware that he had covered up
>   what he started to say, and that he ended
>   quite differently from how he began.
> And yet what he said still made me afraid,
>   because I understood the broken phrase
>   to mean worse perhaps than what he intended.
>   (IX.7–15)

The clumsiness of Virgil's intellectual slip is figured in a linguistic inelegance: having begun the formulation of a sentence he breaks it off unfinished, realizing that its conclusion could only be, in the modern cant phrase, somewhere he doesn't want to go. His "beautiful words," in short, have become phrases that the text itself calls *tronca*, "broken" (line 14). Mere eloquence, in other words, will not suffice; linguistic usage must also correspond to a standard of truth. If it fails to do so, it may well end up in the ugliness of "broken" words; but even if it does not, it will be debarred by its lack of truthfulness alone from being true poetry.

What is needed, as the episode outside the City of Dis goes on to make clear, is a true eloquence that is the eloquence of the true— a (poetic) language, in other words, that reconciles to the maximum possible degree the claims of art with the necessarily more exigent claims of a life rightly ordered in the light of truth.Virgil's "beautiful" but "broken" words are not that kind of poetry, either in the narrative of the *Inferno* or in the world outside (where it is represented, clearly, by the *Aeneid*).True eloquence requires a word that is true, but the ultimate true word, as the Gospel of John attests, is a holy one:

> In the beginning was the Word, and the Word was with God, and the Word was God. (John 1:1)

> I am the way, and the truth, and the life. (John 14:6)

Such is the word that resolves the impasse outside the City of Dis: a messenger from Heaven comes to Virgil and Dante's aid and speaks *parole sante,* "holy words" (IX.105) that instantly put the demons to flight and secure the travelers' admission to the city. Merely persuasive, merely beautiful eloquence—the poetry of a Virgil—is likewise put to flight by eloquence reposing securely on a foundation of truth—the eloquence, perhaps, of the poet Dante. The *Comedy* as a whole will, in fact, turn out to be a journey not only through the afterlife (on the literal level) and through this life (on the allegorical) but also from one kind of word (or poetry, or language) to another: from the "beautiful" but "broken" word of Virgil to the "beautiful" and *true* word of Dante himself, author of the *Comedy* itself, the text that is everything the *Aeneid* is but with (as is also true of its author) the inestimable advantage of being firmly and declaredly Christian as well.

Infernos Pagan and Christian

The working out of this journey from word to word is one that necessarily carries the reader beyond the limits of the *Inferno* into the remainder of the *Comedy*. Yet it is interesting that so little of the framework of the *Inferno* itself is in fact "declaredly" Christian. Of course, the basic idea of Hell rests on Christian tradition and some (actually rather scanty) references in the Hebrew and Christian scriptures; of course, the assumptions with which Dante works and the basis of the morality he uses his text to explore are in all essentials consonant with those of medieval Christianity. But so much in the

Inferno is, if ultimately consonant with Christianity, at least not obviously so. The massive presence of classical culture, literature, history, and mythology, woven as these are into every sheet of the poem's fabric, sees to that. As seen in the *Inferno,* the tensions between these two vastly different and seemingly irreconcilable worlds offer a fascinating display of cultures in conflict and cultures in cooperation on multiple levels. In what follows, I can do no more than raise a few basic questions about their complex relationship and suggest a few tentative answers.

To begin with the most obvious example, Dante's guide, Virgil, comes historically from a non-Christian culture and represents and articulates that culture with his every word, even when doing the bidding or expounding the wisdom of the Christian God. To be sure, Virgil's use of the language of classicism (speaking not of "God" nor of "Jesus Christ," for example, but of "the Emperor who reigns on high," I.124) seems not to inhibit his being perceived by Dante the protagonist in terms more consonant with the culture of Christianity than that of classicism. All the more reason, then, to ask: how well do these two characters from such different worlds really understand each other? (However well that may be, the shock of Virgil's flagrantly pagan appearance as an apparent savior figure responding to Dante's [liturgical] cry of "*Miserere*" [I.65] must have been enormous to an unprepared Christian reader in about 1307, a reader who could not have failed to appreciate the idolatrous implication of such speech.)

Second, the text most visibly present in the *Inferno*'s literary background is, as mentioned above, at least arguably the *Aeneid* rather than the Bible. But Ovid, Lucan, and Statius, among others, amplify the pagan poetic presence in the *Inferno,* too, providing Dante as author with the raw material a mythographer traditionally depends upon and elaborates in creating his own version of a myth. Echoes from the Bible abound in the *Inferno,* and characters from the Bible are often referred to or appear on the infernal stage. But the relationship between classical and biblical literature in the *Inferno* is in various ways asymmetrical. For example, tales from the Hebrew and Christian scriptures are not systematically treated in the *Inferno* as scenes or tales from classical mythology so frequently are, namely, as sources for new versions and variants in a living mythological tradition. Charon, the ferryman from the sixth book of the *Aeneid* is, for example, brilliantly recreated (and, some might say, even improved upon) by Dante in Canto III of the *Inferno*. Why are scenes from the canonical Hebrew and Christian scriptures not similarly retrieved and recast?

Third, the basis of Hell's moral structure, painstakingly described for us by Virgil in Canto XI, is there explicitly ascribed to the writings of Cicero and Aristotle rather than a Christian source—not even the one closest to hand in Dante's culture, the so-(mis)called "Seven Deadly Sins," which are, instead, used as the structuring principle of the poem's representation of Purgatory. The guardians of the damned are not those we usually think of as servants of God but, for the most part, monsters and demons out of mythology. For a Christian Hell, Dante's Inferno looks a lot like a classical Hades. Why?

On one level, such questions seem to admit of ready answers. For the first, even if both happen to be devoted to the search for knowledge and virtue, pagans and Christians (or unaided reason, on the one hand, and reason aided by revelation, on the other) can never be expected to see the world in exactly the same way. They may in effect inhabit different worlds and thus may never be able to completely understand one another. For the second, while it is one thing to recast and even attempt to eclipse the work of a Virgil, a Lucan, or an Ovid poetically ("Let Lucan fall silent. . . . Let Ovid fall silent," XXV.94–97), it would be another thing altogether—a monstrously prideful thing—to treat the scriptural word of God in such a manner. For the third, precisely perhaps because Hell is a realm from which the good things of God are absent (or seem to be—the inscription over the Gate of Hell suggests otherwise), the *Inferno* can be presented in terms—including philosophical ones—that owe more to non-Christian and therefore morally problematic sources than to impeccably orthodox ones.

But the dominance of classical culture in the *Inferno* may be aimed at suggesting not only a predictable association between paganism and sin but also a more contentious one between paganism and Christianity itself—paganism as Christianity's unacknowledged Other; its necessary but now superseded forerunner (along with, but in a different way from, Judaism); its abused and neglected sibling (ditto); its sometimes brainy, sometimes brawny, sometimes noble, sometimes monstrous servant, but one that is not excluded from a kind of redemption insofar as it furthers the aims of its undisputed master, Christianity.

At the very least it is clear that for Dante there was a relation-ship—and one seen as possessing, in certain circumstances, value—between classical, pagan culture and its Christian counterpart. So if in some forms (the Minotaur, say, in Canto XII) paganism is con-nected with sin, in others (Virgil) it is equally closely connected with virtue. In other passages, paganism is shown as intimately con-nected to both sin and virtue at once. As suggested above, it is per-haps a pagan character, Ulysses (Canto XXVI), who most intricately combines, in his own rhetorical self-presentation, elements of an ar-rogant and misguided paganism with intellectual and moral aspira-tions that Dante could happily accept as being characteristically and indeed definitively Christian. Just as the damned pagan Virgil be-comes guide and parent figure to Dante as protagonist, so the damned pagan Ulysses, for all his faults, seems to become a kind of role model and *alter ego* to Dante as thinker and as poet. The problem—the reader's problem as much as Dante's—lies, as ever, in working out the exact nature of the connection and the ethical and theological terms in which it is to be judged.

The *Inferno* as Prologue

However we account for the undeniably strong pagan presence in the *Inferno,* we must remember that it is only the first part of a tri-partite poetic structure, and that it is, within that structure, what medieval logicians would have called the *pars destruens,* or negative portion, of Dante's overall argument. In other words, the *Inferno* pres-ents images of evil, outcomes of bad choices, things the reader should not go out and do because of the consequences, in this world and the next, to which they lead. The *pars construens,* or positive portion, with its images of virtue, outcomes of good choices, and things the reader *should* do (or try to do) is saved for the *Purgatorio* and *Paradiso.*

Whatever conclusion(s) we may arrive at, on this or any other question of overarching importance raised by the *Comedy,* we will never be able to do so in any satisfactory way by reading the *Inferno*

alone. Just as Virgil and Dante hurry past the ultimately (but signif-
icantly) disappointing figure of Satan in Canto XXXIV, so the
reader of the *Inferno* is enjoined not to dwell on a climactic vision
of evil but to move forward, to think of and to pursue the good that
lies beyond. The *Inferno* notoriously ends, in terms of plot, with a
whimper rather than a bang. The bang, indeed the Big Bang, of
Dante's poem is of course reserved for the only place where it could
possibly occur, in the vision of God Himself in Canto XXXIII of
the *Paradiso*, with which both the poem and the protagonist's jour-
ney reach their necessary and appointed end. The attentive reader
has, or should have, known this all along; as far back as Canto I of
the *Inferno*, Virgil had laid out the course of the poem's (and its pro-
tagonist's) journey with unmistakable clarity:

> I will be your guide
> and lead you from here to an eternal place,
> Where you will listen to cries of despair
> and see the ancient tormented spirits
> who lament forever their second death.
> And you will see the souls who are content
> to stay in the fire, because they hope to arrive,
> whenever it may be, among the blessed.
> And then, if you wish to ascend to their side,
> there will be a soul more worthy than I,
> and with her I will leave you when I depart.
>
> (I.113–23)

The promise that Dante's journey would not be fulfilled within
the *Inferno*—that neither character nor reader would be left in Hell
"because thou wilt not leave my soul in hell; nor wilt then give
thy holy one to see corruption" (Ps. 15:10)—recurs at other im-
portant points in the narrative. It occurs first with Beatrice's own
cameo appearance in the flashback of Canto II, promising as it does
the eventual fulfillment of her role in the *Purgatorio* and especially
the *Paradiso*, and then with such darkly allusive clues as Virgil's ap-
probation of Dante's promise to refer what he learns from Brunetto
Latini to Beatrice, if he is lucky enough to reach her:

"I will record what you tell me of my life's course
    and save it with another text to be glossed
        by an enlightening Lady, should I reach her.
And I would like this to be known to you:
    provided only that my conscience is clear,
        I am prepared for whatever Fortune wills.
Oracles like these are not new to my ears.
    And so let Fortune turn her wheel
        as she pleases, and the peasant his hoe."

At this my master cast a backward glance
    over his right cheek at me. Then he said,
        "He listens well who takes note of this."

                                            (XV.88–99)

And many other features of the *Inferno*'s text that look like loose ends turn out, when the reading of the whole *Comedy* is complete, to have functioned as so many markers laying down themes, images, and ideas whose full significance becomes apparent only from the retrospective viewpoint of the reader who has arrived, with the poem's protagonist, at the climactic vision of the ultimate, where all the scattered pages of reality (and of the *Comedy* itself) are bound into a single volume by God's love (*Pd.* XXXIII.85–87). Many readers of the *Comedy* who find themselves tempted to lay it aside a third of the way through may indeed have a sense of an ending when they finish Canto XXXIV of the *Inferno;* but in reality their journey has barely begun.

    Yet before there can be endings, even endings that are not really endings, there must be beginnings—in this instance, the beginning of the story of a poet and politician from Florence who went astray in middle age and found himself in a dark wood both literal and allegorical, a place where any of us, but for the grace of God, might find ourselves; a story that is at once that of a human individual in all his complex particularity and of humanity itself in all its complex diversity; a story that opens "midway through the journey of our life."

Steven Botterill
University of California, Berkeley

Translator's Preface

Halfway through the first canto of the *Inferno*, the shade of Virgil appears to Dante on the barren slope that is drawing him down to perdition. Virgil has been dead for more than 1,300 years, and when Dante first sees him he is

> *chi per lungo silenzio parea fioco*
> one who appeared to be faint through long silence[1]
>
> (I.63)

When Virgil breaks his silence, he is revealed as the poet whom Dante revered above all others—*il mio autore* ("my author," I.85), the character Dante calls him. What Dante the author goes on to do with Virgil is a remarkable act of fictional autobiography. Starting with this passage, here in what would become the next great European epic poem after the *Aeneid*, Virgil will lend his voice to his Italian successor as master poet and guide. By the time Virgil leaves Dante near the summit of Mount Purgatory fading back into the long silence, the mantle has been passed, the next great poet established.

Dante expands on what he means by calling Virgil "his author" by going on to say that he has modeled his own style on Virgil's:

> It is from you alone that I have acquired
> the beautiful style that has won me honor.
>
> (I.86–87)

Dante did write Latin pastoral poetry closely modeled on Virgil's *Eclogues,* but his style as an Italian poet in the *Comedía* also owes much to Virgil, just as Virgil's Latin style in the *Aeneid* owes much to Homer's Greek. Virgil heard Homer's voice as his own, reimagined

---

1. The Italian word *fioco* suggests that he appears to Dante's eyes as hoarse as well as faint (a similar case of synesthesia appears a few lines earlier in "where the sun is mute").

his own voice as Homer's, and in the end produced the authoritative voice of Roman poetry, the voice of Rome's national epic. Dante did the same with Virgil's voice, and what emerged became the authoritative voice of Italian poetry in what has become Italy's national epic. This epic lineage, from Homer to Dante, is beautifully presented and laid claim to in Canto IV of the *Inferno* where Homer, the supreme poet in Limbo, awaits both the returning Virgil and the Italian poet silently (Dante did not know Homer's Greek) and, along with the other great poets of antiquity, welcomes him among their number.

Insofar as it can be distinguished from meaning, style—and the spirit that informs it—is the deepest concern of the translator, whose great task, like Dante's and Virgil's before him, is to hear his author's voice as his own. Dante's voice has been a long time in coming to me, and I don't think I ever could have heard it if I had not first listened hard to Virgil's voice in the *Aeneid*. At first glance their styles seem quite different. Virgil's diction is formal, classical; Dante's is vernacular. Dante's hendecasyllabic verse, with its two three or accentual beats and its rhymed tercet structure, is on the surface nothing like Virgil's quantitative, unrhymed (like all of classical Latin poetry) hexameter line, with its six pulses played off against an underlying accentual pattern. But there are deeper, more fundamental similarities in the verse styles of the two poets. Dante matches Virgil in the plainness and directness that characterizes the vocabulary of both epics; and though his range of diction descends to lower registers in the *Inferno* than Virgil's in the *Aeneid*, Dante's language can rise to any required degree of dignity or formality. He also manages his verse and sentence rhythms in ways that recall the movement of the lines of the *Aeneid*.

Most of the sentences of the *Aeneid* are packaged in two- or three-line units within which there are recursive patterns created by hyperbaton—the artful separation of words that belong together in normal prose word order—patterned around line endings and mid-line breaks. Dante's Italian is not congenial to hyperbaton, but his *terza rima* stanzas create an analogous recursive complexity, and he uses the structure of his verse to zone off clauses and create a sense of order amid the drive of his narrative that, to my ear, recalls the movement of the *Aeneid*'s verse narrative. Both poets are masters of texturing sound and matching it to the sense, and this may be Dante's deepest debt to Virgil, even greater than his many verbal echoes of the Latin poet and his adoption of many of the themes and much of the mood of the Underworld in the sixth book of the *Aeneid*.

The choices I have made in representing the *Inferno* as a poem in English have to do, first, with exactly these matters of diction and verse form and, then, and perhaps more fundamentally, with the voice of the poet as a teller of tales. Dante's range of diction maps well onto the vernacular of contemporary American speech and poetry. John Ciardi first showed this in his 1954 translation, and it remains true today, provided that the translator remains sensitive to the tone of individual passages and phrases. This I have tried to do, moving with Dante from high rhetoric to obscenities and sometimes recording both registers at once.

The choice of verse form is more problematic. Dante's signature interlocking triple rhyme scheme—*ABA BCB CDC* etc.—can and has been replicated in English with some success but at the cost of frequent unnatural inversions, archaisms, and loose or padded translation. Rhyme is always a difficult fit in translation into English; triple rhyme sustained over thousands of lines is extremely compromising. Another consideration is that English rhyme tends to be on the final syllable, calling attention to itself in a way that rhyme in Italian—which tends to be over the last two syllables and as a natural by-product of grammatical inflection and word suffixes—does not. Hearing Dante recited in Italian, one is aware of but not overpowered by the rhymes. And yet what is Dante, even in translation, wholly without rhyme? I have opted to use rhyme in key passages where I think it counts the most: in the inscription over the Gate of Hell; in the apostrophic diatribes against the cities of Italy; in various speeches (the diatribe against Nicholas III and in exchanges of invective analogous to the invective verse form known as *tenzone*); and, most of all, to provide closure to each of the thirty-four cantos, segueing into rhyme toward the end of each canto and concluding with a set of interlocked final rhymes.

Just as important as rhyme in the movement of Dante's verse is the tercet structure and the rhythmic integrity of each line, both of which I have worked to preserve in translation. Dante's eleven-syllable line tends to have only three accentual beats with several

relatively unstressed syllables between each beat. Such a line carries
the reader along quickly, an effect that is often heightened due to
many lines actually having more than eleven syllables, with word-
ending vowels elided before initial vowels. I have, as far as English
allows, incorporated these features into my verse, using lines that
vary in length anywhere from eight to twelve syllables, eleven be-
ing the norm, and limiting the strong stresses to three or four dis-
tributed across the line. This is very nearly a line-for-line translation,
certainly tercet-for-tercet, matching up closely with the facing Ital-
ian text.

In spite of the fact that in the text of his poem he occasionally ad-
dresses the reader, Dante's intended audience, and very likely most of
his first actual audiences, were listeners (as were Virgil's and of course
Homer's). The tradition continued, and reciters still deliver the
Comedía to Italian audiences. (In November 2007, the most popular
clip on YouTube in Italy featured the actor Roberto Benigni recit-
ing Canto V of the *Inferno* to a theater audience.) I have tried to fol-
low suit, composing my translation of Dante (as I did with Homer
and Virgil) for performance in my own voice and, as far as I could,
revising the translation in light of actual readings for audiences.

In this vein I would like to acknowledge and thank first those
who have convened audiences for my readings from the *Inferno*: the
Hall Center for the Humanities at the University of Kansas; Kelly
Fast, Michael Pulsinelli, and their students in the Dante Club of
Shawnee Mission East High School in Kansas City; John Tipton and
the Departments of Classics and of Comparative Literature at the
University of Chicago; and the Classics Department of the Univer-
sity of Georgia. And I would like to express my appreciation to Ben
Graham for his saxophone accompaniment in living room readings.

I am grateful to William Levitan for an early reading of the en-
tire translation and the numerous suggestions he made, as well as for
the enthusiasm he expressed for the project. Gail Polk has also pro-
vided encouragement, advice, and thoughtful criticism throughout
my work on this translation. David Fredrick has given me sound and
cheering advice and substantial assistance. Richard Kay and Marina
de Fazio, my colleagues at the University of Kansas, have also lent
their expertise to this project.

The students in my spring 2008 freshman honors tutorial at the University of Kansas helped improve the translation in various ways. My thanks especially to Bethany Christiansen and Matthew Shepard, both of whom provided invaluable editorial assistance, and to Tashia Dare, who helped compile the Index of the Damned.

I would also like to express my thanks to editors who published parts of the translation in their journals: Lee Chapman (*First Intensity*), Daniel Born (*The Common Review*), and Brandon Holmquest and Steve Dolph (*Calque*).

I would like to thank the readers, anonymous to me, engaged by Hackett and to express my gratitude to Anthony Oldcorn—*doctus, Iuppiter, et laboriosus*—not only for his notes to the volume but also for his telling critiques and sound advice in matters of translation. Meera Dash through her meticulous review of the translation not only has saved me from assorted solecisms and other lapses but also has improved the translation in many places with her perspicacious suggestions. I'm grateful to Carrie Wagner for the elegant design and to Liz Wilson for her work on the diagram and chart of the Inferno. And to Steven Botterill, my thanks for his splendid Introduction.

My wife, Judy Roitman, who understands the ways of poets, has been there for me throughout work on this translation, for which she has my deepest thanks.

Although it may be unusual for an author to dedicate a work to his editor, this translation is nevertheless dedicated to Brian Rak, my longtime friend and editor at Hackett.

Note on the Text

The Italian text substantially accords with that established by the late Giorgio Petrocchi, whose critical edition of the three canticles of Dante's *Comedy* was originally published in *La Commedia secondo l'antica vulgata* (Milan: Mondadori, 1966). In the interest of accommodating English-speaking readers, punctuation in the present edition occasionally diverges from that established by Petrocchi, and new conventions for line indentation and verse paragraphing have been adopted. On four occasions we have preferred from the manuscript tradition a reading other than the one approved by Petrocchi: *orror* instead of *error* (III.31), *maturi* for *marturi* (XIV.48), *ira* in place of *ire* at XXIV.69, and *i borni* for *iborni* (XXVI.14).

Bibliographical Note

Recommended translations of Dante's minor works are *Dante's Lyric Poetry* (edited and translated by Kenelm Foster and Patrick Boyde, 2 vols., Oxford: Clarendon Press, 1967), *Vita nuova* (edited by Dino S. Cervigni and Edward Vasta, Notre Dame, IN: University of Notre Dame Press, 1995), *De vulgari eloquentia* (translated and edited by Steven Botterill, Cambridge: Cambridge University Press, 1996), *Il Convivio* (translated by Richard Lansing, New York: Garland Press, 1990), and *Monarchia* (translated and edited by Prue Shaw, Cambridge: Cambridge University Press, 1995). The standard reference work in Italian, usually dubbed "monumental," is the six-volume *Enciclopedia Dantesca* (Rome: Treccani, 1970–1975), whose compilation was directed by Umberto Bosco. In English, Paget Toynbee's *Dictionary of Proper Names and Notable Matters in the Works of Dante* (1898), revised by Charles S. Singleton (Oxford: Clarendon Press, 1968), is still useful. More recent is the one-volume *Dante Encyclopedia* (New York: Garland Press, 2000), compiled under the general editorship of Richard Lansing. More recently still, medievalist and Dante scholar Christopher Kleinhenz edited the two-volume *Medieval Italy: An Encyclopedia* (New York and London: Routledge, 2004). The authoritative reference work for classical lore is Hubert Cancik and Helmuth Schneider (eds.), *Brill's New Pauly: Encyclopaedia of the Ancient World,* vols. 1 (A–ARI)–10 (OBL-PHE), Leiden and Boston: Brill, 2002–2007. Exegesis of Dante's *Comedy* got off to an early start soon after the author's death with the commentary on the *Inferno* by his son Jacopo Alighieri, and has since continued unabated. Convenient online searchable editions of more than seventy of the major Italian and English commentaries are available through the Dartmouth Dante Project (http://dante.dartmouth.edu/). Italian Dante scholarship privileges readings of single cantos by individual critics. This is the format followed in the periodical *Lectura Dantis: A Forum for Dante Research and Interpretation,* edited by the late Tibor Wlassics, with its three one-volume supplements (I: *Inferno* [Spring 1990], II: *Purgatorio* [1993], III: *Paradiso* [1995]), as well as in the two published volumes of the University of California Press' *Lectura Dantis* (*Inferno*, 1998; *Purgatorio*, 2008). A very useful topical survey of recent scholarship is Rachel Jacoff (ed.), *The Cambridge Companion to Dante*, Second Edition (Cambridge: Cambridge University Press, 2007). The annual *Dante Studies*, the organ of the Dante Society of America, publishes state-of-the-art essays in English on specific cantos and topics.

References to Virgil's *Aeneid* (abbreviated *Aen.*) are to the books and lines of the original Latin text; quotations in English are taken from the translation by Stanley Lombardo (Indianapolis: Hackett Publishing Company, 2005). The Bible is cited in the Douay-Rheims text (Old Testament 1609, New Testament 1582), translated from Jerome's Latin Vulgate, the version that Dante was familiar with.

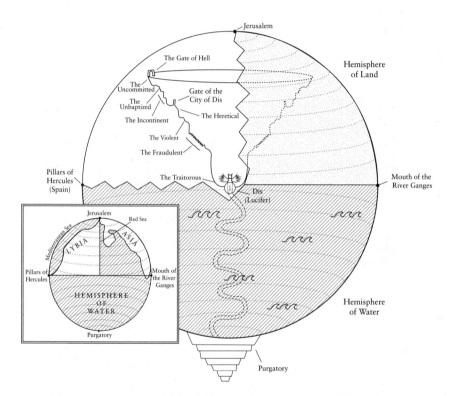

Diagram: Cutaway of the earth, revealing structure of the Inferno

STRUCTURE OF THE INFERNO

Class of Sinner	Location and/or Obstacle	Sub-Class of Sinner	Representative Sinners	Demons & Monsters	Canto
	The Gate of Hell				III
The Uncommitted	The Vestibule of Hell	Neutrals & Cowards	The Man Who Made the Great Refusal		III
	The River Acheron			Charon	III
The Unbaptized	1st Circle: (Limbo)	Unbaptized Infants & Virtuous Pagans	Homer; Aeneas; Saladin; Aristotle		IV
	2nd Circle	The Lustful	Dido; Cleopatra; Helen; Paolo & Francesca	Minos	V
The Incontinent	3rd Circle	The Gluttons	Ciacco	Cerberus	VI
	4th Circle	The Hoarders & the Wasters	Various Clerics, Popes, & Cardinals	Plutus	VII
	5th Circle	The Wrathful & the Sullen	Filippo Argenti		VII–VIII
	The River Styx			Phlegyas	VIII
	The Gate of the City of Dis			Fallen Angels; Furies; Medusa	VIII–IX
The Heretical	6th Circle		Epicurus; Farinata; Frederick II		IX–XI
	The Landslide			The Minotaur	XII
The Violent Against Persons and Their Property	*The River of Blood* 7th Circle; 1st Ring	The Violent . . . . . . against neighbors: the Bloodthirsty & the Plunderers	Ezzelino; Obizzo of Este; Attila	Centaurs	XII
	The Unnatural Wood 7th Circle; 2nd Ring	. . . against self: the Suicides & the Profligates	Piero della Vigna; Jacopo da Santo Andrea;	Harpies	XIII
					XIII

INFERNO

Canto I

Dante, at the age of thirty-five, *comes to his senses to find he has wandered from the true path and is lost in a wild and trackless forest. It is shortly after sunrise and, at the end of the valley, he can see a hill lit by the sun's rays. Taking heart, he begins to climb upward toward the light, but his progress is blocked, first by a prancing leopard, then by a roaring lion, then by a ravening female wolf, or "she-wolf." This third beast so terrifies him that, despairing of scaling the heights, he is forced back down into the darkness below.*

As he retreats, he glimpses a faint figure to whom—whatever he may be, a living man or a ghost—he cries out desperately for help. The figure reveals that

Nel mezzo del cammin di nostra vita
   mi ritrovai per una selva oscura,
3   ché la diritta via era smarrita.
Ahi quanto a dir qual era è cosa dura
   esta selva selvaggia e aspra e forte
6   che nel pensier rinova la paura!
Tant' è amara che poco è piú morte;
   ma per trattar del ben ch'i' vi trovai,
9   dirò de l'altre cose ch'i' v'ho scorte.

Io non so ben ridir com' i' v'intrai,
   tant' era pien di sonno a quel punto
12   che la verace via abbandonai.
Ma poi ch'i' fui al piè d'un colle giunto,
   là dove terminava quella valle
15   che m'avea di paura il cor compunto,
guardai in alto e vidi le sue spalle
   vestite già de' raggi del pianeta
18   che mena dritto altrui per ogne calle.
Allor fu la paura un poco queta,
   che nel lago del cor m'era durata
21   la notte ch'i' passai con tanta pieta.

he is the shade of a Roman poet who sang of Aeneas, a survivor of the fall of Troy. Dante recognizes his beloved Virgil, his chief authority and poetic model. Virgil tells him that he must reach the light by another, less direct route. The she-wolf bars all access to the sun-drenched mountain, but the day will come when she will be driven back to Hell by a messianic Hound that will rid the world of her depravity. Virgil offers to be Dante's guide on the journey that will lead through Hell and Purgatory. Another, worthier guide will accompany him into Paradise. Dante is eager to undertake this pilgrimage.

Midway through the journey of our life
 I found myself within a dark wood,
  for the straight way had now been lost.   3
Ah, how hard it is to describe that wood,
 a wilderness so gnarled and rough
  the very thought of it brings back my fear.   6
Death itself is hardly more bitter;
 but to tell of the good that I found there
  I will speak of the other things I saw.   9

I cannot say just how I entered that wood,
 so full of sleep was I at the point
  when I abandoned the road that runs true.   12
But when I reached the foot of a hill
 that rose up at the end of the valley
  where fear had pierced me through to the heart, 15
I lifted my eyes and saw its shoulders
 already bathed in the light of that planet
  that leads us straight along every path.   18
This calmed a little the lake of my heart
 that had surged with terror all through the night
  that I had just spent so piteously.   21

E come quei che con lena affannata,
uscito fuor del pelago a la riva,
24   si volge a l'acqua perigliosa e guata,
cosí l'animo mio, ch'ancor fuggiva,
si volse a retro a rimirar lo passo
27   che non lasciò già mai persona viva.
Poi ch'èi posato un poco il corpo lasso,
ripresi via per la piaggia diserta,
30   sí che 'l piè fermo sempre era 'l piú basso.
Ed ecco, quasi al cominciar de l'erta,
una lonza leggera e presta molto,
33   che di pel macolato era coverta;
e non mi si partia dinanzi al volto,
anzi 'mpediva tanto il mio cammino,
36   ch'i' fui per ritornar piú volte vòlto.

Temp' era dal principio del mattino,
e 'l sol montava 'n sú con quelle stelle
39   ch'eran con lui quando l'amor divino
mosse di prima quelle cose belle;
sí ch'a bene sperar m'era cagione
42   di quella fiera a la gaetta pelle
l'ora del tempo e la dolce stagione;
ma non sí che paura non mi desse
45   la vista che m'apparve d'un leone.
Questi parea che contra me venisse
con la test' alta e con rabbiosa fame,
48   sí che parea che l'aere ne tremesse.
Ed una lupa, che di tutte brame
sembiava carca ne la sua magrezza,
51   e molte genti fé già viver grame,
questa mi porse tanto di gravezza
con la paura ch'uscia di sua vista,
54   ch'io perdei la speranza de l'altezza.
E qual è quei che volontieri acquista,
e giugne 'l tempo che perder lo face,
57   che 'n tutti suoi pensier piange e s'attrista;

And as a man who, gasping for breath,
  has escaped the sea and wades to shore,
    then turns back and stares at the perilous waves, 24
So too my mind, still racing in flight,
  turned back to wonder at the narrow gorge
    that had never left any traveler alive. 27
I rested a little and then resumed
  my journey across that deserted slope,
    so that my firmer foot was always below. 30
But look there—near the start of the climb
  a leopard prowls, all swift and light
    and covered with a rippling, spotted hide. 33
It was everywhere that I turned my eyes,
  blocking my way at every turn, so that
    again and again I was forced to go back. 36

The time was early morning, and the sun
  was ascending the sky with those very stars
    that rose along with it when Divine Love 39
First set those beautiful things in motion.
  So the hour of day and the sweet season
    were reasons for me to hope for the best 42
From that fierce beast with the gaudy pelt;
  but not so much that I did not feel fear
    at the sight of a lion that then appeared. 45
This one looked to be coming toward me,
  his head held high and roaring with hunger
    so that the very air seemed to be trembling— 48
And then a she-wolf, so emaciated
  she seemed stricken with every kind of craving
    and had already caused many to live in grief. 51
The very sight of this creature burdened me
  with such a weight of desperate fear
    that I lost all hope of attaining the height; 54
And as a man who eagerly racks up gains
  weeps and is wretched in all of his thoughts
    when the time finally comes for him to lose, 57

tal mi fece la bestia sanza pace,
 che, venendomi 'ncontro, a poco a poco
60 mi ripigneva là dove 'l sol tace.

Mentre ch'i' rovinava in basso loco,
 dinanzi a li occhi mi si fu offerto
63 chi per lungo silenzio parea fioco.

Quando vidi costui nel gran diserto,
 "*Miserere* di me," gridai a lui,
66 "qual che tu sii, od ombra od omo certo!"

Rispuosemi: "Non omo, omo già fui,
 e li parenti miei furon lombardi,
69 mantoani per patrïa ambedui.

Nacqui *sub Iulio,* ancor che fosse tardi,
 e vissi a Roma sotto 'l buono Augusto
72 nel tempo de li dèi falsi e bugiardi.

Poeta fui, e cantai di quel giusto
 figliuol d'Anchise che venne di Troia,
75 poi che 'l superbo Ilïón fu combusto.

Ma tu perché ritorni a tanta noia?
 perché non sali il dilettoso monte
78 ch'è principio e cagion di tutta gioia?"

"Or se' tu quel Virgilio e quella fonte
 che spandi di parlar sí largo fiume?"
81 rispuos' io lui con vergognosa fronte.

"O de li altri poeti onore e lume,
 vagliami 'l lungo studio e 'l grande amore
84 che m'ha fatto cercar lo tuo volume.

Tu se' lo mio maestro e 'l mio autore,
 tu se' solo colui da cu' io tolsi
87 lo bello stilo che m'ha fatto onore.

Vedi la bestia per cu' io mi volsi;
 aiutami da lei, famoso saggio,
90 ch'ella mi fa tremar le vene e i polsi."

"A te convien tenere altro vïaggio,"
 rispuose, poi che lagrimar mi vide,
93 "se vuo' campar d'esto loco selvaggio;

So did that restless beast make me feel.
  Advancing always, she kept pushing me back,
    little by little, to where the sun is mute.   60

While I was scrambling down to those depths
  a figure presented itself to my eyes,
    one who appeared to be faint through long silence.   63
When I saw him in that vast and trackless waste,
  I cried out to him: "*Miserere mei,*
    whatever you are, living man or shade!"   66
And he answered me: "Not a living man,
  though once I was. My parents were Lombards,
    both of them natives of Mantua.   69
I was born *sub Julio,* though late,
  and lived in Rome under noble Augustus
    in the time of the false and lying gods.   72
I was a poet, and sang of that just
  son of Anchises, who came out of Troy
    after proud Ilion fell in fire and ash.   75
But you, why do you return to woe so great?
  Why not ascend this blissful mountain,
    the source and cause of every kind of joy?"   78
"Can you be Virgil, then, that great wellspring,
  that wide, spreading stream of eloquence?"
    I blushed with shame as I said this to him.   81
"O glory and light of all other poets,
  may my long study of your works repay me,
    and the love that made me pore over your verse.   84
You are my master, you are my author.
  It is from you alone that I have acquired
    the beautiful style that has won me honor.   87
Look at the beast that makes me turn back.
  Save me from her, glorious sage,
    for she fills me with fear and makes my blood pound!" 90

"You will have to go by another road,"
  he answered me when he saw my tears flow,
    "if you want to escape this wilderness.   93

ché questa bestia, per la qual tu gride,
  non lascia altrui passar per la sua via,
96   ma tanto lo 'mpedisce che l'uccide;
e ha natura sí malvagia e ria,
  che mai non empie la bramosa voglia,
99   e dopo 'l pasto ha piú fame che pria.
Molti son li animali a cui s'ammoglia,
  e piú saranno ancora, infin che 'l veltro
102   verrà, che la farà morir con doglia.
Questi non ciberà terra né peltro,
  ma sapïenza, amore e virtute,
105   e sua nazion sarà tra feltro e feltro.
Di quella umile Italia fia salute
  per cui morí la vergine Cammilla,
108   Eurialo e Turno e Niso di ferute.
Questi la caccerà per ogne villa,
  fin che l'avrà rimessa ne lo 'nferno,
111   là onde 'nvidia prima dipartilla.
Ond' io per lo tuo me' penso e discerno
  che tu mi segui, e io sarò tua guida,
114   e trarrotti di qui per loco etterno;
ove udirai le disperate strida,
  vedrai li antichi spiriti dolenti,
117   ch'a la seconda morte ciascun grida;
e vederai color che son contenti
  nel foco, perché speran di venire
120   quando che sia a le beate genti.
A le quai poi se tu vorrai salire,
  anima fia a ciò piú di me degna:
123   con lei ti lascerò nel mio partire;
ché quello imperador che là sú regna,
  perch' i' fu' ribellante a la sua legge,
126   non vuol che 'n sua città per me si vegna.
In tutte parti impera e quivi regge;
  quivi è la sua città e l'alto seggio:
129   oh felice colui cu' ivi elegge!"

This savage beast that makes you wail
  does not allow any to pass that way.
    She will harry you until she takes your life.   *96*
Her nature is so depraved and vicious
  that her craving can never be satisfied.
    Fed, she is hungrier than before.   *99*
Many are the beasts with whom she mates,
  and there will be more, until the Veltro comes,
    the Hound that will put her to a painful death.   *102*
He will not feed on property or wealth,
  but on wisdom, on love, and on virtue.
    His birthplace will be between Feltro and Feltro,   *105*
And he will be lowly Italy's salvation,
  the land for which the virgin Camilla died
    along with Euryalus, Turnus, and Nisus.   *108*
He will hunt her down through every village
  until he sends her back to Hell below
    from where Envy first sent her into this world.   *111*
Therefore I think that it is best for you
  to follow me. I will be your guide
    and lead you from here to an eternal place,   *114*
Where you will listen to cries of despair
  and see the ancient tormented spirits
    who lament forever their second death.   *117*
And you will see the souls who are content
  to stay in the fire, because they hope to arrive,
    whenever it may be, among the blessed.   *120*
And then, if you wish to ascend to their side,
  there will be a soul more worthy than I,
    and with her I will leave you when I depart.   *123*
For the Emperor who reigns on high
  wills that I, who did not obey his law,
    never gain admittance into His city.   *126*
His rule is everywhere, but there is His reign,
  there is His city and exalted throne.
    Happy are those chosen to share His domain!"   *129*

E io a lui: "Poeta, io ti richeggio
  per quello Dio che tu non conoscesti,
132   acciò ch'io fugga questo male e peggio,
che tu mi meni là dov' or dicesti,
  sí ch'io veggia la porta di san Pietro
135   e color cui tu fai cotanto mesti."
Allor si mosse, e io li tenni dietro.

And I to him: "Poet, I implore you
  by that very God whom you did not know:
    help me escape this and worse ills too.   *132*
Lead me to the place you speak of, so I may go
  and look upon Saint Peter's gate, and see
    those whom you say are full of sorrow."   *135*
Then he set out, and I kept him before me.

Canto II

As all other living creatures *seek their nightly rest, Dante the pilgrim alone sets forth upon his journey. The narrating poet summons his faculties and invokes the Muses' aid. And now the pilgrim, who had eagerly accepted Virgil's proposal to lead him into the realms of the afterlife, hesitates, recalling that his precursors on such a voyage, Aeneas and Saint Paul, were granted this privilege because of their respective roles as founder of Rome and apostle of Christ to the Gentiles. Dante fears his going may be temerarious. Virgil goads*

> Lo giorno se n'andava, e l'aere bruno
> togllieva li animai che sono in terra
> 3   da le fatiche loro; e io sol uno
> m'apparecchiava a sostener la guerra
> sí del cammino e sí de la pietate,
> 6   che ritrarrà la mente che non erra.
> O muse, o alto ingegno, or m'aiutate;
> o mente che scrivesti ciò ch'io vidi,
> 9   qui si parrà la tua nobilitate.
>
> Io cominciai:"Poeta che mi guidi,
> guarda la mia virtù s'ell' è possente,
> 12   prima ch'a l'alto passo tu mi fidi.
> Tu dici che di Silvïo il parente,
> corruttibile ancora, ad immortale
> 15   secolo andò, e fu sensibilmente.
> Però, se l'avversario d'ogne male
> cortese i fu, pensando l'alto effetto
> 18   ch'uscir dovea di lui, e 'l chi e 'l quale,
> non pare indegno ad omo d'intelletto;
> ch'e' fu de l'alma Roma e di suo impero
> 21   ne l'empireo ciel per padre eletto:

Dante's cowardice, assuring him that his journey, like Aeneas' and Paul's, has been willed in Heaven. The woman whom Dante loved in his youth, Beatrice, descended into Limbo, where the Roman poet dwells for all eternity, to urge Virgil to go to Dante's aid. Beatrice in turn was dispatched by the Virgin Mary, who sent Saint Lucy to her to tell her of Dante's need. Virgil's reassurances restore the pilgrim's resolve and ready him once more for the fray.

Day was departing, and the darkening air
    was relieving the creatures who live on Earth
        of all their labors. I alone was left   *3*
To gird myself for the struggle ahead,
    the journey's toil and the toil of pity,
        which unerring memory shall now retrace.   *6*
O Muses, O high Genius, come to my aid.
    O Memory, who wrote down all that I saw,
        here your nobility shall clearly be seen.   *9*

"Poet," I began, "you are my guide.
    Consider whether I am strong enough
        before you trust me to the deeps below.   *12*
You tell how Silvius' father, Aeneas, went,
    while still in his body, to the eternal world
        and was there with all his senses intact.   *15*
But that evil's constant Adversary
    should show him such favor, considering both
        his high legacy and who he himself was,   *18*
Makes perfect sense to a man of reason.
    For he was chosen in the Empyrean
        to be the father of Mother Rome and her realm;   *21*

la quale e 'l quale, a voler dir lo vero,
   fu stabilita per lo loco santo
24   u' siede il successor del maggior Piero.
Per quest' andata onde li dai tu vanto,
   intese cose che furon cagione
27   di sua vittoria e del papale ammanto.
Andovvi poi lo Vas d'elezïone,
   per recarne conforto a quella fede
30   ch'è principio a la via di salvazione.
Ma io, perché venirvi? o chi 'l concede?
   Io non Enëa, io non Paulo sono;
33   me degno a ciò né io né altri 'l crede.
Per che, se del venire io m'abbandono,
   temo che la venuta non sia folle.
36   Se' savio; intendi me' ch'i' non ragiono."

E qual è quei che disvuol ciò che volle
   e per novi pensier cangia proposta,
39   sí che dal cominciar tutto si tolle,
tal mi fec' ïo 'n quella oscura costa,
   perché, pensando, consumai la 'mpresa
42   che fu nel cominciar cotanto tosta.
"S'i' ho ben la parola tua intesa,"
   rispuose del magnanimo quell' ombra,
45   "l'anima tua è da viltade offesa;
la qual molte fïate l'omo ingombra
   sí che d'onrata impresa lo rivolve,
48   come falso veder bestia quand' ombra.
Da questa tema acciò che tu ti solve,
   dirotti perch' io venni e quel ch'io 'ntesi
51   nel primo punto che di te mi dolve.
Io era tra color che son sospesi,
   e donna mi chiamò beata e bella,
54   tal che di comandare io la richiesi.
Lucevan li occhi suoi piú che la stella;
   e cominciommi a dir soave e piana,
57   con angelica voce, in sua favella:

And both Rome and her empire, the truth to tell,
  were founded to serve as the holy place,
    where Saint Peter's successor now has his seat.   24
Aeneas, in the journey you affirm he made,
  came to know things that helped him prevail
    and that led as well to the mantles of popes.   27
Then Paul, the Chosen Vessel, went there
  to bring confirmation from the other world
    of the faith that leads us to salvation.   30
But I, why should I go there? Who permits me?
  I am not Aeneas, I am not Paul.
    Neither I nor anyone thinks me worthy.   33
And so, if I do abandon myself to this journey,
  I fear it may be madness. You are wise,
    you understand better than I can explain."   36

Like a man who unwills what he has willed
  and upon second thought changes his mind
    and finally gives up on the course he began,   39
So was I in the shadow of that slope,
  for my thinking undid the enterprise
    whose first steps had been so precipitous.   42
"If I've understood well what you have said,"
  replied the shade of the great-souled Poet,
    "your spirit is stricken with cowardice,   45
Which often so shrouds a man in doubt
  that he abandons his first noble resolve,
    like a beast that shies when shadows are falling.   48
To free you from this fear I will tell you now
  why I have come and what I was told
    when first I felt pangs of sorrow for you.   51
I was in Limbo when a Lady called me,
  so blessed and so beautiful that I prayed
    she allow me to be of service to her.   54
Her eyes outshone the stars in the sky,
  and when she spoke her voice was as sweet
    and soft as an angel's, as she said to me: 57

'O anima cortese mantoana,
di cui la fama ancor nel mondo dura,
60   e durerà quanto 'l mondo lontana,
l'amico mio, e non de la ventura,
ne la diserta piaggia è impedito
63   sí nel cammin, che vòlt' è per paura;
e temo che non sia già sí smarrito,
ch'io mi sia tardi al soccorso levata,
66   per quel ch'i' ho di lui nel cielo udito.
Or movi, e con la tua parola ornata
e con ciò c'ha mestieri al suo campare,
69   l'aiuta sí ch'i' ne sia consolata.
I' son Beatrice che ti faccio andare;
vegno del loco ove tornar disio;
72   amor mi mosse, che mi fa parlare.
Quando sarò dinanzi al segnor mio,
di te mi loderò sovente a lui.'
75   Tacette allora, e poi comincia' io:
'O donna di virtù, sola per cui
l'umana spezie eccede ogne contento
78   di quel ciel c'ha minor li cerchi sui,
tanto m'aggrada il tuo comandamento,
che l'ubidir, se già fosse, m'è tardi;
81   piú non t'è uo' ch'aprirmi il tuo talento.
Ma dimmi la cagion che non ti guardi
de lo scender qua giuso in questo centro
84   de l'ampio loco ove tornar tu ardi.'
'Da che tu vuo' saver cotanto a dentro,
dirotti brievemente,' mi rispuose,
87   'perch' i' non temo di venir qua entro.
Temer si dee di sole quelle cose
c'hanno potenza di fare altrui male;
90   de l'altre no, ché non son paurose.
I' son fatta da Dio, sua mercé, tale,
che la vostra miseria non mi tange,
93   né fiamma d'esto 'ncendio non m'assale.

'O courteous spirit of Mantua, whose fame
  still endures in the world, and will endure
    as long as the world itself shall last—   60
A friend of mine, who is not Fortune's friend,
  is so entangled on the barren slope
    that he has turned back from the road in fear.   63
From what I have heard of him in Heaven
  I am afraid he may already be so lost
    that I have arisen too late to help him.   66
Go now, and use your beautiful words
  and anything needed for his deliverance.
    Rescue him, so that I might be consoled.   69
I who send you forth am Beatrice,
  come from a place where I long to return.
    Love moved me to do this, love makes me speak.   72
When I am again before my Lord
  I will praise you often in His presence.'
    She fell silent then, and I responded: 75
'Lady of virtue, through whom alone
  humankind transcends what is contained
    by the heaven of least circumference,   78
Your command is so pleasing to me
  that instant obedience would still be too late.
    You have only to reveal to me your will.   81
But tell me the reason you have no fear
  of descending into this central core
    from the spacious region where you long to be?'   84
'Since you have such a deep desire to know,'
  the Lady replied, 'I will tell you briefly
    why I am not afraid to come to this place.   87
One should fear those things alone
  that can cause one harm. Other things, no:
    what causes no harm is not to be feared.   90
I am so made by the grace of God
  that I am untouched by your sorrow and pain,
    nor can I be hurt by these scorching flames.   93

Donna è gentil nel ciel che si compiange
di questo 'mpedimento ov' io ti mando,
96   sí che duro giudicio là sú frange.
Questa chiese Lucia in suo dimando
e disse:—Or ha bisogno il tuo fedele
99   di te, e io a te lo raccomando.—
Lucia, nimica di ciascun crudele,
si mosse, e venne al loco dov' i' era,
102   che mi sedea con l'antica Rachele.
Disse:—Beatrice, loda di Dio vera,
ché non soccorri quei che t'amò tanto,
105   ch'uscí per te de la volgare schiera?
Non odi tu la pieta del suo pianto,
non vedi tu la morte che 'l combatte
108   su la fiumana ove 'l mar non ha vanto?—
Al mondo non fur mai persone ratte
a far lor pro o a fuggir lor danno,
111   com' io, dopo cotai parole fatte,
venni qua giú del mio beato scanno,
fidandomi del tuo parlare onesto,
114   ch'onora te e quei ch'udito l'hanno.'
Poscia che m'ebbe ragionato questo,
li occhi lucenti lagrimando volse,
117   per che mi fece del venir piú presto.
E venni a te cosí com' ella volse:
d'inanzi a quella fiera ti levai
120   che del bel monte il corto andar ti tolse.
Dunque: che è? perché, perché restai,
perché tanta viltà nel core allette,
123   perché ardire e franchezza non hai,
poscia che tai tre donne benedette
curan di te ne la corte del cielo,
126   e 'l mio parlar tanto ben ti promette?"

Quali fioretti dal notturno gelo
chinati e chiusi, poi che 'l sol li 'mbianca,
129   si drizzan tutti aperti in loro stelo,

There is in Heaven a gracious Lady
  with such pity for the plight to which I send you
    that the strict decree above has been broken.   *96*
This Lady summoned Lucy and said to her:
  "Your faithful one now stands in need of you,
    and I deliver him into your care."   *99*
And Lucy, an enemy of everything cruel,
  arose and came to me where I sat
    with venerable Rachel, and said to me: *102*
"Beatrice, true glory of God,
  why do you not go to that man's aid
    who left the common crowd for love of you?   *105*
Do you not hear his pitiful lament
  or see how he is threatened by death
    in the flood that outswells even the sea?"   *108*
No one on Earth was ever so quick
  to gain an advantage or escape from harm
    as I was then upon hearing these words,   *111*
And down I came from my blessed throne,
  placing my trust in your noble speech,
    which honors you and all who have heard it.'
    114
When Beatrice had finished speaking to me
  she averted her eyes that shone with tears,
    which made me all the more eager to come.   *117*
And just as she wished, I came to you
  and rescued you from the beast that hindered
    the short path up the beautiful mountain.   *120*
What is this, then? Why do you hang back?
  Why do you nurse such cowardice?
    Why are you not bold, daring, and free,   *123*
When three such blessed Ladies in Heaven
  are concerned for you, and when my words
    are a pledge to you of so great a good?"   *126*

As little flowers, drooping and closed
  in the chill of night, straighten their stems
    and open up when the sun shines on them,   *129*

tal mi fec' io di mia virtude stanca,
        e tanto buono ardire al cor mi corse,
132   ch'i' cominciai come persona franca:
        "Oh pietosa colei che mi soccorse!
        e te cortese ch'ubidisti tosto
135   a le vere parole che ti porse!
        Tu m'hai con disiderio il cor disposto
        sí al venir con le parole tue,
138   ch'i' son tornato nel primo proposto.
        Or va, ch'un sol volere è d'ambedue:
        tu duca, tu segnore e tu maestro."
141   Cosí li dissi; e poi che mosso fue,
        intrai per lo cammino alto e silvestro.

So too my courage, which had ebbed away;
  and so much good spirit rushed into my heart
    that I said to him, like a man set free: *132*
"How compassionate she who came to my aid,
  and how courteous you, who when you heard
    the true words she spoke, so quickly obeyed!   *135*
And now your words have restored my soul
  and made me so eager to come with you
    that my first intent is once again my goal.   *138*
Let us go now, for though we are two,
  we have one will. You are my master and guide."
    Those were my words, and when he withdrew   *141*
I followed him into the desolate divide.

Canto III

THE INSCRIPTION ON THE GATE OF HELL *is explained by Virgil, who takes Dante by the hand and leads him in. A hideous babel of cries, articulate and inarticulate, strikes their ears. Virgil explains that here, in this the Vestibule of Hell, the Uncommitted, rejected alike by Hell proper and by Heaven, are punished, along with the neutral angels, who sided neither with God nor with Satan. Now, naked, bloody, and pricked on by stinging insects, they pursue a meaningless banner wherever it may lead. They do not merit the pilgrim's attention. Among them Dante recognizes the man "who through cowardice made the Great Refusal."*

'Per me si va ne la città dolente,
   per me si va ne l'etterno dolore,
3   per me si va tra la perduta gente.
Giustizia mosse il mio alto fattore;
   fecemi la divina podestate,
6   la somma sapïenza e 'l primo amore.
Dinanzi a me non fuor cose create
   se non etterne, e io etterno duro.
9   Lasciate ogne speranza, voi ch'intrate'.

Quest parole di colore oscuro
   vid'ïo scritte al sommo d'una porta;
12   per ch'io: "Maestro, il senso lor m'è duro."
Ed elli a me, come persona accorta:
   "Qui si convien lasciare ogne sospetto;
15   ogne viltà convien che qui sia morta.
Noi siam venuti al loco ov' i' t'ho detto
   che tu vedrai le genti dolorose
18   c'hanno perduto il ben de l'intelletto."

Farther along, a crowd of dead souls is gathering on the shore to be ferried over the swamp of Acheron. Despite Virgil's remonstrance, Charon the demon boatman refuses to carry Dante across because he is alive. Before Charon can return, another grieving flock of sinners has assembled. Virgil explains that all those who die in a state of mortal sin instinctively come here, spurred by Divine Justice. Just then, an earthquake occurs and a crimson flash lights up the darkness. Dante loses his senses and falls to the ground.

THROUGH ME IS THE WAY TO THE CITY OF WOE.
THROUGH ME IS THE WAY TO SORROW ETERNAL.
THROUGH ME IS THE WAY TO THE LOST BELOW.   *3*
JUSTICE MOVED MY ARCHITECT SUPERNAL.
I WAS CONSTRUCTED BY DIVINE POWER,
  SUPREME WISDOM, AND LOVE PRIMORDIAL.   *6*
BEFORE ME NO CREATED THINGS WERE
  SAVE THOSE ETERNAL, AND ETERNAL I ABIDE.
  ABANDON ALL HOPE, YOU WHO ENTER.   *9*

These words I saw etched in shadow
  above a gate, and I said: "Master,
  the meaning of these lines is hard for me."   *12*
And he, like one who always knows what to say,
  "All fear and doubt must be forgotten now.
  Here must all cowardice be laid to rest.   *15*
We have come to the place where I foretold
  you would see the souls of the wretched damned
  who have lost the good of the intellect."   *18*

E poi che la sua mano a la mia puose
  con lieto volto, ond' io mi confortai,
21   mi mise dentro a le segrete cose.
Quivi sospiri, pianti e alti guai
  risonavan per l'aere sanza stelle,
24   per ch'io al cominciar ne lagrimai.
Diverse lingue, orribili favelle,
  parole di dolore, accenti d'ira,
27   voci alte e fioche, e suon di man con elle
facevano un tumulto, il qual s'aggira
  sempre in quell' aura sanza tempo tinta,
30   come la rena quando turbo spira.
E io ch'avea d'orror la testa cinta,
  dissi: "Maestro, che è quel ch'i' odo?
33   e che gent' è che par nel duol sí vinta?"

Ed elli a me: "Questo misero modo
  tegnon l'anime triste di coloro
36   che visser sanza 'nfamia e sanza lodo.
Mischiate sono a quel cattivo coro
  de li angeli che non furon ribelli
39   né fur fedeli a Dio, ma per sé fuoro.
Caccianli i ciel per non esser men belli,
  né lo profondo inferno li riceve,
42   ch'alcuna gloria i rei avrebber d'elli."
E io: "Maestro, che è tanto greve
  a lor che lamentar li fa sí forte?"
45   Rispuose: "Dicerolti molto breve.
Questi non hanno speranza di morte,
  e la lor cieca vita è tanto bassa,
48   che 'nvidïosi son d'ogne altra sorte.
Fama di loro il mondo esser non lassa;
  misericordia e giustizia li sdegna:
51   non ragioniam di lor, ma guarda e passa."

E io, che riguardai, vidi una 'nsegna
  che girando correva tanto ratta,
54   che d'ogne posa mi parea indegna;

And when he had placed his hand on mine
  with a cheerful look from which I took comfort,
    he led me among the things that are hidden.   *21*
Here sighs and wailing and lamentation
  echoed so loud through the starless air
    that when I first heard them it made me weep.   *24*
A welter of language, of horrible tongues,
  accents of anger, cries of woe,
    voices shrill and hoarse, and beating hands   *27*
Swirled together in unceasing tumult
  through that ancient, timeless, tainted air,
    like sand when a cyclone whirls it around.   *30*
Horror shrouded my head, and I asked:
  "Master, what is this sound I hear, and who
    are these people so routed by pain?"   *33*

He answered me: "This is the wretched state
  of the sorrowing souls who passed through life
    avoiding infamy but unworthy of praise.   *36*
Mingled with them is the cowardly band
  of angels who neither rebelled against God
    nor were loyal to Him, but to themselves alone.   *39*
Heaven rejects them to preserve its beauty
  and deep Hell will not have them, for fear
    that the damned below might win some glory."   *42*
I asked him: "Master, what pains them so
  that it makes them lament in grief like this?"
    And he answered: "I will be brief.   *45*
Those who are here have no hope of death,
  and their blind existence is so debased
    that they are envious of every other fate.   *48*
The world does not allow them to be known;
  mercy and justice alike disdain them.
    They are of no account. Look and pass on."   *51*

And when I looked again, I saw a banner
  whirling around the circumference so fast
    that it seemed it could not bear to rest.   *54*

e dietro le venía sí lunga tratta
di gente, ch'i' non averei creduto
57   che morte tanta n'avesse disfatta.
Poscia ch'io v'ebbi alcun riconosciuto,
vidi e conobbi l'ombra di colui
60   che fece per viltade il gran rifiuto.
Incontanente intesi e certo fui
che questa era la setta d'i cattivi,
63   a Dio spiacenti e a' nemici sui.
Questi sciaurati, che mai non fur vivi,
erano ignudi e stimolati molto
66   da mosconi e da vespe ch'eran ivi.
Elle rigavan lor di sangue il volto,
che, mischiato di lagrime, a' lor piedi
69   da fastidiosi vermi era ricolto.

E poi ch'a riguardar oltre mi diedi,
vidi genti a la riva d'un gran fiume;
72   per ch'io dissi: "Maestro, or mi concedi
ch'i' sappia quali sono, e qual costume
le fa di trapassar parer sí pronte,
75   com' i' discerno per lo fioco lume."
Ed elli a me: "Le cose ti fier conte
quando noi fermerem li nostri passi
78   su la trista riviera d'Acheronte."
Allor con li occhi vergognosi e bassi,
temendo no 'l mio dir li fosse grave,
81   infino al fiume del parlar mi trassi.

Ed ecco verso noi venir per nave
un vecchio, bianco per antico pelo,
84   gridando: "Guai a voi, anime prave!
Non isperate mai veder lo cielo:
i' vegno per menarvi a l'altra riva
87   ne le tenebre etterne, in caldo e 'n gelo.
E tu che se' costí, anima viva,
pàrtiti da cotesti che son morti."
90   Ma poi che vide ch'io non mi partiva,

And behind the banner there followed
  a long train of people, so many,
    I had not thought death had undone so many.   *57*
Some of them I recognized, and among these
  I picked out the shade of that man
    who through cowardice made the Great Refusal.   *60*
I knew in a flash of certainty
  that these were the sorry lot who displeased
    both God Himself and His enemies.   *63*
These wretches, who never truly lived,
  were naked and pricked from head to toe
    by swarms of horseflies and wasps, whose bites   *66*
And stings streaked their faces with blood
  that mingled with their tears and streamed down
    to be lapped at their feet by loathsome worms.   *69*

Then I raised my eyes to look beyond them
  and saw a crowd on the shore of a river,
    prompting me to ask: "Master, now tell me   *72*
Who these people are and why they seem—
  as it appears to me in this faded light—
    so eager to cross to the other side?"   *75*
And he said to me: "You will be told
  all about this when we halt our steps
    on the dismal shore of the Acheron."   *78*
And so, eyes lowered and full of shame,
  afraid that my words had offended him,
    I kept from talking until we reached the river.   *81*

There we saw, coming toward us in a boat,
  an old man with shriveled white hair
    crying out, "Cursed are you, evil souls!   *84*
Do not hope to see Heaven ever!
  I come to take you to the other shore,
    into eternal darkness, heat, and cold.   *87*
And you, over there, you living soul,
  move away now from those who are dead."
    When he saw that I didn't move, he said: *90*

disse: "Per altra via, per altri porti
       verrai a piaggia, non qui, per passare:
93   piú lieve legno convien che ti porti."
E 'l duca lui: "Caron, non ti crucciare:
       vuolsi cosí colà dove si puote
96   ciò che si vuole, e piú non dimandare."
Quinci fuor quete le lanose gote
       al nocchier de la livida palude,
99   che 'ntorno a li occhi avea di fiamme rote.
Ma quell' anime, ch'eran lasse e nude,
       cangiar colore e dibattero i denti,
102   ratto che 'nteser le parole crude.
Bestemmiavano Dio e lor parenti,
       l'umana spezie e 'l loco e 'l tempo e 'l seme
105   di lor semenza e di lor nascimenti.
Poi si ritrasser tutte quante insieme,
       forte piangendo, a la riva malvagia
108   ch'attende ciascun uom che Dio non teme.
Caron dimonio, con occhi di bragia
       loro accennando, tutte le raccoglie;
111   batte col remo qualunque s'adagia.
Come d'autunno si levan le foglie
       l'una appresso de l'altra, fin che 'l ramo
114   vede a la terra tutte le sue spoglie,
similemente il mal seme d'Adamo
       gittansi di quel lito ad una ad una,
117   per cenni come augel per suo richiamo.
Cosí sen vanno su per l'onda bruna,
       e avanti che sien di là discese,
120   anche di qua nuova schiera s'auna.

"Figliuol mio," disse 'l maestro cortese,
       "quelli che muoion ne l'ira di Dio
123   tutti convegnon qui d'ogne paese;
e pronti sono a trapassar lo rio,
       ché la divina giustizia li sprona,
126   sí che la tema si volve in disio.

"By another way, other ports, not here,
 you will find passage across the shore.
  It is a lighter craft that must carry you." 93
And my guide said to him: "Do not vex yourself,
 Charon. This is willed where there is power
  to do what is willed. Now question us no more." 96
At this the ferryman's grizzled jaws relaxed,
 though his eyes were set in wheels of fire
  as he poled his boat across the bruised swamp. 99
Those exhausted, naked souls turned pale
 and their teeth started to chatter with fear
  as soon as they heard Charon's cruel words. 102
They cursed God and they cursed their parents,
 cursed the human race, the place and time
  and seed of their conception and birth. 105
Then all together, with loud lamentation,
 they drew near to that malignant shore
  that awaits the man who does not fear God. 108
The demon Charon, eyes glowing like coals,
 beckoned to them and collected them all,
  beating those who lingered with the blade of his oar. 111
As leaves in autumn take flight and fall
 one after the other, until the branch
  sees all of its tattered colors on the ground, 114
So too did these, Adam's evil seed,
 cast themselves one by one from that shore
  when the sign was given, like a hawk to its lure. 117
And so they go, over the umber water,
 but before they disembark on the other bank,
  a new crowd gathers on the nearer side. 120

"My son," my gracious master explained,
 "All those who die in the wrath of God
  come together here from every land, 123
Ready and willing to cross the river,
 for Divine Justice so spurs them on
  that their very fear becomes desire. 126

Quinci non passa mai anima buona;
  e però, se Caron di te si lagna,
129   ben puoi sapere omai che 'l suo dir suona."

Finito questo, la buia campagna
  tremò sí forte, che de lo spavento
132   la mente di sudore ancor mi bagna.
La terra lagrimosa diede vento,
  che balenò una luce vermiglia
135   la qual mi vinse ciascun sentimento;
e caddi come l'uom cui sonno piglia.

No virtuous soul ever comes this way,
  and so, if Charon complains of you,
    you understand now what he means to say."   *129*

When he had finished, the darkling plain
  quaked so fearfully that even now
    the memory soaks me with sweat again.   *132*
From the tear-drenched ground up rose a wind
  that flashed a crimson light so terrible
    it overpowered my senses and mind,   *135*
And like a person seized with sleep, I fell.

CANTO IV

ROUSED FROM HIS SWOON *by a clap of thunder, the pilgrim finds himself on the brink of the abyss. At Virgil's bidding, the two poets descend into the First Circle, Limbo. Here, where the unbaptized reside, there are no loud lamentations, only sighs of yearning and regret. This is the place to which Virgil, through no fault of his own, is condemned, along with many others, to live in longing for the salvation he knows he cannot have because he was born before Jesus Christ came into the world to save humankind. In answer to the pilgrim's question, Virgil says that, exceptionally, many Old Testament figures were removed from Limbo by a victorious liberator and taken up to Paradise shortly after his own*

    Ruppemi l'alto sonno ne la testa
      un greve truono, sí ch'io mi riscossi
3   come persona ch'è per forza desta;
    e l'occhio riposato intorno mossi,
      dritto levato, e fiso riguardai
6   per conoscer lo loco dov' io fossi.
    Vero è che 'n su la proda mi trovai
      de la valle d'abisso dolorosa
9   che 'ntrono accoglie d'infiniti guai.
    Oscura e profonda era e nebulosa
      tanto che, per ficcar lo viso a fondo,
12   io non vi discernea alcuna cosa.

    "Or discendiam qua giú nel cieco mondo,"
      cominciò il poeta tutto smorto.
15   "Io sarò primo, e tu sarai secondo."
    E io, che del color mi fui accorto,
      dissi: "Come verrò, se tu paventi
18   che suoli al mio dubbiare esser conforto?"

arrival. The pilgrims make their way through the throng of souls to where a flame lights up the surrounding darkness. This is where those who achieved fame in the non-Christian world are honored. Virgil is greeted by his fellow poets— Homer, Horace, Ovid, and Lucan—and Dante is welcomed as the sixth in their number. Together they enter a noble castle on whose lawns the heroic spirits of the past, as well as the Muslim Saladin, are assembled, watched over by the countless philosophers and scientists of antiquity and of the Arabic Middle Ages. Leaving the other poets and the light behind, Dante and Virgil press on into darkness.

A clap of thunder rumbled in my head
   and broke through my sleep, so that I woke
      with a start, as if someone had shaken me.   *3*
I got to my feet and turned my rested eyes
   in every direction, gazing intently
      to make out the place where I found myself.   *6*
The truth was that I stood on the brink
   of the chasm of grief, the abyss of pain
      that holds the sound of infinite sorrow.   *9*
It was so dark and deep and full of mist
   that although I stared down into its depths
      there was nothing at all that I could discern.   *12*

"Let us descend into the blind world below,"
   the Poet began, his face deathly pale.
      "I will lead the way, and you will follow."   *15*
I saw my guide's pallor, and I asked:
   "How should I come if you are afraid,
      since I look to you when I am in doubt?"   *18*

Ed elli a me:"L'angoscia de le genti
che son qua giú, nel viso mi dipigne
21   quella pietà che tu per tema senti.
Andiam, ché la via lunga ne sospigne."
Cosí si mise e cosí mi fé intrare
24   nel primo cerchio che l'abisso cigne.

Quivi, secondo che per ascoltare,
non avea pianto mai che di sospiri
27   che l'aura etterna facevan tremare;
ciò avvenia di duol sanza martíri,
ch'avean le turbe, ch'eran molte e grandi,
30   d'infanti e di femmine e di viri.
Lo buon maestro a me:"Tu non dimandi
che spiriti son questi che tu vedi?
33   Or vo' che sappi, innanzi che piú andi,
ch'ei non peccaro; e s'elli hanno mercedi,
non basta, perché non ebber battesmo,
36   ch'è porta de la fede che tu credi;
e s' e' furon dinanzi al cristianesmo,
non adorar debitamente a Dio:
39   e di questi cotai son io medesmo.
Per tai difetti, non per altro rio,
semo perduti, e sol di tanto offesi
42   che sanza speme vivemo in disio."

Gran duol mi prese al cor quando lo 'ntesi,
però che gente di molto valore
45   conobbi che 'n quel limbo eran sospesi.
"Dimmi, maestro mio, dimmi, segnore,"
comincia' io per volere esser certo
48   di quella fede che vince ogne errore:
"uscicci mai alcuno, o per suo merto
o per altrui, che poi fosse beato?"
51   E quei che 'ntese il mio parlar coverto,
rispuose:"Io era nuovo in questo stato,
quando ci vidi venire un possente,
54   con segno di vittoria coronato.

And he said: "The anguish of the people
　here below has painted my face
　　with the pity that you mistake for fear.   *21*
Now let us go, for the long journey calls."
　So he entered, and had me enter
　　the <u>First Circle</u> that rings the abyss. levels of hell   *24*

Here was no lamentation, or none
　that could be heard, but only sighs,
　　sighs that made the timeless air tremble,   *27*
Sighs of sadness, but not of torment,
　that arose from crowds many and large,
　　throngs of infants, women, and men.   *30*
My good master said to me: "Do you not wonder
　what spirits are these you see before you?
　　I would have you know, before you go farther,   *33*
That they did not sin. But if they earned merit,
　it did not suffice without the rite of baptism,
　　the portal to the faith that you observe;   *36*
And if they preceded Christianity,
　they did not give the worship owed to God.
　　I myself am counted one of these.   *39*
For these defects, and for no other fault,
　we are lost, but afflicted only so far
　　that we live in longing without any hope."   *42*

My heart beat with sorrow when I heard this,
　for I realized that people of outstanding worth
　　were forever suspended in that Limbo.   *45*
"Tell me, Master, tell me, sir," I began,
　eager to be absolutely sure
　　of the faith that conquers every error,   *48*
"Did anyone ever go forth from here
　by his own merit or that of another
　　to be blessed later?" He knew what I meant   *51*
And answered: "I was new to this state
　when I witnessed a powerful being descend
　　crowned with the insignia of victory.   *54*

Trasseci l'ombra del primo parente,
d'Abèl suo figlio e quella di Noè,
57   di Moïsè legista e ubidente;
Abraàm patrïarca e Davíd re,
Israèl con lo padre e co' suoi nati
60   e con Rachele, per cui tanto fé,
e altri molti, e feceli beati.
E vo' che sappi che, dinanzi ad essi,
63   spiriti umani non eran salvati."

Non lasciavam l'andar perch' ei dicessi,
ma passavam la selva tuttavia,
66   la selva, dico, di spiriti spessi.
Non era lunga ancor la nostra via
di qua dal sonno, quand' io vidi un foco
69   ch'emisperio di tenebre vincia.
Di lungi n'eravamo ancora un poco,
ma non sí ch'io non discernessi in parte
72   ch'orrevol gente possedea quel loco.
"O tu ch'onori scïenzïa e arte,
questi chi son c'hanno cotanta onranza,
75   che dal modo de li altri li diparte?"
E quelli a me:"L'onrata nominanza
che di lor suona sú ne la tua vita,
78   grazïa acquista in ciel che sí li avanza."

Intanto voce fu per me udita:
"Onorate l'altissimo poeta;
81   l'ombra sua torna, ch'era dipartita."
Poi che la voce fu restata e queta,
vidi quattro grand' ombre a noi venire:
84   sembianz' avevan né trista né lieta.

Lo buon maestro cominciò a dire:
"Mira colui con quella spada in mano,
87   che vien dinanzi ai tre sí come sire:

He plucked from here our first parent's shade,
  the shade of Abel and the shade of Noah,
    and that of Moses, obedient lawgiver,   57
Of the patriarch Abraham, and David king,
  Israel along with his father and sons
    and with Rachel, for whom he did so much,   60
And many others. He made them blessed;
  and before these, I would have you know,
    no human soul had achieved salvation."   63

We did not stop walking while he spoke
  but proceeded steadily through a forest,
    a forest, I mean, of thronging souls.   66
We had not gone very far from the spot
  where I had slept, when I saw a fire rising
    triumphant over a hemisphere of shadow.   69
We were still a little distance away
  but close enough that I could dimly discern
    the gloried people who possessed this place.   72
"O Poet who honors knowledge and art,
  who are these whose honor is so great,
    that it sets them apart from all the rest?"   75
And he said to me: "Their glory and fame
  that resound among you in your life above
    win grace in Heaven that advances them here." 78

As he finished I heard another voice saying:
  "Honor the Poet most exalted!
    His shade, which had departed, now returns."   81
After the voice had fallen silent and still,
  I saw four great shades drawing near to us
    with an air that seemed neither joyful nor sad. 84

At this my good master began to speak:
  "Observe the one with the sword in his hand
    leading the other three as their lord.   87

quelli è Omero poeta sovrano;
l'altro è Orazio satiro che vene;
90   Ovidio è 'l terzo, e l'ultimo Lucano.
Però che ciascun meco si convene
nel nome che sonò la voce sola,
93   fannomi onore, e di ciò fanno bene."

Cosí vid' i' adunar la bella scola
di quel segnor de l'altissimo canto
96   che sovra li altri com' aquila vola.
Da ch'ebber ragionato insieme alquanto,
volsersi a me con salutevol cenno,
99   e 'l mio maestro sorrise di tanto;
e piú d'onore ancora assai mi fenno,
ch'e' sí mi fecer de la loro schiera,
102   sí ch'io fui sesto tra cotanto senno.
Cosí andammo infino a la lumera,
parlando cose che 'l tacere è bello,
105   sí com' era 'l parlar colà dov' era.
Venimmo al piè d'un nobile castello,
sette volte cerchiato d'alte mura,
108   difeso intorno d'un bel fiumicello.
Questo passammo come terra dura;
per sette porte intrai con questi savi:
111   giugnemmo in prato di fresca verdura.
Genti v'eran con occhi tardi e gravi,
di grande autorità ne' lor sembianti:
114   parlavan rado, con voci soavi.

Traemmoci cosí da l'un de' canti,
in loco aperto, luminoso e alto,
117   sí che veder si potien tutti quanti.
Colà diritto, sovra 'l verde smalto,
mi fuor mostrati li spiriti magni,
120   che del vedere in me stesso m'essalto.
I' vidi Eletra con molti compagni,
tra ' quai conobbi Ettòr ed Enea,
123   Cesare armato con li occhi grifagni.

That is Homer, the sovereign poet.
  Next comes Horace, the satirist,
    Ovid is third, and behind him Lucan. 90
Since each of them shares with me the title
  announced just now by the solitary voice,
    they do me honor, and in that they do well." 93

And so I saw assembled the noble school
  of that lord of highest poetry
    that soars like an eagle above the rest. 96
After they had talked among themselves awhile
  they turned to me with a gesture of welcome
    that made my master break into a smile. 99
And then they showed me more honor still,
  for they made me one of their company,
    so that I was sixth in that flight of wisdom. 102
In this way we went on into the light
  talking of things better left in silence now,
    just as it was good to speak of them then. 105
We came to the foot of a noble castle
  girded seven times by towering walls
    themselves encircled by a beautiful stream. 108
This we crossed as if on solid ground,
  and I passed through the seven gates with the sages.
    We came into a meadow green with fresh grass 111
Where there were people with grave and solemn eyes
  and great authority in their looks.
    They seldom spoke, and their voices were soft. 114

Then we drew to one side into a place apart
  that was high and open and full of light,
    so we could see them all, each and every one. 117
There in plain view on the enameled green
  the spirits of the great were shown to me.
    To have seen them still exalts my soul. 120
I saw Electra with many companions,
  among whom I knew Aeneas and Hector,
    and Caesar, armed with flashing falcon eyes. 123

Vidi Cammilla e la Pantasilea;
da l'altra parte vidi 'l re Latino
126 che con Lavina sua figlia sedea.

Vidi quel Bruto che cacciò Tarquino,
Lucrezia, Iulia, Marzïa e Corniglia;
129 e solo, in parte, vidi 'l Saladino.

Poi ch'innalzai un poco piú le ciglia,
vidi 'l maestro di color che sanno
132 seder tra filosofica famiglia.

Tutti lo miran, tutti onor li fanno:
quivi vid' ïo Socrate e Platone,
135 che 'nnanzi a li altri piú presso li stanno;

Democrito che 'l mondo a caso pone,
Dïogenès, Anassagora e Tale,
138 Empedoclès, Eraclito e Zenone;

e vidi il buono accoglitor del quale,
Dïascoride dico; e vidi Orfeo,
141 Tulïo e Lino e Seneca morale;

Euclide geomètra e Tolomeo,
Ipocràte, Avicenna e Galïeno,
144 Averoís che 'l gran comento feo.

Io non posso ritrar di tutti a pieno,
però che sí mi caccia il lungo tema,
147 che molte volte al fatto il dir vien meno.

La sesta compagnia in due si scema:
per altra via mi mena il savio duca,
150 fuor de la queta, ne l'aura che trema.

E vegno in parte ove non è che luca.

I saw Camilla and Penthesilea,
  and on the other side King Latinus
    who sat with his daughter Lavinia.   *126*

I saw that Brutus who drove out Tarquin;
  Lucretia, Julia, Marcia, and Cornelia;
    and apart by himself I saw Saladin.   *129*
When I lifted my eyes a little higher
  I saw the master of those who know
    seated with his brood of philosophers.   *132*
All gaze upon him and do him honor.
  There I saw Socrates, and Plato too,
    closest to him and before all the others;   *135*
Anaxagoras, Thales, and Diogenes;
  Democritus, who attributes the world to chance;
    Heraclitus, Zeno, and Empedocles.   *138*
And there too I saw the great herbalist,
  Dioscorides, and also Orpheus,
    Cicero, Linus, Seneca the moralist,   *141*
Euclid, and Ptolemy, the heavens' surveyor,
  Hippocrates, Avicenna, and Galen,
    Averroës too, the great commentator.   *144*

Hurried along by my poem's long intent
  I cannot portray all those who were there,
    and my words often fall short of the event.   *147*
The band of six now dwindled to a pair,
  and my sage guide led me along other lines
    out of the silence into the trembling air,   *150*
And I came to a place where nothing shines.

CANTO V

DANTE AND VIRGIL DESCEND *from the First to the Second Circle. At the entrance, they find the half-human, half-bestial judge of all Hell, Minos, from whom the arriving sinners receive their wordless sentence. When the individual sinner has confessed his or her guilt, Minos wraps his tail around his body, indicating by the number of coils the circle to which the shade's sin condemns it. Minos attempts to dissuade the living Dante from entering, but Virgil silences him. In the darkness of the circle can be heard the roar of a whirlwind and the cries of its hapless victims, the Lustful, who in life allowed themselves to be carried away by the winds of passion. Among those borne upon and buffeted by the wind, Virgil points out a number of famous adulteresses and adulterers from*

Cosí discesi del cerchio primaio
   giú nel secondo, che men loco cinghia
3   e tanto piú dolor, che punge a guaio.
Stavvi Minòs orribilmente, e ringhia:
   essamina le colpe ne l'intrata;
6   giudica e manda secondo ch'avvinghia.
Dico che quando l'anima mal nata
   li vien dinanzi, tutta si confessa;
9   e quel conoscitor de le peccata
vede qual loco d'inferno è da essa;
   cignesi con la coda tante volte
12   quantunque gradi vuol che giú sia messa.
Sempre dinanzi a lui ne stanno molte:
   vanno a vicenda ciascuna al giudizio,
15   dicono e odono e poi son giú volte.
"O tu che vieni al doloroso ospizio,"
   disse Minòs a me quando mi vide,
18   lasciando l'atto di cotanto offizio,

history and legend. Already seized with pity, Dante desires to speak to a pair of shades who are swept along inseparably. Like homing doves, they glide toward him as the wind pauses. One of them, a woman, tells Dante where they were from, what inspired their noble love, and how they died a violent death. Dante, who has recognized Francesca da Rimini, the adulterous wife of Gianciotto Malatesta, asks her how she and her lover first discovered their sexual attraction for one another. By reading together the Arthurian romance of Lancelot and Guinevere, she answers. The book played the same role as Galahalt, the literary adulterers' go-between. Overcome with pity, Dante faints.

And so I descended from the First Circle
   down to the Second, which confines less space
   but much more pain, spurring tortured cries.   *3*
There stands Minos the Terrible, snarling.
   He judges each sinner at the entrance
   and sentences him by coiling his tail.   *6*
What I mean is that when the ill-born soul
   comes before him it confesses completely,
   and Minos, that connoisseur of sin,   *9*
Sees what its just place in Hell should be
   and winds his tail around himself as many times
   as the number of the circle that he assigns.   *12*
They stand in crowds and go one by one,
   each to its judgment. They confess, they hear,
   and then they are hurled into the pit below.   *15*
When I caught his eye, Minos set to one side
   the high duties of his magistracy. "You there,"
   he said, "who approach our grim hospitality,   *18*

"guarda com' entri e di cui tu ti fide;
 non t'inganni l'ampiezza de l'intrare!"
21 E 'l duca mio a lui: "Perché pur gride?
Non impedir lo suo fatale andare:
 vuolsi cosí colà dove si puote
24 ciò che si vuole, e piú non dimandare."

Or incomincian le dolenti note
 a farmisi sentire; or son venuto
27 là dove molto pianto mi percuote.
Io venni in loco d'ogne luce muto,
 che mugghia come fa mar per tempesta,
30 se da contrari venti è combattuto.
La bufera infernal, che mai non resta,
 mena li spirti con la sua rapina;
33 voltando e percotendo li molesta.
Quando giungon davanti a la ruina,
 quivi le strida, il compianto, il lamento;
36 bestemmian quivi la virtù divina.
Intesi ch'a' cosí fatto tormento
 enno dannati i peccator carnali,
39 che la ragion sommettono al talento.

E come li stornei ne portan l'ali
 nel freddo tempo, a schiera larga e piena,
42 cosí quel fiato li spiriti mali
di qua, di là, di giú, di sú li mena;
 nulla speranza li conforta mai,
45 non che di posa, ma di minor pena.
E come i gru van cantando lor lai,
 faccendo in aere di sé lunga riga,
48 cosí vid' io venir, traendo guai,
ombre portate da la detta briga;
 per ch'i' dissi: "Maestro, chi son quelle
51 genti che l'aura nera sí gastiga?"

Beware of entering and watch whom you trust.
  Do not be deceived by the gate's wide mouth."
    And my guide said to him:"Why do you cry out?   *21*
Do not impede his journey ordained on high,
  for this is willed where the power abides
    to do what is willed. Question us no more."   *24*

Now the eternal note of sadness began
  to make itself felt to me, and I came to a place
    where lamentation assaulted my ears,   *27*
A place where all light is dumb but that sounds
  like the sea howling in a hurricane
    when opposing blasts wrestle on the deep.   *30*
There an infernal wind that never rests
  whirls the damned spirits around and around
    with stinging blasts that torture them in flight.   *33*
When they reach the shattered precipice
  the cries, the shrieks, the lamentations rise;
    there they blaspheme the Power Divine.   *36*
I came to understand that those condemned
  to this torment were the souls of the lustful
    who put rational thought below carnal desire.   *39*

As flocks of starlings beat their wings and fly
  in the cold of the year, crowding the air,
    so too that wind drove these accursed souls   *42*
Upward and downward and this way and that,
  without hope of comfort or even lesser pain,
    without hope of repose forevermore.   *45*
And as cranes fall into long lines in the sky,
  chanting their rounds as they wing their way on,
    so too I saw coming, with songs of grief,   *48*
Shadows blown on by the force of that wind.
  And I asked:"Master, who are these people,
    and why does the black air punish them so?"   *51*

"La prima di color di cui novelle
  tu vuo' saper," mi disse quelli allotta,
54   "fu imperadrice di molte favelle.
A vizio di lussuria fu sí rotta,
  che libito fé licito in sua legge,
57   per tòrre il biasmo in che era condotta.
Ell' è Semiramís, di cui si legge
  che succedette a Nino e fu sua sposa:
60   tenne la terra che 'l Soldan corregge.
L'altra è colei che s'ancise amorosa,
  e ruppe fede al cener di Sicheo;
63   poi è Cleopatràs lussurïosa.
Elena vedi, per cui tanto reo
  tempo si volse, e vedi 'l grande Achille,
66   che con amore al fine combatteo.
Vedi París, Tristano"; e piú di mille
  ombre mostrommi e nominommi a dito,
69   ch'amor di nostra vita dipartille.

Poscia ch'io ebbi 'l mio dottore udito
  nomar le donne antiche e ' cavalieri,
72   pietà mi giunse, e fui quasi smarrito.
I' cominciai: "Poeta, volontieri
  parlerei a quei due che 'nsieme vanno,
75   e paion sí al vento esser leggeri."
Ed elli a me: "Vedrai quando saranno
  piú presso a noi; e tu allor li priega
78   per quello amor che i mena, ed ei verranno."
Sí tosto come il vento a noi li piega,
  mossi la voce: "O anime affannate,
81   venite a noi parlar, s'altri nol niega!"
Quali colombe dal disio chiamate
  con l'ali alzate e ferme al dolce nido
84   vegnon per l'aere, dal voler portate;
cotali uscir de la schiera ov' è Dido,
  a noi venendo per l'aere maligno,
87   sí forte fu l'affettüoso grido.

"The first of those whose stories you long
  to learn," my guide began, "was an empress
    with dominion over many tribes and tongues.   *54*
She was so abandoned to sensual vice
  that she made lust legitimate in her laws
    to expunge the shame that she had incurred.   *57*
She is Semiramis. We read of her
  that as widow of Ninus she ascended his throne
    and held the land that the Sultan now rules.   *60*
Beside her is she who cut short her own life
  for love unfaithful to Sychaeus' ashes.
    Next to her is the lascivious Cleopatra.   *63*
Look now at Helen, about whom so many
  seasons of ill revolved, and great Achilles,
    who in his final hour did battle with love.   *66*
See Paris and Tristan!" A thousand shades
  or more he pointed out and named,
    each severed by love from our mortal life.   *69*

After I had listened to my teacher name
  these fair ladies of old and their champions,
    I was seized with pity, bewildered, and lost.   *72*
And I began: "Poet, I would gladly
  speak to those two who go together
    and seem to move so light on the wind."   *75*
He answered me: "Wait until you see them move
  closer to us. Then implore them by the love
    that leads them on, and they will come to you."   *78*
As soon as the wind had whirled them nearer
  I shouted to them: "O troubled souls,
    come speak with us, if no one forbids it."   *81*
As doves summoned by their own desire
  steady their wings and come through the air,
    drawn by love to their sweet nesting place,   *84*
So glided these spirits from Dido's side
  and came to us through the poisoned air,
    so powerful was my heartfelt cry.   *87*

"O animal grazïoso e benigno
　che visitando vai per l'aere perso
90　　　noi che tignemmo il mondo di sanguigno,
se fosse amico il re de l'universo,
　noi pregheremmo lui de la tua pace,
93　　　poi c'hai pietà del nostro mal perverso.
Di quel che udire e che parlar vi piace,
　noi udiremo e parleremo a voi,
96　　　mentre che 'l vento, come fa, ci tace.
Siede la terra dove nata fui
　su la marina dove 'l Po discende
99　　　per aver pace co' seguaci sui.
Amor, ch'al cor gentil ratto s'apprende,
　prese costui de la bella persona
102　　　che mi fu tolta; e 'l modo ancor m'offende.
Amor, ch'a nullo amato amar perdona,
　mi prese del costui piacer sí forte,
105　　　che, come vedi, ancor non m'abbandona.
Amor condusse noi ad una morte.
　Caïna attende chi a vita ci spense."
108　　　Queste parole da lor ci fuor porte.

Quand' io intesi quell' anime offense,
　china' il viso, e tanto il tenni basso,
111　　　fin che 'l poeta mi disse: "Che pense?"
Quando rispuosi, cominciai: "Oh lasso,
　quanti dolci pensier, quanto disio
114　　　menò costoro al doloroso passo!"
Poi mi rivolsi a loro e parla' io,
　e cominciai: "Francesca, i tuoi martíri
117　　　a lagrimar mi fanno tristo e pio.
Ma dimmi: al tempo d'i dolci sospiri,
　a che e come concedette amore
120　　　che conosceste i dubbiosi disiri?"

E quella a me: "Nessun maggior dolore
　che ricordarsi del tempo felice
123　　　ne la miseria; e ciò sa 'l tuo dottore.

"O living soul, so gracious and kind
    to brave the black air and visit us,
        who dyed the Earth the color of blood—   *90*
If the King of the Universe were our friend
    we would pray to Him to grant you peace,
        since you have taken pity on our woe.   *93*
Whatever it pleases you to speak or hear,
    that will we listen to or speak ourselves,
        while the wind is quiet, as the wind is now.   *96*
The city where I was born lies on the shore
    where the river Po comes down to the sea
        with all its tributaries to rest in peace.   *99*
Love, which kindles quickly in the gentle heart,
    impassioned this man with my beautiful form,
        taken from me in a way that still wounds.   *102*
Love, which excuses no beloved from loving,
    filled me with passion so strong for this man,
        that, as you see, it has not left me yet.   *105*
Love led us both to share in one death.
    Caïna awaits him who snuffed out our life."
        These words drifted upon the wind to us.   *108*

When I had heard these wounded souls, I bowed
    my head and kept it low, until the Poet
        finally asked me, "What are you brooding on?"   *111*
When I could speak again, I answered, "Ah,
    how many sweet thoughts, how much desire
        drove these lovers to this sorrowful pass!"   *114*
Then turning to the lovers I spoke again.
    "Francesca, the suffering you endure
        moves me to weep in pity for your pain.   *117*
But tell me this. In that time of sweet sighs,
    how, by what means, did Love grant to you
        the knowledge of your hesitant desires?"   *120*

And she answered: "There is no greater sorrow
    than to recall a time of happiness
        in a time of misery, as your teacher knows.   *123*

Ma s'a conoscer la prima radice
del nostro amor tu hai cotanto affetto,
126   dirò come colui che piange e dice.
Noi leggiavamo un giorno per diletto
di Lancialotto come amor lo strinse;
129   soli eravamo e sanza alcun sospetto.
Per più fiate li occhi ci sospinse
quella lettura, e scolorocci il viso;
132   ma solo un punto fu quel che ci vinse.
Quando leggemmo il disïato riso
esser basciato da cotanto amante,
135   questi, che mai da me non fia diviso,
la bocca mi basciò tutto tremante.
Galeotto fu 'l libro e chi lo scrisse:
138   quel giorno più non vi leggemmo avante."

Mentre che l'uno spirto questo disse,
l'altro piangëa; sí che di pietade
141   io venni men cosí com' io morisse.
E caddi come corpo morto cade.

But if you have so great a desire
  to learn what first made us fall in love,
    I will tell it as one who weeps and tells.   *126*
One day we two were reading for pleasure
  of Love's mastery over Lancelot.
    We were alone, and suspected nothing.   *129*
As we read the story our eyes would meet
  and our faces pale at each other's glance,
    but at one point only did we taste defeat.   *132*
When we read how the longed-for smile was kissed,
  the smile of Guinevere, by her great lover—
    this man, with whom I keep eternal tryst,   *135*
Trembling all over, placed his lips on mine.
  That book and its author were our Galahalt,
    And that day we read not another line."   *138*

While this spirit spoke, the one at her side
  wept with such a piteous sound
    that my senses failed, and as if I had died   *141*
My body fell like a corpse to the ground.

CANTO VI

WHEN HE REGAINS CONSCIOUSNESS, *Dante finds himself in the Third Circle. A steady downpour of filthy sleet and hail soaks the muddy ground. The three-headed guardian Cerberus tears at the sinners with fangs and claws. When he threatens Dante, Virgil silences him by tossing two fistfuls of dirt into his ravenous maw. One of the shades wallowing in the mire addresses Dante familiarly, but Dante fails to recognize him because of his changed appearance. The shade found here among the Gluttons is from Florence, and his name is Ciacco. Since the dead know the future, Dante quizzes Ciacco about faction-riven*

Al tornar de la mente, che si chiuse
   dinanzi a la pietà d'i due cognati,
3   che di trestizia tutto mi confuse,
novi tormenti e novi tormentati
   mi veggio intorno, come ch'io mi mova
6   e ch'io mi volga, e come che io guati.
Io sono al terzo cerchio, de la piova
   etterna, maladetta, fredda e greve;
9   regola e qualità mai non l'è nova.

Grandine grossa, acqua tinta e neve
   per l'aere tenebroso si riversa;
12   pute la terra che questo riceve.
Cerbero, fiera crudele e diversa,
   con tre gole caninamente latra
15   sovra la gente che quivi è sommersa.
Li occhi ha vermigli, la barba unta e atra,
   e 'l ventre largo, e unghiate le mani;
18   graffia li spirti ed iscoia ed isquatra.
Urlar li fa la pioggia come cani;
   de l'un de' lati fanno a l'altro schermo;
21   volgonsi spesso i miseri profani.

Florence. Why is it so divided? What lies in store for it? Are any of its citizens just? Not many, replies Ciacco. Pride, envy, and avarice are Florence's besetting vices. First the White Guelphs will have the upper hand, and then the Blacks. But where, asks Dante, are the Florentine worthies of the past? Among the blackest of souls! Refresh my fame when you return to the world. As Dante and Virgil move on, Virgil tells Dante that all these sinners will suffer more after they have been reunited with their bodies on the Day of Judgment or Doomsday.

When my mind returned, after it had become
   so numb with sorrow that it shut down
      in the face of the two kinfolks' piteous fate,   *3*
New torments and new tormented souls
   surrounded me everywhere that I turned,
      whichever way I directed my gaze.   *6*
I was in the Third Circle, the circle
   of endless, cursed, cold, and heavy rain
      that never varies in measure or in kind.   *9*

Huge hail, polluted mist and snow
   pour down forever through the murky air,
      and the putrid soil reeks under the deluge.   *12*
Cerberus, a grotesque beast and cruel,
   barks like a dog through his three throats
      over the people here submerged.   *15*
He has red eyes, a beard greasy and black,
   an enormous gut, and taloned hands.
      He claws the spirits, flays and mangles them.   *18*
The rain makes these pathetic outcasts
   howl like dogs, and they twist and turn
      trying to shield one side with the other.   *21*

Quando ci scorse Cerbero, il gran vermo,
le bocche aperse e mostrocci le sanne;
24   non avea membro che tenesse fermo.
E 'l duca mio distese le sue spanne,
prese la terra, e con piene le pugna
27   la gittò dentro a le bramose canne.
Qual è quel cane ch'abbaiando agogna,
e si racqueta poi che 'l pasto morde,
30   ché solo a divorarlo intende e pugna,
cotai si fecer quelle facce lorde
de lo demonio Cerbero, che 'ntrona
33   l'anime sí, ch'esser vorrebber sorde.

Noi passavam su per l'ombre che adona
la greve pioggia, e ponavam le piante
36   sovra lor vanità che par persona.
Elle giacean per terra tutte quante,
fuor d'una ch'a seder si levò, ratto
39   ch'ella ci vide passarsi davante.
"O tu che se' per questo 'nferno tratto,"
mi disse, "riconoscimi, se sai:
42   tu fosti, prima ch'io disfatto, fatto."
E io a lui: "L'angoscia che tu hai
forse ti tira fuor de la mia mente,
45   sí che non par ch'i' ti vedessi mai.
Ma dimmi chi tu se' che 'n sí dolente
loco se' messo, e hai sí fatta pena,
48   che, s'altra è maggio, nulla è sí spiacente."

Ed elli a me: "La tua città, ch'è piena
d'invidia sí che già trabocca il sacco,
51   seco mi tenne in la vita serena.
Voi cittadini mi chiamaste Ciacco:
per la dannosa colpa de la gola,
54   come tu vedi, a la pioggia mi fiacco.
E io anima trista non son sola,
ché tutte queste a simil pena stanno
57   per simil colpa." E piú non fé parola.

Cerberus fixed us in his gaze, and the great worm
   spread his jaws wide to bare his fangs,
     and every part of his body quivered.   *24*
My leader stretched out both his hands,
   scooped up earth, and threw fistfuls of it
     into the monster's ravenous gullets.   *27*
Just as a dog who barks when hungry
   will grow quiet when he gulps down food,
     putting all his effort into swallowing,   *30*
So too the foul and ugly faces
   of the demon Cerberus, who peals so loud
     over the damned that they wish they were deaf.   *33*

We were walking over the shades upon whom
   the heavy rain beat down, planting our feet
     on emptiness that seemed like living forms.   *36*
Their shapes sprawled along the ground, all but one
   who lifted himself and sat up
     as soon as he saw us pass before him.   *39*
"You there," he said, "led through this Hell,
   recognize me if you know how.
     You were made before I was unmade."   *42*
And I said to him: "The agony you endure
   may have stolen you from my memory.
     I do not seem to have seen you before.   *45*
But tell me who you are, set in this place
   so grievous, and suffering such punishment
     that if any is greater, none is so foul."   *48*

He answered: "Your city, which is so stuffed
   with envy that it spills from the sack's mouth,
     held me with her in the brightness of life.   *51*
You fellow citizens called me Ciacco,
   and for my sinful gullet engorged like a swine's,
     as you can see, the rain beats me down.   *54*
Wretched soul that I am, I am not alone.
   All these gluttons suffer the same punishment
     for the same sin." And he said no more.   *57*

Io li rispuosi: "Ciacco, il tuo affanno
mi pesa sí, ch'a lagrimar mi 'nvita;
60   ma dimmi, se tu sai, a che verranno
li cittadin de la città partita;
s'alcun v'è giusto; e dimmi la cagione
63   per che l'ha tanta discordia assalita."
E quelli a me: "Dopo lunga tencione
verranno al sangue, e la parte selvaggia
66   caccerà l'altra con molta offensione.
Poi appresso convien che questa caggia
infra tre soli, e che l'altra sormonti
69   con la forza di tal che testé piaggia.
Alte terrà lungo tempo le fronti,
tenendo l'altra sotto gravi pesi,
72   come che di ciò pianga o che n'aonti.
Giusti son due, e non vi sono intesi;
superbia, invidia e avarizia sono
75   le tre faville c'hanno i cuori accesi."

Qui puose fine al lagrimabil suono.
E io a lui: "Ancor vo' che mi 'nsegni
78   e che di piú parlar mi facci dono.
Farinata e 'l Tegghiaio, che fuor sí degni,
Iacopo Rusticucci, Arrigo e 'l Mosca
81   e li altri ch'a ben far puoser li 'ngegni,
dimmi ove sono e fa ch'io li conosca;
ché gran disio mi stringe di savere
84   se 'l ciel li addolcia o lo 'nferno li attosca."
E quelli: "Ei son tra l'anime piú nere;
diverse colpe giú li grava al fondo:
87   se tanto scendi, là i potrai vedere.
Ma quando tu sarai nel dolce mondo,
priegoti ch'a la mente altrui mi rechi:
90   piú non ti dico e piú non ti rispondo."

Li diritti occhi torse allora in biechi;
guardommi un poco e poi chinò la testa:
93   cadde con essa a par de li altri ciechi.

I answered him: "Ciacco, your distress
  weighs upon me so heavily it brings tears
    to my eyes. But tell me, if you know,   60
What will the citizens of the divided town
  come to? Are there any who are just?
    And why has such discord assaulted it?"   63
He answered: "After long contention
  they will come to blood, and the rustic party
    will hunt down the other and do great damage.   66
After three summers that party will falter
  and the other prevail, all through the power
    of one who now is biding his time.   69
For many a year it will hold its head high
  and oppress the other with heavy burdens
    no matter its grief, no matter its shame.   72
Two men are just, yet are not heeded there.
  Pride, envy, and avarice are the three sparks
    that have inflamed all of their hearts."   75

Here he ended his tearful lament.
  I said to him: "Please, tell me more.
    Give me the gift of further speech.   78
Farinata and Tegghiaio, who were so worthy,
  Jacopo Rusticucci, Arrigo, and Mosca,
    and the others who turned their minds to good.   81
Tell me where they are, help me understand,
  for I am gripped by an urgent desire to learn
    whether Heaven soothes or Hell afflicts them."   84
And Ciacco: "They are among Hell's blackest souls,
  sunk to the bottom by an assortment of sins.
    If you descend that far you can see them there.   87
But when you are in the sweet world again
  I beg you to recall my memory to others.
    I tell you no more, and no more answer."   90

His gaze twisted into a squint. He looked
  up at me a moment, then bent his head
    and fell down to lie with the other blind souls.   93

E 'l duca disse a me: "Piú non si desta
di qua dal suon de l'angelica tromba,
96   quando verrà la nimica podesta:
ciascun rivederà la trista tomba,
ripiglierà sua carne e sua figura,
99   udirà quel ch'in etterno rimbomba."

Sí trapassammo per sozza mistura
de l'ombre e de la pioggia, a passi lenti,
102   toccando un poco la vita futura;
per ch'io dissi: "Maestro, esti tormenti
crescerann' ei dopo la gran sentenza,
105   o fier minori, o saran sí cocenti?"
Ed elli a me: "Ritorna a tua scïenza,
che vuol, quanto la cosa è piú perfetta,
108   piú senta il bene, e cosí la doglienza.
Tutto che questa gente maladetta
in vera perfezion già mai non vada,
111   di là piú che di qua essere aspetta."

Noi aggirammo a tondo quella strada,
parlando piú assai ch'i' non ridico;
114   venimmo al punto dove si digrada:
quivi trovammo Pluto, il gran nemico.

My leader said to me: "He wakes no more
   until the sound of the angel's trumpet
      at the coming of the opposing Power.   *96*
Then each will return to his dismal tomb
   to take on again his flesh and form
      and hear that which through all eternity resounds."   *99*

So, through the foul mixture of rain and the dead
   we made our passage with slow steps,
      touching a little on the life ahead.   *102*
I asked: "Master, these torments, how
   will they stand after the Grand Judgment?
      Greater, or less, or no different from now?"   *105*
He answered: "Remember your philosophy,
   which has it that the more a thing is perfect
      the more it feels joy—and misery.   *108*
Although true perfection does not await
   these accursed souls, their being will become
      more complete then than in their present state."   *111*

We continued following the road's weary bend,
   speaking more than I repeat from memory,
      until we came to where we had to descend.   *114*
There we found Plutus, the great enemy.

CANTO VII

THE SCARCELY ARTICULATE MONSTER PLUTUS *bars the entrance to the Fourth Circle, but Virgil deflates him, pointing out that Dante's passage is willed in Heaven and that he, hellish wolf, is impotent to impede it. Here the Avaricious and the Prodigal, divided into two crews, are condemned to roll huge weights, which obstruct their forward vision, in two semicircles until they clash, screaming out hysterical condemnations of the other group's sin, whereupon they turn and roll them in the opposite direction until they clash once more. The tonsured Avaricious, on the left, were all clerics. Virgil remarks that these sinners thought their possessions secure and made no allowance for Fortune. Questioned*

"*P*ape Satàn, pape Satàn aleppe!"
    cominciò Pluto con la voce chioccia;
3   e quel savio gentil, che tutto seppe,
disse per confortarmi: "Non ti noccia
    la tua paura; ché, poder ch'elli abbia,
6   non ci torrà lo scender questa roccia."
Poi si rivolse a quella 'nfiata labbia,
    e disse: "Taci, maladetto lupo!
9   consuma dentro te con la tua rabbia.
Non è sanza cagion l'andare al cupo:
    vuolsi ne l'alto, là dove Michele
12   fé la vendetta del superbo strupo."
Quali dal vento le gonfiate vele
    caggiono avvolte, poi che l'alber fiacca,
15   tal cadde a terra la fiera crudele.
Così scendemmo ne la quarta lacca,
    pigliando piú de la dolente ripa
18   che 'l mal de l'universo tutto insacca.

more closely by Dante, he explains that Fortune is God's minister, an agent of His inscrutable Providence, charged with ensuring that ultimately worthless worldly goods are distributed and redistributed from proprietor to proprietor, never staying in the same hands for long. Crossing the circle to its inner edge, the pilgrims follow a murky stream down into the next circle and the marsh of Styx. Here, in the Fifth Circle, the Wrathful attack each other uncontrollably, while the bubbling slime reveals the presence of the Sullen or Slothful lying passively below the surface. Skirting the swamp, the pilgrims come at last to a tower.

"*P*ape Satàn, pape Satàn aleppe!"
  Plutus greeted us with a cackling voice;
    and my gentle sage, who knew all things,   3
Said to comfort me, "Don't let your fear
  get the better of you. Whatever his power,
    he shall not stop our descent of this rock."   6
He turned then to face that bloated mug
  and spoke. "Silence, hellish wolf,
    and gnaw on your own rage until you choke.   9
This journey down to the hollow depths
  is not without cause. It is willed on high
    where Michael avenged the rebels' arrogance."   12
As sails billowing in the wind collapse
  in a tangled heap when the mainmast snaps,
    so too that cruel beast sprawled on the ground.   15
And so we descended into the fourth abyss,
  taking in more of the aching rim
    that encloses all of the universe's ills.   18

Ahi giustizia di Dio! tante chi stipa
nove travaglie e pene quant' io viddi?
21   e perché nostra colpa sí ne scipa?
Come fa l'onda là sovra Cariddi,
che si frange con quella in cui s'intoppa,
24   cosí convien che qui la gente riddi.

Qui vid' i' gente piú ch'altrove troppa,
e d'una parte e d'altra, con grand' urli,
27   voltando pesi per forza di poppa.
Percotëansi 'ncontro; e poscia pur lí
si rivolgea ciascun, voltando a retro,
30   gridando: "Perché tieni?" e "Perché burli?"
Cosí tornavan per lo cerchio tetro
da ogne mano a l'opposito punto,
33   gridandosi anche loro ontoso metro;
poi si volgea ciascun, quand' era giunto,
per lo suo mezzo cerchio a l'altra giostra.
36   E io, ch'avea lo cor quasi compunto,
dissi: "Maestro mio, or mi dimostra
che gente è questa, e se tutti fuor cherci
39   questi chercuti a la sinistra nostra."
Ed elli a me: "Tutti quanti fuor guerci
sí de la mente in la vita primaia,
42   che con misura nullo spendio ferci.
Assai la voce lor chiaro l'abbaia,
quando vegnono a' due punti del cerchio
45   dove colpa contraria li dispaia.
Questi fuor cherci, che non han coperchio
piloso al capo, e papi e cardinali,
48   in cui usa avarizia il suo soperchio."
E io: "Maestro, tra questi cotali
dovre' io ben riconoscere alcuni
51   che furo immondi di cotesti mali."
Ed elli a me: "Vano pensiero aduni:
la sconoscente vita che i fé sozzi,
54   ad ogne conoscenza or li fa bruni.

Justice of God! Who else could cram together
  all these new torments and punishments I saw?
    And why does our guilt bring us to such ruin?   *21*
As a wave roiling on Charybdis' whirlpool
  breaks against another wave it meets,
    so too these souls in their frantic ring-dance.   *24*

I saw far more here than at any point before,
  on this side and that, with a deafening howl
    rolling along weights that they pushed with their chests.   *27*
They would clash together, and as soon as they did,
  they wheeled around and staggered back with their weights,
    screaming, "Why do you hoard?" and "Why do you waste?" *30*
And so each retraces the dismal arc
  to the opposite point on either side
    reproaching each other with their barren refrains,   *33*
Only to turn when reaching that point
  and follow the semicircle to the next joust.
    This pierced me to the heart, and I said: *36*
"Enlighten me, Master, and tell me,
  who are these people? And the tonsured ones
    over on our left, were they all clergy?"   *39*
He responded: "The minds of all those here
  were so unbalanced in their original lives
    that their spending knew no reason or measure.   *42*
They bark this out clearly enough
  when they come to the circle's opposite points
    where their contrary faults keep them at odds.   *45*
Those without hair covering their heads
  were priests, popes, and cardinals.
    In them avarice reaches its zenith."   *48*
And I said: "Master, among men such as these,
  surely I ought to recognize some
    whose souls were tainted with this kind of sin."   *51*
He answered: "That is a false surmise.
  The lack of discernment that fouled their lives
    has discolored their souls beyond recognition.   *54*

In etterno verranno a li due cozzi:
   questi resurgeranno del sepulcro
57   col pugno chiuso, e questi coi crin mozzi.
Mal dare e mal tener lo mondo pulcro
   ha tolto loro, e posti a questa zuffa:
60   qual ella sia, parole non ci appulcro.
Or puoi, figliuol, veder la corta buffa
   d'i ben che son commessi a la fortuna,
63   per che l'umana gente si rabuffa;
ché tutto l'oro ch'è sotto la luna
   e che già fu, di quest' anime stanche
66   non poterebbe farne posare una."

"Maestro mio," diss' io, "or mi dí anche:
   questa fortuna di che tu mi tocche,
69   che è, che i ben del mondo ha sí tra branche?"
E quelli a me: "Oh creature sciocche,
   quanta ignoranza è quella che v'offende!
72   Or vo' che tu mia sentenza ne 'mbocche.
Colui lo cui saver tutto trascende,
   fece li cieli e diè lor chi conduce
75   sí, ch'ogne parte ad ogne parte splende,
distribuendo igualmente la luce.
   Similemente a li splendor mondani
78   ordinò general ministra e duce
che permutasse a tempo li ben vani
   di gente in gente e d'uno in altro sangue,
81   oltre la difension d'i senni umani;
per ch'una gente impera e l'altra langue,
   seguendo lo giudicio di costei,
84   che è occulto come in erba l'angue.
Vostro saver non ha contasto a lei:
   questa provede, giudica, e persegue
87   suo regno come il loro li altri dèi.
Le sue permutazion non hanno triegue:
   necessità la fa esser veloce;
90   sí spesso vien chi vicenda consegue.

They will butt against each other eternally.
  With fists clenched tight these will rise from the grave,
    while those will rise with close-cropped hair.   *57*
Hoarding and wasting have taken from them
  the beautiful world and set them to brawling.
    I will not dignify it with a nicer word.   *60*
Now you can see, my son, what a mockery,
  a passing game, are Fortune's goods
    that people fight each other to possess.   *63*
All of the gold that is beneath the moon,
  or ever was, would not be enough
    to give rest to even one of these weary souls."   *66*

"Master," I said, "would you tell me more
  about this Fortune you've just now mentioned?
    What is she, with the world's goods in her clutches?"   *69*
And he replied: "O foolish creatures,
  how great is the ignorance that assails you!
    Drink deep from the account I render here.   *72*
That One whose wisdom transcends all
  created the heavens and gave them guides
    so that each part would shine, a mirror to the others,   *75*
Distributing equally all of the light.
  So too for worldly splendors He ordained
    a minister general and a monitor   *78*
To circulate in time all the empty goods
  from nation to nation and race to race,
    beyond any human power to prevent,   *81*
So that one nation rules while another passes,
  all in accordance with Fortune's judgment,
    which lies hidden like a snake in the grass.   *84*
Your wisdom cannot stand up to hers.
  She foresees, judges, and pursues her reign
    just as the other gods all pursue theirs.   *87*
There is no pause in her permutations.
  Necessity compels Fortune to be swift,
    to bring about frequent human changes.   *90*

Quest' è colei ch'è tanto posta in croce
pur da color che le dovrien dar lode,
93   dandole biasmo a torto e mala voce;
ma ella s'è beata e ciò non ode:
con l'altre prime creature lieta
96   volve sua spera e beata si gode.
Or discendiamo omai a maggior pieta;
già ogne stella cade che saliva
99   quand' io mi mossi, e 'l troppo star si vieta."

Noi ricidemmo il cerchio a l'altra riva
sovr' una fonte che bolle e riversa
102   per un fossato che da lei deriva.
L'acqua era buia assai piú che persa;
e noi, in compagnia de l'onde bige,
105   intrammo giú per una via diversa.
In la palude va c'ha nome Stige
questo tristo ruscel, quand' è disceso
108   al piè de le maligne piagge grige.
E io, che di mirare stava inteso,
vidi genti fangose in quel pantano,
111   ignude tutte, con sembiante offeso.
Queste si percotean non pur con mano,
ma con la testa e col petto e coi piedi,
114   troncandosi co' denti a brano a brano.
Lo buon maestro disse: "Figlio, or vedi
l'anime di color cui vinse l'ira;
117   e anche vo' che tu per certo credi
che sotto l'acqua è gente che sospira,
e fanno pullular quest' acqua al summo,
120   come l'occhio ti dice, u' che s'aggira.
Fitti nel limo dicon: 'Tristi fummo
ne l'aere dolce che dal sol s'allegra,
123   portando dentro accidïoso fummo:
or ci attristiam ne la belletta negra.'
Quest' inno si gorgoglian ne la strozza,
126   ché dir nol posson con parola integra."

She is crucified in the mad opinions
  of those who instead should render her praise.
    They blame her unjustly and disgrace her name,   *93*
But blessed as she is, she does not hear it.
  Happy with the other primal creatures,
    she too turns her sphere and exults in bliss.   *96*
Now we descend to even greater grief.
  The stars that were rising when I set out
    are sinking now, and we may not overstay."   *99*

We crossed the circle to its farther edge
  to a point above a boiling spring
    that spills and gathers in the creek of Hell.   *102*
The water was dark, dark as indigo,
  and walking alongside its murky flow
    we descended by an uneven path.   *105*
This sullen stream, when it has made its way
  to the bottom of the barren grey slopes,
    feeds into the marsh known as the Styx.   *108*
As I was standing there, my gaze intent,
  I saw mud-caked people in that morass,
    all of them naked and with looks of rage.   *111*
They were beating each other, not just with their fists,
  but with their heads, their chests, and their feet,
    and they tore each other apart with their teeth.   *114*
My good master said: "You see now, son,
  the souls of those whom wrath overcame,
    and I would also have you know for certain   *117*
That under the swamp are people whose sighs
  make the water at the surface bubble,
    as you see wherever you turn your eyes.   *120*
Stuck in the slime they say, 'Sullen and sad,
  we bore within ourselves a sluggish fog
    while in the sweet air that the sun makes glad;   *123*
Now we mourn like frogs in the black mire.'
  This chant they gurgle deep in their throats
    for they cannot speak the words entire."   *126*

Cosí girammo de la lorda pozza
grand' arco, tra la ripa secca e 'l mézzo,
con li occhi vòlti a chi del fango ingozza.

129

Venimmo al piè d'una torre al da sezzo.

And so we circled the foul pond around,
  watching them swill the swampy water,
    and stepped between the dry and soggy ground   *129*
Until we came at last to the foot of a tower.

Canto VIII

As the pilgrims get closer *to the tower, two signal lights appear on its summit, to which another light from another tower, some distance ahead, responds. In response to Dante's query, Virgil points out that a boat is rapidly approaching across the foggy marsh. The irascible boatman Phlegyas, guardian of the Fifth Circle, thinks Dante is one of his victims, before he is set straight by Virgil. Virgil and Dante climb into the boat, which sinks deeper into the water under Dante's weight. A figure rises from the swamp and accosts Dante. An altercation ensues in which fellow Florentine Filippo Argenti tries to overturn the boat but is thwarted by Virgil. Dante's rightful anger and his wish to see the arrogant spirit*

Io dico, seguitando, ch'assai prima
   che noi fossimo al piè de l'alta torre,
3   li occhi nostri n'andar suso a la cima
per due fiammette che i vedemmo porre,
   e un'altra da lungi render cenno,
6   tanto ch'a pena il potea l'occhio tòrre.
E io mi volsi al mar di tutto 'l senno;
   dissi: "Questo che dice? e che risponde
9   quell' altro foco? e chi son quei che 'l fenno?"
Ed elli a me: "Su per le sucide onde
   già scorgere puoi quello che s'aspetta,
12   se 'l fummo del pantan nol ti nasconde."

Corda non pinse mai da sé saetta
   che sí corresse via per l'aere snella,
15   com' io vidi una nave piccioletta
venir per l'acqua verso noi in quella,
   sotto 'l governo d'un sol galeoto,
18   che gridava: "Or se' giunta, anima fella!"

punished are rewarded when Argenti's equally furious companions turn on him.
Virgil now explains that the fiery City of Dis, whose walls enclose the lower part
of Hell, lies ahead. Phlegyas deposits them unceremoniously on the far shore out-
side the well-guarded city gate. Their way is barred by the fallen angels, who agree,
however, to negotiate with Virgil in private. Dismayed and disheartened, Dante,
ready to retrace his steps, begs him not to go. Virgil affects confidence, trying to
comfort the anxious Dante. The demons shut the gates in Virgil's face, and Vir-
gil returns, momentarily despondent but heartened by the knowledge that their
journey, willed on high, cannot be stayed. Help is on the way.

To continue, I would say that well before
   we came to the high tower's foot
      our eyes had already turned toward its summit,   *3*
Drawn by two flames we saw flickering on top
   and another that answered away in the distance,
      so far off our eyes could barely make it out.   *6*
I turned to that ocean of wisdom and asked,
   "What does this signal mean? And the other,
      how does it answer? And who made them both?"   *9*
And his reply: "You can already make out,
   over the foul waters, what we are awaiting,
      if the fumes off the swamp do not hide it from you."   *12*

No arrow has ever been shot from a bowstring
   to fly through the air nearly as fast
      as the boat that I saw coming toward us then,   *15*
A small craft cutting its way through the water
   under the guidance of a single oarsman,
      who cried out, "Gotcha, you evil soul!"   *18*

"Flegïàs, Flegïàs, tu gridi a vòto,"
   disse lo mio segnore, "a questa volta:
21   piú non ci avrai che sol passando il loto."
Qual è colui che grande inganno ascolta
   che li sia fatto, e poi se ne rammarca,
24   fecesi Flegïàs ne l'ira accolta.
Lo duca mio discese ne la barca,
   e poi mi fece intrare appresso lui;
27   e sol quand' io fui dentro parve carca.

Tosto che 'l duca e io nel legno fui,
   segando se ne va l'antica prora
30   de l'acqua piú che non suol con altrui.
Mentre noi corravam la morta gora,
   dinanzi mi si fece un pien di fango,
33   e disse: "Chi se' tu che vieni anzi ora?"
E io a lui: "S'i' vegno, non rimango;
   ma tu chi se', che sí se' fatto brutto?"
36   Rispuose: "Vedi che son un che piango."
E io a lui: "Con piangere e con lutto,
   spirito maladetto, ti rimani;
39   ch'i' ti conosco, ancor sie lordo tutto."
Allor distese al legno ambo le mani;
   per che 'l maestro accorto lo sospinse,
42   dicendo: "Via costà con li altri cani!"
Lo collo poi con le braccia mi cinse;
   basciommi 'l volto e disse: "Alma sdegnosa,
45   benedetta colei che 'n te s'incinse!
Quei fu al mondo persona orgogliosa;
   bontà non è che sua memoria fregi:
48   cosí s'è l'ombra sua qui furïosa.
Quanti si tegnon or là sú gran regi
   che qui staranno come porci in brago,
51   di sé lasciando orribili dispregi!"
E io: "Maestro, molto sarei vago
   di vederlo attuffare in questa broda
54   prima che noi uscissimo del lago."

"Phlegyas, Phlegyas, you shout in vain,"
  my master said, "in vain this time.
  You have us only to the swamp's other side."   *21*
Like a man who learns that he has been swindled
  and is consumed with bitter resentment,
  so Phlegyas seethed in his smothering rage.   *24*
My leader got into the boat and had me
  come aboard after, and only when I stepped in
  did the craft seem to shift with its cargo.   *27*

As soon as he and I were both aboard
  the ancient prow moved off, cutting the water
  more deeply than with its usual passengers.   *30*
While we were coursing through that dead morass
  a mud-daubed figure rose up before me
  and said, "Who are you, come before your time?"   *33*
I answered: "I may come, but not for keeps.
  But who are you, who have become such slime?"
  And he said: "As you see, I am one who weeps."   *36*
And I said: "Then weep and moan on, stuck in this pit,
  and may your soul be damned right here where it steeps!
  I know you, even if you are covered with shit."   *39*
Then he stretched out both his hands toward the boat,
  but my master, alert, shoved him away,
  saying, "Back where you belong, with the other dogs!" *42*
Then he put his arms around my neck,
  kissed my cheek, and said, "Indignant soul,
  blessed is she, the mother who bore you.   *45*
In the world above he was an arrogant man.
  His memory is graced with no goodness at all,
  and so his shade rages violently here.   *48*
How many up there who think of themselves
  as great lords will lie here like pigs in the slop,
  and leave behind only contempt for their names." *51*
And I said: "Master, I would really like
  to see this man dipped deep in the soup
  before you and I take leave of the lake."   *54*

Ed elli a me: "Avante che la proda
ti si lasci veder, tu sarai sazio:
57   di tal disïo convien che tu goda."
Dopo ciò poco vid' io quello strazio
far di costui a le fangose genti,
60   che Dio ancor ne lodo e ne ringrazio.
Tutti gridavano: "A Filippo Argenti!"
e 'l fiorentino spirito bizzarro
63   in sé medesmo si volvea co' denti.

Quivi il lasciammo, che piú non ne narro;
ma ne l'orecchie mi percosse un duolo,
66   per ch'io avante l'occhio intento sbarro.
Lo buon maestro disse: "Omai, figliuolo,
s'appressa la città c'ha nome Dite,
69   coi gravi cittadin, col grande stuolo."
E io: "Maestro, già le sue meschite
là entro certe ne la valle cerno,
72   vermiglie come se di foco uscite
fossero." Ed ei mi disse: "Il foco etterno
ch'entro l'affoca le dimostra rosse,
75   come tu vedi in questo basso inferno."

Noi pur giugnemmo dentro a l'alte fosse
che vallan quella terra sconsolata:
78   le mura mi parean che ferro fosse.
Non sanza prima far grande aggirata,
venimmo in parte dove il nocchier forte
81   "Usciteci," gridò: "qui è l'intrata."
Io vidi piú di mille in su le porte
da ciel piovuti, che stizzosamente
84   dicean: "Chi è costui che sanza morte
va per lo regno de la morta gente?"
E 'l savio mio maestro fece segno
87   di voler lor parlar segretamente.
Allor chiusero un poco il gran disdegno
e disser: "Vien tu solo, e quei sen vada
90   che sí ardito intrò per questo regno.

He answered: "Before we even sight shore
   your wish will be granted. It is fitting
      that you be gratified in such a desire."   *57*
Soon after that I saw the mud-caked people
   tear the flesh of that man so badly
      that I still praise God and thank Him for it.   *60*
"Get Filippo Argenti," they all cried at once,
   and then that fiendish Florentine spirit
      turned his own teeth onto himself.   *63*

We left him there, and I say no more of him.
   Then there beat upon my ears the sound of pain,
      at which I strained my vision forward.   *66*
My good master said: "And now, my son,
   the city called Dis is just ahead,
      with its stern citizens and great garrison.   *69*
I said: "Master, I can already make out
   the minarets there, down in the valley,
      as red as if they had been in the fire."   *72*
And he said to me: "The eternal fire
   that blazes inside makes them glow red,
      just as you see, in this lower part of Hell."   *75*

We came at last to the bottomless moats,
   the outer defense of that dismal city
      whose walls seemed to me to be forged of iron.   *78*
It was not until we had made a great loop
   that we came to a place where the boatman barked,
      "Outta my boat! This is the entrance."   *81*
Above the gate I saw a thousand or more
   of the angels who fell like rain from Heaven,
      crying scornfully, "Who is this who dares   *84*
to go without death through death's own kingdom?"
   My wise master made a gesture to show
      that he wished to speak to them in private.   *87*
At this they concealed their great disdain somewhat,
   saying, "You, come on solo—but he goes back,
      who entered so boldly into this realm,   *90*

Sol si ritorni per la folle strada:
 pruovi, se sa; ché tu qui rimarrai,
93 che li ha' iscorta sí buia contrada."

Pensa, lettor, se io mi sconfortai
 nel suon de le parole maladette,
96 ché non credetti ritornarci mai.

"O caro duca mio, che piú di sette
 volte m'hai sicurtà renduta e tratto
99 d'alto periglio che 'ncontra mi stette,
non mi lasciar," diss' io, "cosí disfatto;
 e se 'l passar piú oltre ci è negato,
102 ritroviam l'orme nostre insieme ratto."
E quel segnor che lí m'avea menato,
 mi disse: "Non temer; ché 'l nostro passo
105 non ci può tòrre alcun: da tal n'è dato.
Ma qui m'attendi, e lo spirito lasso
 conforta e ciba di speranza buona,
108 ch'i' non ti lascerò nel mondo basso."

Cosí sen va, e quivi m'abbandona
 lo dolce padre, e io rimagno in forse,
111 che sí e no nel capo mi tenciona.
Udir non potti quello ch'a lor porse;
 ma ei non stette là con essi guari,
114 che ciascun dentro a pruova si ricorse.
Chiuser le porte que' nostri avversari
 nel petto al mio segnor, che fuor rimase
117 e rivolsesi a me con passi rari.
Li occhi a la terra e le ciglia avea rase
 d'ogne baldanza, e dicea ne' sospiri:
120 "Chi m'ha negate le dolenti case!"
E a me disse: "Tu, perch' io m'adiri,
 non sbigottir, ch'io vincerò la prova,
123 qual ch'a la difension dentro s'aggiri.

Back alone on his own foolish way.
  See if he can! For you will stay here,
    you who have led him through regions so dark."   *93*

Imagine, Reader, how my heart must have sunk
  at the sound of these black curses, for I thought
    I would never again return to this world.   *96*

"Dear leader and guide! Seven times or more
  you have restored my confidence, and saved me
    from great dangers that would have beaten me down.   *99*
Do not leave me now," I cried, "undone like this!
  If we are not permitted to go any farther,
    let us quickly retrace our steps together."   *102*
And that great lord, who had led me there,
  said, "Do not be afraid. No one can take
    this passage from us, by such a One granted.   *105*
Wait for me here. Comfort your weary soul
  and feed it with good hope, for I will never
    abandon you here in the world below."   *108*

So off he goes, a father gentle and kind,
  and leaves me there, and I remain in doubt,
    with Yes and No contending in my mind.   *111*
I could not hear what he proposed to them,
  but he was not with them long before they all
    jostled each other to get inside the wall.   *114*
Then our adversaries closed the gates of the city
  in the face of my lord, who remained outside
    and with deliberate steps made his way back to me.   *117*
His eyes were fixed on the ground, and his brow
  shorn of boldness, as he sighed to himself,
    "Who has denied me the sinners' houses?"   *120*
And to me he said: "Feel no dismay
  at my vexation, for I will prevail,
    whatever they contrive to block our way.   *123*

Questa lor tracotanza non è nova;
 ché già l'usaro a men segreta porta,
126 la qual sanza serrame ancor si trova.
Sovr' essa vedestù la scritta morta:
 e già di qua da lei discende l'erta,
129 passando per li cerchi sanza scorta,
tal che per lui ne fia la terra aperta."

There is nothing new in their insolence,
  for they showed it once at a gate less secret
    that is still unbarred and without defense.   *126*
You saw already the dead inscription. On this side,
  already descending the declivity,
    navigating the circles without a guide,   *129*
Comes one who will unlock for us this city."

Canto IX

VIRGIL TRIES TO CONCEAL *his own discomfiture and put on a good face. Dante, however, senses his guide's less than complete assurance and asks, generically but pointedly, whether any soul from Limbo ever ventured this far down in Hell. Virgil replies that he himself made the descent once before, summoned by the Thessalian witch Erichtho to bring back a soul condemned to the lowest circle. Looking up to the top of the city's watchtower, Dante is terrified to see the monstrous blood-dripping Furies, identified one by one by Virgil. They threaten to bring the Gorgon Medusa to turn Dante to stone. Virgil urges Dante to look away, covering his eyes as an added precaution. The author invites the reader to*

Quel color che viltà di fuor mi pinse
    veggendo il duca mio tornare in volta,
3   piú tosto dentro il suo novo ristrinse.
Attento si fermò com' uom ch'ascolta;
    ché l'occhio nol potea menare a lunga
6   per l'aere nero e per la nebbia folta.
"Pur a noi converrà vincer la punga,"
    cominciò el, "se non . . . Tal ne s'offerse.
9   Oh quanto tarda a me ch'altri qui giunga!"
I' vidi ben sí com' ei ricoperse
    lo cominciar con l'altro che poi venne,
12   che fur parole a le prime diverse;
ma nondimen paura il suo dir dienne,
    perch' io traeva la parola tronca
15   forse a peggior sentenzia che non tenne.

"In questo fondo de la trista conca
    discende mai alcun del primo grado,
18   che sol per pena ha la speranza cionca?"

consider the allegorical meaning of this episode. A fearsome crashing announces the arrival of a Rescuer from Heaven striding resolutely over the Stygian swamp. The Necessary Angel opens the unresisting gate of Hell, reprimands its recalcitrant guardians, and returns whence he came. The pilgrims now enter the city without further challenge. Inside the walls they are confronted with a vast necropolis in which the unlidded sepulchres, ringed with fire, echo with the tortured cries of their inhabitants. Virgil reveals that those punished in this, the Sixth Circle, are the heretics.

The pallor that cowardice brought to my face
  when I saw my leader turn and retreat
    restored his own color all the more quickly.   *3*
He stopped, alert as a man who listens
  because his eyes cannot take him very far
    through the black air and dripping fog.   *6*
"We still ought to win this fight," he began,
  "unless—but so great a Lady offered us help!
    Ah, it is taking so long for someone to come."   *9*
I was well aware that he had covered up
  what he started to say, and that he ended
    quite differently from how he began.   *12*
And yet what he said still made me afraid,
  because I understood the broken phrase
    to mean worse perhaps than what he intended.   *15*

"Does anyone from the First Circle,
  where the sole punishment is loss of hope,
    ever descend this low into the pit?"   *18*

Questa question fec' io; e quei "Di rado
   incontra," mi rispuose, "che di noi
21   faccia il cammino alcun per qual io vado.
Ver è ch'altra fïata qua giú fui,
   congiurato da quella Eritón cruda
24   che richiamava l'ombre a' corpi sui.
Di poco era di me la carne nuda,
   ch'ella mi fece intrar dentr' a quel muro,
27   per trarne un spirto del cerchio di Giuda.
Quell' è 'l piú basso loco e 'l piú oscuro,
   e 'l piú lontan dal ciel che tutto gira:
30   ben so 'l cammin; però ti fa sicuro.
Questa palude che 'l gran puzzo spira
   cigne dintorno la città dolente,
33   u' non potemo intrare omai sanz' ira."

E altro disse, ma non l'ho a mente;
   però che l'occhio m'avea tutto tratto
36   ver' l'alta torre a la cima rovente,
dove in un punto furon dritte ratto
   tre furïe infernal di sangue tinte,
39   che membra feminine avieno e atto,
e con idre verdissime eran cinte;
   serpentelli e ceraste avien per crine,
42   onde le fiere tempie erano avvinte.
E quei, che ben conobbe le meschine
   de la regina de l'etterno pianto,
45   "Guarda," mi disse, "le feroci Erine.
Quest' è Megera dal sinistro canto;
   quella che piange dal destro è Aletto;
48   Tesifón è nel mezzo"; e tacque a tanto.
Con l'unghie si fendea ciascuna il petto;
   battiensi a palme e gridavan sí alto,
51   ch'i' mi strinsi al poeta per sospetto.
"Vegna Medusa: sí 'l farem di smalto,"
   dicevan tutte riguardando in giuso;
54   "mal non vengiammo in Tesëo l'assalto."

I posed this question, and he responded,
  "Rarely does it happen that any of us
    make the journey I am making now, 21
But once before I did make the descent,
  driven by Erichtho's spells, the cruel witch
    who summoned shades back to their corpses. 24
My flesh had not long been stripped from me
  when she forced me to slip within these walls
    and fetch a soul from the circle of Judas. 27
There is no place lower or more black,
  or farther from the shining wheel of Heaven.
    I know the way well; you can be sure of that. 30
This swamp that reeks of foul decay
  completely surrounds the City of Woe.
    We cannot enter now without violence." 33

He said more that I do not remember,
  for my eye had drawn all my attention
    up the sides of the tower to its fiery summit, 36
Where all of a sudden there appeared
  three hellish Furies, stained with blood.
    They had the bodies and bearing of women, 39
But bright green hydras circled their waists
  and for hair they had serpents, slithering and horned,
    that twined around their dread, savage brows. 42
My master knew them at once, these handmaidens
  of the queen of eternal lamentation,
    and said to me, "See the Furies glare! 45
That is Megaera on the left, and on the right
  is Allecto, wailing. Between them Tisiphone,
    Grief's middle child." With that he fell silent. 48
They clawed their breasts with their nails, beat them
  with their fists, and cried out so loudly
    that out of fear I pressed close to the Poet. 51
"Let Medusa come, and we'll turn him to stone,"
  they said, looking down. "We went wrong,
    not avenging Theseus' raid." 54

"Volgiti 'n dietro e tien lo viso chiuso;
   ché se 'l Gorgón si mostra e tu 'l vedessi,
57   nulla sarebbe di tornar mai suso."
Cosí disse 'l maestro; ed elli stessi
   mi volse, e non si tenne a le mie mani,
60   che con le sue ancor non mi chiudessi.

O voi ch'avete li 'ntelletti sani,
   mirate la dottrina che s'asconde
63   sotto 'l velame de li versi strani.

E già venía su per le torbide onde
   un fracasso d'un suon, pien di spavento,
66   per cui tremavano amendue le sponde,
non altrimenti fatto che d'un vento
   impetüoso per li avversi ardori,
69   che fier la selva e sanz' alcun rattento
li rami schianta, abbatte e porta fori;
   dinanzi polveroso va superbo,
72   e fa fuggir le fiere e li pastori.
Li occhi mi sciolse e disse: "Or drizza il nerbo
   del viso su per quella schiuma antica
75   per indi ove quel fummo è piú acerbo."
Come le rane innanzi a la nimica
   biscia per l'acqua si dileguan tutte,
78   fin ch'a la terra ciascuna s'abbica,
vid' io piú di mille anime distrutte
   fuggir cosí dinanzi ad un ch'al passo
81   passava Stige con le piante asciutte.
Dal volto rimovea quell' aere grasso,
   menando la sinistra innanzi spesso;
84   e sol di quell' angoscia parea lasso.
Ben m'accorsi ch'elli era da ciel messo,
   e volsimi al maestro; e quei fé segno
87   ch'i' stessi queto ed inchinassi ad esso.
Ahi quanto mi parea pien di disdegno!
   Venne a la porta e con una verghetta
90   l'aperse, che non v'ebbe alcun ritegno.

"Turn around and keep your eyes shut.
    If the Gorgon appears and you even glance,
        there will be no return to the world above."   *57*
As my master said this, he took me himself,
    spun me around, and not trusting my hands,
        covered my eyes with his hands as well.   *60*

You readers who are of sound understanding,
    look well at the teaching that conceals itself
        under the veil of these strange verses.   *63*

And now there came over the turbulent water
    a crashing sound full of fear and terror
        that made both of the marsh's shorelines tremble.   *66*
It was like a blast of air given momentum
    by opposing waves of heat, the kind of wind
        that smashes through a forest without restraint,   *69*
Splinters the branches, snaps and sweeps them off,
    and rushing onward in a cloud of dust
        puts all the animals and shepherds to flight.   *72*
He freed my eyes and said: "Now look out there
    over the ancient foam and focus your vision
        where that cloud of smoke is most intense."   *75*
As frogs at the threat of a water-snake
    will scatter and flee in every direction
        until all of them are huddled on shore,   *78*
More than a thousand ruined spirits I saw
    fleeing before one who strode along
        with dry soles over the swamp of Styx.   *81*
The air hung thick, and with his left hand
    he often fanned his face, weary,
        it seemed, of only this annoyance.   *84*
I was well aware he was sent from Heaven,
    and I turned to my master, who made a sign
        that I should stay quiet and bow before him.   *87*
How full of disdain he appeared to me!
    He came to the gate and with a slender wand
        opened it without any resistance.   *90*

"O cacciati del ciel, gente dispetta,"
　cominciò elli in su l'orribil soglia,
93　　"ond' esta oltracotanza in voi s'alletta?
Perché recalcitrate a quella voglia
　a cui non puote il fin mai esser mozzo,
96　　e che piú volte v'ha cresciuta doglia?
Che giova ne le fata dar di cozzo?
　Cerbero vostro, se ben vi ricorda,
99　　ne porta ancor pelato il mento e 'l gozzo."
Poi si rivolse per la strada lorda,
　e non fé motto a noi, ma fé sembiante
102　　d'omo cui altra cura stringa e morda
che quella di colui che li è davante;
　e noi movemmo i piedi inver' la terra,
105　　sicuri appresso le parole sante.

Dentro li 'ntrammo sanz' alcuna guerra;
　e io, ch'avea di riguardar disio
108　　la condizion che tal fortezza serra,
com' io fui dentro, l'occhio intorno invio:
　e veggio ad ogne man grande campagna,
111　　piena di duolo e di tormento rio.
Sí come ad Arli, ove Rodano stagna,
　sí com' a Pola, presso del Carnaro
114　　ch'Italia chiude e suoi termini bagna,
fanno i sepulcri tutt' il loco varo,
　cosí facevan quivi d'ogne parte,
117　　salvo che 'l modo v'era piú amaro;
ché tra li avelli fiamme erano sparte,
　per le quali eran sí del tutto accesi,
120　　che ferro piú non chiede verun' arte.
Tutti li lor coperchi eran sospesi,
　e fuor n'uscivan sí duri lamenti,
123　　che ben parean di miseri e d'offesi.
E io: "Maestro, quai son quelle genti
　che, seppellite dentro da quell' arche,
126　　si fan sentir coi sospiri dolenti?"

Standing tall upon that horrible threshold,
  "O outcasts from Heaven," he began, "a people
    despised, what makes you cling to your insolence?   *93*
Why do you kick against the Divine Will
  whose purpose can never be rescinded
    and that many times has increased your pain?   *96*
Do you think it helps to butt against Fate?
  Your Cerberus, as you will recall,
    got his chin and gullet peeled for that."   *99*
Then he returned along the mucky road
  and never spoke to us. He looked as though
    he were distracted, beset with other cares   *102*
Than those of the people there before him.
  When he was gone we advanced toward the city,
    his holy words having stiffened our spines.   *105*

We entered and met no challenge within.
  I, who had a strong desire to discover
    what it was like inside that fortress,   *108*
Began casting my eyes in every direction
  and saw all around me an enormous plain
    full of terrible distress and pain.   *111*
Just as at Arles, where the Rhone grows stagnant,
  and at Pola, near the Gulf of Quarnerno,
    which shelters Italy and bathes her borders,   *114*
The sepulchres make the terrain uneven—
  so too in this place, on every side,
    but with one horrifying difference.   *117*
For the tombs were kindled thickly with fire
  that caused them to glow like red-hot iron,
    iron far hotter than any forge requires.   *120*
The tombs' lids were all open, and the cries
  that issued from within them were so tortured
    they could only have come from the wretched damned. *123*
I said: "Master, who are these people
  entombed in these sarcophagi,
    whose laments proclaim their suffering?"   *126*

E quelli a me: "Qui son li eresïarche
con lor seguaci, d'ogne setta, e molto
129   piú che non credi son le tombe carche.
Simile qui con simile è sepolto,
e i monimenti son piú e men caldi."
132   E poi ch'a la man destra si fu vòlto,
passammo tra i martíri e li alti spaldi.

He answered me: "Here the great heretics grieve
  with their followers from every sect.
  The tombs are more crowded than you would believe.   *129*
Like is sepulchred with like, and the fiery blast
  is more or less hot in various monuments."
  He took a turn to the right then, and we passed   *132*
Between the torments and looming battlements.

CANTO X

THE PILGRIMS FOLLOW A PATH *through the Sixth Circle that leads among the sepulchres. Dante, seeing that they are open, is eager to see who is buried in them. They will be sealed, replies Virgil, on the Day of Judgment. The pilgrims are crossing the zone in which the shades of the Epicureans, who did not believe that the soul was immortal, have found the after-death burial they expected. As they walk by, their conversation is suddenly interrupted by a voice that comes from one of the tombs. The speaker, a fellow Tuscan, has recognized Dante's Florentine accent. Virgil urges Dante to turn around and see the great Ghibelline champion Farinata, about whose whereabouts he had previously questioned the glutton Ciacco. Virgil recommends that Dante address him respectfully. Farinata quizzes Dante about his forebears and, when Dante tells him who they were, identifies them as belonging to the rival Guelph faction and therefore among his bitter enemies. Twice the Ghibellines drove them out, exults Farinata. But not the third time, replies Dante. The third time, which pays for all, your side was defeated. At this point, as unexpected as the voice of Farinata had been, another shade rears up from the same tomb, peering around for his son, who, given their intellectual parity, ought, he thinks, to be with Dante. The pilgrim recognizes*

Ora sen va per un secreto calle,
    tra 'l muro de la terra e li martíri,
3   lo mio maestro, e io dopo le spalle.
"O virtù somma, che per li empi giri
    mi volvi," cominciai, "com' a te piace,
6   parlami, e sodisfammi a' miei disiri.
La gente che per li sepolcri giace
    potrebbesi veder? già son levati
9   tutt' i coperchi, e nessun guardia face."
E quelli a me: "Tutti saran serrati
    quando di Iosafàt qui torneranno
12   coi corpi che là sú hanno lasciati.

90

Cavalcante dei Cavalcanti, the father of Guido, the Florentine poet who "held in scorn" the person to whom Virgil is leading him. The shade interprets Dante's use of the past tense as evidence that his son is dead and falls down backward in despair. Ignoring Cavalcante, the Stoic Farinata continues where he left off, expressing his dismay at the news Dante has brought him. But Dante himself will soon learn how hard it is to come back from exile. Why, Farinata asks, do the Florentines persecute my family so? Because of the bloody battle of Montaperti, replies Dante. I was not the only warrior who fought there, says Farinata, but I was the only one who spoke out against the destruction of Florence after the Ghibelline victory. Dante asks why, if the dead can see into the future, they don't appear to know what is happening on Earth at present. Farinata replies that the closer events approach, the more clouded their vision becomes. Dante asks him to tell Cavalcante that his son Guido is not dead. Farinata informs him that among the others condemned to this circle is the Hohenstaufen Emperor Frederick II. Virgil tells Dante, who is mulling over Farinata's hostile prophecy, to wait for Beatrice, who will clarify his destiny.

Along a path that wound its secret way
 between the torments and the city's wall
  my master went, and I stayed close behind.   *3*
"Supreme Virtue," I said to him,
 "leading me around these sinful circles
  as you please, satisfy my desire to know.   *6*
The people lying in these sepulchres,
 might they be seen? The lids are open,
  and no one keeps guard." And he answered: *9*
"These tombs will all be closed when their inhabitants
 return here below from Jehoshaphat
  with the bodies they abandoned up above.   *12*

Suo cimitero da questa parte hanno
  con Epicuro tutti suoi seguaci,
15   che l'anima col corpo morta fanno.
Però a la dimanda che mi faci
  quinc' entro satisfatto sarà tosto,
18   e al disio ancor che tu mi taci."
E io: "Buon duca, non tegno riposto
  a te mio cuor se non per dicer poco,
21   e tu m'hai non pur mo a ciò disposto."

"O Tosco che per la città del foco
  vivo ten vai cosí parlando onesto,
24   piacciati di restare in questo loco.
La tua loquela ti fa manifesto
  di quella nobil patrïa natio,
27   a la qual forse fui troppo molesto."
Subitamente questo suono uscío
  d'una de l'arche; però m'accostai,
30   temendo, un poco piú al duca mio.
Ed el mi disse: "Volgiti! Che fai?
  Vedi là Farinata che s'è dritto:
33   da la cintola in sú tutto 'l vedrai."
Io avea già il mio viso nel suo fitto;
  ed el s'ergea col petto e con la fronte
36   com' avesse l'inferno a gran dispitto.
E l'animose man del duca e pronte
  mi pinser tra le sepulture a lui,
39   dicendo: "Le parole tue sien conte."
Com' io al piè de la sua tomba fui,
  guardommi un poco, e poi, quasi sdegnoso,
42   mi dimandò: "Chi fuor li maggior tui?"
Io ch'era d'ubidir disideroso,
  non gliel celai, ma tutto gliel' apersi;
45   ond' ei levò le ciglia un poco in suso;
poi disse: "Fieramente furo avversi
  a me e a miei primi e a mia parte,
48   sí che per due fïate li dispersi."

Buried in this branch of the cemetery
  are Epicurus and all his sect, who make
    the soul and body die a single death.   *15*
You will soon, in any case, have satisfaction
  as to the question that you posed to me—
    as well as for the wish that you withhold."   *18*
And I said: "My trusted guide, I would not hide
  my heart from you except to speak more briefly,
    for this is what you have always had me do."   *21*

"O Tuscan, speaking with such civility
  as you go alive through the city of fire,
    may it please you to stop a while in this place.   *24*
Your manner and accent clearly show you to be
  a native son of that noble city
    to which I perhaps caused too much harm."   *27*
The sound of this voice issued so suddenly
  from one of the monumental coffins
    that in fear I drew closer to my guide,   *30*
Who said, "What are you doing? Turn around!
  Look at Farinata there, who has risen upright.
    You will see him all from the waist on up."   *33*
I had already fixed my eyes on his
  as he rose with chest and brow thrown back
    as if he had nothing but scorn for Hell.   *36*
The assured and ready hands of my guide
  were pushing me through the tombs to him,
    and he told me, "See that your words are apt."   *39*
When I was at the foot of Farinata's tomb
  he looked me over briefly, and then asked,
    "Who were your ancestors?" as if with disdain.   *42*
I was eager to comply, and hid
  nothing from him but told him all,
    at which he lifted his brows a little,   *45*
And then said, "They were hostile to me,
  and so not once but twice I scattered them,
    enemies to my family and to my party."   *48*

"S'ei fur cacciati, ei tornar d'ogne parte,"
rispuos' io lui, "l'una e l'altra fïata;
51   ma i vostri non appreser ben quell' arte."

Allor surse a la vista scoperchiata
un'ombra, lungo questa, infino al mento:
54   credo che s'era in ginocchie levata.
Dintorno mi guardò, come talento
avesse di veder s'altri era meco;
57   e poi che 'l sospecciar fu tutto spento,
piangendo disse: "Se per questo cieco
carcere vai per altezza d'ingegno,
60   mio figlio ov' è? e perché non è teco?"
E io a lui: "Da me stesso non vegno:
colui ch'attende là per qui mi mena
63   forse cui Guido vostro ebbe a disdegno."
Le sue parole e 'l modo de la pena
m'avean di costui già letto il nome;
66   però fu la risposta cosí piena.
Di súbito drizzato gridò: "Come?
dicesti 'elli ebbe'? non viv' elli ancora?
69   non fiere li occhi suoi lo dolce lume?"
Quando s'accorse d'alcuna dimora
ch'io facëa dinanzi a la risposta,
72   supin ricadde e piú non parve fora.

Ma quell' altro magnanimo, a cui posta
restato m'era, non mutò aspetto,
75   né mosse collo, né piegò sua costa;
e sé continüando al primo detto,
"S'elli han quell' arte," disse, "male appresa,
78   ciò mi tormenta piú che questo letto.
Ma non cinquanta volte fia raccesa
la faccia de la donna che qui regge,
81   che tu saprai quanto quell' arte pesa.

"If they were driven out, they always returned
  from every quarter," I answered him,
    "an art your people have hardly learned."   *51*

Then there rose beside him another shade
  in the open tomb. Visible from his chin up,
    he seemed as if he had risen onto his knees.   *54*
He looked about me as though he wanted
  to see someone else in my company,
    and when this hope was disappointed,   *57*
He said, weeping, "If it is your genius
  by which you journey through this blind prison,
    where is my son, and why is he not with you?"   *60*
I said to him: "I do not come on my own.
  My guide over there leads me through this place,
    perhaps to someone your Guido held in scorn."   *63*
His words and the mode of his punishment
  had already announced his name to me,
    and this is why my response was so full.   *66*
Straightening up suddenly, he cried out:
  "Did you say 'held'? Is he not still alive?
    Does the sweet light not still fall on his eyes?"   *69*
When he perceived my hesitation
  in answering, he fell supine again,
    and after that he appeared no more.   *72*

But the other one, that great soul at whose request
  I had stopped, kept the same expression
    and did not turn his head or bend his waist.   *75*
Picking up his speech where he had left off,
  He said, "And if they have learned that art badly,
    that torments me more than this bed of flames.   *78*
But the face of that Lady who rules here below
  will not be relit fifty times in the sky
    before you will learn the true weight of that art.   *81*

E se tu mai nel dolce mondo regge,
   dimmi: perché quel popolo è sí empio
84   incontr' a' miei in ciascuna sua legge?"
Ond' io a lui: "Lo strazio e 'l grande scempio
   che fece l'Arbia colorata in rosso,
87   tal orazion fa far nel nostro tempio."
Poi ch'ebbe sospirando il capo mosso,
   "A ciò non fu' io sol," disse, "né certo
90   sanza cagion con li altri sarei mosso.
Ma fu' io solo, là dove sofferto
   fu per ciascun di tòrre via Fiorenza,
93   colui che la difesi a viso aperto."

"Deh, se riposi mai vostra semenza,"
   prega' io lui, "solvetemi quel nodo
96   che qui ha 'nviluppata mia sentenza.
El par che voi veggiate, se ben odo,
   dinanzi quel che 'l tempo seco adduce,
99   e nel presente tenete altro modo."
"Noi veggiam, come quei c'ha mala luce,
   le cose," disse, "che ne son lontano;
102   cotanto ancor ne splende il sommo duce.
Quando s'appressano o son, tutto è vano
   nostro intelletto; e s'altri non ci apporta,
105   nulla sapem di vostro stato umano.
Però comprender puoi che tutta morta
   fia nostra conoscenza da quel punto
108   che del futuro fia chiusa la porta."

Allor, come di mia colpa compunto,
   dissi: "Or direte dunque a quel caduto
111   che 'l suo nato è co' vivi ancor congiunto;
e s'i' fui, dianzi, a la risposta muto,
   fate i saper che 'l fei perché pensava
114   già ne l'error che m'avete soluto."

And, so may you return to that sweet world again;
  tell me, why is that city so merciless
    against my kindred in all of its laws?"   84
I said: "The great devastation and the slaughter
  that dyed the waters of the Arbia red
    cause such prayers to be said in our temple."   87
He sighed, shook his head, and then said to me,
  "I was not alone there, nor would I ever
    have moved with the others without great cause.   90
But when all the others were complicit,
  agreeing to make an end of Florence, I,
    I alone, stood forth in her defense."   93

"Yes, and so may your seed sometime find peace,"
  I entreated him, "would you solve for me
    a problem that has tied my mind in knots?   96
It appears, if I have heard correctly,
  that you see beforehand what time will bring,
    but it is not so when it comes to the present."   99
"We see best," he said, "like one in dim light,
  the things that are farther away in the distance.
    So much does the High Ruler still shine on us.   102
But when they are near, or present, our intellect
  is wholly useless. Unless someone brings word
    we have no knowledge of your human state.   105
And so, you can readily comprehend
  that our understanding will be forever dead
    the moment the door of the future is closed."   108

Then, feeling as if I were at fault, I said,
  "Will you tell the one who fell back beside you
    that his son is still among the living?   111
And, to explain my silence to his question before,
  tell him that at that time I labored under
    the misunderstanding you cleared up for me."   114

E già 'l maestro mio mi richiamava;
per ch'i' pregai lo spirto piú avaccio
117   che mi dicesse chi con lu' istava.
Dissemi: "Qui con piú di mille giaccio:
qua dentro è 'l secondo Federico
120   e 'l Cardinale; e de li altri mi taccio."

Indi s'ascose; e io inver' l'antico
poeta volsi i passi, ripensando
123   a quel parlar che mi parea nemico.
Elli si mosse; e poi, cosí andando,
mi disse: "Perché se' tu sí smarrito?"
126   E io li sodisfeci al suo dimando.
"La mente tua conservi quel ch'udito
hai contra te," mi comandò quel saggio;
129   "e ora attendi qui," e drizzò 'l dito:
"quando sarai dinanzi al dolce raggio
di quella il cui bell' occhio tutto vede,
132   da lei saprai di tua vita il vïaggio."
Appresso mosse a man sinistra il piede:
lasciammo il muro e gimmo inver' lo mezzo
135   per un sentier ch'a una valle fiede,
che 'nfin là sú facea spiacer suo lezzo.

My master now was calling me back,
   and so in great haste I asked the spirit
      to tell me those who were in there with him. *117*
He said: "Here I lie with more than a thousand.
   The second Frederick is in this tomb,
      the Cardinal too. I do not speak of the rest." *120*

With that he withdrew. I turned my steps
   toward the ancient Poet, meditating upon
      the words that seemed so hostile to me. *123*
He set out, and then, as we walked on,
   he asked me, "Why are you so lost in thought?"
      And so I told him what he wanted to know. *126*
"Keep in memory what you have heard
   against yourself," the sage commanded,
      and, raising a finger, "Now hear my word. *129*
When you are bathed in the sweet radiance
   of her whose beautiful eyes see all,
      your journey through life will finally make sense." *132*
With that he turned to the left, and we
   abandoned the wall, traveling where
      a path led inward and down to a valley *135*
Whose stench disgusted us even up there.

CANTO XI

A STEEP LANDSLIPPED EMBANKMENT *leads down from the Sixth Circle to the Seventh. To accustom their senses to the putrid stench that wells up from below, Virgil and Dante take refuge behind the tomb that holds heretical pope Anastasius II. Dante's guide takes advantage of the pause to explain the moral topography of the circles that lie below. There are three circles remaining. The first holds the Violent, who sinned through force, and is subdivided into three rings according to the object against which that force was directed: their neighbors, themselves, or God Himself. A further distinction is made between violence against persons (and, in the case of God, the would-be violence of blasphemy) and violence against property (in God's case, sins against the order of His creation—sodomy and usury). More grievous than those of the Violent are the sins of the Fraudulent, who employ reason, the special gift of humankind, to harm*

     In su l'estremità d'un'alta ripa
       che facevan gran pietre rotte in cerchio,
3   venimmo sopra piú crudele stipa;
     e quivi, per l'orribile soperchio
       del puzzo che 'l profondo abisso gitta,
6   ci raccostammo, in dietro, ad un coperchio
       d'un grand' avello, ov' io vidi una scritta
       che dicea: 'Anastasio papa guardo,
9   lo qual trasse Fotin de la via dritta.'
     "Lo nostro scender conviene esser tardo,
       sí che s'ausi un poco in prima il senso
12   al tristo fiato; e poi no i fia riguardo."
     Cosí 'l maestro; e io "Alcun compenso,"
       dissi lui, "trova che 'l tempo non passi
15   perduto." Ed elli: "Vedi ch'a ciò penso."

others. The Fraudulent too are further subdivided: into those who defrauded their unsuspecting neighbors, punished in the Eighth Circle, and the Traitors, who had a special bond of trust with their victims, a bond they violated. This last category is punished in the Ninth Circle, which is also the last. Dante asks: What of the sinners we saw outside the walls of Dis: the Lustful, the Gluttonous, the Avaricious, and the Prodigal, the Wrathful, and the Sullen? Virgil reminds him that Aristotle's Nicomachean Ethics *distinguished three dispositions rejected by Heaven—bestial rage (violence), malice (fraud and treachery), and the less heinous sins of incontinence, which condemn the sinner but do not hurt other victims. Incontinence is punished outside the walls. In a corollary, with another reference to Aristotle, this time to the* Physics, *as well as to the book of Genesis, Virgil explains why usury constitutes violence against God.*

Arriving at the edge of a high embankment
   formed by a circle of huge broken rocks,
      we looked down upon an even crueler pen.   3
And here, because of the overwhelming
   putrid stench that the abyss exuded,
      we drew back and took cover behind the lid   6
Of a great tomb, on which I saw an inscription
   that read: I HOLD POPE ANASTASIUS,
      WHOM PHOTINUS SEDUCED FROM THE RIGHT PATH.   9
"We must delay our descent a while, until
   our senses can stomach that vile stench.
      Then we will not notice it so much."   12
Thus my master, and I said to him: "Could you
   find some profitable way to pass the time?"
      And he said: "I was thinking the same thing myself."   15

"Figliuol mio, dentro da cotesti sassi,"
  cominciò poi a dir, "son tre cerchietti
18   di grado in grado, come que' che lassi.
Tutti son pien di spirti maladetti;
  ma perché poi ti basti pur la vista,
21   intendi come e perché son costretti.
D'ogne malizia, ch'odio in cielo acquista,
  ingiuria è 'l fine, ed ogne fin cotale
24   o con forza o con frode altrui contrista.
Ma perché frode è de l'uom proprio male,
  piú spiace a Dio; e però stan di sotto
27   li frodolenti, e piú dolor li assale.
Di vïolenti il primo cerchio è tutto;
  ma perché si fa forza a tre persone,
30   in tre gironi è distinto e costrutto.
A Dio, a sé, al prossimo si pòne
  far forza, dico in loro e in lor cose,
33   come udirai con aperta ragione.
Morte per forza e ferute dogliose
  nel prossimo si danno, e nel suo avere
36   ruine, incendi e tollette dannose;
onde omicide e ciascun che mal fiere,
  guastatori e predon, tutti tormenta
39   lo giron primo per diverse schiere.
Puote omo avere in sé man vïolenta
  e ne' suoi beni; e però nel secondo
42   giron convien che sanza pro si penta
qualunque priva sé del vostro mondo,
  biscazza e fonde la sua facultade,
45   e piange là dov' esser de' giocondo.
Puossi far forza ne la deïtade,
  col cor negando e bestemmiando quella,
48   e spregiando natura e sua bontade;
e però lo minor giron suggella
  del segno suo e Soddoma e Caorsa
51   e chi, spregiando Dio col cor, favella.

"My son," he began, "within these rocks
are three lesser circles, each of them set
    below another, like the ones you have left.   *18*
All are filled with spirits of the damned,
but so that you will know as soon as you see them,
    hear how and why these souls are constrained.   *21*
Injustice is the end of every malice
hated in Heaven, and every such end,
    whether by force or by fraud, injures another.   *24*
But since fraud is an evil peculiar to man,
it displeases God more, and so the fraudulent
    are lower down, and assailed by more pain.   *27*
The whole First Circle houses the violent,
but since three persons may be targets of violence,
    it is divided into three concentric rings.   *30*
To God, to oneself, and to one's neighbor,
violence may be done, to each of these
    and to their property, as I will make clear.   *33*
Death by violence and grievous wounds
may undo one's neighbor; pillage and arson
    and ruinous extortion may destroy his goods;   *36*
Therefore all murderers and all who assault
another unjustly, who despoil and plunder,
    the first ring torments in various groups.   *39*
A man may lay violent hands on himself
and his own possessions, and such a sinner
    pours out empty remorse in the second ring,   *42*
Anyone who deprives himself of your world,
who squanders and gambles his goods away
    and ends up weeping where he should be glad.   *45*
Violence may be done against the Godhead
by heartfelt denial and blasphemy,
    and holding Nature's bounty in contempt;   *48*
And so the smallest ring seals with its mark
both Sodom and Cahors, and those who speak
    despising the Deity in their hearts.   *51*

La frode, ond' ogne coscïenza è morsa,
    può l'omo usare in colui che 'n lui fida
54   e in quel che fidanza non imborsa.
Questo modo di retro par ch'incida
    pur lo vinco d'amor che fa natura;
57   onde nel cerchio secondo s'annida
ipocresia, lusinghe e chi affattura,
    falsità, ladroneccio e simonia,
60   ruffian, baratti e simile lordura.
Per l'altro modo quell' amor s'oblia
    che fa natura, e quel ch'è poi aggiunto,
63   di che la fede spezïal si cria;
onde nel cerchio minore, ov' è 'l punto
    de l'universo in su che Dite siede,
66   qualunque trade in etterno è consunto."

E io: "Maestro, assai chiara procede
    la tua ragione, e assai ben distingue
69   questo baràtro e 'l popol ch'e' possiede.
Ma dimmi: quei de la palude pingue,
    che mena il vento, e che batte la pioggia,
72   e che s'incontran con sí aspre lingue,
perché non dentro da la città roggia
    sono ei puniti, se Dio li ha in ira?
75   e se non li ha, perché sono a tal foggia?"

Ed elli a me "Perché tanto delira,"
    disse, "lo 'ngegno tuo da quel che sòle?
78   o ver la mente dove altrove mira?
Non ti rimembra di quelle parole
    con le quai la tua Etica pertratta
81   le tre disposizion che 'l ciel non vole,
incontenenza, malizia e la matta
    bestialitade? e come incontenenza
84   men Dio offende e men biasimo accatta?
Se tu riguardi ben questa sentenza,
    e rechiti a la mente chi son quelli
87   che sú di fuor sostegnon penitenza,

Fraud, by which every conscience is gnawed,
  may be practiced upon one who trusts in us,
    or upon one who has entrusted no confidence.   *54*
The latter seems to sever only the bond
  of natural love of neighbor, and hence
    the Second Circle is the nesting place   *57*
For hypocrites, parasites, and sorcerers,
  counterfeiters, thieves, and simoniacs,
    panderers, grafters, and other such filth.   *60*
The other kind of fraud that violates trust
  obliterates the bond of natural affection
    and forsakes the love that depends on faith,   *63*
And therefore in the smallest circle of all,
  at the universe's center and the seat of Dis,
    every traitor is consumed forevermore."   *66*

And I said: "Master, your explanation
  is most clear and distinguishes well
    the parts of this chasm and the people it holds.   *69*
But tell me, the souls in the sickening swamp,
  and those the wind drives, and those the rain pelts,
    and those who collide with such harsh words,   *72*
Why are they not punished in this charred city
  if God's wrath is upon them? And if it is not,
    why do they suffer such a sorry fate?"   *75*

He said to me: "Where has your accustomed
  intelligence gone? Why are you raving?
    Down what blind alley does your mind wander?   *78*
Do you not remember your Aristotle?
  How his *Ethics* describes, and deals with at length,
    the three dispositions rejected by Heaven—   *81*
Incontinence, malice, and bestial rage—
  and how one of these three, incontinence,
    offends God less and so incurs less blame?   *84*
If you examine this doctrine carefully
  and call to mind who those people are
    who are punished up there outside the walls,   *87*

tu vedrai ben perché da questi felli
    sien dipartiti, e perché men crucciata
90   la divina vendetta li martelli."

"O sol che sani ogne vista turbata,
    tu mi contenti sí quando tu solvi,
93   che, non men che saver, dubbiar m'aggrata.
Ancora in dietro un poco ti rivolvi,"
    diss'io, "là dove di' ch'usura offende
96   la divina bontade, e 'l groppo solvi."

"Filosofia," mi disse, "a chi la 'ntende,
    nota, non pure in una sola parte,
99   come natura lo suo corso prende
dal divino 'ntelletto e da sua arte;
    e se tu ben la tua Fisica note,
102   tu troverai, non dopo molte carte,
che l'arte vostra quella, quanto pote,
    segue, come 'l maestro fa 'l discente;
105   sí che vostr' arte a Dio quasi è nepote.
Da queste due, se tu ti rechi a mente
    lo Genesí dal principio, convene
108   prender sua vita e avanzar la gente;
e perché l'usuriere altra via tene,
    per sé natura e per la sua seguace
111   dispregia, poi ch'in altro pon la spene.
Ma seguimi oramai che 'l gir mi piace;
    ché i Pesci guizzan su per l'orizzonta,
114   e 'l Carro tutto sovra 'l Coro giace,
e 'l balzo via là oltra si dismonta."

You will see clearly why they are kept apart
 from these sinners, and why Divine Vengeance
  smites them less cruelly then it does those here."   *90*

"O Sun who heals every clouded vision,
 you satisfy me so when you resolve my doubts
  that doubting pleases me no less than knowing,"   *93*
I said to him, "But go back a little
 to your account of usury as an offense
  against Divine Goodness, and untie that knot."   *96*

"Philosophy," he said, "properly understood,
 observes, and not in one place alone,
  how Nature herself sets her course   *99*
By the Divine Intellect and by Its art.
 And if you pay attention to your *Physics*,
  you will find, after not too many pages,   *102*
That your own art, as far as it can,
 follows Nature as the pupil his master.
  Your art, then, is a kind of grandchild of God.   *105*
By Nature and Art, if you remember
 the opening verses of Genesis,
  the human race must endure and prosper.   *108*
But because the usurer takes another course
 he despises both Nature and her disciple,
  investing his hope in something worse.   *111*
But follow me now, for I wish to go.
 Pisces flickers on the dawn horizon,
  and in the northwest the Wagon swings low,   *114*
And our next descent is still farther on."

Canto XII

THE LOOSE, ROCKY DESCENT *down into the Seventh Circle is treacherous, and the way is guarded by the misbegotten Cretan Minotaur, part man, part bull, slain by Theseus. When Virgil challenges him, the violent guardian of the Circle of the Violent is seized with a fit of impotent rage. As they scramble by him, Virgil explains that, on his previous journey through Hell, this landslide had not yet occurred. It happened, in fact, as a result of the earthquake that accompanied Christ's visit to Hell to liberate the meritorious souls from Limbo. The pilgrims now approach the River of Blood, in which the first group of the Violent, the Violent against Their Neighbors, watched over by the impulsive*

Era lo loco ov' a scender la riva
venimmo, alpestro e, per quel che v'er' anco,
3   tal, ch'ogne vista ne sarebbe schiva.
Qual è quella ruina che nel fianco
di qua da Trento l'Adice percosse,
6   o per tremoto o per sostegno manco,
che da cima del monte, onde si mosse,
al piano è sí la roccia discoscesa,
9   ch'alcuna via darebbe a chi sú fosse:
cotal di quel burrato era la scesa;
e 'n su la punta de la rotta lacca
12   l'infamïa di Creti era distesa
che fu concetta ne la falsa vacca;
e quando vide noi, sé stesso morse,
15   sí come quei cui l'ira dentro fiacca.
Lo savio mio inver' lui gridò: "Forse
tu credi che qui sia 'l duca d'Atene,
18   che sú nel mondo la morte ti porse?
Pàrtiti, bestia, ché questi non vene
ammaestrato da la tua sorella,
21   ma vassi per veder le vostre pene."

Centaurs, are more or less deeply immersed. Challenged by the Centaur Nessus, Virgil desires to speak with Chiron, who observes how Dante's living feet stir the stones. Virgil requests an escort, and Chiron instructs Nessus to guide them along the river's edge. They see tyrants, ancient and modern, plunged up to their eyebrows in the hot blood. The shade of assassin Guy de Montfort is covered to the neck. Highwaymen and brigands are less deeply immersed. The river gets shallower and shallower until it becomes possible to ford it. His task accomplished, Nessus turns to recross the stream and rejoin his fellow Centaurs.

The place where we came to descend the gorge
　　was rugged and, given what else we saw there,
　　　would make anyone turn and look away.　　　　　　　*3*
Like the huge landslide that rattled the Alps
　　in the Adige valley this side of Trento,
　　　when earthquakes or erosion brought the cliff down,　　*6*
And sent a tumble of rocks from the summit,
　　where the slide was triggered, down to the plain
　　　in such a way as to allow a descent—　　　　　　　*9*
Such was the descent of that ravine;
　　and on the edge of that splintered scree
　　　sprawled the Minotaur, the infamy of Crete　　　　*12*
Who was conceived in the artificial cow.
　　When he saw us coming, he bit himself
　　　as if consumed by some inward rage.　　　　　　　*15*
My sage cried out to him: "Perhaps you think
　　this is Theseus, the Duke of Athens
　　　who dealt you your death in the world above.　　　*18*
Out of our way, beast! This man does not come
　　schooled by your sister. No, his journey is to see
　　　how all your punishment is exacted here."　　　　*21*

Qual è quel toro che si slaccia in quella
c'ha ricevuto già 'l colpo mortale,
24   che gir non sa, ma qua e là saltella,
vid' io lo Minotauro far cotale;
e quello accorto gridò: "Corri al varco;
27   mentre ch'e' 'nfuria, è buon che tu ti cale."
Cosí prendemmo via giú per lo scarco
di quelle pietre, che spesso moviensi
30   sotto i miei piedi per lo novo carco.

Io gia pensando; e quei disse: "Tu pensi
forse a questa ruina, ch'è guardata
33   da quell' ira bestial ch'i' ora spensi.
Or vo' che sappi che l'altra fïata
ch'i' discesi qua giú nel basso inferno,
36   questa roccia non era ancor cascata.
Ma certo poco pria, se ben discerno,
che venisse colui che la gran preda
39   levò a Dite del cerchio superno,
da tutte parti l'alta valle feda
tremò sí, ch'i' pensai che l'universo
42   sentisse amor, per lo qual è chi creda
piú volte il mondo in caòsso converso;
e in quel punto questa vecchia roccia,
45   qui e altrove, tal fece riverso.
Ma ficca li occhi a valle, ché s'approccia
la riviera del sangue in la qual bolle
48   qual che per vïolenza in altrui noccia."

Oh cieca cupidigia e ira folle,
che sí ci sproni ne la vita corta,
51   e ne l'etterna poi sí mal c'immolle!

Io vidi un'ampia fossa in arco torta,
come quella che tutto 'l piano abbraccia,
54   secondo ch'avea detto la mia scorta;

As a bull who breaks loose just as he receives
  a mortal blow can no longer run
    but bucks and thrashes this way and that,   *24*
So too the Minotaur. And my wary guide:
  "Run for the slope! It would be best
    for you to get down while he is in his rage."   *27*
And so the two of us picked our way down
  over the rubble of stones, which slid
    and shifted under my unfamiliar weight.   *30*

I was thinking as I went along, and he asked,
  "Are you wondering about this landslide, guarded
    by that bestial fury I just now gentled?   *33*
I would have you know that the previous time
  I descended this far into lower Hell
    this rock had not yet cascaded down.   *36*
But certainly, if my reckoning is right,   Jesus
  shortly before He harrowed Hell, and bore away
    the great plunder of the topmost circle,   *39*
The reeking abyss trembled so hard
  that I thought the universe was in the grip
    of the love by which, as some believe,   *42*
The world has often been reduced to chaos.
  It was at that moment that this ancient rock,
    here and elsewhere, tumbled in avalanche.   *45*
But fix your eyes down below, for we are near
  the River of Blood, in which are cooked
    those whose violence has injured others."   *48*

O blind greed and maniacal rage
  that prick and goad us in this too short-lived flesh
    and then boil us down in the life eternal!   *51*

I saw a wide trench bent in an arc
  that seemed to go on and ring the plain,
    just as my guide had earlier explained.   *54*

e tra 'l piè de la ripa ed essa, in traccia
  corrien centauri, armati di saette,
57   come solien nel mondo andare a caccia.
Veggendoci calar, ciascun ristette,
  e de la schiera tre si dipartiro
60   con archi e asticciuole prima elette;
e l'un gridò da lungi: "A qual martiro
  venite voi che scendete la costa?
63   Ditel costinci; se non, l'arco tiro."
Lo mio maestro disse: "La risposta
  farem noi a Chirón costà di presso:
66   mal fu la voglia tua sempre sí tosta."
Poi mi tentò, e disse: "Quelli è Nesso,
  che morí per la bella Deianira,
69   e fé di sé la vendetta elli stesso.
E quel di mezzo, ch'al petto si mira,
  è il gran Chirón, il qual nodrí Achille;
72   quell' altro è Folo, che fu sí pien d'ira.
Dintorno al fosso vanno a mille a mille,
  saettando qual anima si svelle
75   del sangue piú che sua colpa sortille."

Noi ci appressammo a quelle fiere isnelle:
  Chirón prese uno strale, e con la cocca
78   fece la barba in dietro a le mascelle.
Quando s'ebbe scoperta la gran bocca,
  disse a' compagni: "Siete voi accorti
81   che quel di retro move ciò ch'el tocca?
Cosí non soglion far li piè d'i morti."
  E 'l mio buon duca, che già li er' al petto,
84   dove le due nature son consorti,
rispuose: "Ben è vivo, e sí soletto
  mostrar li mi convien la valle buia;
87   necessità 'l ci 'nduce, e non diletto.
Tal si partì da cantare alleluia
  che mi commise quest' officio novo:
90   non è ladron, né io anima fuia.

Between the trench and the embankment's foot
  Centaurs galloped in single file, armed with arrows
    just as for the hunt in the world above.   *57*
When they saw us descending they all stopped,
  and then three peeled off from the company
    with choice arrows notched onto their bowstrings.   *60*
They were still a ways off when one cried out,
  "Bound for what torment do you descend the slope?
    Tell me from there, or I draw my bow."   *63*
My master said: "We will make our reply
  to Chiron, there at your side. Your own will
    was always hasty. It has cost you before."   *66*
Then he nudged me with his elbow, saying,
  "That is Nessus, who died for the beautiful
    Deianira and avenged his own death.   *69*
The one in the middle, head bowed to his chest,
  is the great Chiron, who raised Achilles.
    The other is Pholus, who was so full of rage.   *72*
Around the trench they go in their thousands,
  shooting any spirit who pulls himself
    out of the blood more than his guilt allows."   *75*

As we drew closer to these agile beasts
  Chiron took out an arrow and with its nock
    brushed his beard back beside either jaw;   *78*
And when he had uncovered that great mouth of his,
  he observed to his fellows, "Have you noticed
    that the one who follows moves what he touches?   *81*
The feet of the dead do not do that."
  And my good leader, who was now at the chest
    of the Centaur, where his two natures met,   *84*
Replied, "Yes, he is alive, and all alone,
  and I must show him this chasm's murk.
    Necessity, not pleasure, brings us here.   *87*
She who gave me this new duty came
  from singing Alleluia. He is no
    robber, nor am I the spirit of a thief,   *90*

Ma per quella virtù per cu' io movo
　li passi miei per sí selvaggia strada,
93　　　danne un de' tuoi, a cui noi siamo a provo,
　e che ne mostri là dove si guada,
　　e che porti costui in su la groppa,
96　　　ché non è spirto che per l'aere vada."
Chirón si volse in su la destra poppa,
　e disse a Nesso: "Torna, e sí li guida,
99　　　e fa cansar s'altra schiera v'intoppa."

Or ci movemmo con la scorta fida
　lungo la proda del bollor vermiglio,
102　　　dove i bolliti facieno alte strida.
Io vidi gente sotto infino al ciglio;
　e 'l gran centauro disse: "E' son tiranni
105　　　che dier nel sangue e ne l'aver di piglio.
Quivi si piangon li spietati danni;
　quivi è Alessandro, e Dïonisio fero
108　　　che fé Cicilia aver dolorosi anni.
E quella fronte c'ha 'l pel cosí nero,
　è Azzolino; e quell' altro ch'è biondo,
111　　　è Opizzo da Esti, il qual per vero
fu spento dal figliastro sú nel mondo."
　Allor mi volsi al poeta, e quei disse:
114　　　"Questi ti sia or primo, e io secondo."

Poco piú oltre il centauro s'affisse
　sovr' una gente che 'nfino a la gola
117　　　parea che di quel bulicame uscisse.
Mostrocci un'ombra da l'un canto sola,
　dicendo: "Colui fesse in grembo a Dio
120　　　lo cor che 'n su Tamisi ancor si cola."
Poi vidi gente che di fuor del rio
　tenean la testa e ancor tutto 'l casso;
123　　　e di costoro assai riconobb' io.

But by that Power through which I move
  step by step down so brutal a road,
    give us one of your band as an escort,   *93*
Someone who could help us find the ford
  and ferry this one over on his back,
    since he is no spirit who walks upon air."   *96*
Chiron turned to his right and said to Nessus,
  "Go back and guide them. If another detachment
    bars your path, pull rank and make them yield."   *99*

And so we moved on with our trusty escort
  along the edge of the seething crimson
    where the scalded souls uttered piercing shrieks.   *102*
I saw people in it as deep as their eyebrows,
  and the great Centaur said, "These were tyrants
    eager to spill blood as they grabbed others' goods. *105*
Here they lament their pitiless crimes.
  Alexander is here and cruel Dionysius
    who made Sicily endure decades of woe.   *108*
And that brow there that has hair so black
  is Ezzelino; and that other one, blond,
    is Obizzo of Este, who up in the world   *111*
Was killed, in truth, by his bastard son."
  At this I turned to the Poet, who said,
    "Let him now be first for you, and me second."   *114*

A little farther on the Centaur paused
  before some people who could be seen
    up to their throats in the boiling stream.   *117*
He showed us a spirit alone on one side,
  saying, "That one clove, in the bosom of God's church,
    the heart that still seeps blood on the Thames." *120*
Then I saw some who had not only their heads
  but their entire chests above the stream,
    and among these there were many I knew.   *123*

Cosí a piú a piú si facea basso
   quel sangue, sí che cocea pur li piedi;
126   e quindi fu del fosso il nostro passo.
"Sí come tu da questa parte vedi
   lo bulicame che sempre si scema,"
129   disse 'l centauro, "voglio che tu credi
che da quest' altra a piú a piú giú prema
   lo fondo suo, infin ch'el si raggiunge
132   ove la tirannia convien che gema.
La divina giustizia di qua punge
   quell'Attila che fu flagello in terra,
135   e Pirro e Sesto; e in etterno munge
le lagrime, che col bollor diserra,
   a Rinier da Corneto, a Rinier Pazzo,
138   che fecero a le strade tanta guerra."
Poi si rivolse e ripassossi 'l guazzo.

And so lower and lower the blood's level sank
  until it just braised the soles of their feet,
    and this was the place where we found the ford.   *126*
"Just as you see that the boiling stream here
  grows ever more shallow," the Centaur said,
    "you must take my word for it that over there   *129*
The bed of the stream gets deeper and deeper
  until it makes a circle and comes around
    to the place where tyranny groans forever.   *132*
There Divine Justice stings Attila, who
  was a scourge on Earth, and torments eternally
    Pyrrhus and Sextus; and milks the tears, too,   *135*
Of those brigands who made the roads run with blood,
  Rinier of Corneto and Rinier Pazzo,
    their eyes now unlocked by the boiling flood."   *138*
Then he crossed back where the stream was shallow.

Canto XIII

BEFORE NESSUS HAS HAD TIME *to recross the stream, the pilgrims find themselves in a tangled forest that is anything but an orderly and well-kept orchard. In the gnarled and twisted trees, the foul Harpies, part bird, part woman, make their nests. Virgil alerts Dante to the fact that they are in the Second Ring of the Violent, that of the Violent against Self. Lamentations issue from the wood, but there is no one to be seen.*

To disprove Dante's supposition that the sufferers are hidden in the woods, Virgil invites him to break off a twig from one of the trees. When Dante does so, the tree itself cries out and bleeds. Like steam and sap hissing from an unseasoned firebrand, a sibilant voice oozes from the broken stub. Virgil begs the tree-shade to forgive Dante's violence. Snapping off the twig was the only way to overcome his protégé's incredulity, even though he himself had described a similar phenomenon in his Aeneid. *He invites the sufferer to reveal his identity, which he does, in an extended, figuratively complex discourse. He is Piero della*

Non era ancor di là Nesso arrivato,
    quando noi ci mettemmo per un bosco
3   che da neun sentiero era segnato.
Non fronda verde, ma di color fosco;
    non rami schietti, ma nodosi e 'nvolti;
6   non pomi v'eran, ma stecchi con tòsco.
Non han sí aspri sterpi né sí folti
    quelle fiere selvagge che 'n odio hanno
9   tra Cecina e Corneto i luoghi cólti.
Quivi le brutte Arpie lor nidi fanno,
    che cacciar de le Strofade i Troiani
12   con tristo annunzio di futuro danno.
Ali hanno late, e colli e visi umani,
    piè con artigli, e pennuto 'l gran ventre;
15   fanno lamenti in su li alberi strani.

Vigna, the emperor Frederick II's confidant, whose official letters were held up as rhetorical models of diplomatic correspondence. He committed suicide to preserve his honor when accused of high treason. He further explains how the very trees are the souls of suicides. Having rejected their human forms, they fall into the wood and take on this inferior, vegetable form.

The Harpies torment them almost inadvertently, breaking off twigs to build their nests. When Doomsday comes, the resurrected bodies of the sinners will hang forever suspended from their branches. At this point, the naked figures of two spendthrifts appear crashing through the undergrowth, pursued by fierce jet-black hounds. One tries to hide in one of the bushes but is torn limb from limb by the dogs. The lacerated bush, its broken branches dripping blood, asks why Jacopo da Santo Andrea tried to use him as a shield. The bush asks Dante and Virgil to gather up his dispersed leaves, confessing that he was a suicide from Dante's faction-vexed city of Florence.

Nor had Nessus reached the other shore
  when we stepped into a brooding wood
    that was not marked by any trail.   3
No leaves of green there, but rather of dusk;
  no branches grown smooth, but gnarled and twisted;
    no fruits clustered there, rather poisonous thorns.   6
Nor do wild beasts live in brush so thick
  and rough, not even those that abhor the tilled fields
    in the lowlands between Cecina and Corneto.   9
Here the Harpies nest, those foul creatures
  who drove the Trojans from the Strophades
    with dismal omens of troubles in store.   12
They have wide wings, human necks and faces,
  taloned feet, and great feathered bellies.
    Perched in the strange trees they croak their laments.   15

E 'l buon maestro "Prima che piú entre,
sappi che se' nel secondo girone,"
18   mi cominciò a dire, "e sarai mentre
che tu verrai ne l'orribil sabbione.
Però riguarda ben; sí vederai
21   cose che torrien fede al mio sermone."
Io sentia d'ogne parte trarre guai
e non vedea persona che 'l facesse;
24   per ch'io tutto smarrito m'arrestai.
Cred' ïo ch'ei credette ch'io credesse
che tante voci uscisser, tra quei bronchi,
27   da gente che per noi si nascondesse.
Però disse 'l maestro: "Se tu tronchi
qualche fraschetta d'una d'este piante,
30   li pensier c'hai si faran tutti monchi."
Allor porsi la mano un poco avante
e colsi un ramicel da un gran pruno;
33   e 'l tronco suo gridò: "Perché mi schiante?"
Da che fatto fu poi di sangue bruno,
ricominciò a dir: "Perché mi scerpi?
36   non hai tu spirto di pietade alcuno?
Uomini fummo, e or siam fatti sterpi:
ben dovrebb' esser la tua man piú pia,
39   se state fossimo anime di serpi."
Come d'un stizzo verde ch'arso sia
da l'un de' capi, che da l'altro geme
42   e cigola per vento che va via,
sí de la scheggia rotta usciva insieme
parole e sangue; ond' io lasciai la cima
45   cadere, e stetti come l'uom che teme.

"S'elli avesse potuto creder prima,"
rispuose 'l savio mio, "anima lesa,
48   ciò c'ha veduto pur con la mia rima,
non averebbe in te la man distesa;
ma la cosa incredibile mi fece
51   indurlo ad ovra ch'a me stesso pesa.

My good master said: "Before you enter
  any deeper here, know that you are now
    in the second ring, and will remain here   *18*
Until you come to the agonizing sand.
  Look well, therefore, and you shall see things
    you would not believe if I told them to you."   *21*
I heard sounds of wailing all around me
  and saw no one there who made the sounds.
    Completely bewildered, I stopped in my tracks.   *24*
I think my master saw that I believed
  those voices echoing among the tree trunks
    came from people who were hidden from us,   *27*
So he said to me, "If you will pluck even
  a little branch from one of the trees,
    your present thoughts will all be cut short."   *30*
When he said that, I stretched out my hand
  and snapped off a twig from a great thorn bush,
    and the stub cried out, "Why do you break me?"   *33*
Then, after it had become dark with blood
  it cried out again, "Why do you tear me?
    Do you have no spirit of pity at all?   *36*
We were men once and have now become brush.
  Surely your hand would have shown more mercy
    had we been merely the souls of vipers and asps."   *39*
A green firebrand with flames at one end
  and hot sap dripping out from the other
    will hiss as the air within it escapes.   *42*
So too from that broken twig words and blood
  oozed out together. I let the tip fall
    and stood there like a man in the grip of fear.   *45*

"O wounded spirit," my sage replied,
  "if he had been able to believe beforehand
    what he had never seen except in my verse,   *48*
He would never have lifted his hand against you.
  But the reality here was so hard to believe
    that I put him to this test, which also grieves me.   *51*

Ma dilli chi tu fosti, sí che 'n vece
  d'alcun' ammenda tua fama rinfreschi
54   nel mondo sú, dove tornar li lece."
E 'l tronco: "Sí col dolce dir m'adeschi,
  ch'i' non posso tacere; e voi non gravi
57   perch' ïo un poco a ragionar m'inveschi.
Io son colui che tenni ambo le chiavi
  del cor di Federigo, e che le volsi,
60   serrando e diserrando, sí soavi,
che dal secreto suo quasi ogn' uom tolsi;
  fede portai al glorïoso offizio,
63   tanto ch'i' ne perde' li sonni e ' polsi.
La meretrice che mai da l'ospizio
  di Cesare non torse li occhi putti,
66   morte comune e de le corti vizio,
infiammò contra me li animi tutti;
  e li 'nfiammati infiammar sí Augusto,
69   che ' lieti onor tornaro in tristi lutti.
L'animo mio, per disdegnoso gusto,
  credendo col morir fuggir disdegno,
72   ingiusto fece me contra me giusto.
Per le nove radici d'esto legno
  vi giuro che già mai non ruppi fede
75   al mio segnor, che fu d'onor sí degno.
E se di voi alcun nel mondo riede,
  conforti la memoria mia, che giace
78   ancor del colpo che 'nvidia le diede."

Un poco attese, e poi "Da ch'el si tace,"
  disse 'l poeta a me, "non perder l'ora;
81   ma parla, e chiedi a lui, se piú ti piace."
Ond' ïo a lui: "Domandal tu ancora
  di quel che credi ch'a me satisfaccia;
84   ch'i' non potrei, tanta pietà m'accora."
Perciò ricominciò: "Se l'om ti faccia
  liberamente ciò che 'l tuo dir priega,
87   spirito incarcerato, ancor ti piaccia

But tell him who you were, so that he might
  by way of amends refresh your fame
    in the world above, where he will return."   *54*
And the injured branch said: "Your sweet words bait me
  out of my silence. May it not burden you
    if I ensnare myself a little in talk.   *57*
I am the one who held both the keys
  to Frederick's heart, and I turned them
    so softly when I locked and unlocked   *60*
That I kept his secrets from almost everyone.
  So faithful was I to this glorious duty
    that I lost both sleep and the pulse of life.   *63*
The whore who never turned her harlot's eyes
  from the house of Caesar—and this vice
    is the common downfall of courts everywhere—   *66*
Inflamed all hearts and minds against me,
  and they, inflamed, so inflamed Augustus
    that my accolades turned to mournful grief.   *69*
My mind, in a scornful mood, reflected
  that by dying I might escape from scorn,
    and this made me unjust to my just self.   *72*
By the roots of this new tree I swear to you
  that never did I break faith with my lord,
    who was himself so worthy of honor.   *75*
And if one of you returns to the world,
  comfort my memory, which now lies low
    beneath the blow that Envy delivered."   *78*

After a moment's hesitation the Poet said,
  "Do not lose time while he is silent.
    Ask him now, if you want to know more."   *81*
To which I replied: "Please ask him for me
  whatever you think will make me content,
    for I am too overwhelmed with pity to ask."   *84*
So he began again: "Imprisoned spirit,
  if you wish this man to fulfill your request,
    may it please you now to explain further   *87*

di dirne come l'anima si lega
in questi nocchi; e dinne, se tu puoi,
90   s'alcuna mai di tai membra si spiega."

Allor soffiò il tronco forte, e poi
si convertí quel vento in cotal voce:
93   "Brievemente sarà risposto a voi.
Quando si parte l'anima feroce
dal corpo ond' ella stessa s'è disvelta,
96   Minòs la manda a la settima foce.
Cade in la selva, e non l'è parte scelta;
ma là dove fortuna la balestra,
99   quivi germoglia come gran di spelta.
Surge in vermena e in pianta silvestra:
l'Arpie, pascendo poi de le sue foglie,
102   fanno dolore, e al dolor fenestra.
Come l'altre verrem per nostre spoglie,
ma non però ch'alcuna sen rivesta,
105   ché non è giusto aver ciò ch'om si toglie.
Qui le strascineremo, e per la mesta
selva saranno i nostri corpi appesi,
108   ciascuno al prun de l'ombra sua molesta."

Noi eravamo ancora al tronco attesi,
credendo ch'altro ne volesse dire,
111   quando noi fummo d'un romor sorpresi,
similemente a colui che venire
sente 'l porco e la caccia a la sua posta,
114   ch'ode le bestie, e le frasche stormire.
Ed ecco due da la sinistra costa,
nudi e graffiati, fuggendo sí forte,
117   che de la selva rompieno ogne rosta.
Quel dinanzi: "Or accorri, accorri, morte!"
E l'altro, cui pareva tardar troppo,
120   gridava: "Lano, sí non furo accorte
le gambe tue a le giostre dal Toppo!"
E poi che forse li fallia la lena,
123   di sé e d'un cespuglio fece un groppo.

How the soul is bound in these gnarled bushes,
  and tell us, if you can, whether any soul
    ever finds release from such knotted limbs."   *90*

Then the stub puffed hard, until its breath
  transformed itself into a voice that said,
    "You will be answered, although in brief.   *93*
When the violent soul departs the body
  from which it has torn itself out by the root,
    Minos assigns it to the Seventh Circle.   *96*
It falls into the wood, to no special place,
  but wherever random Fortune casts it down,
    and there it sprouts up like a grain of spelt   *99*
And grows into a bush of wild, tangled shoots.
  Then the Harpies come to taste its leaves,
    giving it both pain and the means to express it.   *102*
In the final hour we will come like the rest
  for our mortal spoils, but not to clothe ourselves,
    for it is not right for a man to possess again   *105*
What he has robbed from himself. No, we will drag
  our bodies here to hang in this mournful wood,
    each on the thorn bush of its malignant shade."   *108*

We remained intent on the stub, thinking that
  it might have still more it wished to tell us,
    but then, like a hunter who becomes aware   *111*
Of a boar approaching his post in the woods,
  crashing through the branches with the dogs on his trail,
    we were surprised by a sudden uproar.   *114*
Two naked and torn figures on our left
  were running so hard in desperate flight
    that they cleared a path through the tangled brush.   *117*
The one in front was shouting, "Death be quick,"
  and the other, feeling he was running too slow,
    "Lano, your feet didn't move this fast   *120*
When you ran away from the fight at the Toppo!"
  and then, as he was gasping and out of breath,
    he dove for cover under a bush.   *123*

Di rietro a loro era la selva piena
di nere cagne, bramose e correnti
126   come veltri ch'uscisser di catena.
In quel che s'appiattò miser li denti,
e quel dilaceraro a brano a brano;
129   poi sen portar quelle membra dolenti.

Presemi allor la mia scorta per mano,
e menommi al cespuglio che piangea
132   per le rotture sanguinenti in vano.
"O Iacopo," dicea, "da Santo Andrea,
che t'è giovato di me fare schermo?
135   che colpa ho io de la tua vita rea?"
Quando 'l maestro fu sovr' esso fermo,
disse: "Chi fosti, che per tante punte
138   soffi con sangue doloroso sermo?"
Ed elli a noi: "O anime che giunte
siete a veder lo strazio disonesto
141   c'ha le mie fronde sí da me disgiunte,
raccoglietele al piè del tristo cesto.
I' fui de la città che nel Batista
144   mutò 'l primo padrone; ond' ei per questo
sempre con l'arte sua la farà trista;
e se non fosse che 'n sul passo d'Arno
147   rimane ancor di lui alcuna vista,
que' cittadin che poi la rifondarno
sovra 'l cener che d'Attila rimase,
150   avrebber fatto lavorare indarno.
Io fei gibetto a me de le mie case."

The wood behind him was packed with dogs,
  jet-black bitches as ravenous and swift
    as greyhounds just released from their chains.   *126*
They sunk their teeth in the one who sat trembling,
  and when they had torn his body to pieces
    they carried off all those ghastly limbs.   *126*

My guide and escort then took me by the hand
  and led me beside the shattered bush
    that wept in vain through its bleeding stumps: *132*
"O Jacopo da Santo Andrea,
  what good has it done you to use me as a screen?
    What blame do I have for your guilty life?"   *135*
My master peered down on the bush and said,
  "Who were you, sighing out just now
    your sorrowful speech through all your bloody tips?"   *138*
And he said to us: "O souls who have arrived
  just in time to see the shameful slaughter
    that has torn my leaves from me like this,   *141*
Collect them at this wretched bush's base.
  I was from the city that changed her first patron
    for the Baptist, for which the one who gave place   *144*
Will plague her forever with his wars.
  And if at the Arno's bridge there was no trace
    or fading semblance of that ancient god, Mars,   *147*
Those citizens who built her up again
  when Attila made ashes of what used to be
    would have performed their labor all in vain.   *150*
I turned my house into my gallows tree."

Canto XIV

As a fellow citizen *of the Florentine suicide, Dante piously gathers his scattered leaves. With their backs to the encircling wood, he and Virgil now face the Third Ring of the Circle of the Violent, a sandy desert plain, on which a constant rain of fire and brimstone falls. Here several categories of naked sinners are spread-eagled or crouch, although the majority run apparently aimlessly in various bands. All are subsumed under the general heading of the Violent against God. All, being naked, are burned by the fiery flakes in spite of their efforts to fend them off.*

Poi che la carità del natio loco
   mi strinse, raunai le fronde sparte
3   e rende'le a colui, ch'era già fioco.
Indi venimmo al fine ove si parte
   lo secondo giron dal terzo, e dove
6   si vede di giustizia orribil arte.
A ben manifestar le cose nove,
   dico che arrivammo ad una landa
9   che dal suo letto ogne pianta rimove.
La dolorosa selva l'è ghirlanda
   intorno, come 'l fosso tristo ad essa;
12   quivi fermammo i passi a randa a randa.
Lo spazzo era una rena arida e spessa,
   non d'altra foggia fatta che colei
15   che fu da' piè di Caton già soppressa.

O vendetta di Dio, quanto tu dei
   esser temuta da ciascun che legge
18   ciò che fu manifesto a li occhi mei!

D'anime nude vidi molte gregge
   che piangean tutte assai miseramente,
21   e parea posta lor diversa legge.

The first sinner Dante observes is the legendary (and unrepentant) blasphemer Capaneus, struck down by Jove on the walls of the ancient city of Thebes. A stream derived from Phlegethon, the River of Blood, crosses the desert plain in a paved canal. Virgil describes its curious source on the island of Crete. The cloud of steam above it forms a natural umbrella and protects Dante and Virgil from the fiery rain.

Wrung by love for the place of my birth
  I gathered up the leaves and gave them back
    to him whose voice had by now grown hoarse.   *3*
Then we came to the border that separates
  the second ring from the third, and where
    the dreadful art of justice is revealed.   *6*
In order to make these new things clearer,
  I will say that we reached the rim of a plain
    that rips out every last plant from its bed.   *9*
The dismal wood forms a garland around it,
  as around the wood runs the bloody ditch.
    We stopped our steps at the plain's very edge.   *12*
The ground before us was deep and dense sand,
  not unlike the desert floor that once
    was trod by the feet of Roman Cato.   *15*

Vengeance of God, how you should be feared
  by everyone who reads this account
    of what was revealed to my eyes in that place!   *18*

I saw many herds of naked souls,
  all of them wailing miserably,
    but each group seemed subject to different laws.   *21*

Supin giacea in terra alcuna gente,
   alcuna si sedea tutta raccolta,
24   e altra andava continüamente.
Quella che giva 'ntorno era piú molta,
   e quella men che giacëa al tormento,
27   ma piú al duolo avea la lingua sciolta.
Sovra tutto 'l sabbion, d'un cader lento,
   piovean di foco dilatate falde,
30   come di neve in alpe sanza vento.
Quali Alessandro in quelle parti calde
   d'Indïa vide sopra 'l süo stuolo
33   fiamme cadere infino a terra salde,
per ch'ei provide a scalpitar lo suolo
   con le sue schiere, acciò che lo vapore
36   mei si stingueva mentre ch'era solo:
tale scendeva l'etternale ardore;
   onde la rena s'accendea, com' esca
39   sotto focile, a doppiar lo dolore.
Sanza riposo mai era la tresca
   de le misere mani, or quindi or quinci
42   escotendo da sé l'arsura fresca.

I' cominciai: "Maestro, tu che vinci
   tutte le cose, fuor che ' demon duri
45   ch'a l'intrar de la porta incontra uscinci,
chi è quel grande che non par che curi
   lo 'ncendio e giace dispettoso e torto,
48   sí che la pioggia non par che 'l maturi?"
E quel medesmo, che si fu accorto
   ch'io domandava il mio duca di lui,
51   gridò: "Qual io fui vivo, tal son morto.
Se Giove stanchi 'l suo fabbro da cui
   crucciato prese la folgore aguta
54   onde l'ultimo dí percosso fui;
o s'elli stanchi li altri a muta a muta
   in Mongibello a la focina negra,
57   chiamando 'Buon Vulcano, aiuta, aiuta!'

Some were lying supine on the ground,
  some were crouching down, huddled,
    while others circled endlessly around.   *24*
Those in motion were far more numerous,
  while those who lay in torment were fewer
    though their tongues gave freer voice to their pain.   *27*
Over all the sand, huge flakes of fire
  drifted down in a slow, steady cadence,
    like snow that falls in windless mountains.   *30*
They fell like the flames that Alexander,
  in the torrid regions of India,
    saw fall on his army and settle to Earth,   *33*
And he ordered his men to stomp on the ground
  and put out each single fiery flake
    so as not to be faced with a huge conflagration.   *36*
So too this eternal fire descended
  and the sand that it fell upon was ignited
    like tinder under flint, to double the pain.   *39*
The dance of the wretched hands continued
  without any pause, this way and that way,
    as they tried to beat off each fresh new burn.   *42*

"Master," I said, "who have overcome all,
  except for those intransigent demons
    who blocked our path at the gate above,   *45*
Who is that great one who seems so unconcerned
  about the fire, but lies there disdainful,
    scowling, as if the rain does not ripen his torment?"   *48*
And that very soul, who was well aware
  of the question about him posed to my guide,
    cried out, "What I was living, that I am dead.   *51*
Even if Jove wears out the blacksmith
  who hammered out for his rage the jagged bolt
    that struck me through on my last day above,   *54*
And even if he wears out all the others
  at the clanging black forge in Mongibello,
    crying, 'Help me, Vulcan, Vulcan, help me!'   *57*

sí com' el fece a la pugna di Flegra,
    e me saetti con tutta sua forza:
60   non ne potrebbe aver vendetta allegra."
Allora il duca mio parlò di forza
    tanto, ch'i' non l'avea sí forte udito:
63   "O Capaneo, in ciò che non s'ammorza
la tua superbia, se' tu piú punito;
    nullo martiro, fuor che la tua rabbia,
66   sarebbe al tuo furor dolor compito."
Poi si rivolse a me con miglior labbia,
    dicendo: "Quei fu l'un d'i sette regi
69   ch'assiser Tebe; ed ebbe e par ch'elli abbia
Dio in disdegno, e poco par che 'l pregi;
    ma, com' io dissi lui, li suoi dispetti
72   sono al suo petto assai debiti fregi.
Or mi vien dietro, e guarda che non metti,
    ancor, li piedi ne la rena arsiccia;
75   ma sempre al bosco tien li piedi stretti."

Tacendo divenimmo là 've spiccia
    fuor de la selva un picciol fiumicello,
78   lo cui rossore ancor mi raccapriccia.
Quale del Bulicame esce ruscello
    che parton poi tra lor le peccatrici,
81   tal per la rena giú sen giva quello.
Lo fondo suo e ambo le pendici
    fatt' era 'n pietra, e ' margini dallato;
84   per ch'io m'accorsi che 'l passo era lici.
"Tra tutto l'altro ch'i' t'ho dimostrato,
    poscia che noi intrammo per la porta
87   lo cui sogliare a nessuno è negato,
cosa non fu da li tuoi occhi scorta
    notabile com' è 'l presente rio,
90   che sovra sé tutte fiammelle ammorta."
Queste parole fuor del duca mio;
    per ch'io 'l pregai che mi largisse 'l pasto
93   di cui largito m'avëa il disio.

Just as he did in the fight at Phlegra,
   and shoots them at me with all his might,
      he still would not have a happy vengeance."   60
Then my guide spoke with much more force
   than I had ever heard him use before:
      "Capaneus, because your pride is unquenched   63
The punishments you bear are so much the greater.
   No torment in Hell but your own unchecked rage
      would be painful enough to match your fury."   66
Then with a gentler look he turned to me
   and said, "That was one of the seven kings
      who laid siege to Thebes. He held God in contempt   69
When he was alive, and seems to do so now.
   But, as I said to him, his spite and scorn
      are adornments worthy of his own black heart.   72
Now come along behind me, and take care
   that you do not step upon the burning sand
      but keep your feet back, close to the wood."   75

We walked in silence and came to a place
   where a little stream bubbles out from the wood.
      That stream's deep red still makes my skin crawl.   78
There flows from the Bulicame a rivulet
   that the prostitutes share among themselves.
      So ran this stream, stained and soiled through the sand.   81
Both the stream's bed and its sloping banks
   were made of stone, as were both of its quays,
      and there I saw where our path might lie.   84
"Of all the things I have shown to you
   since we made our way through that sleepless gate
      that denies entrance to no one who comes,   87
Nothing has been so remarkable
   as the stream that you see before you now,
      which snuffs out every flame above its course."   90
These were the words of my guide, and I
   asked him to serve to me the repast
      for which he had whet my appetite.   93

"In mezzo mar siede un paese guasto,"
diss' elli allora, "che s'appella Creta,
96   sotto 'l cui rege fu già 'l mondo casto.

Una montagna v'è che già fu lieta
d'acqua e di fronde, che si chiamò Ida;
99   or è diserta come cosa vieta.

Rëa la scelse già per cura fida
del mio figliuolo, e per celarlo meglio,
102   quando piangea, vi facea far le grida.

Dentro dal monte sta dritto un gran veglio,
che tien volte le spalle inver' Dammiata
105   e Roma guarda come süo speglio.

La sua testa è di fin oro formata,
e puro argento son le braccia e 'l petto,
108   poi è di rame infino a la forcata;

da indi in giuso è tutto ferro eletto,
salvo che 'l destro piede è terra cotta;
111   e sta 'n su quel, piú che 'n su l'altro, eretto.

Ciascuna parte, fuor che l'oro, è rotta
d'una fessura che lagrime goccia,
114   le quali, accolte, fóran quella grotta.

Lor corso in questa valle si diroccia;
fanno Acheronte, Stige e Flegetonta;
117   poi sen van giú per questa stretta doccia,

infin, là dove piú non si dismonta,
fanno Cocito; e qual sia quello stagno
120   tu lo vedrai, però qui non si conta."

E io a lui: "Se 'l presente rigagno
si diriva cosí dal nostro mondo,
123   perché ci appar pur a questo vivagno?"

Ed elli a me: "Tu sai che 'l loco è tondo;
e tutto che tu sie venuto molto,
126   pur a sinistra, giú calando al fondo,

non se' ancor per tutto 'l cerchio vòlto;
per che, se cosa n'apparisce nova,
129   non de' addur maraviglia al tuo volto."

"In the middle of the sea lies a wasteland,"
  he then began, "by the name of Crete,
    under whose king the world was once chaste.   *96*
In that land is a mountain called Ida,
  once green and well watered, but now
    no more than a desert, parched and old.   *99*
In ancient days Rhea chose this mountain
  as her son's cradle, and to conceal him better
    she had her priests raise shouts when he cried.   *102*
Within the mountain stands an enormous statue
  of an Old Man, his back toward Damietta,
    his gaze toward Rome as toward a mirror.   *105*
His head is fashioned of the finest gold,
  his arms and chest are made of pure silver,
    then down to the crotch he is formed of bronze,   *108*
And down from there he is solid iron
  except the right foot, which is terra-cotta,
    and on this he places most of his weight.   *111*
A crack runs through every part but the gold,
  and this crack drips with tears, which then collect
    and force a passage through the cavern there.   *114*
Running through rocks they find their way down here
  and form Acheron, Styx, and Phlegethon.
    Then they continue through this narrow channel   *117*
Down to where nothing farther descends
  and form Cocytus. What that pool is like
    you shall see, so I do not describe it now."   *120*
And I said to him: "If this stream before us here
  flows as you describe down from our world,
    why does it appear only at this frontier?"   *123*
He replied: "This place, as you know,
  is circular, and though you have journeyed far,
    turning ever leftward down to the pit below,   *126*
you have not yet come completely around,
  so if something new appears to us,
    there is nothing in that that should astound."   *129*

E io ancor: "Maestro, ove si trova
Flegetonta e Letè? ché de l'un taci,
*132*e l'altro di' che si fa d'esta piova."
"In tutte tue question certo mi piaci,"
rispuose, "ma 'l bollor de l'acqua rossa
*135*dovea ben solver l'una che tu faci.
Letè vedrai, ma fuor di questa fossa,
là dove vanno l'anime a lavarsi
*138*quando la colpa pentuta è rimossa."
Poi disse: "Omai è tempo da scostarsi
dal bosco; fa che di retro a me vegne:
*141*li margini fan via, che non son arsi,
e sopra loro ogne vapor si spegne."

"Master, where are Phlegethon," I asked again,
  "and Lethe? About the one you are silent,
    and the other you say is formed from these tears."   *132*
"Your questions," he replied, "truly please me,
  but you have already seen one of them answered
    in the boiling red water. Lethe you shall see,   *135*
Not in this great sewer, but on the other side
  where the souls go to wash themselves—
    their sins repented—and to be purified."   *138*
Then he said: "It is time now to leave the wood.
  Stay right behind me. The margins that frame
    the stream are not hot; they will be our road   *141*
And will quench above them every falling flame."

CANTO XV

LEAVING BEHIND THE WOOD OF SUICIDES *and following one of the raised embankments built to contain the steaming river that appears with different names in different parts of Hell, Virgil and Dante are able to escape the scalding brimstone falling on the barren desert, symbol of the barrenness of its nonprocreative denizens. They are approached by a group of sinners running below them across the sands. One of them recognizes and is recognized by Dante.*

It is the distinguished poet and author Brunetto Latini, who addresses Dante with paternal admiration and affection, sentiments filially reciprocated by Dante:

Ora cen porta l'un de' duri margini;
   e 'l fummo del ruscel di sopra aduggia,
3   sí che dal foco salva l'acqua e li argini.
Quali Fiamminghi tra Guizzante e Bruggia,
   temendo 'l fiotto che 'nver' lor s'avventa,
6   fanno lo schermo perché 'l mar si fuggia;
e quali Padoan lungo la Brenta,
   per difender lor ville e lor castelli,
9   anzi che Carentana il caldo senta:
a tale imagine eran fatti quelli,
   tutto che né sí alti né sí grossi,
12   qual che si fosse, lo maestro félli.

Già eravam da la selva rimossi
   tanto, ch'i' non avrei visto dov' era,
15   perch' io in dietro rivolto mi fossi,
quando incontrammo d'anime una schiera
   che venian lungo l'argine, e ciascuna
18   ci riguardava come suol da sera
guardare uno altro sotto nuova luna;
   e sí ver' noi aguzzavan le ciglia
21   come 'l vecchio sartor fa ne la cruna.

What fortune brings you here like this before your death? Who is your guide? I
knew in life that you were destined for great things, though the uncouth Floren-
tines, closer to barbarous Fiesole than to enlightened Rome, were bound to treat
you with hostility.—Let Florence and Fortune do their worst. I care nothing for
them.—The sinners here were all intellectuals, writers, and clerics, who oriented
their sexuality where it could not reproduce. My own eternity lies in my book.

At this, Brunetto turns and sprints off like a runner about to win the race
and claim the prize.

We are moving along one of the hard banks,
 and steam from the rivulet forms a canopy
  that shelters the stream bed from the fire.   *3*
As the Flemings, fearing the incoming tide
 between Wissant and Bruges construct dikes
  to keep the sea from overwhelming them,   *6*
And as the Paduans do the same
 along the Brenta to protect castle and town
  before the snows up in Carentana melt,   *9*
So too were these embankments built,
 except that the builder, whoever he was,
  made them neither so thick nor so high.   *12*

We had already left the dismal wood
 so far behind, that if I had turned to look
  I would not have been able to make it out,   *15*
When we met a troop of souls advancing
 alongside the bank, and each of them
  looked at us as men peer at each other   *18*
Under a crescent moon in early evening,
 knitting their brows as an old tailor does
  when he squints hard at the eye of a needle.   *21*

Cosí adocchiato da cotal famiglia,
   fui conosciuto da un, che mi prese
24   per lo lembo e gridò: "Qual maraviglia!"
E io, quando 'l suo braccio a me distese,
   ficcaï li occhi per lo cotto aspetto,
27   sí che 'l viso abbrusciato non difese
la conoscenza süa al mio 'ntelletto;
   e chinando la mano a la sua faccia,
30   rispuosi: "Siete voi qui, ser Brunetto?"
E quelli: "O figliuol mio, non ti dispiaccia
   se Brunetto Latino un poco teco
33   ritorna 'n dietro e lascia andar la traccia."
I' dissi lui: "Quanto posso, ven preco;
   e se volete che con voi m'asseggia,
36   faròl, se piace a costui che vo seco."
"O figliuol," disse, "qual di questa greggia
   s'arresta punto, giace poi cent' anni
39   sanz' arrostarsi quando 'l foco il feggia.
Però va oltre: i' ti verrò a' panni;
   e poi rigiugnerò la mia masnada,
42   che va piangendo i suoi etterni danni."
Io non osava scender de la strada
   per andar par di lui; ma 'l capo chino
45   tenea com' uom che reverente vada.

El cominciò: "Qual fortuna o destino
   anzi l'ultimo dí qua giú ti mena?
48   e chi è questi che mostra 'l cammino?"
"Là sú di sopra, in la vita serena,"
   rispuos' io lui, "mi smarri' in una valle,
51   avanti che l'età mia fosse piena.
Pur ier mattina le volsi le spalle:
   questi m'apparve, tornand' ïo in quella,
54   e reducemi a ca per questo calle."
Ed elli a me: "Se tu segui tua stella,
   non puoi fallire a glorïoso porto,
57   se ben m'accorsi ne la vita bella;

So was I being eyed, when one of them
  recognized me, and taking hold of my hem
    he cried out, "How miraculous!"   *24*
As he was reaching out his arm to me
  I fixed my eyes on his scorched visage
    and looked so hard that his baked features   *27*
Did not prevent me from knowing him
  and, stretching my hand down toward his face,
    I asked, "Ser Brunetto, are you here?"   *30*
And he said, "My son, do not be displeased
  if Brunetto Latini turns back with you
    a little while, and lets the line go on."   *33*
"I beg you to do so with all my heart,"
  I said, "and if you want me to sit with you,
    I will do that, if it please my companion."   *36*
"My son," he said, "whoever from this flock
  stops for even a moment must lie one hundred years
    and cannot brush away the afflicting fire.   *39*
Therefore, go on, and I will come with you
  close behind your hem, and then rejoin my band
    who go lamenting their eternal loss."   *42*
I did not dare descend from the road
  to walk beside him, but I kept my head bowed
    and went on as one who walks in reverence.   *45*

He began: "What fortune, or what destiny,
  leads you down here before your final hour,
    and who is this one showing you the way?"   *48*
"In the bright life above," I answered him,
  "I became lost in a trackless valley
    before my span of years had reached their end.   *51*
Just yesterday morning I put it behind me
  but was returning into it, when he appeared,
    and now he leads me home along this path."   *54*
And he responded: "If you follow your star,
  you will surely sail into a glorious port,
    if I learned anything in that beautiful life.   *57*

e s'io non fossi sí per tempo morto,
 veggendo il cielo a te cosí benigno,
60   dato t'avrei a l'opera conforto.
 Ma quello ingrato popolo maligno
  che discese di Fiesole *ab* antico,
63   e tiene ancor del monte e del macigno,
 ti si farà, per tuo ben far, nimico;
  ed è ragion, ché tra li lazzi sorbi
66   si disconvien fruttare al dolce fico.
 Vecchia fama nel mondo li chiama orbi;
  gent' è avara, invidiosa e superba:
69   dai lor costumi fa che tu ti forbi.
 La tua fortuna tanto onor ti serba,
  che l'una parte e l'altra avranno fame
72   di te; ma lungi fia dal becco l'erba.
 Faccian le bestie fiesolane strame
  di lor medesme, e non tocchin la pianta,
75   s'alcuna surge ancora in lor letame,
 in cui riviva la sementa santa
  di que' Roman che vi rimaser quando
78   fu fatto il nido di malizia tanta."

 "Se fosse tutto pieno il mio dimando,"
  rispuos' io lui, "voi non sareste ancora
81   de l'umana natura posto in bando;
 ché 'n la mente m'è fitta, e or m'accora,
  la cara e buona imagine paterna
84   di voi quando nel mondo ad ora ad ora
 m'insegnavate come l'uom s'etterna:
  e quant' io l'abbia in grado, mentr' io vivo
87   convien che ne la mia lingua si scerna.
 Ciò che narrate di mio corso scrivo,
  e serbolo a chiosar con altro testo
90   a donna che saprà, s'a lei arrivo.
 Tanto vogl' io che vi sia manifesto,
  pur che mia coscïenza non mi garra,
93   ch'a la Fortuna, come vuol, son presto.

And if death had not come to me so soon,
  I would have, seeing the heavens favor you so,
    supported you in everything you did.   *60*
But that ungrateful and malignant stock
  who came down in the old days from Fiesole
    and are still as rough and crude as granite   *63*
Will hate you for all the good you have done,
  and not without reason, for the sweet fig tree
    should not bear fruit among the bitter sorbs.   *66*
The old stories say that they are blind,
  a people given to envy, greed, and pride.
    You must cleanse yourself of all their ways.   *69*
Your fortune holds such honor in store
  that hunger for you will goad both parties,
    but the grass will lie a long way from the goat.   *72*
Let these Fiesolan beasts eat each other like straw
  on their heap of dung and not touch the plant,
    if any still grows there, in which survives   *75*
The sacred seed of the ancient Romans
  who remained there even when it became
    a breeding place for so much malice."   *78*

"If I could have all my prayers answered,"
  I said to him, "you would still be alive
    and not hounded in exile from the world of men,   *81*
For the image of you is fixed in my mind
  and saddens my heart. Kind as a father
    and as dear, you taught me hour by hour   *84*
How man may make himself eternal,
  and while I am still alive I must express
    the gratitude that I feel toward you.   *87*
I will record what you tell me of my life's course
  and save it with another text to be glossed
    by an enlightening Lady, should I reach her.   *90*
And I would like this to be known to you:
  provided only that my conscience is clear,
    I am prepared for whatever Fortune wills.   *93*

Non è nuova a li orecchi miei tal arra:
   però giri Fortuna la sua rota
96   come le piace, e 'l villan la sua marra."

Lo mio maestro allora in su la gota
   destra si volse in dietro e riguardommi;
99   poi disse: "Bene ascolta chi la nota."

Né per tanto di men parlando vommi
   con ser Brunetto, e dimando chi sono
102   li suoi compagni piú noti e piú sommi.
Ed elli a me: "Saper d'alcuno è buono;
   de li altri fia laudabile tacerci,
105   ché 'l tempo saria corto a tanto suono.
In somma sappi che tutti fur cherci
   e litterati grandi e di gran fama,
108   d'un peccato medesmo al mondo lerci.
Priscian sen va con quella turba grama,
   e Francesco d'Accorso anche; e vedervi,
111   s'avessi avuto di tal tigna brama,
colui potei che dal servo de' servi
   fu trasmutato d'Arno in Bacchiglione,
114   dove lasciò li mal protesi nervi.
Di piú direi; ma 'l venire e 'l sermone
   piú lungo esser non può, però ch'i' veggio
117   là surger nuovo fummo del sabbione.
Gente vien con la quale esser non deggio.
   Sieti raccomandato il mio Tesoro,
120   nel qual io vivo ancora, e piú non cheggio."
Poi si rivolse e parve di coloro
   che corrono a Verona il drappo verde
123   per la campagna; e parve di costoro
quelli che vince, non colui che perde.

Oracles like these are not new to my ears.
And so let Fortune turn her wheel
as she pleases, and the peasant his hoe."   *96*

At this my master cast a backward glance
over his right cheek at me. Then he said,
"He listens well who takes note of this."   *99*

Yet I went on speaking with Ser Brunetto
and asked him who of his companions
are most notable and most eminent.   *102*
He answered: "It is good to know of some of them;
for the rest, silence would be more laudable,
for there is not time enough to name them all.   *105*
Suffice it to say, they were all of them clerics,
great men of letters and of fame equally great,
defiled in the world by the selfsame sin.   *108*
Priscian is one of that mournful flock,
Francesco d'Accorso too. And you could see,
if you wanted to see such filthy vermin,   *111*
The one moved by the Servant of Servants
from the Arno to the Bacchiglione,
where he left that distended piece of flesh and nerves. *114*
There is more I could say, but I am banned
from further speech now, for I see in the distance
a new cloud of smoke rising from the sand   *118*
That signals the arrival of another corps,
which I must not join. Keep well my *Treasure*,
in which I still live. I ask no more."   *120*
He turned back then, and he seemed like one
who runs for the green cloth in the footrace
across Verona's field, nor did he run   *123*
Like one who loses, but one who takes first place.

Canto XVI

WITHIN EARSHOT OF A ROARING CATARACT *that can be heard ahead, Dante and Virgil are approached by three naked shades, cruelly scorched by the rain of fire, who recognize the cut of Dante's clothes as Florentine. Forbidden to halt, these fellow Florentine noblemen circle below the levee where Dante walks. They are Tegghiaio Aldobrandi, Jacopo Rusticucci, and Guido Guerra; Dante had eagerly asked Ciacco about the first two in Canto VI.*

Overcome with emotion, Dante is ready to fling himself onto the burning sand to embrace them out of reverence and affection. Invoking future fame for

Già era in loco onde s'udia 'l rimbombo
de l'acqua che cadea ne l'altro giro,
3   simile a quel che l'arnie fanno rombo,
quando tre ombre insieme si partiro,
correndo, d'una torma che passava
6   sotto la pioggia de l'aspro martiro.
Venian ver' noi, e ciascuna gridava:
"Sòstati tu ch'a l'abito ne sembri
9   essere alcun di nostra terra prava."
Ahimè, che piaghe vidi ne' lor membri,
ricenti e vecchie, da le fiamme incese!
12   Ancor men duol pur ch'i' me ne rimembri.
A le lor grida il mio dottor s'attese;
volse 'l viso ver' me, e "Or aspetta,"
15   disse, "a costor si vuole esser cortese.
E se non fosse il foco che saetta
la natura del loco, i' dicerei
18   che meglio stesse a te che a lor la fretta."

Ricominciar, come noi restammo, ei
l'antico verso; e quando a noi fuor giunti,
21   fenno una rota di sé tutti e trei.

the poet, they ask for news of Florence. Do the chivalric virtues still reside there or are they gone forever? They have been driven out by the "new people," the greedy upstarts who think only of profit, replies Dante. Thanking him for his forthrightness, the trio takes flight while Virgil and Dante continue toward the crash of waters falling over the sheer drop into the next circle. In a mysterious ritual, Virgil flings the cord that girded Dante's waist down over the cliff. In response to this signal, a strange figure is soon perceived hovering up toward them through the fog and filthy air.

And now I was in a place where I could hear
   the drone of water pouring into the next ring,
      like the hum that bees make around their hives,   *3*
When three shades together at a run
   from a company that was passing by
      veered off under that bitter rain.   *6*
They came toward us, each of them crying,
   "You there, stop—your clothes give you away.
      You seem to hail from our depraved city."   *9*
Ah, the wounds I saw covering their bodies,
   burned in by the flames, wounds old and new.
      It pains me even now just to remember.   *12*
My teacher listened to their cries, and then,
   turning his face toward mine, said, "Wait now,
      these souls deserve our courtesy;   *15*
And were it not for the piercing darts of fire
   that are natural to this place, I would say
      that haste was more befitting of you than them."   *18*

When we stopped, the three began once more
   their endless songs of pain, and when they reached us
      they formed themselves into a turning wheel.   *21*

Qual sogliono i campion far nudi e unti,
   avvisando lor presa e lor vantaggio,
24   prima che sien tra lor battuti e punti,
cosí rotando, ciascuno il visaggio
   drizzava a me, sí che 'n contraro il collo
27   faceva ai piè continüo vïaggio.
E "Se miseria d'esto loco sollo
   rende in dispetto noi e nostri prieghi,"
30   cominciò l'uno, "e 'l tinto aspetto e brollo,
la fama nostra il tuo animo pieghi
   a dirne chi tu se', che i vivi piedi
33   cosí sicuro per lo 'nferno freghi.
Questi, l'orme di cui pestar mi vedi,
   tutto che nudo e dipelato vada,
36   fu di grado maggior che tu non credi:
nepote fu de la buona Gualdrada;
   Guido Guerra ebbe nome, e in sua vita
39   fece col senno assai e con la spada.
L'altro, ch'appresso me la rena trita,
   è Tegghiaio Aldobrandi, la cui voce
42   nel mondo sú dovria esser gradita.
E io, che posto son con loro in croce,
   Iacopo Rusticucci fui, e certo
45   la fiera moglie piú ch'altro mi nuoce."

S'i' fossi stato dal foco coperto,
   gittato mi sarei tra lor di sotto,
48   e credo che 'l dottor l'avria sofferto;
ma perch' io mi sarei brusciato e cotto,
   vinse paura la mia buona voglia
51   che di loro abbracciar mi facea ghiotto.
Poi cominciai: "Non dispetto, ma doglia
   la vostra condizion dentro mi fisse,
54   tanta che tardi tutta si dispoglia,
tosto che questo mio segnor mi disse
   parole per le quali i' mi pensai
57   che qual voi siete, tal gente venisse.

As champion wrestlers, naked and oiled,
  will eye their holds and lines of attack
    before they mix it up with lunges and blows,   *24*
So each of them, wheeling, kept his face turned
  in my direction, always twisting his neck
    in counterpoint to his feet's forward motion.   *27*
One of them began: "If the misery
  of this desert, and our burnt, hairless faces,
    bring us and our prayers into contempt,   *30*
Let our fame move your spirit to tell us
  who you are, walking without care
    on living feet through the world below.   *33*
The one before me, whose prints I trample,
  though he goes naked and his skin is peeled,
    was of higher rank than you would believe.   *36*
His name is Guido Guerra, the noble grandson
  of good Gualdrada, and in his lifetime
    he accomplished much with counsel and sword.   *39*
And this one, who treads the sand behind me,
  is Tegghiaio Aldobrandi, whose voice
    should have been more welcome in the world above.   *42*
And I, who am posted with them in pain,
  was Jacopo Rusticucci. Truly, my wife's ferocity
    has done me more harm than anything else."   *45*

Had there only been some shelter from the fire
  I would gladly have cast myself down in their midst,
    and I think my teacher would have indulged me.   *48*
As it was, since I would have been seared and baked,
  fear overcame the good will that made me
    hunger and thirst to embrace those men.   *51*
"It was not contempt, but sorrow," I began,
  "that your condition inspired within me,
    sorrow so deep it will not go away soon,   *54*
When my master here first spoke to me
  words that made me think that men such as you,
    so worthy of respect, might be approaching.   *57*

Di vostra terra sono, e sempre mai
l'ovra di voi e li onorati nomi
60   con affezion ritrassi e ascoltai.
Lascio lo fele e vo per dolci pomi
promessi a me per lo verace duca;
63   ma 'nfino al centro pria convien ch'i' tomi."
"Se lungamente l'anima conduca
le membra tue," rispuose quelli ancora,
66   "e se la fama tua dopo te luca,
cortesia e valor dí se dimora
ne la nostra città sí come suole,
69   o se del tutto se n'è gita fora;
ché Guiglielmo Borsiere, il qual si duole
con noi per poco e va là coi compagni,
72   assai ne cruccia con le sue parole."

"La gente nuova e i súbiti guadagni
orgoglio e dismisura han generata,
75   Fiorenza, in te, sí che tu già ten piagni."
Cosí gridai con la faccia levata;
e i tre, che ciò inteser per risposta,
78   guardar l'un l'altro com' al ver si guata.
"Se l'altre volte sí poco ti costa,"
rispuoser tutti, "il satisfare altrui,
81   felice te se sí parli a tua posta!
Però, se campi d'esti luoghi bui
e torni a riveder le belle stelle,
84   quando ti gioverà dicere 'I' fui,'
fa che di noi a la gente favelle."
Indi rupper la rota, e a fuggirsi
87   ali sembiar le gambe loro isnelle.
Un amen non saria possuto dirsi
tosto cosí com' e' fuoro spariti;
90   per ch'al maestro parve di partirsi.

Io lo seguiva, e poco eravam iti,
che 'l suon de l'acqua n'era sí vicino,
93   che per parlar saremmo a pena uditi.

I am from your land, and I have always
  heard your honored names, heard your deeds,
    and passed them on with great affection.   *60*
I am leaving the bitter, and seek the sweet fruits
  that my truthful leader has promised me,
    but first I must go all the way down to the core."   *63*
"So may your soul long govern your limbs,"
  the shade replied, "and so may your fame
    shine on after you when you are gone,   *66*
Only tell us if courtesy and valor still
  remain in our city as once they did,
    or if they are gone from it forever.   *69*
For Guiglielmo Borsiere over there,
  who has suffered with us only a short time now,
    afflicts us greatly with the words he speaks."   *72*

"The newcomers with their sudden windfalls
  have engendered in you such arrogance and glut,
    that already you lament it, Florence!"   *75*
I cried out these words with face uplifted,
  and they realized that this was my answer
    and looked at each other, knowing it was the truth.   *78*
"If it costs you so little all the time,"
  they replied together, "to satisfy others,
    happy are you to be able to speak as you wish.   *81*
And so if you escape from these dark places
  and return to see the beautiful stars,
    when it makes you glad to say, 'I was there,'   *84*
Make sure that people hear our story."
  Then they broke their wheel and took flight,
    running so nimbly their legs seemed like wings.   *87*
An "Amen" could not have been said
  as quickly as these spirits vanished.
    And so my master thought it was time to leave.   *90*

I followed him, and we had not gone far
  when the sound of the water became so loud
    any words spoken would have been drowned.   *93*

Come quel fiume c'ha proprio cammino
prima dal Monte Viso 'nver' levante,
96   da la sinistra costa d'Apennino,
che si chiama Acquacheta suso, avante
che si divalli giú nel basso letto,
99   e a Forlí di quel nome è vacante,
rimbomba là sovra San Benedetto
de l'Alpe per cadere ad una scesa
102   ove dovea per mille esser recetto;
cosí, giú d'una ripa discoscesa,
trovammo risonar quell' acqua tinta,
105   sí che 'n poc' ora avria l'orecchia offesa.
Io avea una corda intorno cinta,
e con essa pensai alcuna volta
108   prender la lonza a la pelle dipinta.
Poscia ch'io l'ebbi tutta da me sciolta,
sí come 'l duca m'avea comandato,
111   porsila a lui aggroppata e ravvolta.
Ond' ei si volse inver' lo destro lato,
e alquanto di lunge da la sponda
114   la gittò giuso in quell' alto burrato.
"E' pur convien che novità risponda,"
dicea fra me medesmo, "al novo cenno
117   che 'l maestro con l'occhio sí seconda."
Ahi quanto cauti li uomini esser dienno
presso a color che non veggion pur l'ovra,
120   ma per entro i pensier miran col senno!
El disse a me: "Tosto verrà di sovra
ciò ch'io attendo e che il tuo pensier sogna;
123   tosto convien ch'al tuo viso si scovra."

Sempre a quel ver c'ha faccia di menzogna
de' l'uom chiuder le labbra fin ch'el puote,
126   però che sanza colpa fa vergogna;
ma qui tacer nol posso; e per le note
di questa comedía, lettor, ti giuro,
129   s'elle non sien di lunga grazia vòte,

There is a river, the first to hold its course
  down Mount Viso and east to the sea
    under the Apennines' northern slope.   *96*
It is called Acquacheta before it descends
  from the high slopes into its bed below
    until at Forlì it gives up its name.   *99*
As it roars above San Benedetto dell'Alpe
  and thunders down in a single cataract
    that could just as well have fed a thousand,   *102*
So too, down a precipitous bank
  we found the blackened water resounding,
    so loud it soon would have damaged our ears.   *105*
I had a cord cinched around my waist
  with which I once had thought to capture
    the leopard with the dappled hide.   *108*
After I had taken off this cord,
  complying with my master's request,
    I handed it to him knotted and coiled.   *111*
He stepped back and, twisting to his right,
  flung it out far from the edge of the cliff
    and down into the depth of that abyss.   *114*
"Something strange," I thought to myself,
  "will surely answer this strange signal
    that my master follows with his eyes."   *117*
One cannot be too careful with this kind,
  who not only see everything you do
    but also have the power to read your mind!   *120*
He said to me: "It will rise up to the light—
  what I look for and you try to imagine.
    Soon it will be visible to your sight."   *123*

When it comes to truth that wears a liar's face
  a man should keep his mouth shut, if possible,
    for through no fault of his can it bring disgrace.   *126*
But I can't be silent here. Reader, I swear
  by the notes of this Comedy, by the favor
    that I hope it will enjoy forever,   *129*

ch'i' vidi per quell' aere grosso e scuro
venir notando una figura in suso,
132　　　maravigliosa ad ogne cor sicuro,
sí come torna colui che va giuso
talora a solver l'àncora ch'aggrappa
135　　　o scoglio o altro che nel mare è chiuso,
che 'n sú si stende e da piè si rattrappa.

I saw through that thick and murky air
  a figure swimming upward—fearful
    even to a heart that beats without care—   *132*
Like a diver coming back up after he
  has gone down to free an anchor that has been
    hooked on a reef or a shelf undersea,   *135*
His arms extended and his feet tucked in.

Canto XVII

SUMMONED BY VIRGIL, *the three-natured monster Geryon swims up from the depths of the Eighth Circle and beaches himself on the rim. Virgil goes to parlay with him, suggesting that Dante complete his reconnaissance of the Circle of the Violent by visiting the Usurers, who squat near the edge of the pit unprotected from the rain of fire and brimstone. Unrecognizably burned, the*

"Ecco la fiera con la coda aguzza,
    che passa i monti e rompe i muri e l'armi!
3   Ecco colei che tutto 'l mondo appuzza!"
Sí cominciò lo mio duca a parlarmi;
    e accennolle che venisse a proda,
6   vicino al fin d'i passeggiati marmi.
E quella sozza imagine di froda
    sen venne, e arrivò la testa e 'l busto,
9   ma 'n su la riva non trasse la coda.
La faccia sua era faccia d'uom giusto,
    tanto benigna avea di fuor la pelle,
12   e d'un serpente tutto l'altro fusto;
due branche avea pilose insin l'ascelle;
    lo dosso e 'l petto e ambedue le coste
15   dipinti avea di nodi e di rotelle.
Con piú color, sommesse e sovraposte
    non fer mai drappi Tartari né Turchi,
18   né fuor tai tele per Aragne imposte.
Come talvolta stanno a riva i burchi,
    che parte sono in acqua e parte in terra,
21   e come là tra li Tedeschi lurchi
lo bivero s'assetta a far sua guerra,
    cosí la fiera pessima si stava
24   su l'orlo ch'è di pietra e 'l sabbion serra.

once-noble usurers are identified by their family coats of arms, now reduced to
business logos. Most of them are Florentine, with one exception from Padua.
The pilgrim returns to Virgil, who is already mounted on the back of Geryon.
A terrified Dante is persuaded to mount too, and, after a hair-raising descent,
Geryon deposits them safely in the next circle and shoots off out of sight.

"Behold the beast with the barbed tail
   that breaches mountains and shatters shields and walls.
   Behold the one who makes the whole world stink."   *3*
So my leader began to speak to me
   as he beckoned the monster to come come ashore
   near where our marble footpath had ended.   *6*
And that loathsome image of treachery
   came on, and beached his head and chest
   but did not draw his tail onto the bank.   *9*
His face was the face of a righteous man—
   his features above seemed kindly enough—
   but his trunk below was more like a serpent.   *12*
From his armpits down his two paws were shaggy.
   His back and chest and both of his flanks
   were tattooed in a pattern of knots and wheels.   *15*
No Turk or Tartar ever wove a brocade
   with a design so colorful and intricate,
   nor did Arachne ever weave such a web.   *18*
As boats sometimes lie at the shore,
   their sterns in the water and their bows on land;
   and just as among the guzzling Germans   *21*
A beaver backs into water to begin his war,
   so this worst of beasts lay stretched on the brink
   of the stone ledge that bordered the sand.   *24*

Nel vano tutta sua coda guizzava,
  torcendo in sú la venenosa forca
27   ch'a guisa di scorpion la punta armava.
Lo duca disse: "Or convien che si torca
  la nostra via un poco insino a quella
30   bestia malvagia che colà si corca."

Però scendemmo a la destra mammella,
  e diece passi femmo in su lo stremo,
33   per ben cessar la rena e la fiammella.
E quando noi a lei venuti semo,
  poco piú oltre veggio in su la rena
36   gente seder propinqua al loco scemo.
Quivi 'l maestro "Acciò che tutta piena
  esperïenza d'esto giron porti,"
39   mi disse, "va, e vedi la lor mena.
Li tuoi ragionamenti sian là corti;
  mentre che torni, parlerò con questa,
42   che ne conceda i suoi omeri forti."

Cosí ancor su per la strema testa
  di quel settimo cerchio tutto solo
45   andai, dove sedea la gente mesta.
Per li occhi fora scoppiava lor duolo;
  di qua, di là soccorrien con le mani
48   quando a' vapori, e quando al caldo suolo:
non altrimenti fan di state i cani
  or col ceffo or col piè, quando son morsi
51   o da pulci o da mosche o da tafani.
Poi che nel viso a certi li occhi porsi,
  ne' quali 'l doloroso foco casca,
54   non ne conobbi alcun; ma io m'accorsi
che dal collo a ciascun pendea una tasca
  ch'avea certo colore e certo segno,
57   e quindi par che 'l loro occhio si pasca.

His whole tail quivered out in the void,
  twisting upward its venomous fork
    whose tip was barbed like a scorpion's sting.   *27*
My leader said: "We must veer off now
  a little way and bend our steps there,
    where that malevolent beast has beached himself."   *30*

We got off the dike on the right-hand side
  and took ten steps over along the edge,
    keeping clear of the sand and the flames.   *33*
When we came to the beast, I raised my eyes
  and saw a knot of souls a little farther on,
    sitting on the sand near the gaping abyss.   *36*
Here my master said: "In order to have
  full experience of this circle of Hell,
    go and see how these souls are punished.   *39*
But your conversation must be brief. Meanwhile,
  I will have a word or two with this one here
    to hitch us a ride upon his strong shoulders."   *42*

And so I went on all by myself
  along the edge of that Seventh Circle
    where these people sat in their misery.   *45*
Out of their eyes burst forth their sorrow,
  and they beat their hands now here, now there,
    against the fiery flakes and the burning ground.   *48*
Dogs in the summer will act the same way,
  now with their muzzles, now with their paws,
    when bitten by fleas or buzzing flies.   *51*
When I fixed my gaze on the faces of those
  upon whom the doleful fire descends
    I recognized not a single one, but I did see,   *54*
Hanging from the neck of each sinner there,
  pouches of distinct color and design,
    and each soul feasted his eyes on his own.   *57*

E com' io riguardando tra lor vegno,
in una borsa gialla vidi azzurro
60   che d'un leone avea faccia e contegno.
Poi, procedendo di mio sguardo il curro,
vidine un'altra come sangue rossa,
63   mostrando un'oca bianca piú che burro.
E un che d'una scrofa azzurra e grossa
segnato avea lo suo sacchetto bianco,
66   mi disse: "Che fai tu in questa fossa?
Or te ne va; e perché se' vivo anco,
sappi che 'l mio vicin Vitalïano
69   sederà qui dal mio sinistro fianco.
Con questi Fiorentin son padoano:
spesse fïate mi 'ntronan li orecchi
72   gridando: 'Vegna 'l cavalier sovrano,
che recherà la tasca con tre becchi!'"
Qui distorse la bocca e di fuor trasse
75   la lingua, come bue che 'l naso lecchi.
E io, temendo no'l piú star crucciasse
lui che di poco star m'avea 'mmonito,
78   torna'mi in dietro da l'anime lasse.

Trova' il duca mio ch'era salito
già su la groppa del fiero animale,
81   e disse a me: "Or sie forte e ardito.
Omai si scende per sí fatte scale;
monta dinanzi, ch'i' voglio esser mezzo,
84   sí che la coda non possa far male."
Qual è colui che sí presso ha 'l riprezzo
de la quartana, c'ha già l'unghie smorte,
87   e triema tutto pur guardando 'l rezzo,
tal divenn' io a le parole porte;
ma vergogna mi fé le sue minacce,
90   che innanzi a buon segnor fa servo forte.
I' m'assettai in su quelle spallacce;
sí volli dir, ma la voce non venne
93   com' io credetti: 'Fa che tu m'abbracce.'

When I got among them I saw, for instance,
   a yellow purse emblazoned with azure
      fashioned into the figure of a lion.   *60*
Then, as I passed my eyes over the scene,
   I saw another that was as red as blood
      with a goose upon it whiter than butter.   *63*
And one of them, whose own white pouch
   displayed in azure a pregnant sow,
      said to me, "What are you doing in this ditch?   *66*
Get out of here! But since you are still alive,
   know that I am warming a seat for my neighbor,
      Vitaliano, who will sit at my left.   *69*
I am a Paduan among these Florentines,
   and they shout into my ears and make them ring,
      saying, "Let the sovereign knight come down here   *72*
Who will bring the pouch with three goats on it."
   Then he twisted up his mouth and stuck out
      his tongue, just like an ox licking his nose.   *75*
Afraid that a longer stay would anger my guide,
   who had warned me not to wear out my welcome,
      I turned my back on these wretched souls.   *78*

I found my leader already mounted
   upon the ferocious creature's back,
      and he said to me, "Be strong and be bold;   *81*
From now on we descend on stairs like these.
   Climb on in front. I want to be in the middle
      so that the tail can do you no harm."   *84*
As a man so close to a fit of shivering
   from quartan fever that his nails are white
      and he trembles all over at the sight of shade,   *87*
So I began to shiver at my master's words;
   but shame, which makes a servant brave
      in a good master's presence, admonished me.   *90*
I got myself seated up on those shoulders
   and wanted to say, "Make sure that you hold me,"
      but my voice didn't sound as I thought it would.   *93*

Ma esso, ch'altra volta mi sovvenne
    ad altro forse, tosto ch'i' montai
96   con le braccia m'avvinse e mi sostenne;
e disse: "Gerïon, moviti omai:
    le rote larghe, e lo scender sia poco;
99   pensa la nova soma che tu hai."
Come la navicella esce di loco
    in dietro in dietro, sí quindi si tolse;
102   e poi ch'al tutto si sentí a gioco,
là 'v' era 'l petto, la coda rivolse,
    e quella tesa, come anguilla, mosse,
105   e con le branche l'aere a sé raccolse.

Maggior paura non credo che fosse
    quando Fetonte abbandonò li freni,
108   per che 'l ciel, come pare ancor, si cosse;
né quando Icaro misero le reni
    sentí spennar per la scaldata cera,
111   gridando il padre a lui "Mala via tieni!"
che fu la mia, quando vidi ch'i' era
    ne l'aere d'ogne parte, e vidi spenta
114   ogne veduta fuor che de la fera.
Ella sen va notando lenta lenta;
    rota e discende, ma non me n'accorgo
117   se non che al viso e di sotto mi venta.
Io sentia già da la man destra il gorgo
    far sotto noi un orribile scroscio,
120   per che con li occhi 'n giú la testa sporgo.
Allor fu' io piú timido a lo stoscio,
    però ch'i' vidi fuochi e senti' pianti;
123   ond' io tremando tutto mi raccoscio.
E vidi poi, ché nol vedea davanti,
    lo scendere e 'l girar per li gran mali
126   che s'appressavan da diversi canti.

Come 'l falcon ch'è stato assai su l'ali,
    che sanza veder logoro o uccello
129   fa dire al falconiere "Omè, tu cali!"

No matter. He who had come to my aid before
  in other perils, clasped me in his arms
    and held me steady as soon as I mounted,   *96*
And then said, "Move on now, Geryon.
  Keep your circles wide and your descent slow.
    Remember the new burden that you bear now."   *99*
As a ship backs up from out of its slip
  little by little, so too Geryon;
    and when he could feel that he had free play,   *102*
Turning his tail to where his chest had been,
  he extended and plied it like a sinuous eel,
    gathering the air to himself with his paws.   *105*

I do not think Phaethon felt more fear
  when the reins fell from his hands as his horses
    bolted, scorching the sky as still can be seen—   *108*
Nor did poor Icarus when he felt the feathers
  molting from his back, the wax all melted
    and his father crying, "Wrong way, son!"—   *111*
Than the fear I felt when I saw that I
  was in midair, and on every side
    I could see nothing at all except the beast.   *114*
He goes on swimming, slowly, slowly,
  wheels and descends, but I am only aware
    of the wind on my face and up from below.   *117*
And now off to my right I heard the torrent
  thunder far down through the shuddering air,
    so I stretched my head out, but when I looked down   *120*
I found myself more terrified of falling,
  and the sight of the fires and sound of wailing
    made me tremble and hold on more tightly.   *123*
Then I saw what I had not yet recognized—
  the grand sweep of evils exposed when we banked
    drawing ever closer as we descended.   *126*

As a falcon that has been too long on the wing
  and has sighted neither lure nor bird
    makes the falconer cry, "Ah, you're descending,"   *129*

discende lasso onde si move isnello,
 per cento rote, e da lunge si pone
132   dal suo maestro, disdegnoso e fello;
cosí ne puose al fondo Gerïone
 al piè al piè de la stagliata rocca,
135   e, discarcate le nostre persone,
si dileguò come da corda cocca.

And through many weary circles comes down again
  to where it set out swiftly and finally alights
    far from its master, full of sullen disdain—   *132*
So too Geryon set us in place;
  and having dropped off his human cargo
    at the very foot of the sheer cliff face,   *135*
He vanished like an arrow shot from a bow.

Canto XVIII

THE EIGHTH CIRCLE, CALLED MALEBOLGE, *is described. This is where Dante and Virgil now find themselves. They must make their way to the central pit and the final circle by crossing the bridges over the ten concentric bolgias or trenches in which the sinners are punished. Approaching the First Bolgia they observe two columns of sinners, whipped on by demons in opposite directions.*

Luogo è in inferno detto Malebolge,
    tutto di pietra di color ferrigno,
3   come la cerchia che dintorno il volge.
Nel dritto mezzo del campo maligno
    vaneggia un pozzo assai largo e profondo,
6   di cui *suo loco* dicerò l'ordigno.
Quel cinghio che rimane adunque è tondo
    tra 'l pozzo e 'l piè de l'alta ripa dura,
9   e ha distinto in dieci valli il fondo.
Quale, dove per guardia de le mura
    piú e piú fossi cingon li castelli,
12   la parte dove son rende figura,
tale imagine quivi facean quelli;
    e come a tai fortezze da' lor sogli
15   a la ripa di fuor son ponticelli,
cosí da imo de la roccia scogli
    movien che ricidien li argini e ' fossi
18   infino al pozzo che i tronca e raccogli.

In questo luogo, de la schiena scossi
    di Gerïon, trovammoci; e 'l poeta
21   tenne a sinistra, e io dietro mi mossi.
A la man destra vidi nova pieta,
    novo tormento e novi frustatori,
24   di che la prima bolgia era repleta.

Those coming toward them are the Panderers, among them the Bolognese Vene-
dico Caccianemico. Those on the other side, including the mythological figure of
Jason, are the Seducers. To view them Dante and Virgil mount the bridge that
leads to the next bolgia. In the Second Bolgia, the Flatterers, among them Alessio
Interminei from Lucca and the Roman courtesan Thais, are wallowing in feces.

There is a region in Hell called Malebolge,
 all of stone the color of iron,
  as is the wall that runs around it.   *3*
Right in the middle of this expanse of sin
 yawns a great pit, very wide and deep,
  which I will describe in its own place below.   *6*
The circular belt between the central pit
 and the foot of the surrounding high, hard bank
  has its bottom divided into ten valleys.   *9*
Picture one trench after another, encircling
 a castle's walls for added protection.
  This is the figure that is presented   *12*
By the successive trenches in Malebolge.
 And just as in such a stronghold there run
  bridges from the thresholds to the outer bank, *15*
So from the rim of the cliff ribs run like spokes,
 spanning the ditches and their embankments
  down to the pit that cuts off and collects them. *18*

It was in this place that we found ourselves
 when Geryon shook us off his back. The Poet
  headed to the left, and I fell in behind.   *21*
On the right I saw new forms of piteous woe,
 new torments, and tormentors armed with whips
  cramming the First Trench's entire circuit. *24*

Nel fondo erano ignudi i peccatori;
dal mezzo in qua ci venien verso 'l volto,
27   di là con noi, ma con passi maggiori,
come i Roman per l'essercito molto,
l'anno del giubileo, su per lo ponte
30   hanno a passar la gente modo colto,
che da l'un lato tutti hanno la fronte
verso 'l castello e vanno a Santo Pietro,
33   da l'altra sponda vanno verso 'l monte.
Di qua, di là, su per lo sasso tetro
vidi demon cornuti con gran ferze,
36   che li battien crudelmente di retro.
Ahi come facean lor levar le berze
a le prime percosse! già nessuno
39   le seconde aspettava né le terze.

Mentr' io andava, li occhi miei in uno
furo scontrati; e io sí tosto dissi:
42   "Già di veder costui non son digiuno."
Per ch'ïo a figurarlo i piedi affissi;
e 'l dolce duca meco si ristette,
45   e assentio ch'alquanto in dietro gissi.
E quel frustato celar si credette
bassando 'l viso; ma poco li valse,
48   ch'io dissi: "O tu che l'occhio a terra gette,
se le fazion che porti non son false,
Venedico se' tu Caccianemico.
51   Ma che ti mena a sí pungenti salse?"
Ed elli a me: "Mal volontier lo dico;
ma sforzami la tua chiara favella,
54   che mi fa sovvenir del mondo antico.
I' fui colui che la Ghisolabella
condussi a far la voglia del marchese,
57   come che suoni la sconcia novella.
E non pur io qui piango bolognese;
anzi n'è questo loco tanto pieno,
60   che tante lingue non son ora apprese

At the bottom were the sinners, walking naked.
　On our side they walked toward us; on the other,
　　the same way as us, but with longer strides.　　27
So too the Romans have developed a plan
　when this Jubilee year jams their city
　　for all the people to pass over the bridge:　　30
On one side all of them face the Castle
　and these continue on to Saint Peter's
　　while the others go toward Giordano's low hill.　　33
On this side and that, all along the dark rock,
　I saw horned demons with enormous scourges
　　who lashed them fiercely from behind.　　36
Ah, how the devils made them lift their heels
　at the very first blow! None of them waited
　　for a taste of the second, much less the third.　　39

As I made my way my gaze happened to fall
　on one of the sinners, and instantly I said,
　　"My eyes have had a taste of him before."　　42
And so I stopped to make out who he was,
　and my gentle leader stopped when I did
　　and let me retrace my steps a little.　　45
That scourged soul thought he could hide himself,
　lowering his face, but it didn't help much,
　　for I said, "You, with your eyes on the ground,　　48
Unless the features that you wear are lying,
　you are Venedico Caccianemico.
　　But what brings you to such pungent sauces?"　　51
He said to me, "Unwillingly I speak,
　but your plain talk, which brings that old world
　　back to my mind, compels me to tell you.　　54
I was the one who led Ghisolabella,
　my own sister, to do the marquis' bidding,
　　however they report the ugly story.　　57
And I am not the only Bolognese
　lamenting here. This place is so full of us,
　　that not so many tongues are still taught to say　　60

a dicer 'sipa' tra Sàvena e Reno;
e se di ciò vuoi fede o testimonio,
63   rècati a mente il nostro avaro seno."
Cosí parlando il percosse un demonio
de la sua scurïada, e disse: "Via,
66   ruffian! qui non son femmine da conio."

I' mi raggiunsi con la scorta mia;
poscia con pochi passi divenimmo
69   là 'v' uno scoglio de la ripa uscia.
Assai leggeramente quel salimmo;
e vòlti a destra su per la sua scheggia,
72   da quelle cerchie etterne ci partimmo.
Quando noi fummo là dov' el vaneggia
di sotto per dar passo a li sferzati,
75   lo duca disse: "Attienti, e fa che feggia
lo viso in te di quest' altri mal nati,
ai quali ancor non vedesti la faccia
78   però che son con noi insieme andati."
Del vecchio ponte guardavam la traccia
che venía verso noi da l'altra banda,
81   e che la ferza similmente scaccia.
E 'l buon maestro, sanza mia dimanda,
mi disse: "Guarda quel grande che vene,
84   e per dolor non par lagrime spanda:
quanto aspetto reale ancor ritene!
Quelli è Iasón, che per cuore e per senno
87   li Colchi del monton privati féne.
Ello passò per l'isola di Lenno
poi che l'ardite femmine spietate
90   tutti li maschi loro a morte dienno.
Ivi con segni e con parole ornate
Isifile ingannò, la giovinetta
93   che prima avea tutte l'altre ingannate.
Lasciolla quivi, gravida, soletta;
tal colpa a tal martiro lui condanna;
96   e anche di Medea si fa vendetta.

'*Sipa*' for '*sì*' between the Sàvena and Reno.
    And if you want confirmation of this,
        recall to mind our money-grubbing hearts." *63*
As he was speaking a demon struck him
    hard with his scourge, and said, "Beat it, pimp!
        There ain't no pussy to hustle here." *66*

At this point I rejoined my escort,
    and we came, after not too many steps,
        up to a ridge that led out from the bank. *69*
We got up onto this quite easily
    and turned to the right upon its spine,
        leaving those eternal circlings behind. *72*
When we came to the place where the bridge yawns
    to allow the scourged souls to pass below,
        my leader said, "Stop here, and let the sight *75*
Of these other ill-born shades strike your eyes.
    You have not seen their faces yet,
        for they have been going the same way as us." *78*
From the old bridge we viewed the sad parade
    coming toward us from the other side,
        driven on likewise by the demons' lash. *81*
My good master, without any question from me,
    said, "Look at that great one coming over there,
        who despite his pain seems not to shed a tear. *84*
What a royal demeanor he still retains!
    That is Jason, whose courage and guile
        fleeced the Colchians of their golden ram. *87*
He passed through the island of Lemnos once,
    the bold women there having pitilessly
        delivered every last man among them to death. *90*
There, with fine gestures and honeyed words,
    he deceived the young Hypsipyle,
        who earlier had deceived all of the rest. *93*
He left her pregnant and all alone,
    and his guilt condemns him to the fitting torment
        by which Medea is also avenged. *96*

Con lui sen va chi da tal parte inganna;
e questo basti de la prima valle
99   sapere e di color che 'n sé assanna."

Già eravam là 've lo stretto calle
con l'argine secondo s'incrocicchia,
102   e fa di quello ad un altr' arco spalle.
Quindi sentimmo gente che si nicchia
ne l'altra bolgia e che col muso scuffa,
105   e sé medesma con le palme picchia.
Le ripe eran grommate d'una muffa,
per l'alito di giú che vi s'appasta,
108   che con li occhi e col naso facea zuffa.
Lo fondo è cupo sí, che non ci basta
loco a veder sanza montare al dosso
111   de l'arco, ove lo scoglio piú sovrasta.
Quivi venimmo; e quindi giú nel fosso
vidi gente attuffata in uno sterco
114   che da li uman privadi parea mosso.

E mentre ch'io là giú con l'occhio cerco,
vidi un col capo sí di merda lordo,
117   che non parëa s'era laico o cherco.
Quei mi sgridò: "Perché se' tu sí gordo
di riguardar piú me che li altri brutti?"
120   E io a lui: "Perché, se ben ricordo,
già t'ho veduto coi capelli asciutti,
e se' Alessio Interminei da Lucca:
123   però t'adocchio piú che li altri tutti."
Ed elli allor, battendosi la zucca:
"Qua giú m'hanno sommerso le lusinghe
126   ond' io non ebbi mai la lingua stucca."
Appresso ciò lo duca "Fa che pinghe,"
mi disse, "il viso un poco piú avante,
129   sí che la faccia ben con l'occhio attinghe

With him go all who deceive in this way,
  and let this be enough for you to know
    of the first valley and those crushed in its jaws."   *99*

We now had come to the intersection
  of the narrow path and second embankment,
    which forms the abutment for another arch.   *102*
From there we heard the sound of people moaning
  in the next ditch, snorting through their snouts,
    and the slap of their palms against their own skin.   *105*
The banks were caked and crusted with mold
  from the vapor below that condensed on them
    and launched an assault on the eyes and the nose.   *108*
The murk at the bottom remained impenetrable
  until we climbed to the hump of the arch,
    where the ridge rises to its highest point.   *111*
When we got there I saw down in the ditch
  people plunged into some kind of muck
    like human waste in an endless latrine.   *114*

Searching the scene, I saw one whose head
  was so slimed with shit that you could not tell
    whether he was a cleric or laity.   *117*
He bawled at me: "Why turn your hungry gaze
  on me, more than these other shitheads?"
    I answered: "Because, if I remember right,   *120*
I have seen you before—when your hair was dry—
  and you are Alessio Interminei of Lucca.
    And so more than the rest you've caught my eye."   *123*
And he answered me as he pummeled that mop,
  "My tongue never tired of laying on thick
    the flatteries that have sunk me down in this slop."   *126*
Then my leader said: "Move your gaze to a space
  that lies a bit farther in that direction
    so that your eyes may admire the face   *129*

di quella sozza e scapigliata fante
  che là si graffia con l'unghie merdose,
132   e or s'accoscia e ora è in piedi stante.
Taïde è, la puttana che rispuose
  al drudo suo quando disse 'Ho io grazie
135   grandi apo te?': 'Anzi maravigliose!'
E quinci sian le nostre viste sazie."

Of that miserable disheveled slut
  scratching herself with her shit-encrusted nails.
    She will sometimes stand and sometimes squat.   *132*
That, you should know, is Thais the whore, who,
  when her lover asked her, 'Do you hold me dear?'
    answered, 'More than dear. No, I adore you!'   *135*
And that is all that we need to see over here."

Canto XIX

THE CANTO OPENS WITH AN AUTHORIAL ASIDE, *a solemn warning to the Simoniacs, who turn a financial profit from religion. From the height of the third bridge, Dante and Virgil look down on the Third Bolgia, where they see countless holes, each with a pair of wriggling legs protruding. Oily flames play on the soles of the sinners, who are buried head down. Dante is intrigued by a darker, more intense flame that licks the feet of one of the sinners, and Virgil offers to take him down among them. They descend the far embankment.*

In his reply to Dante's inquiry, the sinner he had singled out addresses Dante as "Boniface." He is a recent pope, Nicholas III, and the hole he occupies is

O Simon mago, o miseri seguaci
  che le cose di Dio, che di bontate
3   deon essere spose, e voi rapaci
per oro e per argento avolterate,
  or convien che per voi suoni la tromba,
6   però che ne la terza bolgia state.
Già eravamo, a la seguente tomba,
  montati de lo scoglio in quella parte
9   ch'a punto sovra mezzo 'l fosso piomba.
O somma sapïenza, quanta è l'arte
  che mostri in cielo, in terra e nel mal mondo,
12   e quanto giusto tua virtú comparte!

Io vidi per le coste e per lo fondo
  piena la pietra livida di fóri,
15   d'un largo tutti e ciascun era tondo.
Non mi parean men ampi né maggiori
  che que' che son nel mio bel San Giovanni,
18   fatti per loco d'i battezzatori;

reserved for those who held the most powerful office in Christendom. Boniface VIII, the reigning pope, will join him in it when he dies in 1303; so will his successor Clement V. Dante gives the pope a lesson in the true spirit of the Gospels and reprimands the Christian emperor Constantine the Great for making his donation (a forgery, as it would later turn out), the root of the Church's subsequent corruption, to Pope Sylvester. Virgil then carries Dante up out of the bolgia onto the fourth bridge.

O Simon Magus, O wretches that trod
  in his steps, rapacious traders who exchange
    gold or silver for the things of God   *3*
That should be of righteousness the brides—
  for all of you now the trumpet must sound,
    since the third fold holds you between its sides!   *6*
We now had come to the next charnel trench,
  having climbed to that part of the rocky bridge
    that overhangs the middle of the ditch.   *9*
O Supreme Wisdom, how great are Your designs
  in Heaven, on Earth, and in the world below!
    How just the portions Your power assigns!   *12*

I saw that on the sides and on the bottom
  the dark stone was full of holes, all of them
    perfectly round and of the same size.   *15*
They seemed to me no smaller or larger
  than those that serve as baptismal fonts
    in San Giovanni, my beautiful church,   *18*

177

l'un de li quali, ancor non è molt' anni,
    rupp' io per un che dentro v'annegava:
21   e questo sia suggel ch'ogn' omo sganni.
Fuor de la bocca a ciascun soperchiava
    d'un peccator li piedi e de le gambe
24   infino al grosso, e l'altro dentro stava.
Le piante erano a tutti accese intrambe;
    per che sí forte guizzavan le giunte,
27   che spezzate averien ritorte e strambe.
Qual suole il fiammeggiar de le cose unte
    muoversi pur su per la strema buccia,
30   tal era lí dai calcagni a le punte.

"Chi è colui, maestro, che si cruccia
    guizzando piú che li altri suoi consorti,"
33   diss' io, "e cui piú roggia fiamma succia?"
Ed elli a me: "Se tu vuo' ch'i' ti porti
    là giú per quella ripa che piú giace,
36   da lui saprai di sé e de' suoi torti."
E io: "Tanto m'è bel, quanto a te piace:
    tu se' segnore, e sai ch'i' non mi parto
39   dal tuo volere, e sai quel che si tace."

Allor venimmo in su l'argine quarto;
    volgemmo e discendemmo a mano stanca
42   là giú nel fondo foracchiato e arto.
Lo buon maestro ancor de la sua anca
    non mi dipuose, sí mi giunse al rotto
45   di quel che si piangeva con la zanca.
"O qual che se' che 'l di sú tien di sotto,
    anima trista come pal commessa,"
48   comincia' io a dir, "se puoi, fa motto."
Io stava come 'l frate che confessa
    lo perfido assessin, che, poi ch'è fitto,
51   richiama lui per che la morte cessa.
Ed el gridò: "Se' tu già costí ritto,
    se' tu già costí ritto, Bonifazio?
54   Di parecchi anni mi mentí lo scritto.

One of which I broke open, not many years past,
　　to rescue someone who was drowning inside—
　　　and let this be my seal to set everyone straight.　　*21*
Sticking out of the mouth of each hole,
　　from the soles of the feet down to the thighs,
　　　were the legs of a sinner; the rest was inside.　　*24*
They all had the soles of both feet on fire,
　　and this made their legs twitch so hard
　　　they could have snapped ropes or cables in two.　　*27*
As flames on an oily object play
　　on the outer surface only, so too these flames
　　　played on their soles from heel to toe.　　*30*

"Who is that one there, master," I asked,
　　"writhing and twitching more than the others
　　　and sucked upon by a redder flame?"　　*33*
And he said: "If you want, I will carry you down
　　by that gentler slope on the other side,
　　　so you yourself can learn his sins from him."　　*36*
And I answered: "I will do as you wish.
　　You are my lord. You know I won't stray from your will,
　　　and you know even what I leave unsaid."　　*39*

And so we came onto the fourth embankment,
　　turned to our left and then descended
　　　down to the perforated, narrow bottom.　　*42*
My good master did not set me down
　　until he had carried me to the very hole
　　　where the shanks of the sinner danced with pain.　　*45*
I began to speak to him: "Wretched soul,
　　whoever you are, planted upside down
　　　like an inverted fence post, speak if you can."　　*48*
I was standing there like a friar hearing confession
　　from an assassin, who, after he is fixed,
　　　calls the priest back to delay his death.　　*51*
And he cried: "Are you already standing there,
　　already standing up there, Boniface?
　　　Then the Writ has misled me by several years.　　*54*

Se' tu sí tosto di quell' aver sazio
per lo qual non temesti tòrre a 'nganno
57   la bella donna, e poi di farne strazio?"

Tal mi fec' io, quai son color che stanno,
per non intender ciò ch'è lor risposto,
60   quasi scornati, e risponder non sanno.
Allor Virgilio disse: "Dilli tosto:
'Non son colui, non son colui che credi'";
63   e io rispuosi come a me fu imposto.
Per che lo spirto tutti storse i piedi;
poi, sospirando e con voce di pianto,
66   mi disse: "Dunque che a me richiedi?
Se di saper ch'i' sia ti cal cotanto,
che tu abbi però la ripa corsa,
69   sappi ch'i' fui vestito del gran manto;
e veramente fui figliuol de l'orsa,
cupido sí per avanzar li orsatti,
72   che sú l'avere e qui me misi in borsa.
Di sotto al capo mio son li altri tratti
che precedetter me simoneggiando,
75   per le fessure de la pietra piatti.
Là giú cascherò io altresí quando
verrà colui ch'i' credea che tu fossi,
78   allor ch'i' feci 'l súbito dimando.
Ma piú è 'l tempo già che i piè mi cossi
e ch'i' son stato cosí sottosopra,
81   ch'el non starà piantato coi piè rossi:
ché dopo lui verrà di piú laida opra,
di ver' ponente, un pastor sanza legge,
84   tal che convien che lui e me ricuopra.
Nuovo Iasón sarà, di cui si legge
ne' Maccabei; e come a quel fu molle
87   suo re, cosí fia lui chi Francia regge."

Io non so s'i' mi fui qui troppo folle,
ch'i' pur rispuosi lui a questo metro:
90   "Deh, or mi dí: quanto tesoro volle

Have you already been glutted by the profits
  that emboldened you to seduce that virgin,
    the Bride of Christ, and then violate her?"   *57*

I felt like someone who has been mocked
  without understanding what has been said
    and so just stands there unable to answer.   *60*
Then Virgil said: "Tell him quickly,
  'I am not he, not the one that you think.'"
    And so I responded as I was told.   *63*
At that, both of the spirit's feet writhed,
  and then, sighing, he said in a tearful voice,
    "Then what is it that you want of me?   *66*
If you care so much to know who I am
  that you came down the bank to find this out,
    you might as well know I wore the great mantle,   *69*
And as an Orsini, a true son of the she-bear,
  I was so eager to profit my cubs
    that I lined pockets there as I line this one here.   *72*
Beneath my head are all the other popes
  who preceded me in simony,
    mashed down into fissures deep in the rock.   *75*
I will be thrust down there in succession
  when that one comes who I thought you were
    when I suddenly blurted out my question.   *78*
But I have already cooked my feet longer
  suspended in this upside-down position
    than he will stay planted with his feet aglow,   *81*
For after him will come from the west of France
  a lawless shepherd even more loathsome,
    one worthy to cover both him and me.   *84*
He will be a new Jason, like the one we read of
  in Maccabees, whose king was so easily led,
    and he will find the French king equally pliant."   *87*

I do not know whether I went too far
  when I answered him, without missing a beat,
    "Tell me then, just how much treasure   *90*

Nostro Segnore in prima da san Pietro
ch'ei ponesse le chiavi in sua balía?
93   Certo non chiese se non 'Viemmi retro.'
Né Pier né li altri tolsero a Matia
oro od argento, quando fu sortito
96   al loco che perdé l'anima ria.
Però ti sta, ché tu se' ben punito;
e guarda ben la mal tolta moneta
99   ch'esser ti fece contra Carlo ardito.
E se non fosse ch'ancor lo mi vieta
la reverenza de le somme chiavi
102   che tu tenesti ne la vita lieta,
io userei parole ancor piú gravi;
ché la vostra avarizia il mondo attrista,
105   calcando i buoni e sollevando i pravi.
Di voi pastor s'accorse il Vangelista,
quando colei che siede sopra l'acque
108   puttaneggiar coi regi a lui fu vista;
quella che con le sette teste nacque,
e da le diece corna ebbe argomento,
111   fin che virtute al suo marito piacque.
Fatto v'avete dio d'oro e d'argento;
e che altro è da voi a l'idolatre,
114   se non ch'elli uno, e voi ne orate cento?
Ahi, Costantin, di quanto mal fu matre,
non la tua conversion, ma quella dote
117   che da te prese il primo ricco patre!"

E mentr' io li cantava cotai note,
o ira o coscïenza che 'l mordesse,
120   forte spingava con ambo le piote.
I' credo ben ch'al mio duca piacesse,
con sí contenta labbia sempre attese
123   lo suon de le parole vere espresse.
Però con ambo le braccia mi prese;
e poi che tutto su mi s'ebbe al petto,
126   rimontò per la via onde discese.

Did our Lord require of Saint Peter
  before he entrusted him with a Key?
    He asked nothing, surely, except 'Follow me.'   *93*
Nor did Peter, or any apostle you will,
  take gold from Matthias when he was chosen to fill
    the place that was lost when the Guilty Soul fell.   *96*
So stay right here, for you are punished well,
  and guard the ill-gotten gains that prompted you
    to pit yourself against Charles of Anjou.   *99*
And if I were not restrained by my reverence
  for the Great Keys, the Keys that you once
    held and turned in the life of ease,   *102*
I would use even harsher words than these,
  for the greed you enjoyed makes the whole world sad,
    trampling the good and exalting the bad.   *105*
The Evangelist John saw shepherds like you
  in the woman who sprawls on the water's blue
    and whores herself out to the kings of the Earth,   *108*
The woman who had seven heads at birth
  and whose power derived from the ten horns she had
    (as long as virtue made her bridegroom glad).   *111*
You have made a god of gold and silver,
  and how are you different from an idolater,
    except that you pray to a hundred and he to one?   *114*
Ah, Constantine, it was not your conversion
  but your Donation, the dowry that first
    made a pope rich—Oh, what shameful evil it nursed!"   *117*

The whole time I chanted these notes to him,
  he, whether bitten by anger or conscience,
    thrashed away hard with both of his feet.   *120*
I think my leader was both pleased and impressed,
  to judge by his contented look as he listened
    to the sound of true words truly expressed.   *123*
He wrapped both of his arms around me then,
  and, gathering me up onto his chest,
    climbed the path by which he'd come down.   *126*

Né si stancò d'avermi a sé distretto,
   sí men portò sovra 'l colmo de l'arco
129   che dal quarto al quinto argine è tragetto.
Quivi soavemente spuose il carco,
   soave per lo scoglio sconcio ed erto
132   che sarebbe a le capre duro varco.
Indi un altro vallon mi fu scoperto.

Nor did he tire of embracing me
  until he had carried me up to the ridge
    that crosses from the fourth to the fifth levee.   *129*
Here my master gently set down his load,
  gently, because the bridge was craggy and sheer,
    even for a goat a difficult road.   *132*
Another valley opened up to me here.

CANTO XX

MOUNTED ON THE FOURTH BRIDGE, *Dante looks down into the Fourth Bolgia, where the Soothsayers, who claimed to see forward into the future, are punished by having their heads on backward. Dante weeps to see our human image so distorted, but Virgil reprimands him, warning him not to question God's justice. He points out the ancient augurs Amphiaraus, Tiresias, and Arruns and the witch Manto.*

The connection between Manto and Virgil's birthplace of Mantua elicits a long digression on the city's origins (lines 57–99). Others punished in this

Di nova pena mi conven far versi
    e dar matera al ventesimo canto
3   de la prima canzon, ch'è d'i sommersi.
Io era già disposto tutto quanto
    a riguardar ne lo scoperto fondo,
6   che si bagnava d'angoscioso pianto;
e vidi gente per lo vallon tondo
    venir, tacendo e lagrimando, al passo
9   che fanno le letane in questo mondo.
Come 'l viso mi scese in lor piú basso,
    mirabilmente apparve esser travolto
12   ciascun tra 'l mento e 'l principio del casso,
ché da le reni era tornato 'l volto,
    e in dietro venir li convenia,
15   perché 'l veder dinanzi era lor tolto.
Forse per forza già di parlasia
    si travolse cosí alcun del tutto;
18   ma io nol vidi, né credo che sia.

Se Dio ti lasci, lettor, prender frutto
    di tua lezione, or pensa per te stesso
21   com' io potea tener lo viso asciutto,

bolgia include the ancient Eurypylus and the moderns Michael Scot (astrologer to Emperor Frederick II), Guido Bonatti (who cast horoscopes for Frederick II, Ezzelino da Romano, and Guido da Montefeltro), and Asdente, the cobbler from Parma. But time presses, and the pilgrims must hurry on; so, apart from Manto, the women necromancers go unnamed.

A strange punishment I now put into verse,
  and so give substance to the twentieth canto
    of the first canticle, which treats those below.   *3*
I was now as ready as I could ever be
  to peer down into the uncovered depths
    that were bathed with tears of bitter anguish,   *6*
And through the circular valley I saw a people
  advancing slowly, silent and weeping,
    at the solemn pace of our world's processions.   *9*
As my gaze lowered itself to their bodies,
  each of them seemed to be strangely distorted
    between the chin and the top of the chest.   *12*
Their heads were twisted around to the rear,
  and as they proceeded they had to walk backward,
    deprived as they were of looking ahead.   *15*
It may be that sometimes a man has a palsy
  that contorts him like this, but I have not seen it,
    and I do not believe it is possible.   *18*

So that by God's grace, Reader, you may benefit
  from these pages, ask yourself now
    how I could ever have kept my cheeks dry   *21*

quando la nostra imagine di presso
vidi sí torta, che 'l pianto de li occhi
24   le natiche bagnava per lo fesso.

Certo io piangea, poggiato a un de' rocchi
del duro scoglio, sí che la mia scorta
27   mi disse: "Ancor se' tu de li altri sciocchi?
Qui vive la pietà quand' è ben morta;
chi è piú scellerato che colui
30   che al giudicio divin passion comporta?
Drizza la testa, drizza, e vedi a cui
s'aperse a li occhi d'i Teban la terra;
33   per ch'ei gridavan tutti: 'Dove rui,
Anfïarao? perché lasci la guerra?'
E non restò di ruinare a valle
36   fino a Minòs che ciascheduno afferra.
Mira c'ha fatto petto de le spalle;
perché volse veder troppo davante,
39   di retro guarda e fa retroso calle.
Vedi Tiresia, che mutò sembiante
quando di maschio femmina divenne,
42   cangiandosi le membra tutte quante;
e prima, poi, ribatter li convenne
li duo serpenti avvolti, con la verga,
45   che rïavesse le maschili penne.
Aronta è quel ch'al ventre li s'atterga,
che ne' monti di Luni, dove ronca
48   lo Carrarese che di sotto alberga,
ebbe tra ' bianchi marmi la spelonca
per sua dimora; onde a guardar le stelle
51   e 'l mar non li era la veduta tronca.
E quella che ricuopre le mammelle,
che tu non vedi, con le trecce sciolte,
54   e ha di là ogne pilosa pelle,
Manto fu, che cercò per terre molte;
poscia si puose là dove nacqu' io;
57   onde un poco mi piace che m'ascolte.

When I saw before me our human form
  so contorted that the tears of the eyes
    rolled down to bathe the cleft of the buttocks.   24

Of course I wept, leaning on one of the stones
  of the hard crag, so that my escort
    said to me, "Are you still one of the fools?   27
Pity survives here where pity is dead.
  Can anyone be more impious
    than one who grieves at the judgment of God?   30
Raise your head—raise it!—and see the man
  whom the gaping Earth took before the Thebans' eyes,
    at which they all cried, 'What's the big rush,   33
Amphiaraus? Why leave the war now?'
  But he did not stop, and plunged all the way down
    headlong to Minos, who seizes each soul.   36
See how he has made a breast of his back.
  Because he wanted to see too far ahead
    he faces behind and walks backward too.   39
See Tiresias, who was transmuted
  from male to female, assuming the form
    of a woman's body in every detail;   42
And afterward he had to strike with his staff
  the two entwined serpents a second time
    before he could resume his masculine form.   45
That one whose back faces Tiresias' belly
  is Arruns, who among the hills of Luni,
    where Carrara's peasants scratch out a living,   48
Lived in a cave among the white marbles
  from which his view could roam unobstructed
    through the starry heavens and across to the sea.   51
And the woman there who with her loose tresses
  shrouds her breasts away from your eyes
    and whose pubic hair too is on the wrong side,   54
Was Manto, who searched through many lands
  and finally settled in the place I was born.
    Please hear me a little on this subject.   57

Poscia che 'l padre suo di vita uscío
e venne serva la città di Baco,
60   questa gran tempo per lo mondo gio.
Suso in Italia bella giace un laco,
a piè de l'Alpe che serra Lamagna
63   sovra Tiralli, c'ha nome Benaco.
Per mille fonti, credo, e piú si bagna
tra Garda e Val Camonica e Pennino
66   de l'acqua che nel detto laco stagna.
Loco è nel mezzo là dove 'l trentino
pastore e quel di Brescia e 'l veronese
69   segnar poria, s'e' fesse quel cammino.
Siede Peschiera, bello e forte arnese
da fronteggiar Bresciani e Bergamaschi,
72   ove la riva 'ntorno piú discese.
Ivi convien che tutto quanto caschi
ciò che 'n grembo a Benaco star non può,
75   e fassi fiume giú per verdi paschi.
Tosto che l'acqua a correr mette co,
non piú Benaco, ma Mencio si chiama
78   fino a Governol, dove cade in Po.
Non molto ha corso, ch'el trova una lama,
ne la qual si distende e la 'mpaluda;
81   e suol di state talor esser grama.
Quindi passando la vergine cruda
vide terra, nel mezzo del pantano,
84   sanza coltura e d'abitanti nuda.
Lí, per fuggire ogne consorzio umano,
ristette con suoi servi a far sue arti,
87   e visse, e vi lasciò suo corpo vano.
Li uomini poi che 'ntorno erano sparti
s'accolsero a quel loco, ch'era forte
90   per lo pantan ch'avea da tutte parti.
Fer la città sovra quell' ossa morte;
e per colei che 'l loco prima elesse,
93   Mantüa l'appellar sanz' altra sorte.

After her father had departed from life
  and Bacchus' city had become enslaved,
    Manto wandered the world for quite some time.   60
Up there, in fair Italy, at the foot
  of the mountains that border Germany
    above Tyrol, lies a lake called Benaco.   63
A thousand springs or more, I believe, bathe
  the region between Garda, Val Camonica,
    and Pennino, and all that water pools into a lake.   66
In the middle is an island where three dioceses meet,
  and the bishops of Trent, Brescia, and Verona
    might each give their blessing if they ever went there. 69
Peschiera, a beautiful stronghold
  built to confront the Bergamese and Brescians,
    sits at the lowest point of the shoreline.   72
All of the water that Lake Benaco
  cannot hold in its bosom must tumble down
    into a river that flows through green pastures.   75
At the point where the river leaves its source,
  it is called the Mincio, a name that sticks
    all the way to Governol, where it joins the Po.   78
It does not run far until it comes to the lowlands,
  flat ground where it fans out into a marsh
    that is sometimes unwholesome in summertime.   81
When the ungentled virgin passed that way
  she saw land in the middle of that swamp,
    untilled and devoid of inhabitants.   84
There, to avoid any contact with man
  she stopped with her servants, practiced her arts,
    lived her life, and left only a husk.   87
After she died, the people scattered thereabouts
  settled in that spot, a strong location
    because of the marsh that surrounded it.   90
They built a city over those dead bones
  and called it (without further augury)
    Mantua, after her who first chose the place.   93

Già fuor le genti sue dentro piú spesse,
　prima che la mattia da Casalodi
96　　da Pinamonte inganno ricevesse.
Però t'assenno che, se tu mai odi
　originar la mia terra altrimenti,
99　　la verità nulla menzogna frodi."

E io: "Maestro, i tuoi ragionamenti
　mi son sí certi e prendon sí mia fede,
102　　che li altri mi sarien carboni spenti.
Ma dimmi, de la gente che procede,
　se tu ne vedi alcun degno di nota;
105　　ché solo a ciò la mia mente rifiede."
Allor mi disse: "Quel che da la gota
　porge la barba in su le spalle brune,
108　　fu—quando Grecia fu di maschi vòta,
sí ch'a pena rimaser per le cune—
　augure, e diede 'l punto con Calcanta
111　　in Aulide a tagliar la prima fune.
Euripilo ebbe nome, e cosí 'l canta
　l'alta mia tragedía in alcun loco:
114　　ben lo sai tu che la sai tutta quanta.
Quell' altro che ne' fianchi è cosí poco,
　Michele Scotto fu, che veramente
117　　de le magiche frode seppe 'l gioco.
Vedi Guido Bonatti; vedi Asdente,
　ch'avere inteso al cuoio e a lo spago
120　　ora vorrebbe, ma tardi si pente.
Vedi le triste che lasciaron l'ago,
　la spuola e 'l fuso, e fecersi 'ndivine;
123　　fecer malie con erbe e con imago.

Ma vienne omai, ché già tiene 'l confine
　d'amendue li emisperi e tocca l'onda
126　　sotto Sobilia Caino e le spine;

The population there was larger once,
  before Casalodi in his folly
    was tricked by the treacherous Pinamonte.   *96*
So be advised: should you ever hear
  any other account of my city's origin,
    let no fabrication shortchange the truth."   *99*

And I said: "Master, the account you give
  is so sure and so compelling to me
    any rival would be no more than dead coals.   *102*
But tell me, of the people passing by,
  do you see any that are worthy of note?
    My mind keeps going back to that."   *105*
He answered: "That one there, whose beard reaches
  down from his cheeks to his swarthy shoulders,
    was once a soothsayer. This was when men and boys   *108*
Were so scarce in Greece you could hardly find one
  in any cradle. Along with Calchas
    he augured the cutting and running at Aulis.   *111*
Eurypylus was his name. You know well
  where my high tragedy sings of him,
    for you know the poem all the way through.   *114*
That other one, who is so lean in the hips,
  was Michael Scot, a true virtuoso
    in playing the game of fraudulent magic.   *117*
See Guido Bonatti and Asdente,
  who wishes now he had kept his attention
    on his leather and thread but repents too late.   *120*
See the wretched women who became soothsayers,
  abandoning their needles, their spools, and spindles,
    to cast dark spells with effigies and herbs.   *123*

But come, for already Cain with his thorns
  is setting on the waves below Seville
    and is now on the cusp of the hemispheres' horns,   *126*

e già iernotte fu la luna tonda:
ben ten de' ricordar, ché non ti nocque
129   alcuna volta per la selva fonda."
Sí mi parlava, e andavamo introcque.

And since the moon last night did you some good
 you must remember that it was full already
  when you were wandering deep in the wood." 129
We were walking along when he said this to me.

Canto XXI

As they reach the crest *of the bridge over the impenetrable blackness of the Fifth Bolgia, Dante, peering down, is able to make out nothing but a tarry ebullience on the surface below. It reminds him of the bubbling pitch used by the shipbuilders of the bustling Venetian Arsenal to caulk their vessels. All at once Virgil grabs Dante and pulls him to one side as a fearsome black demon rushes by bearing a sinner on his back, whom he flings down off the bridge, hurrying back for more. The sinner rises to the surface of the pitch and is taunted and lacerated by other demons whom Dante had not observed because they were hidden beneath the bridge.*

Virgil warns Dante to remain in hiding and walks confidently ahead to parlay with them. Once on the other side of the bridge, Virgil is surrounded

> Cosí di ponte in ponte, altro parlando
> che la mia comedía cantar non cura,
> 3   venimmo; e tenavamo 'l colmo, quando
> restammo per veder l'altra fessura
> di Malebolge e li altri pianti vani;
> 6   e vidila mirabilmente oscura.
> Quale ne l'arzanà de'Viniziani
> bolle l'inverno la tenace pece
> 9   a rimpalmare i legni lor non sani,
> ché navicar non ponno—in quella vece
> chi fa suo legno novo e chi ristoppa
> 12   le coste a quel che piú vïaggi fece;
> chi ribatte da proda e chi da poppa;
> altri fa remi e altri volge sarte;
> 15   chi terzeruolo e artimon rintoppa—:
> tal, non per foco ma per divin'arte,
> bollia là giuso una pegola spessa,
> 18   che 'nviscava la ripa d'ogne parte.

by the snarling demons, who call for their leader Malacoda to negotiate with
him. More confident than ever after their exchange, Virgil invites Dante to
join them; he does so, not without trepidation. Malacoda explains that at
this point the bridge over the next bolgia has collapsed, and he offers the
wayfarers an escort detail to the next bridge, located, he assures them, farther
along. A suspicious Dante tries to persuade Virgil not to accept, but his guide
tells him to take heart, making light of the threat. The squad moves off to
the sound of an unusual military fanfare.

So from bridge to bridge, talking of things
   that do not concern my Comedy,
      we came along, and when we reached the top   *3*
There we stopped to see the next canyon
   of Malebolge, the next vain lamentation,
      and when I looked I saw it was strangely dark.   *6*
As the Venetians in their Arsenal
   during winter simmer pots of sticky pitch
      to seal the timbers of unsound ships,   *9*
Because they cannot sail then, and instead
   one lays out a new hull, another caulks the ribs
      of a vessel that has seen many a voyage,   *12*
One hammers at the prow, another at the stern,
   some turn out oars while others twist ropes,
      and another patches the jib and the mainsail—   *15*
So too a thick pitch was boiling below,
   not by fire but by Divine Art,
      and it stuck like glue all over the banks.   *18*

I' vedea lei, ma non vedëa in essa
        mai che le bolle che 'l bollor levava,
21   e gonfiar tutta, e riseder compressa.

Mentr' io là giú fisamente mirava,
        lo duca mio, dicendo "Guarda, guarda!"
24   mi trasse a sé del loco dov' io stava.
Allor mi volsi come l'uom cui tarda
        di veder quel che li convien fuggire
27   e cui paura súbita sgagliarda,
che, per veder, non indugia 'l partire:
        e vidi dietro a noi un diavol nero
30   correndo su per lo scoglio venire.
Ahi quant' elli era ne l'aspetto fero!
        e quanto mi parea ne l'atto acerbo,
33   con l'ali aperte e sovra i piè leggero!
L'omero suo, ch'era aguto e superbo,
        carcava un peccator con ambo l'anche,
36   e quei tenea de' piè ghermito 'l nerbo.
Del nostro ponte disse: "O Malebranche,
        ecco un de li anzïan di Santa Zita!
39   Mettetel sotto, ch'i' torno per anche
a quella terra, che n'è ben fornita:
        ogn' uom v'è barattier, fuor che Bonturo;
42   del no, per li denar, vi si fa *ita*."

Là giú 'l buttò, e per lo scoglio duro
        si volse; e mai non fu mastino sciolto
45   con tanta fretta a seguitar lo furo.
Quel s'attuffò, e tornò sú convolto;
        ma i demon che del ponte avean coperchio,
48   gridar: "Qui non ha loco il Santo Volto!
qui si nuota altrimenti che nel Serchio!
        Però, se tu non vuo' di nostri graffi,
51   non far sopra la pegola soverchio."

I saw the pitch, but in it I saw nothing
   except the bubbles the boiling caused,
      seething in a mass and then settling down.   *21*

While my eyes were fixed on the simmering tar,
   my guide exclaimed, "Watch out, watch out!"
      and pulled me to his side from where I stood.   *24*
Then I turned around like someone who
   cannot help looking at what he must flee,
      so stricken is he with sudden fear,   *27*
Though his backward glance doesn't hinder his flight,
   and I saw behind us a black devil
      coming up at a run along the crag.   *30*
Ah, how savage he was to look upon,
   and how ferocious in action he seemed,
      with his wings spread out and light on his feet.   *33*
Slung over one of his huge, square shoulders
   were the haunches of a sinner, clenched tight
      where the devil's nails sank into his heels.   *36*
He announced from our bridge: "O Malebranche,
   here's one of the elders of Saint Zita in Lucca.
      Send him under while I go back for more.   *39*
That city is well supplied with them—
   everyone's on the take there—except Bonturo!—
      and they all make Yes out of No for cash."   *42*

And he hurled him down, then turned back
   on the flinty crag; a mastiff unchained
      never took off so swiftly after a thief.   *45*
The sinner sank under and came up butt first,
   and the devils, from their shelter under the bridge,
      cried, "There's no place here for the Holy Face!   *48*
You're not swimming in the Serchio here,
   so unless you want a taste of our hooks
      don't stick out an inch above the black tar!"   *51*

Poi l'addentar con piú di cento raffi,
　disser: "Coverto convien che qui balli,
54　　sí che, se puoi, nascosamente accaffi."

Non altrimenti i cuoci a' lor vassalli
　fanno attuffare in mezzo la caldaia
57　　la carne con li uncin, perché non galli.
Lo buon maestro "Acciò che non si paia
　che tu ci sia," mi disse, "giú t'acquatta
60　　dopo uno scheggio, ch'alcun schermo t'aia;
e per nulla offension che mi sia fatta,
　non temer tu, ch'i' ho le cose conte,
63　　per ch'altra volta fui a tal baratta."
Poscia passò di là dal co del ponte;
　e com' el giunse in su la ripa sesta,
66　　mestier li fu d'aver sicura fronte.
Con quel furore e con quella tempesta
　ch'escono i cani a dosso al poverello
69　　che di súbito chiede ove s'arresta,
usciron quei di sotto al ponticello,
　e volser contra lui tutt'i runcigli;
72　　ma el gridò: "Nessun di voi sia fello!
Innanzi che l'uncin vostro mi pigli,
　traggasi avante l'un di voi che m'oda,
75　　e poi d'arruncigliarmi si consigli."
Tutti gridaron: "Vada Malacoda!";
　per ch'un si mosse—e li altri stetter fermi—
78　　e venne a lui dicendo: "Che li approda?"

"Credi tu, Malacoda, qui vedermi
　esser venuto," disse 'l mio maestro,
81　　"sicuro già da tutti vostri schermi,
sanza voler divino e fato destro?
　Lascian' andar, ché nel cielo è voluto
84　　ch'i' mostri altrui questo cammin silvestro."

Then they jabbed him with more than a hundred prongs
  and said, "You'll have to dance under cover,
    so do your dirty deals down there if you can."   *54*

No differently do cooks have their kitchen help
  use their forks to push the brisket down
    into the broth so it can't float up.   *57*
My good master said to me: "They must not catch
  a glimpse of you. Crouch down over here
    behind this crag, and it will shield you from view.   *60*
However outrageous they may be toward me,
  do not be afraid. This is not unforeseen,
    and I know from times past how to deal with this crew.   *63*
Then he went on beyond the head of the bridge
  and when he arrived at the sixth embankment
    he had to put on a confident front.   *66*
With the all the sound and fury of dogs
  unleashed on some beggar who stops in his tracks
    and does his begging from the spot where he stands,   *69*
The demons rushed out from under the bridge
  and pointed all their grapples against him,
    but he cried out: "Don't any of you get nasty.   *72*
Before you touch me with your hooks,
  one of you step forward to hear me out,
    and then decide about gaffing me."   *75*
They all shouted: "Get Malacoda out here!"
  Then the rest stood still, but one demon
    stepped forward, saying, "What good will it do him?"   *78*

"Do you think, Malacoda," my master said,
  "that you see me here, having made it this far
    completely secure against all your snares,   *81*
Without Divine Will and Fate on my side?
  Let us pass, for it is willed in Heaven
    that I show another this dreadful path."   *84*

Allor li fu l'orgoglio sí caduto,
ch'e' si lasciò cascar l'uncino a' piedi,
87   e disse a li altri: "Omai non sia feruto."
E 'l duca mio a me: "O tu che siedi
tra li scheggion del ponte quatto quatto,
90   sicuramente omai a me ti riedi."
Per ch'io mi mossi e a lui venni ratto;
e i diavoli si fecer tutti avanti,
93   sí ch'io temetti ch'ei tenesser patto;
cosí vid' io già temer li fanti
ch'uscivan patteggiati di Caprona,
96   veggendo sé tra nemici cotanti.
I' m'accostai con tutta la persona
lungo 'l mio duca, e non torceva li occhi
99   da la sembianza lor ch'era non buona.
Ei chinavan li raffi e "Vuo' che 'l tocchi,"
diceva l'un con l'altro, "in sul groppone?"
102   E rispondien: "Sí, fa che gliel' accocchi."
Ma quel demonio che tenea sermone
col duca mio, si volse tutto presto
105   e disse: "Posa, posa, Scarmiglione!"
Poi disse a noi: "Piú oltre andar per questo
iscoglio non si può, però che giace
108   tutto spezzato al fondo l'arco sesto.
E se l'andare avante pur vi piace,
andatevene su per questa grotta;
111   presso è un altro scoglio che via face.
Ier, piú oltre cinqu' ore che quest' otta,
mille dugento con sessanta sei
114   anni compié che qui la via fu rotta.
Io mando verso là di questi miei
a riguardar s'alcun se ne sciorina;
117   gite con lor, che non saranno rei."

"Tra'ti avante, Alichino, e Calcabrina,"
cominciò elli a dire, "e tu, Cagnazzo;
120   e Barbariccia guidi la decina.

At that the demon's pride was so crushed
  that he let the hook fall at his feet
    and told the others, "None of you touch him."   *87*
Then my leader called to me: "All right,
  it's safe. Come out now over here to me
    from where you are crouching among the rocks."   *90*
And so I made my way quickly across to his side.
  Now the devils all pressed several steps forward
    and I was afraid their agreement was void.   *93*
I saw soldiers once filing out of Caprona
  in great fear, though under pledge of safe conduct,
    when they saw the enemy surrounding them.   *96*
I pressed up to my leader as close as I could
  and huddled beside him, keeping my eyes
    on the demons' looks, which were far from good.   *99*
They did lower their forks, but one of them said,
  "Should I give him a little touch on the ass?"
    And the others answered, "Yeah, let him have it."   *102*
But then the demon with whom my master
  had been speaking wheeled around and snapped,
    "You mangy dog! Down, Scarmiglione, down!"   *105*
Then he said to us: "You can't go farther
  along this crag, because the sixth arch
    lies all shattered at the canyon's bottom.   *108*
But if you still want to pursue your journey
  make your way along the bank over here.
    Another arch close by will lead you across.   *111*
Five hours later than now, yesterday marked
  one thousand two hundred sixty-six years
    since a tremor reduced the bridge to ruins.   *114*
I was just dispatching some of my troops there
  to see if any sinners have come up for air.
    You can go with them; they will not hurt you."   *117*

"Alichino, you clown, and Calcabrina, get up here,"
  he called out, "you too, Mad Dog Cagnazzo.
    Barbariccia the Beard will lead the squad.   *120*

Libicocco vegn' oltre e Draghignazzo,
Cirïatto sannuto e Graffiacane

123 e Farfarello e Rubicante pazzo.
Cercate 'ntorno le boglienti pane;
costor sian salvi infino a l'altro scheggio

126 che tutto intero va sovra le tane."

"Omè, maestro, che è quel ch'i' veggio?"
diss' io, "deh, sanza scorta andianci soli,

129 se tu sa' ir; ch'i' per me non la cheggio.
Se tu se' sí accorto come suoli,
non vedi tu ch'e' digrignan li denti

132 e con le ciglia ne minaccian duoli?"
Ed elli a me: "Non vo' che tu paventi;
lasciali digrignar pur a lor senno,

135 ch'e' fanno ciò per li lessi dolenti."
Per l'argine sinistro volta dienno;
ma prima avea ciascun la lingua stretta

138 coi denti, verso lor duca, per cenno;
ed elli avea del cul fatto trombetta.

Lover-boy Libicocco and our little Dragon come too,
  and Ciriatto the Tusker, Flea-bag Graffiacane,
    Farfarello the Butterfly, and Crazy Rubicante.   *123*
Go scout around the boiling glue,
  and get these two safe to the next crag
    that spans the pit and hasn't broken down."   *126*

"O Master," I said, "what is this I see?
  If you know the way, let's go on alone
    without any escort. I don't want any.   *129*
If you are still as wary as you always have been
  you must see how they are grinding their teeth.
    You can read in their eyebrows the harm they mean."   *132*
"I would not have you be as frightened as you are,"
  my master said. "Let them grind their teeth—
    and their looks are for those simmering in the tar."   *135*
They wheeled to the left and onto the bank,
  but each of them stuck his tongue out first
    as a salute to their commander's rank,   *138*
And he from his rump gave a trumpeting burst.

CANTO XXII

REFLECTING ON THE INAUSPICIOUS TRUMPET VOLUNTARY, *Dante and Virgil step off on their forced march accompanied by the squad of ten fierce demons. His eyes glued to the pitch, Dante observes a number of sinners breach the surface, lining up along the banks of the bolgia like frogs with their snouts out of the water. All dive down below when the Malebranche approach, except for one, who is hooked by the hair by Graffiacane and held up for the others to torment. The unfortunate Grafter is from Navarre in Spain.*

The anonymous Navarrese fixer names a couple of other bribe-takers from Sardinia who are under the pitch and offers to make a deal. If the demons set

Io vidi già cavalier muover campo,
    e cominciare stormo e far lor mostra,
3   e talvolta partir per loro scampo;
corridor vidi per la terra vostra,
    o Aretini, e vidi gir gualdane,
6   fedir torneamenti e correr giostra;
quando con trombe, e quando con campane,
    con tamburi e con cenni di castella,
9   e con cose nostrali e con istrane;
né già con sí diversa cennamella
    cavalier vidi muover né pedoni,
12   né nave a segno di terra o di stella.

Noi andavam con li diece demoni.
    Ahi fiera compagnia! ma ne la chiesa
15   coi santi, e in taverna coi ghiottoni.
Pur a la pegola era la mia 'ntesa,
    per veder de la bolgia ogne contegno
18   e de la gente ch'entro v'era incesa.

him down and back off, he will give a secret whistle to his companions, who will
surface thinking the coast is clear. Reluctantly, the demons, suspicious but avid
for prey, agree and hide behind the bank. Instead of keeping his end of the bar-
gain, the Navarrese dives under before they can catch him, leaving Calcabrina
and Alichino to squabble among themselves, grapple above the pitch, and finally
fall in. In the ensuing confusion Dante and his guide slip away.

I have in my life seen horsemen breaking camp,
   starting an assault and making their muster,
      and sometimes retiring in retreat;   *3*
I have seen light cavalry scouting your land,
   men of Arezzo, and I have seen raids begun,
      tournaments starting, and the running of jousts,   *6*
Some signaled with trumpets, some with bells,
   with drumbeats and with flags or lights from castles,
      with signals native and signs exotic—   *9*
But never have I seen cavalry charge, or soldiers
   advance, or ships set sail by lighthouse or star,
      signaled by an instrument as strange as that pipe!   *12*

So with these ten demons we made our way.
   Rough company, but as the saying goes,
      in church with saints, with drunks in the tavern.   *15*
All my attention was focused on the pitch,
   to learn everything I could about this trench
      and about the people burning within it.   *18*

Come i dalfini, quando fanno segno
a' marinar con l'arco de la schiena
21 che s'argomentin di campar lor legno,
talor cosí, ad alleggiar la pena,
mostrav' alcun de' peccatori 'l dosso
24 e nascondea in men che non balena.
E come a l'orlo de l'acqua d'un fosso
stanno i ranocchi pur col muso fuori,
27 sí che celano i piedi e l'altro grosso,
sí stavan d'ogne parte i peccatori;
ma come s'appressava Barbariccia,
30 cosí si ritraén sotto i bollori.
I' vidi, e anco il cor me n'accapriccia,
uno aspettar cosí, com' elli 'ncontra
33 ch'una rana rimane e l'altra spiccia;
e Graffiacan, che li era piú di contra,
li arrunciglió le 'mpegolate chiome
36 e trassel sú, che mi parve una lontra.
I' sapea già di tutti quanti 'l nome,
sí li notai quando fuorono eletti,
39 e poi ch'e' si chiamaro, attesi come.
"O Rubicante, fa che tu li metti
li unghioni a dosso, sí che tu lo scuoi!"
42 gridavan tutti insieme i maladetti.
E io:"Maestro mio, fa, se tu puoi,
che tu sappi chi è lo sciagurato
45 venuto a man de li avversari suoi."
Lo duca mio li s'accostò allato;
domandollo ond'ei fosse, e quei rispuose:
48 "I' fui del regno di Navarra nato.
Mia madre a servo d'un segnor mi puose,
che m'avea generato d'un ribaldo,
51 distruggitor di sé e di sue cose.
Poi fui famiglia del buon re Tebaldo;
quivi mi misi a far baratteria,
54 di ch'io rendo ragione in questo caldo."

As dolphins breach and arch their backs
  signaling mariners on the high seas
    to take precautions to save their ships,   *21*
So too sometimes one of the sinners,
  to lessen his pain, would show his back
    and then hide it quicker than a lightning flash.   *24*
And as at the edge of water in a ditch
  frogs sit with only their muzzles exposed,
    submerging their feet and the rest of their bulk,   *27*
So were the sinners on each side of this ditch;
  but as soon as Barbariccia approached
    they would sink back under the boiling tar.   *30*
I saw—and my heart still skips a beat—
  one of them waiting, just as you might see
    one frog linger while others flash away.   *33*
And Graffiacane, who was nearest to him,
  hooked him by his long, tarred hair
    and hauled him up as if he were an otter.   *36*
I already knew all the devils' names,
  for I noted them well when they were picked
    and paid attention when they called each other.   *39*
"Get your claws into him, Rubicante,"
  the whole crew of fiends shouted at once.
    "Sink them in deep and rip his skin off!"   *42*
And I said: "Master, find out if you can
  who this is, this miserable soul
    who has fallen into his enemies' hands."   *45*
My leader came up close to his side, asking
  where he was from, and he replied,
    "I was born in the kingdom of Navarre.   *48*
My mother sent me to work for a lord
  after my father, a liar and gambler,
    ruined himself and all he was worth.   *51*
Then I was in the house of good King Thibault,
  where as his official I was on the take,
    and now my accounts are squared in this heat."   *54*

E Cirïatto, a cui di bocca uscia
   d'ogne parte una sanna come a porco,
57   li fé sentir come l'una sdruscia.
Tra male gatte era venuto 'l sorco;
   ma Barbariccia il chiuse con le braccia
60   e disse: "State in là, mentr' io lo 'nforco."
E al maestro mio volse la faccia;
   "Domanda," disse, "ancor, se piú disii
63   saper da lui, prima ch'altri 'l disfaccia."
Lo duca dunque: "Or dí: de li altri rii
   conosci tu alcun che sia latino
66   sotto la pece?" E quelli: "I' mi partii,
poco è, da un che fu di là vicino.
   Cosí foss' io ancor con lui coperto,
69   ch'i' non temerei unghia né uncino!"
E Libicocco "Troppo avem sofferto,"
   disse e preseli 'l braccio col runciglio,
72   sí che, stracciando, ne portò un lacerto.
Draghignazzo anco i volle dar di piglio
   giuso a le gambe; onde 'l decurio loro
75   si volse intorno intorno con mal piglio.
Quand' elli un poco rappaciati fuoro,
   a lui, ch'ancor mirava sua ferita,
78   domandò 'l duca mio sanza dimoro:
"Chi fu colui da cui mala partita
   di' che facesti per venire a proda?"
81   Ed ei rispuose: "Fu frate Gomita,
quel di Gallura, vasel d'ogne froda,
   ch'ebbe i nemici di suo donno in mano,
84   e fé sí lor, che ciascun se ne loda.
Danar si tolse e lasciolli di piano,
   sí com' e' dice; e ne li altri offici anche
87   barattier fu non picciol, ma sovrano.
Usa con esso donno Michel Zanche
   di Logodoro; e a dir di Sardigna
90   le lingue lor non si sentono stanche.

Then Ciriatto, who had a tusk like a boar's
  protruding from either side of his mouth,
    made him feel how each one could rip.   *57*
The mouse had fallen among the cats;
  but Barbariccia circled his arms around him
    and said, "Stand back while I cage him in,"   *60*
And then he turned to my master and said,
  "If you want to ask him more, go ahead,
    before one of them tears him limb from limb."   *63*
And so my leader asked him, "Tell us, then,
  of the other sinners under the pitch,
    do you know any who are Italian?"   *66*
He said: "I just now left one from nearby Sardinia.
  I wish I were still under cover with him,
    so I wouldn't be trembling at claws and hooks."   *69*
And Libicocco cried: "We've put up with too much!"
  and hooked his arm with a grapple that tore
    a piece of muscle out through his skin.   *72*
Draghignazzo made a move to hook him
  around the legs, but at this their sergeant
    turned on them all with an ugly look.   *75*
When all of them had all simmered down a little,
  my leader immediately asked the sinner,
    who still looked in amazement at his open wound,   *78*
"From whose side do you say you made
  an unfortunate departure to come ashore?"
    And he answered: "It was Fra Gomita,   *81*
That vessel of fraud out of Gallura,
  who had his lord's enemies in his hand,
    and won their praise for how he dealt with them.   *84*
He took their cash and soft-pedaled them out,
  to hear him tell it; and in his other deals
    he was anything but a small-time player.   *87*
Don Michel Zanche of Logudoro
  always hangs out with him. The two of them
    never shut up—'Sardinia this,' 'Sardinia that.'   *90*

Omè, vedete l'altro che digrigna;
 i' direi anche, ma i' temo ch'ello
93   non s'apparecchi a grattarmi la tigna."

E 'l gran proposto, vòlto a Farfarello
 che stralunava li occhi per fedire,
96   disse: "Fatti 'n costà, malvagio uccello!"
 "Se voi volete vedere o udire,"
 ricominciò lo spaürato appresso,
99   "Toschi o Lombardi, io ne farò venire;
 ma stieno i Malebranche un poco in cesso,
 sí ch'ei non teman de le lor vendette;
102   e io, seggendo in questo loco stesso,
 per un ch'io son, ne farò venir sette
 quand' io suffolerò, com' è nostro uso
105   di fare allor che fori alcun si mette."
 Cagnazzo a cotal motto levò 'l muso,
 crollando 'l capo, e disse: "Odi malizia
108   ch'elli ha pensata per gittarsi giuso!"
 Ond' ei, ch'avea lacciuoli a gran divizia,
 rispuose: "Malizioso son io troppo,
111   quand' io procuro a' mia maggior trestizia."
 Alichin non si tenne e, di rintoppo
 a li altri, disse a lui: "Se tu ti cali,
114   io non ti verrò dietro di gualoppo,
 ma batterò sovra la pece l'ali.
 Lascisi 'l collo, e sia la ripa scudo,
117   a veder se tu sol piú di noi vali."

O tu che leggi, udirai nuovo ludo:
 ciascun da l'altra costa li occhi volse,
120   quel prima, ch'a ciò fare era piú crudo.
 Lo Navarrese ben suo tempo colse;
 fermò le piante a terra, e in un punto
123   saltò e dal proposto lor si sciolse.
 Di che ciascun di colpa fu compunto,
 ma quei piú che cagion fu del difetto;
126   però si mosse e gridò: "Tu se' giunto!"

Oh shit, look at that one grinding his teeth.
  I would keep on talking, but I'm afraid
    he's gearing up to scratch where I itch." 93

The sergeant master turned to Farfarello,
  who was rolling his eyes preparing to strike,
    and said, "Get back there, you flying turd." 96
"If you want to see some Tuscans or Lombards,"
  the frightened sinner began again,
    "I can get a bunch to come over here. 99
Just have these Malebranche back off a little
  so the Italians think the coast is clear,
    and I, sitting on this very spot, 102
All by myself, can get seven to come
  just by whistling. That's the signal we have
    when any of us gets out of the pitch." 105
When he heard this, Cagnazzo raised his snout
  and said, shaking his head, "Listen to the trick
    this guy's come up with so he can jump back in." 108
And the sinner, who was flush with swindles,
  replied, "I would have to be awfully rotten
    to bring more suffering upon my own." 111
Alichino no longer held himself back,
  and said, arguing against the others,
    "If you dive in I won't just run after you; 114
I'll be beating my wings above the pitch.
  Let's leave the ridge and hide behind the bank,
    and we'll see if you get the better of us." 117

Listen now, Reader, to new entertainment.
  They all turned to look toward the other side,
    led by the one who had been most against it. 120
The Navarrese timed it well. Feet planted
  firmly on the ground, he made a sudden leap
    and broke away from the squadron's leader. 123
Then each of them felt the sting of remorse,
  not least of all the one who caused their blunder,
    Alichino, who flew out shouting, "Gotcha!" 126

Ma poco i valse: ché l'ali al sospetto
non potero avanzar; quelli andò sotto,
129 e quei drizzò volando suso il petto:
non altrimenti l'anitra di botto,
quando 'l falcon s'appressa, giú s'attuffa,
132 ed ei ritorna sú crucciato e rotto.
Irato Calcabrina de la buffa,
volando dietro li tenne, invaghito
135 che quei campasse per aver la zuffa;
e come 'l barattier fu disparito,
cosí volse li artigli al suo compagno,
138 e fu con lui sopra 'l fosso ghermito.
Ma l'altro fu bene sparvier grifagno
ad artigliar ben lui, e amendue
141 cadder nel mezzo del bogliente stagno.
Lo caldo sghermitor súbito fue;
ma però di levarsi era neente,
144 sí avieno inviscate l'ali sue
Barbariccia, con li altri suoi dolente,
quattro ne fé volar da l'altra costa
147 con tutt' i raffi, e assai prestamente
di qua, di là discesero a la posta;
porser li uncini verso li 'mpaniati,
150 ch'eran già cotti dentro da la crosta.
E noi lasciammo lor cosí 'mpacciati.

But it did him no good: his wings were no match
  for the other's fear. The Navarrese went under,
    and the demon, in flight, turned his chest upward.   *129*
It was like a wild duck diving suddenly under
  at a falcon's approach, and the bird of prey
    veering upward again, vexed and beaten.   *132*
Calcabrina, angry at being played for a fool,
  went flying after him, eager for the sinner
    to make his escape so he could pick a fight.   *135*
And when the grafter had vanished in the tar,
  he turned his talons on his companion,
    and above the ditch they grappled in flight.   *138*
But Alichino was no fledgling falcon
  and clawed him back, as into the middle
    of the boiling pitch they both tumbled down.   *141*
At once the searing heat ungrappled them,
  but there was no way for them to get out
    with their wings ensnared in the viscous gum.   *144*
Barbariccia, groaning with the rest of the crew,
  dispatched four by air to the opposite bank,
    each armed with a gaffe. Off they flew   *147*
And came down into position, hooks thrust
  toward their companions coated with pitch,
    the two demons already cooked in their crust.   *150*
There we left them, floundering around the ditch.

Canto XXIII

AS VIRGIL AND DANTE TRUDGE ON IN SILENCE, *Dante reflects on the instance he has just observed of the biter bit, and he realizes that they are still exposed to the demons' revenge. In fact the Malebranche are in hot pursuit. Seizing the opportunity, Virgil scrambles down the sloping bank into the Sixth Bolgia, where their pursuers are barred from following them. They find themselves among the Hypocrites, who move at a snail's pace under their unbearably heavy leaden cloaks, deceptively gilded on the outside.*

As he expresses to Virgil his curiosity to know exactly who they are, Dante is addressed by two of them, Catalano and Loderingo from Bologna, former

Taciti, soli, sanza compagnia
    n'andavam l'un dinanzi e l'altro dopo,
3   come frati minor vanno per via.
Vòlt' era in su la favola d'Isopo
    lo mio pensier per la presente rissa,
6   dov' el parlò de la rana e del topo;
ché piú non si pareggia 'mo' e 'issa'
    che l'un con l'altro fa, se ben s'accoppia
9   principio e fine con la mente fissa.
E come l'un pensier de l'altro scoppia,
    cosí nacque di quello un altro poi,
12   che la prima paura mi fé doppia.
Io pensava cosí: 'Questi per noi
    sono scherniti con danno e con beffa
15   sí fatta, ch' assai credo che lor nòi.
Se l'ira sovra 'l mal voler s'aggueffa,
    ei ne verranno dietro piú crudeli
18   che 'l cane a quella lievre ch'elli acceffa.'
Già mi sentia tutti arricciar li peli
    de la paura e stava in dietro intento,
21   quand' io dissi: "Maestro, se non celi

papal appointees as chief magistrates of Florence. They identify the crucified
figures they are treading underfoot as the high priests of the Pharisees and mem-
bers of the Sanhedrin, who tried Jesus Christ and handed him over to the Ro-
man governor for execution. Finally, showing them how they can resume their
steady descent, the hypocrites sarcastically reveal that, in this circle of fraud and
deceit, Dante and more especially his guide Virgil have naively allowed them-
selves to be fooled by the wiles of the devils.

Silent, alone, without company,
   we walked on, one ahead, the other behind,
      as Franciscan mendicants go when they travel.   *3*
The brawl we'd just witnessed reminded me
   of Aesop and that fable of his,
      the old story of the frog and the mouse.   *6*
When you compare the two side by side,
   especially how each began and ended,
      they are just as alike as "at present" and "now."   *9*
My reflections on the fable brought to light
   another idea that gave me pause,
      something that doubled my original fear.   *12*
I thought: "They have been fooled because of us,
   and insult has been added to injury,
      so I think that they must be really annoyed.   *15*
And if their malice becomes entwined with rage,
   they're going to come after us more ferociously
      than the jaws of a dog closing down on a hare."   *18*
Already I felt my hair bristle with fear
   as I went along intent on what was behind,
      and I said, "Master, unless you can hide us   *21*

te e me tostamente, i' ho pavento
d'i Malebranche. Noi li avem già dietro;
24   io li 'magino sí, che già li sento."
E quei: "S'i' fossi di piombato vetro,
l'imagine di fuor tua non trarrei
27   piú tosto a me, che quella dentro 'mpetro.
Pur mo venieno i tuo' pensier tra ' miei,
con simile atto e con simile faccia,
30   sí che d'intrambi un sol consiglio fei.
S'elli è che sí la destra costa giaccia,
che noi possiam ne l'altra bolgia scendere,
33   noi fuggirem l'imaginata caccia."

Già non compié di tal consiglio rendere,
ch'io li vidi venir con l'ali tese
36   non molto lungi, per volerne prendere.
Lo duca mio di súbito mi prese,
come la madre ch'al romore è desta
39   e vede presso a sé le fiamme accese,
che prende il figlio e fugge e non s'arresta,
avendo piú di lui che di sé cura,
42   tanto che solo una camiscia vesta;
e giú dal collo de la ripa dura
supin si diede a la pendente roccia,
45   che l'un de' lati a l'altra bolgia tura.
Non corse mai sí tosto acqua per doccia
a volger ruota di molin terragno,
48   quand' ella piú verso le pale approccia,
come 'l maestro mio per quel vivagno,
portandosene me sovra 'l suo petto,
51   come suo figlio, non come compagno.
A pena fuoro i piè suoi giunti al letto
del fondo giú, ch'e' furon in sul colle
54   sovresso noi; ma non lí era sospetto:
ché l'alta provedenza che lor volle
porre ministri de la fossa quinta,
57   poder di partirs' indi a tutti tolle.

Pretty quickly, I'm going to be very nervous
　　about the Malebranche. They're after us,
　　　　and I imagine I can hear them already."　　　　　24
And he said to me: "If I were leaded glass,
　　I would not reflect your outward appearance
　　　　more quickly than I sense your inner state.　　　27
Just now your thoughts mingled with mine,
　　looking and feeling exactly the same,
　　　　and I've made both into a single plan.　　　　　30
If it turns out that the slope that lies on the right
　　allows us a way down to the next ditch,
　　　　we will slip away from this imagined pursuit."　　33

He had not finished outlining his plan
　　when I saw them coming with wings outstretched
　　　　and closing fast with murderous intent.　　　　36
My master instantly snatched me up
　　like a mother who awakes to the crackling
　　　　roar of fire, and seeing the flames close by,　　39
Snatches up her son and rushes out,
　　thinking so much of him rather than herself
　　　　that she doesn't wait to put on more than a shift.　42
Then he leapt from the rough shoulder of the ridge
　　and started to slide on his back down the slope
　　　　that formed the near side of the lower trench.　　45
Water has never flowed so fast through a sluice,
　　when it rushes from the stream to turn the paddles
　　　　of a mill's grinding wheel, as my master went　　48
Careening down that bank while carrying me
　　upon his chest, not as someone would hold
　　　　a mere companion, but would hold his own son.　51
At the moment his feet had touched the floor
　　of the chasm below, there the demons were,
　　　　peering from the height directly above us.　　　54
But there was nothing to fear, for high Providence,
　　which set them as ministers of the Fifth Trench,
　　　　denies them the power ever to leave it.　　　　57

Là giú trovammo una gente dipinta
che giva intorno assai con lenti passi,
60   piangendo e nel sembiante stanca e vinta.
Elli avean cappe con cappucci bassi
dinanzi a li occhi, fatte de la taglia
63   che in Clugní per li monaci fassi.
Di fuor dorate son, sí ch'elli abbaglia;
ma dentro tutte piombo, e gravi tanto,
66   che Federigo le mettea di paglia.
Oh in etterno faticoso manto!
Noi ci volgemmo ancor pur a man manca
69   con loro insieme, intenti al tristo pianto;
ma per lo peso quella gente stanca
venía sí pian, che noi eravam nuovi
72   di compagnia ad ogne mover d'anca.
Per ch'io al duca mio: "Fa che tu trovi
alcun ch'al fatto o al nome si conosca,
75   e li occhi, sí andando, intorno movi."

E un che 'ntese la parola tosca,
di retro a noi gridò: "Tenete i piedi,
78   voi che correte sí per l'aura fosca!
Forse ch'avrai da me quel che tu chiedi."
Onde 'l duca si volse e disse: "Aspetta,
81   e poi secondo il suo passo procedi."
Ristetti, e vidi due mostrar gran fretta
de l'animo, col viso, d'esser meco;
84   ma tardavali 'l carco e la via stretta.
Quando fuor giunti, assai con l'occhio bieco
mi rimiraron sanza far parola;
87   poi si volsero in sé, e dicean seco:
"Costui par vivo a l'atto de la gola;
e s'e' son morti, per qual privilegio
90   vanno scoperti de la grave stola?"
Poi disser me: "O Tosco, ch'al collegio
de l'ipocriti tristi se' venuto,
93   dir chi tu se' non avere in dispregio."

Down there we found a painted people
  stepping slowly in circumambulation,
    weeping, weary, and with an air of defeat.   60
They wore cloaks with cowls pulled down low
  over their eyes, cut in the style
    of vestments made for the monks of Cluny.   63
The outside of the cloaks was dazzling gold,
  but inside they were solid lead, so heavy
    the ones Frederick used were as light as straw—   66
A weary mantle for all eternity!
  Turning to the left, we walked along with them,
    intent upon their sorrowful weeping,   69
But because of their load, the exhausted souls
  proceeded so slowly that we drew alongside
    new companions at every step we took.   72
So after a while I said to my guide,
  "Could you look around as we walk, and discover
    someone well known for his deeds or his name?"   75

Then one of them recognized my Tuscan speech
  and called out from behind, "Slow down, you two,
    running like that through the dusky air.   78
Perhaps you can get from me what you want."
  At this my leader turned to me and said,
    "Wait for him, and then walk at his pace."   81
I paused, and saw two who evinced
  great mental haste to catch up with me
    but were slowed by their burden and the narrow way.   84
When they reached me, they looked in silence
  for some time at me with a suspicious eye,
    and finally turned to each other and said,   87
"This man seems alive from the way his throat moves,
  and if they are both dead, then why is it
    they do not have to wear the heavy stole?"   90
Then they said to me: "O Tuscan,
  cloistered now among the sad hypocrites,
    do not disdain to tell us who you are."   93

E io a loro: "I' fui nato e cresciuto
  sovra 'l bel fiume d'Arno a la gran villa,
96   e son col corpo ch'i' ho sempre avuto.
Ma voi chi siete, a cui tanto distilla
  quant' i' veggio dolor giú per le guance?
99   e che pena è in voi che sí sfavilla?"
E l'un rispuose a me: "Le cappe rance
  son di piombo sí grosse, che li pesi
102   fan cosí cigolar le lor bilance.
Frati godenti fummo, e bolognesi;
  io Catalano e questi Loderingo
105   nomati, e da tua terra insieme presi
come suole esser tolto un uom solingo,
  per conservar sua pace; e fummo tali,
108   ch'ancor si pare intorno dal Gardingo."

Io cominciai: "O frati, i vostri mali . . .";
  ma piú non dissi, ch'a l'occhio mi corse
111   un, crucifisso in terra con tre pali.
Quando mi vide, tutto si distorse,
  soffiando ne la barba con sospiri;
114   e 'l frate Catalan, ch'a ciò s'accorse,
mi disse: "Quel confitto che tu miri,
  consigliò i Farisei che convenia
117   porre un uom per lo popolo a' martíri.
Attraversato è, nudo, ne la via,
  come tu vedi, ed è mestier ch'el senta
120   qualunque passa, come pesa, pria.
E a tal modo il socero si stenta
  in questa fossa, e li altri dal concilio
123   che fu per li Giudei mala sementa."
Allor vid' io maravigliar Virgilio
  sovra colui ch'era disteso in croce
126   tanto vilmente ne l'etterno essilio.
Poscia drizzò al frate cotal voce:
  "Non vi dispiaccia, se vi lece, dirci
129   s'a la man destra giace alcuna foce

And I answered: "I was born and grew up
  by the beautiful Arno, in the splendid town,
  and this is the body I have always had.   *96*
But who are you? The tears I see on your cheeks
  distill great sorrow. And what chastisement
  is this upon you that shines so bright?"   *99*
One of them replied: "The golden cloaks
  are made of lead so thick that their weight
  makes our frames creak like overladen scales.   *102*
We were Jovial Friars from Bologna.
  My name is Catalano and he is Loderingo,
  and we were chosen together by your city   *105*
The way one man alone is usually chosen
  to keep the peace. How well we did that
  can still be seen around the Gardingo."   *108*

I began: "Friars, the evils that you . . ."
  but I said no more, for my eye caught a figure
  crucified with three stakes upon the ground.   *111*
When he saw me he writhed all over,
  breathing heavy sighs into his beard.
  Fra Catalano saw this and said to me,   *114*
"The one transfixed here before your gaze
  advised the Pharisees that it was expedient
  that one man should die for everyone's good.   *117*
He is stretched out naked across the road,
  as you see, and he must feel the weight
  of each of us when we pass this way.   *120*
His father-in-law, too, lies extended
  across the floor of this ditch, as do all
  of that council, an evil seed for the Jews."   *123*
Then I saw Virgil marvel over this man
  stretched out there in the shape of a cross
  so vilely in the eternal exile.   *126*
Then he addressed the friar and said,
  "If you are allowed, may it not displease you
  to tell us if some passage slopes up on the right *129*

onde noi amendue possiamo uscirci,
   sanza costrigner de li angeli neri
132   che vegnan d'esto fondo a dipartirci."
Rispuose adunque: "Piú che tu non speri
   s'appressa un sasso che da la gran cerchia
135   si move e varca tutt' i vallon feri,
salvo che 'n questo è rotto e nol coperchia;
   montar potrete su per la ruina,
138   che giace in costa e nel fondo soperchia."

Lo duca stette un poco a testa china;
   poi disse: "Mal contava la bisogna
141   colui che i peccator di qua uncina."
E 'l frate: "Io udi' già dire a Bologna
   del diavol vizi assai, tra ' quali udi'
144   ch'elli è bugiardo e padre di menzogna."
Appresso il duca a gran passi sen gí,
   turbato un poco d'ira nel sembiante;
147   ond' io da li 'ncarcati mi parti'
dietro a le poste de le care piante.

That will lead us out of here without the need
  of recruiting the help of those black angels
    to provide transportation out of this ditch."   *132*
And he replied:"Nearer than you hope
  is a ridge that runs from the great outer wall
    and marches in spans over all the valleys   *135*
Except for this one, where it is broken down.
  You will be able to climb through the tumbled rocks
    lying against the side and piled up in a heap."   *138*

My guide stood for a moment with bowed head.
  "That one who hooks sinners over there
    gave a poor account of this matter," he said.   *141*
And the friar:"Among the vices the devil plies,
  as they say in Bologna, not the least is that
    he is a liar, and the father of lies."   *144*
Then, with great strides, my guide went ahead
  disturbed a little and looking quite angry,
    and I took my leave of the burdened dead,   *147*
Following the feet that were dear to me.

Canto XXIV

As he reacts to the changing weather *of Virgil's facial expressions, first betokening anxiety, then resolution, Dante is like the peasant who at first takes the hoarfrost for snow, but quickly rejoices when the frozen dew melts in the February sun. Arriving at the ruined bridge, Virgil takes Dante into his arms and together they climb laboriously out of the Sixth Bolgia. Once out, Dante is not allowed to linger and catch his breath. As they cross the next bridge, over the murky Seventh Bolgia, an angry voice is heard uttering indistinguishable words in the darkness below. Approaching closer, they see that on the opposite*

    In quella parte del giovanetto anno
      che 'l sole i crin sotto l'Aquario tempra
3   e già le notti al mezzo dí sen vanno,
    quando la brina in su la terra assempra
      l'imagine di sua sorella bianca,
6   ma poco dura a la sua penna tempra,
    lo villanello a cui la roba manca,
      si leva, e guarda, e vede la campagna
9   biancheggiar tutta; ond' ei si batte l'anca,
    ritorna in casa, e qua e là si lagna,
      come 'l tapin che non sa che si faccia;
12   poi riede, e la speranza ringavagna,
    veggendo 'l mondo aver cangiata faccia
      in poco d'ora, e prende suo vincastro
15   e fuor le pecorelle a pascer caccia.

    Cosí mi fece sbigottir lo mastro
      quand' io li vidi sí turbar la fronte,
18   e cosí tosto al mal giunse lo 'mpiastro;
    ché, come noi venimmo al guasto ponte,
      lo duca a me si volse con quel piglio
21   dolce ch'io vidi prima a piè del monte.

side the bolgia is teeming with exotic reptiles while naked human figures, their hands bound by snakes, run among them. A serpent bites one of these figures in the neck, and he instantly crumbles to dust, only to spring up again, just as the Phoenix is said to rise from its ashes. Though dazed, when interrogated by Virgil he reveals, with a show of violence, that he is Vanni Fucci, a Black Guelph from Pistoia. Dante presses him further, to find out what sin he is guilty of. Ashamed, the sinner admits he was a thief and, to avenge his humiliation by Dante, prophesies the ultimate defeat of Dante's party, the White Guelphs.

When the year is young, and the sun
  is warming his locks under Aquarius
    and the nights are almost as short as the days,   *3*
When frost copies on the woods and fields
  the likeness of her wintry sister,
    but the quill she draws with soon becomes blunt,   *6*
Then the peasant whose fodder is running low
  gets up in the morning, looks out, and sees
    the fields all white. He slaps his thigh,   *9*
Goes back inside, and grumbles for a while,
  worries, frets, doesn't know what to do;
    but then he goes back out and hope returns   *12*
When he sees how quickly the face of the world
  has changed its expression. He takes his crook
    and drives his sheep out to hunt for pasture.   *15*

My master likewise caused me dismay
  when I saw his brow so anxious and troubled,
    but just as quickly a remedy appeared.   *18*
For when we came to the shattered bridge
  my guide turned to me with that gentle look
    that I saw first at the foot of the mountain.   *21*

Le braccia aperse, dopo alcun consiglio
   eletto seco riguardando prima
24   ben la ruina, e diedemi di piglio.
E come quei ch'adopera ed estima,
   che sempre par che 'nnanzi si proveggia,
27   cosí, levando me sú ver' la cima
d'un ronchione, avvisava un'altra scheggia
   dicendo: "Sovra quella poi t'aggrappa;
30   ma tenta pria s'è tal ch'ella ti reggia."
Non era via da vestito di cappa,
   ché noi a pena, ei lieve e io sospinto,
33   potavam sú montar di chiappa in chiappa.
E se non fosse che da quel precinto
   piú che da l'altro era la costa corta,
36   non so di lui, ma io sarei ben vinto.
Ma perché Malebolge inver' la porta
   del bassissimo pozzo tutta pende,
39   lo sito di ciascuna valle porta
che l'una costa surge e l'altra scende;
   noi pur venimmo al fine in su la punta
42   onde l'ultima pietra si scoscende.
La lena m'era del polmon sí munta
   quand' io fui sú, ch'i' non potea piú oltre,
45   anzi m'assisi ne la prima giunta.

"Omai convien che tu cosí ti spoltre,"
   disse 'l maestro; "ché, seggendo in piuma,
48   in fama non si vien, né sotto coltre;
sanza la qual chi sua vita consuma,
   cotal vestigio in terra di sé lascia,
51   qual fummo in aere e in acqua la schiuma.
E però leva sú; vinci l'ambascia
   con l'animo che vince ogne battaglia,
54   se col suo grave corpo non s'accascia.
Piú lunga scala convien che si saglia;
   non basta da costoro esser partito.
57   Se tu mi 'ntendi, or fa sí che ti vaglia."

After thinking it over a moment or two
  and examining the rubble, he spread
    his arms out and wrapped them around me. 24
And, like a person who plans every move
  and seems to see everything in advance,
    while he was lifting me up toward the top 27
Of one great rock he was already mapping
  the handhold to follow, saying, "Grab that one next,
    but test it to see if it will bear your weight." 30
It was no route for those wearing thick cloaks,
  for we, light as he was and I with his support,
    could hardly make it from one ledge to another. 33
And except for the fact that on that embankment
  the slope was shorter than on the other side—
    I don't know about him, but I would have been beat. 36
But because Malebolge all slopes inward
  to the bottom of the central pit,
    each of the valleys is situated 39
So that one side towers over the other.
  At long last, however, we reached the point
    where the last stone breaks off from the edge. 42
I had so little breath left in my lungs
  after the ascent, I could go no farther,
    and I sat down as soon as I got to the top. 45

"You're going to have to stop being so lazy,"
  my master said. "No one attains fame
    propped on down pillows or under coverlets, 48
And without fame you will waste your life
  and leave no more of yourself on Earth
    than smoke in the air or foam on water. 51
So stop gasping and get up! Conquer your breath
  with the spirit that wins all of its battles
    if it doesn't surrender to the weight of its body. 54
There is a longer ladder yet to be climbed.
  It is not enough to have left those souls behind.
    If you understand me, do something about it!" 57

Leva'mi allor, mostrandomi fornito
 meglio di lena ch'i' non mi sentia,
60 e dissi: "Va, ch'i' son forte e ardito."

Su per lo scoglio prendemmo la via,
 ch'era ronchioso, stretto e malagevole,
63 ed erto piú assai che quel di pria.
Parlando andava per non parer fievole;
 onde una voce uscí de l'altro fosso,
66 a parole formar disconvenevole.
Non so che disse, ancor che sovra 'l dosso
 fossi de l'arco già che varca quivi;
69 ma chi parlava ad ira parea mosso.
Io era vòlto in giú, ma li occhi vivi
 non poteano ire al fondo per lo scuro;
72 per ch'io: "Maestro, fa che tu arrivi
da l'altro cinghio e dismontiam lo muro;
 ché, com' i' odo quinci e non intendo,
75 cosí giú veggio e neente affiguro."
"Altra risposta," disse, "non ti rendo
 se non lo far; ché la dimanda onesta
78 si de' seguir con l'opera tacendo."

Noi discendemmo il ponte da la testa
 dove s'aggiugne con l'ottava ripa,
81 e poi mi fu la bolgia manifesta:
e vidivi entro terribile stipa
 di serpenti, e di sí diversa mena
84 che la memoria il sangue ancor mi scipa.
Piú non si vanti Libia con sua rena;
 ché se chelidri, iaculi e faree
87 produce, e cencri con anfisibena,
né tante pestilenzie né sí ree
 mostrò già mai con tutta l'Etïopia
90 né con ciò che di sopra al Mar Rosso èe.
Tra questa cruda e tristissima copia
 corrëan genti nude e spaventate,
93 sanza sperar pertugio o elitropia:

I got up then, pretending not to be
  nearly as winded as I felt, and said,
    "Go ahead now. I'm strong and determined."   *60*

We took the way that led up the ridge,
  a tortuous path hedged in by rocks,
    and far steeper than the last one we crossed.   *63*
I was talking as I went, so I would not seem
  so exhausted, when a voice, ill suited
    for forming words, came out of the ditch.   *66*
I don't know what it said, being as yet
  at the crown of the arch that crosses there,
    but the one that spoke seemed driven to rage.   *69*
I turned my gaze below, but my eyes could not pierce
  the shroud of darkness down to the bottom,
    so I said, "Master, would you please go down   *72*
To the next bank? Let's descend the wall,
  for from this point I can't understand what I hear,
    and when I look down there I can't see a thing."   *75*
"The only reply," he said, "that I will give
  is just to do it, for a proper request
    should be met with action performed in silence."   *78*

We came down at the end of the bridge
  where it abuts the eighth embankment,
    and the ditch's contents were revealed to me.   *81*
I saw within it a terrifying mass
  of serpents, snakes of so many strange kinds
    that the memory of it still chills my blood.   *84*
Libya can boast of nothing like this,
  for rich as it is in trail-scorchers and dart snakes,
    plow-adders, line-winders, and two-headed asps,   *87*
It has never had, with Ethiopia thrown in,
  and all of the lands along the Red Sea,
    so many, or such evil vipers as these.   *90*
And amid this cruel and hideous swarm
  people were running, naked and panicked,
    with no place to hide and no magic stone.   *93*

con serpi le man dietro avean legate;
quelle ficcavan per le ren la coda
96   e 'l capo, ed eran dinanzi aggroppate.
Ed ecco a un ch'era da nostra proda,
s'avventò un serpente che 'l trafisse
99   là dove 'l collo a le spalle s'annoda.
Né O sí tosto mai né I si scrisse,
com' el s'accese e arse, e cener tùtto
102   convenne che cascando divenisse;
e poi che fu a terra sí distrutto,
la polver si raccolse per sé stessa
105   e 'n quel medesmo ritornò di butto.
Cosí per li gran savi si confessa
che la fenice more e poi rinasce,
108   quando al cinquecentesimo anno appressa;
erba né biado in sua vita non pasce,
ma sol d'incenso lagrime e d'amomo,
111   e nardo e mirra son l'ultime fasce.
E qual è quel che cade, e non sa como,
per forza di demon ch'a terra il tira,
114   o d'altra oppilazion che lega l'omo,
quando si leva, che 'ntorno si mira
tutto smarrito de la grande angoscia
117   ch'elli ha sofferta, e guardando sospira:
tal era 'l peccator levato poscia.
Oh potenza di Dio, quant' è severa,
120   che cotai colpi per vendetta croscia!

Lo duca il domandò poi chi ello era;
per ch'ei rispuose: "Io piovvi di Toscana,
123   poco tempo è, in questa gola fiera.
Vita bestial mi piacque e non umana,
sí come a mul ch'i' fui; son Vanni Fucci
126   bestia, e Pistoia mi fu degna tana."
E ïo al duca: "Dilli che non mucci,
e domanda che colpa qua giú 'l pinse;
129   ch'io 'l vidi omo di sangue e di crucci."

Their hands were bound behind their backs with snakes
  whose heads and tails transfixed their loins
    and were tied in knots in front of their bellies.   *96*
A serpent suddenly shot after one
  who was near our bank and buried its fangs
    at the knot that joins the neck to the shoulders.   *99*
An *o* or an *i* was never written as fast
  as that soul caught fire and burned to a crisp,
    reduced to nothing but a pile of ashes;   *102*
But when he was undone on the ground like this,
  the dust reassembled all by itself
    and instantly resumed its previous form.   *105*
In the same way, learned men say,
  the Phoenix dies and is born again
    on the evening of its five hundredth year.   *108*
It does not feed on grasses or grain,
  but on tears of incense and on amomum,
    and its last nest is feathered with nard and myrrh.   *111*
Like someone who falls without knowing how,
  either because some devil drags him down
    or because he is seized with paralysis,   *114*
And when he gets up he looks around stunned,
  completely bewildered by the great anguish
    he is suffering, and then stares ahead sighing—   *117*
So too that sinner when he rose to his feet.
  Oh, the power of God! What stern severity
    that showers down blow upon blow in vengeance!   *120*

My guide then asked him who he was,
  to which he answered: "Not long ago
    I poured down from Tuscany to this savage throat.   *123*
A bestial life, not a human one, pleased me,
  mule that I was. I am Vanni Fucci,
    the beast, and Pistoia was my chosen lair."   *126*
I said to my guide: "Tell him not to leave,
  and ask him what sin got him down here,
    for I knew him as a bloody, violent man."   *129*

E 'l peccator, che 'ntese, non s'infinse,
ma drizzò verso me l'animo e 'l volto,
132 e di trista vergogna si dipinse;
poi disse:"Piú mi duol che tu m'hai colto
ne la miseria dove tu mi vedi,
135 che quando fui de l'altra vita tolto.
Io non posso negar quel che tu chiedi;
in giú son messo tanto perch' io fui
138 ladro a la sagrestia d'i belli arredi,
e falsamente già fu apposto altrui.
Ma perché di tal vista tu non godi,
141 se mai sarai di fuor da' luoghi bui,
apri li orecchi al mio annunzio, e odi.
Pistoia in pria d'i Neri si dimagra;
144 poi Fiorenza rinova gente e modi.
Tragge Marte vapor di Val di Magra
ch'è di torbidi nuvoli involuto;
147 e con tempesta impetüosa e agra
sovra Campo Picen fia combattuto;
ond' ei repente spezzerà la nebbia,
150 sí ch'ogne Bianco ne sarà feruto.
E detto l'ho perché doler ti debbia!"

The sinner heard me, and did not dissemble.
 In fact, he turned all his attention toward me
  and blushed with bitter shame. Then he said: *132*
"It causes me more pain that you have caught me
 in the misery where you see me now
  than I felt when I left the other life.   *135*
I have no choice but to answer your question.
 They put me so far down here in Hell
  because I stole from the church's treasury   *138*
And let the blame fall on an innocent man.
 But so that you may not triumph in this sight
  if you ever get out of this desolate place,   *141*
Open your ears now to what Vanni Fucci says:
 Pistoia first rids herself of the Blacks,
  then Florence changes her people and her ways.   *144*
But from Val di Magra Mars will awaken
 a lightning bolt wrapped in threatening clouds,
  and a sudden and bitter storm will break   *147*
As they rush to combat on Campo Piceno,
 from where suddenly the mist and fog will be rent
  so that every White will feel the blow.   *150*
And I tell you this to make you lament."

CANTO XXV

PISTOIAN THIEF VANNI FUCCI *makes an obscene gesture leveled at God and is silenced, his arms bound by two snakes. He flees before the Centaur Cacus can catch up with him. Dante and Virgil's ensuing exchange is interrupted by the appearance of three shades who are looking for a lost companion. One of them is assailed by a six-legged reptile, which clings to him until their two forms, human and reptilian, fuse into a monstrous hybrid, which slowly squirms away.*

Al fine de le sue parole il ladro
  le mani alzò con amendue le fiche,
3   gridando: "Togli, Dio, ch'a te le squadro!"
Da indi in qua mi fuor le serpi amiche,
  perch' una li s'avvolse allora al collo,
6   come dicesse 'Non vo' che piú diche';
e un'altra a le braccia, e rilegollo,
  ribadendo sé stessa sí dinanzi,
9   che non potea con esse dare un crollo.

Ahi Pistoia, Pistoia, ché non stanzi
  d'incenerarti sí che piú non duri,
12   poi che 'n mal fare il seme tuo avanzi?

Per tutt' i cerchi de lo 'nferno scuri
  non vidi spirto in Dio tanto superbo,
15   non quel che cadde a Tebe giú da' muri.
El si fuggí che non parlò piú verbo;
  e io vidi un centauro pien di rabbia
18   venir chiamando: "Ov' è, ov' è l'acerbo?"
Maremma non cred' io che tante n'abbia,
  quante bisce elli avea su per la groppa
21   infin ove comincia nostra labbia.

A second serpent darts at one of the other two, pierces his navel, and falls to the ground. As smoke pours from the wound and the serpent's mouth, they begin, slowly and uncannily, to exchange shapes at a distance, until the serpent has become a man and the man a serpent. Dante recognizes the only thief in the group whose human form, at least for now, has not been stolen.

When he had finished speaking, the thief
  raised his hands and made figs with both fists,
    crying out, "Take them, God. These are for you!"   *3*
And that is when snakes and I became friends,
  for one of them coiled around his neck
    as if to say, "You will speak no more,"   *6*
And another snake constricted his arms,
  lashing them so firmly in front
    that he could not even wiggle them.   *9*

Ah, Pistoia, Pistoia! Why don't you decree
  your own incineration, since you are more
    evil than even your founders could be?   *12*

In all of Hell, through all its dark circles,
  I saw no spirit so arrogant toward God,
    not even he who fell from the walls of Thebes.   *15*
Vanni Fucci fled without another word.
  Then I saw a Centaur come up, shouting with rage,
    "Which way did he go? Where's the crude one?"   *18*
Maremma's swamps can't have as many reptiles
  as crawled along this Centaur's back
    up to where our human torso begins;   *21*

Sovra le spalle, dietro da la coppa,
  con l'ali aperte li giacea un draco;
24   e quello affuoca qualunque s'intoppa.
Lo mio maestro disse: "Questi è Caco,
  che, sotto 'l sasso di monte Aventino,
27   di sangue fece spesse volte laco.
Non va co' suoi fratei per un cammino,
  per lo furto che frodolente fece
30   del grande armento ch'elli ebbe a vicino;
onde cessar le sue opere biece
  sotto la mazza d'Ercule, che forse
33   gliene diè cento, e non sentí le diece."

Mentre che sí parlava, ed el trascorse,
  e tre spiriti venner sotto noi,
36   de' quai né io né 'l duca mio s'accorse,
se non quando gridar: "Chi siete voi?"
  per che nostra novella si ristette,
39   e intendemmo pur ad essi poi.
Io non li conoscea; ma ei seguette,
  come suol seguitar per alcun caso,
42   che l'un nomar un altro convenette,
dicendo: "Cianfa dove fia rimaso?"
  per ch'io, acciò che 'l duca stesse attento,
45   mi puosi 'l dito su dal mento al naso.

Se tu se' or, lettore, a creder lento
  ciò ch'io dirò, non sarà maraviglia,
48   ché io che 'l vidi, a pena il mi consento.

Com'io tenea levate in lor le ciglia,
  e un serpente con sei piè si lancia
51   dinanzi a l'uno, e tutto a lui s'appiglia.
Co' piè di mezzo li avvinse la pancia
  e con li anterïor le braccia prese;
54   poi li addentò e l'una e l'altra guancia;

And on his shoulders just behind his neck
  a dragon crouched with outstretched wings,
    ready to breathe fire on whomever it met.   *24*
My master said:"That is Cacus,
  who beneath the rock of Mount Aventine,
    time after time made a lake of blood.   *27*
He does not travel in his brothers' company,
  on account of the cunning theft he made
    of the great herd that pastured near his lair.   *30*
It was for this his crooked ways were ended
  by Hercules' club, who dealt him perhaps
    a hundred blows, though he felt only ten."   *33*

While he spoke, the Centaur galloped past,
  and three spirits came up from below
    unnoticed by either my guide or me   *36*
Until they cried out:"Who are you two?"
  At this we broke off our conversation
    and gave our attention to them alone.   *39*
I did not know them, but it happened,
  as it often turns out by coincidence,
    that one of them had cause to name another,   *42*
Saying, "Where in Hell can Cianfa be?"
  When I heard this, I alerted my leader
    by placing a finger over my lips.   *45*

If, Reader, you are slow to believe
  what I'm about to say, it will be no surprise,
    for I, who saw it, hardly believe it myself.   *48*

While I kept my wide open eyes on them
  a six-legged serpent suddenly shot up
    onto one's chest and clamped on tight.   *51*
It clasped his belly with its middle feet
  and with its forefeet took hold of his arms,
    then stuck its fangs into both of his cheeks;   *54*

li diretani a le cosce distese,
  e miseli la coda tra 'mbedue
57   e dietro per le ren sú la ritese.
Ellera abbarbicata mai non fue
  ad alber sí, come l'orribil fiera
60   per l'altrui membra avviticchiò le sue.
Poi s'appiccar, come di calda cera
  fossero stati, e mischiar lor colore,
63   né l'un né l'altro già parea quel ch'era:
come procede innanzi da l'ardore,
  per lo papiro suso, un color bruno
66   che non è nero ancora e 'l bianco more.
Li altri due 'l riguardavano, e ciascuno
  gridava:"Omè, Agnel, come ti muti!
69   Vedi che già non se' né due né uno."
Già eran li due capi un divenuti,
  quando n'apparver due figure miste
72   in una faccia, ov' eran due perduti.
Fersi le braccia due di quattro liste;
  le cosce con le gambe e 'l ventre e 'l casso
75   divenner membra che non fuor mai viste.
Ogne primaio aspetto ivi era casso:
  due e nessun l'imagine perversa
78   parea; e tal sen gio con lento passo.

Come 'l ramarro sotto la gran fersa
  dei dí canicular, cangiando sepe,
81   folgore par se la via attraversa,
sí pareva, venendo verso l'epe
  de li altri due, un serpentello acceso,
84   livido e nero come gran di pepe;
e quella parte onde prima è preso
  nostro alimento, a l'un di lor trafisse;
87   poi cadde giuso innanzi lui disteso.
Lo trafitto 'l mirò, ma nulla disse;
  anzi, co' piè fermati, sbadigliava
90   pur come sonno o febbre l'assalisse.

It spread its hind feet onto his thighs
  and inserted its tail right in between them
    bending it upward to touch the small of his back.   *57*
Ivy has never clung to a tree
  the way this horrible beast entwined
    its own limbs around the other's body.   *60*
And then, as if they were made of hot wax,
  they stuck together, and as their colors mixed
    neither one seemed what it had been at first.   *63*
It was just the way a dark color moves
  before a flame across a sheet of paper
    not yet charred black, though the white dies away.   *66*
The other two spirits were looking on,
  and each cried, "Look at you change, Agnello!
    Already you are neither two nor one!"   *69*
But the two heads had by now become one,
  and then we saw the two profiles merging
    into one face, where both were lost.   *72*
Two arms were fashioned out of four limbs;
  the thighs, the legs, the belly, the chest
    became body parts never seen before.   *75*
Each former feature was blotted out;
  the perverse figure was double and none,
    and such as it was, it moved on at a crawl.   *78*

As a lizard darts like quicksilver through hedges
  under the Dog Star's terrible scourge,
    and flashes like lightning if it crosses the road,   *81*
So too a small fiery serpent appeared,
  purple and black like crushed peppercorns,
    and made for the bellies of the other two.   *84*
It transfixed one of them in that part
  through which we receive our first nourishment,
    then fell down before him, stretched on the ground.   *87*
The soul it had pierced gazed down on it
  but said nothing, just stood there and yawned
    as if drowsy with sleep or weak with fever.   *90*

Elli 'l serpente e quei lui riguardava;
   l'un per la piaga e l'altro per la bocca
93   fummavan forte, e 'l fummo si scontrava.

Taccia Lucano omai là dov' e' tocca
   del misero Sabello e di Nasidio,
96   e attenda a udir quel ch'or si scocca.
Taccia di Cadmo e d'Aretusa Ovidio,
   ché se quello in serpente e quella in fonte
99   converte poetando, io non lo 'nvidio;
ché due nature mai a fronte a fronte
   non trasmutò sí ch'amendue le forme
102   a cambiar lor matera fosser pronte.

Insieme si rispuosero a tai norme,
   che 'l serpente la coda in forca fesse,
105   e 'l feruto ristrinse insieme l'orme.
Le gambe con le cosce seco stesse
   s'appiccar sí, che 'n poco la giuntura
108   non facea segno alcun che si paresse.
Togliea la coda fessa la figura
   che si perdeva là, e la sua pelle
111   si facea molle, e quella di là dura.
Io vidi intrar le braccia per l'ascelle,
   e i due piè de la fiera, ch'eran corti,
114   tanto allungar quanto accorciavan quelle.
Poscia li piè di rietro, insieme attorti,
   diventaron lo membro che l'uom cela,
117   e 'l misero del suo n'avea due porti.
Mentre che 'l fummo l'uno e l'altro vela
   di color novo, e genera 'l pel suso
120   per l'una parte e da l'altra il dipela,
l'un si levò e l'altro cadde giuso,
   non torcendo però le lucerne empie,
123   sotto le quai ciascun cambiava muso.
Quel ch'era dritto, il trasse ver' le tempie,
   e di troppa matera ch'in là venne
126   uscir li orecchi de le gote scempie;

He eyed the serpent; the serpent eyed him.
  Smoke poured out from his wound and from
    the reptile's mouth, and the two smokes met.   *93*

Let Lucan fall silent, where his poem tells
  of putrefied Sabellus and swollen Nasidius,
    and let him wait for what my poem will let fly.   *96*
Let Ovid fall silent, for if in his verse
  he transforms Cadmus into a snake
    and Arethusa into a babbling fountain,   *99*
I am not envious, for he never transmuted
  two different natures face to face, so that their forms
    readily interchanged their substances.   *102*

Their transformation had a strange symmetry:
  a fork developed in the tail of the reptile
    while the wounded man's feet were welded together.   *105*
His calves and thighs were stuck fast to each other,
  adhering so firmly it became impossible
    to see any sign of a seam or juncture,   *108*
While the snake's cloven tail took on the shape
  that the other had lost, and its skin grew soft
    as the skin of the other grew scaly and tough.   *111*
I saw the man's arms shrink into his armpits,
  and the reptile's forefeet, which had been short,
    grow longer in proportion to the other's loss.   *114*
Its two hind feet then twisted together
  and became the member that men conceal,
    while the wretch's own manhood grew feet and claws.   *117*
The smoke enveloped both of the figures
  with a new color, propagating hair
    on one part while stripping hair from another.   *120*
One rose up and the other fell down,
  but neither turned aside those baleful eyes
    even as their muzzles underneath were changing.   *123*
The one standing erect contracted his face
  up toward the temples, and from the leftover skin
    ears were extruded from the smooth, flat cheeks.   *126*

ciò che non corse in dietro e si ritenne
di quel soverchio, fé naso a la faccia
129   e le labbra ingrossò quanto convenne.
Quel che giacëa, il muso innanzi caccia,
e li orecchi ritira per la testa
132   come face le corna la lumaccia;
e la lingua, ch'avëa unita e presta
prima a parlar, si fende, e la forcuta
135   ne l'altro si richiude; e 'l fummo resta.
L'anima ch'era fiera divenuta,
suffolando si fugge per la valle,
138   e l'altro dietro a lui parlando sputa.
Poscia li volse le novelle spalle,
e disse a l'altro: "I' vo' che Buoso corra,
141   com' ho fatt' io, carpon per questo calle."

Cosí vid' io la settima zavorra
mutare e trasmutare; e qui mi scusi
144   la novità se fior la penna abborra.
E avvegna che li occhi miei confusi
fossero alquanto e l'animo smagato,
147   non poter quei fuggirsi tanto chiusi,
ch'i' non scorgessi ben Puccio Sciancato;
ed era quel che sol, di tre compagni
150   che venner prima, non era mutato;
l'altr' era quel che tu, Gaville, piagni.

The excess mass that did not shift around back
  provided material for a nose on the face
    and to thicken the lips to proportionate size.   *129*
The one that lay prone elongated his snout
  and retracted his ears back into his head,
    the way that snails draw in their horns.   *132*
And just as his tongue, which had been intact
  and capable of speech, now split apart,
    so too the forked tongue fused, and then the smoke cleared.   *135*
The soul that had become a wild animal
  ran off hissing down the valley floor,
    and the other, who could speak now, spat as it ran.   *138*
Then he turned his new shoulders back on it
  and said to the third, "I want Buoso to run
    along this road on all fours, as I have done!"   *141*

So I saw the baggage in the seventh hold
  transform and transmute; the utter strangeness
    explains why my quill could not be controlled.   *144*
And although my vision was in disarray
  and my mind was somewhat bewildered,
    these souls could not so easily sneak away   *147*
That I could not make out among the three
  Puccio Sciancato. It was this one alone
    who remained unchanged. The other was he   *150*
For whom you, village of Gaville, still groan.

Canto XXVI

AFTER IRONICALLY CONGRATULATING FLORENCE *for the distinction of having so many thieves in Hell, Dante cautiously proceeds with his exploration of the Eighth Bolgia. As he leans precariously from the bridge, the sight he sees below reminds him of a swarm of fireflies on a summer night. Moving over the floor of the bolgia, in fact, he sees countless tongues of flame, which he realizes conceal within them the souls of the sinners. One flame that particularly attracts his attention is split in a forked tongue. Within it, says Virgil, are not one but*

G odi, Fiorenza, poi che se' sí grande
   che per mare e per terra batti l'ali,
3   e per lo 'nferno tuo nome si spande!
Tra li ladron trovai cinque cotali
   tuoi cittadini onde mi ven vergogna,
6   e tu in grande orranza non ne sali.
Ma se presso al mattin del ver si sogna,
   tu sentirai, di qua da picciol tempo,
9   di quel che Prato, non ch'altri, t'agogna.
E se già fosse, non saria per tempo.
   Cosí foss' ei, da che pur esser dee!
12   ché piú mi graverà, com' piú m'attempo.

Noi ci partimmo, e su per le scalee
   che n'avea fatto i borni a scender pria,
15   rimontò 'l duca mio e trasse mee;
e proseguendo la solinga via,
   tra le schegge e tra ' rocchi de lo scoglio
18   lo piè sanza la man non si spedia.
Allor mi dolsi, e ora mi ridoglio
   quando drizzo la mente a ciò ch'io vidi,
21   e piú lo 'ngegno affreno ch'i' non soglio,

two Greek heroes, Ulysses (or Odysseus) and Diomedes, two of the warriors most responsible for the defeat and destruction of Troy. In the Odyssey, a sequel to the Iliad, Ulysses was also, like Aeneas and like Dante, a famous exile and a wanderer and a seeker. No wonder Dante is eager to hear how his journeying ended. At Virgil's request, the overreaching Ulysses describes how he persuaded his comrades to follow him on his final and most ambitious (and fatal) voyage.

Rejoice, O Florence, for so great have you grown
    that your wingspan extends over land and sea,
      and even through Hell your name is known.   3
Among the thieves I found five who were
    your citizens, which fills me with shame
      and hardly lifts you to heights of honor.   6
But if dreams we have near morning are true,
    you will feel, before too much time goes by,
      what Prato, and others, crave for you.   9
Were it done now, it would be none too soon,
    and would that it were, since it must be done
      and will weigh on me more as my life wears on.   12

We left that place, and my leader climbed
    the same stairs that the jutting stones had made
      for our descent. Then he hoisted me up,   15
And we made our solitary way
    through the rocks and along the splintered ridge
      where the foot could not advance without the hand.   18
I grieved then, and I grieve again now
    when I turn my mind to what I saw there,
      and now I rein in my native genius   21

perché non corra che virtù nol guidi;
sí che, se stella bona o miglior cosa
24   m'ha dato 'l ben, ch'io stessi nol m'invidi.

Quante 'l villan ch'al poggio si riposa,
nel tempo che colui che 'l mondo schiara
27   la faccia sua a noi tien meno ascosa,
come la mosca cede a la zanzara,
vede lucciole giú per la vallea,
30   forse colà dov' e' vendemmia e ara:
di tante fiamme tutta risplendea
l'ottava bolgia, sí com' io m'accorsi
33   tosto che fui là 've 'l fondo parea.
E qual colui che si vengiò con li orsi
vide 'l carro d'Elia al dipartire,
36   quando i cavalli al cielo erti levorsi,
che nol potea sí con li occhi seguire,
ch'el vedesse altro che la fiamma sola,
39   sí come nuvoletta, in sú salire:
tal si move ciascuna per la gola
del fosso, ché nessuna mostra 'l furto,
42   e ogne fiamma un peccatore invola.
Io stava sovra 'l ponte a veder surto,
sí che s'io non avessi un ronchion preso,
45   caduto sarei giú sanz' esser urto.
E 'l duca, che mi vide tanto atteso,
disse:"Dentro dai fuochi son li spirti;
48   catun si fascia di quel ch'elli è inceso."
"Maestro mio," rispuos' io, "per udirti
son io piú certo; ma già m'era avviso
51   che cosí fosse, e già voleva dirti:
chi è 'n quel foco che vien sí diviso
di sopra, che par surger de la pira
54   dov' Eteòcle col fratel fu miso?"

Rispuose a me:"Là dentro si martira
Ulisse e Dïomede, e cosí insieme
57   a la vendetta vanno come a l'ira;

To keep it from running where virtue won't lead,
  so that if a kind star or something yet better
    has endowed me with wit, I might not abuse it. *24*

In the season when he who lights the world
  lingers, hiding his face least from us,
    and at twilight the fly yields to the mosquito, *27*
A shepherd resting on a hill will see
  swarms of fireflies twinkling along the valley
    where perhaps he plows, perhaps gathers grapes— *30*
With so many flames was the entire Eighth Trench
  aglow, as I realized when I reached the point
    where I could see all the way to the bottom. *33*
And as the prophet who was avenged by bears
  saw Elijah's chariot when it took flight,
    the horses rising straight up to heaven *36*
Faster than his eyes could ever follow,
  so that all he could see was a little cloud
    of shooting flame ascending the sky, *39*
So too each flame moved along the gullet
  of this trench, for not one betrayed its theft,
    though each stole away a sinner inside. *42*
I was standing on the bridge, leaning out to see,
  and had I not caught hold of a pier of rock
    I would have fallen below without a push. *45*
And my guide, seeing me so intent,
  explained, "The spirits are inside the fires.
    Each robes himself with that which burns him." *48*
"Master," I replied, "hearing you say so
  makes me certain, but I had already thought
    that this was the case and was about to ask: *51*
Who is in that fire so cleft at the top
  that it seems it could have risen from the pyre
    where Eteocles and his brother were laid?" *54*

He answered me: "Ulysses and Diomedes
  are tormented there, eternal comrades
    in punishment as once they were in wrath. *57*

e dentro da la lor fiamma si geme
l'agguato del caval che fé la porta
60   onde uscí de' Romani il gentil seme.
Piangevisi entro l'arte per che, morta,
Deïdamìa ancor si duol d'Achille,
63   e del Palladio pena vi si porta."
"S'ei posson dentro da quelle faville
parlar," diss' io, "maestro, assai ten priego
66   e ripriego, che 'l priego vaglia mille,
che non mi facci de l'attender niego
fin che la fiamma cornuta qua vegna;
69   vedi che del disio ver' lei mi piego!"
Ed elli a me: "La tua preghiera è degna
di molta loda, e io però l'accetto;
72   ma fa che la tua lingua si sostegna.
Lascia parlare a me, ch'i' ho concetto
ciò che tu vuoi; ch'ei sarebbero schivi,
75   perch' e' fuor greci, forse del tuo detto."

Poi che la fiamma fu venuta quivi
dove parve al mio duca tempo e loco,
78   in questa forma lui parlare audivi:
"O voi che siete due dentro ad un foco,
s'io meritai di voi mentre ch'io vissi,
81   s'io meritai di voi assai o poco
quando nel mondo li alti versi scrissi,
non vi movete; ma l'un di voi dica
84   dove, per lui, perduto a morir gissi."

Lo maggior corno de la fiamma antica
cominciò a crollarsi mormorando,
87   pur come quella cui vento affatica;
indi la cima qua e là menando,
come fosse la lingua che parlasse,
90   gittò voce di fuori e disse: "Quando
mi diparti' da Circe, che sottrasse
me piú d'un anno là presso a Gaeta,
93   prima che sí Enëa la nomasse,

Within their flame they lament the Wooden Horse,
   the stratagem that opened the gates of Troy
      through which the noble seed of Rome set forth.   *60*
Trapped within they lament the craft by which
   Deidamia still mourns Achilles in death,
      and for the stolen Palladium they pay the price."   *63*
"If they are able to speak from within
   those burning tongues, I pray you, Master,
      and multiply my prayer a thousand times,   *66*
Do not refuse to let me wait here until
   the horned flame comes near. You see
      how strongly desire inclines me toward it."   *69*
And he said to me: "Your prayer
   is praiseworthy, and so I grant it.
      But see that you restrain your tongue   *72*
And let me do the talking. I understand
   just what you want, but because they were Greeks
      they might be scornful of what you would say."   *75*

When the double flame came close enough
   that it seemed to my guide the right time and place,
      I heard him speak in a manner like this: *78*
"O you who are paired within one fire,
   if I deserved anything of you while I lived,
      deserved anything of you either great or small,   *81*
When in the world I wrote high poetry,
   stop for a moment, and let one of you tell
      where he wandered lost and met his death."   *84*

The greater horn of that ancient flame
   began to quiver and murmur low
      as if it were a candle vexed by the wind;   *87*
And then, wagging its tip back and forth
   as if it were a speaking tongue, the flame
      flung out a voice and said, "When I left   *90*
Circe, who had held me back
   a year or more on her isle near Gaeta,
      before Aeneas gave it that name,   *93*

né dolcezza di figlio, né la pieta
del vecchio padre, né 'l debito amore
96   lo qual dovea Penelopè far lieta,
vincer potero dentro a me l'ardore
ch'i' ebbi a divenir del mondo esperto
99   e de li vizi umani e del valore;
ma misi me per l'alto mare aperto
sol con un legno e con quella compagna
102   picciola da la qual non fui diserto.
L'un lito e l'altro vidi infin la Spagna,
fin nel Morrocco, e l'isola d'i Sardi,
105   e l'altre che quel mare intorno bagna.
Io e' compagni eravam vecchi e tardi
quando venimmo a quella foce stretta
108   dov' Ercule segnò li suoi riguardi
acciò che l'uom piú oltre non si metta;
da la man destra mi lasciai Sibilia,
111   da l'altra già m'avea lasciata Setta.
'O frati,' dissi, 'che per cento milia
perigli siete giunti a l'occidente,
114   a questa tanto picciola vigilia
d'i nostri sensi ch'è del rimanente
non vogliate negar l'esperïenza,
117   di retro al sol, del mondo sanza gente.
Considerate la vostra semenza:
fatti non foste a viver come bruti,
120   ma per seguir virtute e canoscenza.'
Li miei compagni fec' io sí aguti,
con questa orazion picciola, al cammino,
123   che a pena poscia li avrei ritenuti;
e volta nostra poppa nel mattino,
de' remi facemmo ali al folle volo,
126   sempre acquistando dal lato mancino.
Tutte le stelle già de l'altro polo
vedea la notte, e 'l nostro tanto basso,
129   che non surgëa fuor del marin suolo.

Neither the sweet thought of my son, nor reverence
  for my old father, nor the love I owed
    Penelope and that would have made her glad   *96*
Could overcome my burning desire
  for experience of the wide world above
    and of men's vices and their valor.   *99*
I put forth on the deep, open sea
  with one ship only, and a skeleton crew
    of companions who had not deserted me.   *102*
I saw one coast, then another, as far as Spain,
  as far as Morocco; I saw Sardinia
    and the other islands lapped by the waves.   *105*
My crew and I were old and slow
  when we pulled into the narrow straits
    where Hercules had set up his pillars   *108*
To mark where men should not pass beyond.
  I had left Seville on the starboard side
    and off the port left Ceuta behind.   *111*
'Brothers,' I said, 'who through a hundred
  thousand perils have reached the West,
    do not deny to the last glimmering hour   *114*
Of consciousness that remains to us
  experience of the unpeopled world
    that lies beyond the setting sun.   *117*
Consider the seed from which you were born!
  You were not made to live like brute animals
    but to live in pursuit of virtue and knowledge!'   *120*
This little speech steeled my crew's hearts
  and made them so eager for the voyage ahead
    I could hardly have restrained them afterward.   *123*
We swung the stern toward the morning light
  and made our oars wings for our last, mad run,
    the ship's left side always gaining on the right.   *126*
All of the stars around the opposite pole
  now shone in the night, while our own was so low
    it did not rise above the ocean's roll.   *129*

Cinque volte racceso e tante casso
     lo lume era di sotto da la luna,
132   poi che 'ntrati eravam ne l'alto passo,
quando n'apparve una montagna, bruna
     per la distanza, e parvemi alta tanto
135   quanto veduta non avëa alcuna.
Noi ci allegrammo, e tosto tornò in pianto;
     ché de la nova terra un turbo nacque
138   e percosse del legno il primo canto.
Tre volte il fé girar con tutte l'acque;
     a la quarta levar la poppa in suso
141   e la prora ire in giú, com' altrui piacque,
infin che 'l mar fu sovra noi richiuso."

Five times had we seen it wax and wane,
  the light on the underside of the moon,
    since we began our journey on the main,   *132*
And then a mountain loomed in the sky,
  still dim and distant, but it seemed to me
    I had never seen any mountain so high.   *135*
We shouted for joy, but our joy now
  turned into grief, for a whirlwind roared
    out of the new land and struck the ship's prow.   *138*
Three times it spun her around in the water,
  and the fourth time around, up the stern rose
    and the prow plunged down, as pleased Another,   *141*
Until above us we felt the waters close."

Canto XXVII

THE FLAME CONTAINING ULYSSES AND DIOMEDES *moves away, and another flame approaches. Moving like a tongue and forming words, it asks the newcomers for news of Romagna. Is the shade's homeland in peace or at war? With Virgil's encouragement, Dante replies that hostilities in the region are temporarily suspended in a kind of armed truce. Asked who he is, the spirit in the flame—whom the early commentators identify as the mercenary captain Guido da Montefeltro—agrees to tell his story, so confident is he that his interlocutor can never go back on earth to reveal what he is about to learn. Guido made a career*

Già era dritta in sú la fiamma e queta
per non dir piú, e già da noi sen gia
3   con la licenza del dolce poeta,
quand' un'altra, che dietro a lei venía,
ne fece volger li occhi a la sua cima
6   per un confuso suon che fuor n'uscia.
Come 'l bue cicilian che mugghiò prima
col pianto di colui, e ciò fu dritto,
9   che l'avea temperato con sua lima,
mugghiava con la voce de l'afflitto,
sí che, con tutto che fosse di rame,
12   pur el pareva dal dolor trafitto;
cosí, per non aver via né forame
dal principio nel foco, in suo linguaggio
15   si convertïan le parole grame.
Ma poscia ch'ebber colto lor vïaggio
su per la punta, dandole quel guizzo
18   che dato avea la lingua in lor passaggio,
udimmo dire: "O tu a cu' io drizzo
la voce e che parlavi mo lombardo,
21   dicendo 'Istra ten va, piú non t'adizzo,'

as a cunning military strategist but decided late in life to save his soul by becoming a Franciscan friar. When the pope found out that he was now an obedient member of the Church, he summoned the friar to him and asked for his military counsel against the rival Colonna family. Guido, at first reluctant, agreed when Pope Boniface VIII offered him preemptive absolution. When Guido died, however, and Saint Francis came to carry his soul into Heaven, a theologically informed demon from Hell claimed it instead, pointing out that the astute Guido had been hoodwinked, since one cannot unwill a sin and then go on to commit it.

The flame, which was no longer speaking now,
   stood erect and quiet, and with the consent
      of the gentle Poet, moved away from us   *3*
When another one that followed behind
   called our attention to its flickering crown
      by the confused sound that issued from it.   *6*
As the Sicilian bull (whose first sound was the cry
   of the artisan—and it served him right—
      who molded and filed the statue's form)   *9*
Used to bellow with the voice of its victim,
   and so seemed itself, though it was hollow bronze,
      to be transfixed with the worst kind of pain—   *12*
So too these wretched and muffled words,
   having no way out of their fiery source,
      were converted into the language of fire.   *15*
But when they found their way to the flame's peak
   they gave to it the same vibration
      they had received from the tongue that spoke them,   *18*
And we heard it say: "You, to whom I direct
   my voice, I heard just now a trace of Lombard
      when you said, 'Be off now, I press you no more.'   *21*

perch' io sia giunto forse alquanto tardo,
non t'incresca restare a parlar meco;
24   vedi che non incresce a me, e ardo!
Se tu pur mo in questo mondo cieco
caduto se' di quella dolce terra
27   latina ond' io mia colpa tutta reco,
dimmi se Romagnuoli han pace o guerra;
ch'io fui d'i monti là intra Orbino
30   e 'l giogo di che Tever si diserra."

Io era in giuso ancora attento e chino,
quando il mio duca mi tentò di costa,
33   dicendo: "Parla tu; questi è latino."
E io, ch'avea già pronta la risposta,
sanza indugio a parlare incominciai:
36   "O anima che se' là giú nascosta,
Romagna tua non è, e non fu mai,
sanza guerra ne' cuor de' suoi tiranni;
39   ma 'n palese nessuna or vi lasciai.
Ravenna sta come stata è molt' anni:
l'aguglia da Polenta la si cova,
42   sí che Cervia ricuopre co' suoi vanni.
La terra che fé già la lunga prova
e di Franceschi sanguinoso mucchio,
45   sotto le branche verdi si ritrova.
E 'l mastin vecchio e 'l nuovo da Verrucchio,
che fecer di Montagna il mal governo,
48   là dove soglion fan d'i denti succhio.
Le città di Lamone e di Santerno
conduce il lïoncel dal nido bianco,
51   che muta parte da la state al verno.
E quella cu' il Savio bagna il fianco,
cosí com' ella sie' tra 'l piano e 'l monte,
54   tra tirannia si vive e stato franco.
Ora chi se', ti priego che ne conte;
non esser duro piú ch'altri sia stato,
57   se 'l nome tuo nel mondo tegna fronte."

Although I may have arrived a little late,
  may it not irk you to stop and speak with me.
    You see that I am not irked, and I am on fire!   24
If it is only recently that you fell
  into this blind world from sweet Italy's land,
    from where I bring with me all my guilt,   27
Tell me if Romagna is at peace or war,
  for I was from the mountains between Urbino
    and the ridge from which the Tiber springs."   30

I was still bent down, intent on the flame,
  when my master gave my ribs a nudge
    and said, "You speak; this one is Italian."   33
My answer to him was already well rehearsed,
  and without further delay I began,
    saying, "O soul, hidden down there,   36
Your Romagna is not, nor ever has been,
  without strife in its tyrannous rulers' hearts,
    but when I left she was not openly at war.   39
Ravenna is now as she has been for years.
  The Eagle of Polenta broods over her
    so as to cover Cervia with its wings.   42
The land that endured the long ordeal
  and reduced the French knights to a bloody heap
    finds itself again beneath the green claws.   45
Verruchio's mastiffs, both the old and the young,
  who dealt so harshly with Montagna,
    bore holes with their teeth as they always have done.   48
The Little Lion of the White Den rules
  the cities on the Lamone and the Santerno
    and changes sides from summer to winter.   51
And the town whose side the Savio bathes—
  just as it straddles mountain and plain,
    so too it lives between tyranny and freedom.   54
And now, I ask you, tell us who you are.
  Do not refuse one who has not refused you,
    so may your name in the world be proud."   57

Poscia che 'l foco alquanto ebbe rugghiato
al modo suo, l'aguta punta mosse
60   di qua, di là, e poi diè cotal fiato:
"S'i' credesse che mia risposta fosse
a persona che mai tornasse al mondo,
63   questa fiamma staria sanza piú scosse;
ma però che già mai di questo fondo
non tornò vivo alcun, s'i' odo il vero,
66   sanza tema d'infamia ti rispondo.
Io fui uom d'arme, e poi fui cordigliero,
credendomi, sí cinto, fare ammenda;
69   e certo il creder mio venía intero,
se non fosse il gran prete, a cui mal prenda!,
che mi rimise ne le prime colpe;
72   e come e *quare,* voglio che m'intenda.
Mentre ch'io forma fui d'ossa e di polpe
che la madre mi diè, l'opere mie
75   non furon leonine, ma di volpe.
Li accorgimenti e le coperte vie
io seppi tutte, e sí menai lor arte,
78   ch'al fine de la terra il suono uscie.
Quando mi vidi giunto in quella parte
di mia etade ove ciascun dovrebbe
81   calar le vele e raccoglier le sarte,
ciò che pria mi piacëa, allor m'increbbe,
e pentuto e confesso mi rendei;
84   ahi miser lasso! e giovato sarebbe.
Lo principe d'i novi Farisei,
avendo guerra presso a Laterano,
87   e non con Saracin né con Giudei,
ché ciascun suo nimico era cristiano,
e nessun era stato a vincer Acri
90   né mercatante in terra di Soldano,
né sommo officio né ordini sacri
guardò in sé, né in me quel capestro
93   che solea fare i suoi cinti piú macri.

After the flame had roared for a while
  in its own way, the sharp point flickered
    to and fro, and then breathed out these words: *60*
"If I believed that my answer were made
  to one who might ever return to the world
    this flame would be still and quiver no more;   *63*
But since, if what I hear is true, no one
  has ever returned alive from this abyss,
    I answer you without fear of disgrace.   *66*
I was a man of arms, but thereafter wore,
  to make amends, the cord of a Franciscan,
    and my trust in this would have been rewarded,   *69*
If not for the Great Priest—and may he suffer!
  He sent me back to my old sinful ways,
    and I want you to hear me tell how and why.   *72*
While I still had the form of flesh and bones
  my mother gave me, my actions were not
    like those of the lion, but of the fox.   *75*
I knew all the tricks, every subterfuge,
  and I practiced the art of deception so well
    that my fame spread to the ends of the Earth.   *78*
But when I saw that I had arrived
  at that stage of life when it befits a man
    to lower his sails and coil up his ropes,   *81*
What had pleased me before began then to grieve.
  I repented, confessed, and turned to God,
    and—oh, wretched me!—it would have worked,   *84*
But the Prince of the Latter-Day Pharisees
  had a war on his hands near the Lateran.
    He was not fighting Saracens or Jews;   *87*
His enemies were Christians, down to a man,
  not one of whom had gone to conquer Acre
    or get rich as a trader in the Sultan's land.   *90*
This Prince who had no regard for his office,
  for his own holy orders or my friar's cord
    (that used to make those who wore it grow lean),   *93*

Ma come Costantin chiese Silvestro
d'entro Siratti a guerir de la lebbre,
96 cosí mi chiese questi per maestro
a guerir de la sua superba febbre;
domandommi consiglio, e io tacetti
99 perché le sue parole parver ebbre.
E' poi ridisse: 'Tuo cuor non sospetti;
finor t'assolvo, e tu m'insegna fare
102 sí come Penestrino in terra getti.
Lo ciel poss' io serrare e diserrare,
come tu sai; però son due le chiavi
105 che 'l mio antecessor non ebbe care.'
Allor mi pinser li argomenti gravi
là 've 'l tacer mi fu avviso 'l peggio,
108 e dissi: 'Padre, da che tu mi lavi
di quel peccato ov' io mo cader deggio,
lunga promessa con l'attender corto
111 ti farà trïunfar ne l'alto seggio.'
Francesco venne poi, com' io fu' morto,
per me; ma un d'i neri cherubini
114 li disse: 'Non portar; non mi far torto.
Venir se ne dee giú tra ' miei meschini
perché diede 'l consiglio frodolente,
117 dal quale in qua stato li sono a' crini;
ch'assolver non si può chi non si pente,
né pentere e volere insieme puossi
120 per la contradizion che nol consente.'
Oh me dolente! come mi riscossi
quando mi prese dicendomi: 'Forse
123 tu non pensavi ch'io löico fossi!'
A Minòs mi portò; e quelli attorse
otto volte la coda al dosso duro;
126 e poi che per gran rabbia la si morse,
disse: 'Questi è d'i rei del foco furo';
per ch'io là dove vedi son perduto,
129 e sí vestito, andando, mi rancuro."

This Prince sought me out. As Constantine
    sent for Sylvester from up on Soracte
        to cure his leprosy, this Prince sent for me   96
To doctor the fever of his pride.
    He asked my counsel, and I stayed quiet,
        for he sounded as if he were crazy or drunk.   99
Then he spoke again: 'Do not mistrust me.
    I absolve you in advance, so now you teach me
        how to throw Penestrino to the ground.   102
I can lock and unlock Heaven, as you know.
    There are two keys, a pair whose value
        my predecessor did not seem to understand.'   105
The arguments became so weighty
    that silence seemed the worse of two paths,
        and I said, 'Father, since you absolve me   108
Of the sin into which I now must fall—
    long on promise but short on delivery—
        that's how to triumph upon your High Seat.'   111
When I died, Francis came for my soul,
    but one of the black angels said to him,
        'Hands off this one, don't do me wrong!   114
Down he goes to the ranks of my slaves,
    for he gave a liar's counsel, and since that time
        I have been waiting to clutch him by the hair.   117
He who does not repent cannot be absolved,
    nor can one repent a thing while he wills it,
        for that is a contradiction in terms.'   120
Ah me, in my sorrow! What a shock it was
    when he seized me and said, 'It may surprise you
        to learn that the devil is a logician!'   123
He took me to Minos, and Minos coiled his tail
    eight times around his hard, scaly back,
        and then bit it in his rage and pronounced,   126
'This sinner gets the fire befitting a thief.'
    And so I am lost where you see me here,
        and robed like this I go in bitter grief."   129

Quand' elli ebbe 'l suo dir cosí compiuto,
la fiamma dolorando si partio,
132   torcendo e dibattendo 'l corno aguto.
Noi passamm' oltre, e io e 'l duca mio,
su per lo scoglio infino in su l'altr' arco
135   che cuopre 'l fosso in che si paga il fio
a quei che scommettendo acquistan carco.

It spoke no more, and when it fell silent
  the sorrowful flame took its leave of us,
    Tossing its flickering horn as it went.   *132*
We moved on then, my guide and I, along
  the rocky cliff and to the arch that soared
    over the next ditch, where all those belong   *135*
Who pay for the sin of sowing discord.

Canto XXVIII

THE POET WONDERS HOW *anyone could describe what he now saw, even in prose, unhampered by rhyme or meter. If all the wounded victims of the countless terrible battles fought in Italy's south were to be brought together in one place, the sight would not equal that of the mutilations of the Ninth Bolgia, where the Sowers of Discord are punished with retaliation. The pilgrim sees a shade whose torso is split from chin to anus. Exhibiting his entrails, he reveals that he is Mohamed, condemned as a renegade Christian. Ahead of him is Ali, his son-in-law, cleft from the chin up. Dividers in life, their bodies are divided in death. When Mohamed learns that Dante is still alive, he asks him to warn*

> Chi poria mai pur con parole sciolte
> dicer del sangue e de le piaghe a pieno
> ch'i' ora vidi, per narrar piú volte?

3

> Ogne lingua per certo verria meno
> per lo nostro sermone e per la mente
> c'hanno a tanto comprender poco seno.

6

> S'el s'aunasse ancor tutta la gente
> che già, in su la fortunata terra
> di Puglia, fu del suo sangue dolente

9

> per li Troiani e per la lunga guerra
> che de l'anella fé sí alte spoglie,
> come Livïo scrive, che non erra,

12

> con quella che sentio di colpi doglie
> per contastare a Ruberto Guiscardo;
> e l'altra il cui ossame ancor s'accoglie

15

> a Ceperan, là dove fu bugiardo
> ciascun Pugliese, e là da Tagliacozzo,
> dove sanz' arme vinse il vecchio Alardo;

18

> e qual forato suo membro e qual mozzo
> mostrasse, d'aequar sarebbe nulla
> il modo de la nona bolgia sozzo.

21

heretic Fra Dolcino of his impending capture and execution. Pier da Medicina,
another sufferer, would have him warn the two foremost citizens of Fano that
they will soon be betrayed and drowned by one-eyed Malatesta of Rimini. He
also identifies Curio, who urged Caesar to cross the Rubicon, thereby sowing
discord within the Roman Republic, and Mosca dei Lamberti, who counseled
the death of Buondelmonte, introducing bloody factionalism into Florence. Fi-
nally Dante sees a headless trunk approaching, holding up his severed head like
a lantern before him. He is the Provençal poet Bertran de Born who set enmity
between Henry II of England and his son, the future Henry III.

Who could ever tell, even in unfettered prose,
   and even if he told the tale many times,
      the blood and the wounds that I saw now?   *3*
Surely no tongue would be up to the task,
   for neither our speech nor our memory
      has the capacity to embrace so much.   *6*
If all the people could be assembled again
   who in Italy's ill-destined south
      bewailed the blood that the Trojans shed,   *9*
And those from the long campaign that ended
   with bushels of rings from Roman corpses,
      as Livy, who does not err, records,   *12*
Along with all those crippled by wounds
   in the many battles against Robert Guiscard,
      and those whose bones are still collected   *15*
At Ceperano, where the Apulians
   deserted their posts, and at Tagliacozzo,
      where old Alardo won more by tactics than arms,   *18*
And if some would display their mangled limbs
   and others their stumps—it would not begin
      to equal the horror of Malebolge's Ninth Trench.   *21*

Già veggia, per mezzul perdere o lulla,
   com'io vidi un, cosí non si pertugia,
24   rotto dal mento infin dove si trulla.
Tra le gambe pendevan le minugia;
   la corata pareva e 'l tristo sacco
27   che merda fa di quel che si trangugia.
Mentre che tutto in lui veder m'attacco,
   guardommi e con le man s'aperse il petto,
30   dicendo: "Or vedi com' io mi dilacco!
vedi come storpiato è Mäometto!
   Dinanzi a me sen va piangendo Alí,
33   fesso nel volto dal mento al ciuffetto.
E tutti li altri che tu vedi qui,
   seminator di scandalo e di scisma
36   fuor vivi, e però son fessi cosí.
Un diavolo è qua dietro che n'accisma
   sí crudelmente, al taglio de la spada
39   rimettendo ciascun di questa risma,
quand' avem volta la dolente strada;
   però che le ferite son richiuse
42   prima ch'altri dinanzi li rivada.
Ma tu chi se' che 'n su lo scoglio muse,
   forse per indugiar d'ire a la pena
45   ch'è giudicata in su le tue accuse?"
"Né morte 'l giunse ancor, né colpa 'l mena,"
   rispuose 'l mio maestro, "a tormentarlo;
48   ma per dar lui esperïenza piena,
a me, che morto son, convien menarlo
   per lo 'nferno qua giú di giro in giro;
51   e quest' è ver cosí com' io ti parlo."

Piú fuor di cento che, quando l'udiro,
   s'arrestaron nel fosso a riguardarmi
54   per maraviglia, oblïando il martiro.
"Or dí a fra Dolcin dunque che s'armi,
   tu che forse vedra' il sole in breve,
57   s'ello non vuol qui tosto seguitarmi,

If a cask were missing one of its staves
  it would not gape so wide as one I saw there,
    cleft from his chin down to where he farts.   *24*
His entrails were hanging between his legs,
  and the vital organs could be seen, along with
    the foul sack that turns our food into shit.   *27*
While I gazed at him, completely entranced,
  he looked up at me, and with his hands
    pulled his chest open, saying, "Now see how   *30*
I tear myself, see Mohamed mangled!
  In front of me goes Ali, shedding tears,
    his face split from forelock to chin.   *33*
And all the others you see here cultivated
  discord and schism when they were alive,
    and that is the reason they all are gashed.   *36*
Behind us back there is posted a devil
  who adorns us so cruelly, subjecting
    each of this lot to the edge of his sword   *39*
Every time we circle this sorrowful road,
  for all of our wounds have closed up before
    we come face to face with the demon again.   *42*
But who are you, musing up there on the ridge,
  buying time, perhaps, before the punishment
    your self-accusations have pronounced on you?"   *45*
"Death has not yet touched him," my master said,
  "nor does guilt lead him to be tormented.
    It is so he may have experience of all   *48*
That I, who myself am dead, have the duty
  of leading him down through the circles of Hell;
    and this is as true as I am talking to you."   *51*

More than a hundred, when they heard him,
  stood still in the ditch to look at me,
    forgetting their torment in their wonder.   *54*
"Then you, who perhaps will see the sun soon,
  should tell Fra Dolcino, if he would rather not
    follow me down here before his time is up,   *57*

sí di vivanda, che stretta di neve
non rechi la vittoria al Noarese,
60 　　　ch'altrimenti acquistar non saria leve."
Poi che l'un piè per girsene sospese,
Mäometto mi disse esta parola;
63 　　　indi a partirsi in terra lo distese.

Un altro, che forata avea la gola
e tronco 'l naso infin sotto le ciglia,
66 　　　e non avea mai ch'una orecchia sola,
ristato a riguardar per maraviglia
con li altri, innanzi a li altri aprí la canna,
69 　　　ch'era di fuor d'ogne parte vermiglia,
e disse: "O tu cui colpa non condanna
e cu' io vidi in su terra latina,
72 　　　se troppa simiglianza non m'inganna,
rimembriti di Pier da Medicina,
se mai torni a veder lo dolce piano
75 　　　che da Vercelli a Marcabò dichina.
E fa sapere a' due miglior da Fano,
a messer Guido e anco ad Angiolello,
78 　　　che, se l'antiveder qui non è vano,
gittati saran fuor di lor vasello
e mazzerati presso a la Cattolica
81 　　　per tradimento d'un tiranno fello.
Tra l'isola di Cipri e di Maiolica
non vide mai sí gran fallo Nettuno,
84 　　　non da pirate, non da gente argolica.
Quel traditor che vede pur con l'uno,
e tien la terra che tale qui meco
87 　　　vorrebbe di vedere esser digiuno,
farà venirli a parlamento seco;
poi farà sí, ch'al vento di Focara
90 　　　non sarà lor mestier voto né preco."
E io a lui: "Dimostrami e dichiara,
se vuo' ch'i' porti sú di te novella,
93 　　　chi è colui da la veduta amara."

To stock up his mountain retreat with provisions,
    or the snow will present to the Novarese
        a victory not otherwise easily won."   60
Mohamed had already begun to move on
    when he paused in mid-step to tell me this,
        then he planted his foot on the ground and left.   63

Another, who had his throat pierced through
    and a slash in his nose up to his eyebrows,
        and just one ear left on the side of his head,   66
Stopped with the rest to gaze in wonder,
    and in front of them all pulled open his windpipe,
        where his neck was stained with blood, and said,   69
"You, who are not condemned by guilt
    and whom I saw above in Italy,
        unless a close resemblance has fooled me,   72
Remember Pier da Medicina
    if you ever return to see the sweet plain
        that slopes from Vercelli to Marcabò.   75
And tell this to the two best men of Fano,
    Messer Guido and Angiolello,
        that unless our foresight here is useless,   78
They will be thrown off their ship near Cattolica,
    weighted with stones like a fishing net,
        through the treachery of an evil tyrant.   81
Between the islands of Cyprus and Majorca
    Neptune never witnessed a crime so great
        committed by pirates or crews of Greeks.   84
That traitor who sees with only one eye
    and rules that city, which a soul here with me
        wishes he had abstained from seeing,   87
Will make them come to hold talks, and then
    deal with them so that they will never need
        to pray or make vows to the wind off Focara."   90
And I said to him, "If you would like me to take
    news of you above, show me the man
        who found the sight of that city bitter."   93

Allor puose la mano a la mascella
d'un suo compagno e la bocca li aperse,
96   gridando: "Questi è desso, e non favella.
Questi, scacciato, il dubitar sommerse
in Cesare, affermando che 'l fornito
99   sempre con danno l'attender sofferse."
Oh quanto mi pareva sbigottito
con la lingua tagliata ne la strozza
102   Curïo, ch'a dir fu cosí ardito!

E un ch'avea l'una e l'altra man mozza,
levando i moncherin per l'aura fosca,
105   sí che 'l sangue facea la faccia sozza,
gridò: "Ricordera'ti anche del Mosca,
che disse, lasso! 'Capo ha cosa fatta,'
108   che fu mal seme per la gente tosca."
E io li aggiunsi: "E morte di tua schiatta";
per ch'elli, accumulando duol con duolo,
111   sen gio come persona trista e matta.

Ma io rimasi a riguardar lo stuolo,
e vidi cosa ch'io avrei paura,
114   sanza piú prova, di contarla solo;
se non che coscïenza m'assicura,
la buona compagnia che l'uom francheggia
117   sotto l'asbergo del sentirsi pura.
Io vidi certo, e ancor par ch'io 'l veggia,
un busto sanza capo andar sí come
120   andavan li altri de la trista greggia;
e 'l capo tronco tenea per le chiome,
pesol con mano a guisa di lanterna:
123   e quel mirava noi e dicea: "Oh me!"
Di sé facea a sé stesso lucerna,
ed eran due in uno e uno in due;
126   com' esser può, quei sa che sí governa.
Quando diritto al piè del ponte fue,
levò 'l braccio alto con tutta la testa
129   per appressarne le parole sue,

He took hold of one of his companions
  by the jaw and pried open his mouth, crying,
    "This is the one, and he does not speak!   *96*
In exile, he banished the doubts of Caesar,
  avowing that if a man is prepared
    he can only suffer injury by delay."   *99*
Ah, how horror-stricken he seemed to me,
  with his tongue cut off in his throat, Curio,
    once such a courageous orator.   *102*

Now one who had both his hands lopped off
  raised his stumps up through the dull air
    so their oozing blood defiled his whole face,   *105*
And cried, "You will remember Mosca, too,
  the wretch who said, 'What's done is done,'
    which was the seed of woe for the Tuscans."   *108*
To this I added, "And death to your sons."
  He went off then, heaping sorrow on sorrow,
    like someone out of his mind with grief.   *111*

I stayed to view the hordes. And I saw there
  something that without further proof
    I would hesitate even to mention;   *114*
But conscience—that noble companion
  that emboldens a man under the armor
    of feeling himself pure—conscience reassures me.   *117*
The truth is I saw, and seem to see still,
  a trunk without a head moving along
    just like the others in that sorry herd.   *120*
It was holding its severed head by the hair,
  swinging it back and forth like a lantern,
    and the head was looking at us, saying, "Ah me."   *123*
It was making of itself a lamp for itself,
  and they were two in one and one in two.
    How this can be, only He who ordains it knows.   *126*
When he had arrived at the foot of the bridge
  he lifted high the hand holding his head
    to bring his words up close to our ears,   *129*

che fuoro: "Or vedi la pena molesta,
tu che, spirando, vai veggendo i morti:
132   vedi s'alcuna è grande come questa.
E perché tu di me novella porti,
sappi ch'i' son Bertram dal Bornio, quelli
135   che diedi al re giovane i ma' conforti.
Io feci il padre e 'l figlio in sé ribelli;
Achitofèl non fé piú d'Absalone
138   e di Davíd coi malvagi punzelli.
Perch' io parti' cosí giunte persone,
partito porto il mio cerebro, lasso!,
141   dal suo principio ch'è in questo troncone.
Cosí s'osserva in me lo contrapasso."

And those words were, "Look now at my pain,
  you there, breathing, as you go to view the dead,
    and see if any other is as great as mine.   *132*
And so that you may carry news of me,
  know that I am Bertran de Born,
    who gave evil counsel to young king Henry.   *135*
I made the father and the son rebel
  against each other. Absalom and David
    were not prodded more wickedly by Ahitophel.   *138*
Since I parted persons so closely united
  I carry my brain parted, so piteously,
    from this trunk on which it once resided.   *141*
This is how retribution is observed in me."

CANTO XXIX

DANTE LINGERS, AS IF PARALYZED *by the mayhem he has witnessed, but Virgil urges him on, pointing out how little time they have left. Striding after his guide, Dante admits that what had made him hesitate was the sight of Geri del Bello, one of his own relatives, pointing at him accusingly from the ditch, angry because his violent death had not yet been avenged. On the bridge over the Tenth (and final) Bolgia, they are greeted with agonizing lamentations that make Dante block his ears. In the bolgia below him, it is as if all the sick and crippled from all of Tuscany's and Sardinia's most insalubrious regions had been*

La molta gente e le diverse piaghe
    avean le luci mie sí inebrïate,
3   che de lo stare a piangere eran vaghe.
Ma Virgilio mi disse:"Che pur guate?
    perché la vista tua pur si soffolge
6   là giú tra l'ombre triste smozzicate?
Tu non hai fatto sí a l'altre bolge;
    pensa, se tu annoverar le credi,
9   che miglia ventidue la valle volge.
E già la luna è sotto i nostri piedi;
    lo tempo è poco omai che n'è concesso,
12   e altro è da veder che tu non vedi."
"Se tu avessi," rispuos' io appresso,
    "atteso a la cagion per ch'io guardava,
15   forse m'avresti ancor lo star dimesso."
Parte sen giva, e io retro li andava,
    lo duca, già faccendo la risposta,
18   e soggiugnendo:"Dentro a quella cava
dov' io tenea or li occhi sí a posta,
    credo ch'un spirto del mio sangue pianga
21   la colpa che là giú cotanto costa."

gathered together in one place—in a leper colony without beds. Two scurvy
shades sit propped together like cooking pots in a kitchen, scratching away at
their scabs. When Virgil reveals that Dante is still alive, they topple to the ground
in shock. In response to Dante's question, one of them identifies himself as
Griffolino d'Arezzo, burnt alive by the fatuous Albero of Siena, disappointed
because Griffolino couldn't teach him to fly. The other is Capocchio. Both were
alchemists or Falsifiers of Metals.

The multitude of people with wounds of all kinds
   had now so blurred the lights of my eyes
      that I longed only to linger and weep;   *3*
But Virgil said to me, "What are you still
   looking at? Why is your gaze still down there
      among those miserable, mutilated shades?   *6*
No other trench had this effect on you.
   If you care to count these souls, keep in mind
      that this valley's circumference is twenty-two miles,   *9*
And the moon is already beneath our feet.
   The time allotted us is growing short,
      and there is more to see than what you see here."   *12*
"If you had considered," I responded,
   "the reason I wanted to stand there and gaze,
      you might have allowed me a longer stay."   *15*
He had already left, and I was following
   a little behind when I made my reply,
      and now I added, "Down in that pit   *18*
Into which I was just now staring
   I believe that a spirit of my own blood
      laments the sin that costs so dearly down there."   *21*

277

Allor disse 'l maestro: "Non si franga
lo tuo pensier da qui innanzi sovr' ello.

24   Attendi ad altro, ed ei là si rimanga;
ch'io vidi lui a piè del ponticello
mostrarti e minacciar forte col dito,

27   e udi' 'l nominar Geri del Bello.
Tu eri allor sí del tutto impedito
sovra colui che già tenne Altaforte,

30   che non guardasti in là, sí fu partito."
"O duca mio, la vïolenta morte
che non li è vendicata ancor," diss' io,

33   "per alcun che de l'onta sia consorte,
fece lui disdegnoso; ond' el sen gio
sanza parlarmi, sí com' ïo estimo:

36   e in ciò m'ha el fatto a sé piú pio."

Cosí parlammo infino al loco primo
che de lo scoglio l'altra valle mostra,

39   se piú lume vi fosse, tutto ad imo.
Quando noi fummo sor l'ultima chiostra
di Malebolge, sí che i suoi conversi

42   potean parere a la veduta nostra,
lamenti saettaron me diversi,
che di pietà ferrati avean li strali;

45   ond' io li orecchi con le man copersi.
Qual dolor fora, se de li spedali
di Valdichiana tra 'l luglio e 'l settembre

48   e di Maremma e di Sardigna i mali
fossero in una fossa tutti 'nsembre,
tal era quivi, e tal puzzo n'usciva

51   qual suol venir de le marcite membre.
Noi discendemmo in su l'ultima riva
del lungo scoglio, pur da man sinistra;

54   e allor fu la mia vista piú viva
giú ver' lo fondo, là 've la ministra
de l'alto Sire infallibil giustizia

57   punisce i falsador che qui registra.

Then the master said, "Don't let your thoughts
    break on that shore any more. Put your mind
        on something else, and let him remain below;   24
For I saw him down there under the bridge
    pointing his finger and threatening you,
        and I heard them call him Geri del Bello.   27
You were then so completely absorbed
    with the former master of Altaforte
        that you didn't look there until he was gone."   30
"Sir," I said, "it was his violent death,
    which has not been avenged by any of us,
        who now live on as partners in shame,   33
That made him indignant. This was why, I think,
    he went on his way without speaking to me,
        and this makes me pity him all the more."   36

We spoke in this way until we arrived
    at the first point on the arch that would have shown,
        had there been more light, the next valley's floor.   39
And when we were far enough above
    the final enclosure of Malebolge
        to see the lay brothers in Hell's cloister,   42
Strange lamentations shot through me like arrows
    whose barbed shafts were iron-tipped with pity,
        and at once I covered my ears with my hands.   45
It was as if the sick from all the hospitals
    of Valdichiana and of Maremma
        and of Sardinia, during the sweltering months   48
From July to September, were in one ditch—
    such was the suffering here, and the putrid stench
        of gangrenous limbs rose through the air.   51
We came down onto the last embankment
    of the long ridge, always keeping to the left,
        and then my eyes became more quick to see   54
Down into the depths, where the ministress
    of the Lord on High, infallible Justice,
        punishes every falsifier in her registry.   57

Non credo ch'a veder maggior tristizia
 fosse in Egina il popol tutto infermo,
60   quando fu l'aere sí pien di malizia,
che li animali, infino al picciol vermo,
 cascaron tutti, e poi le genti antiche,
63   secondo che i poeti hanno per fermo,
si ristorar di seme di formiche;
 ch'era a veder per quella oscura valle
66   languir li spirti per diverse biche.
Qual sovra 'l ventre e qual sovra le spalle
 l'un de l'altro giacea, e qual carpone
69   si trasmutava per lo tristo calle.
Passo passo andavam sanza sermone,
 guardando e ascoltando li ammalati,
72   che non potean levar le lor persone.

Io vidi due sedere a sé poggiati,
 com' a scaldar si poggia tegghia a tegghia,
75   dal capo al piè di schianze macolati;
e non vidi già mai menare stregghia
 a ragazzo aspettato dal segnorso,
78   né a colui che mal volontier vegghia,
come ciascun menava spesso il morso
 de l'unghie sopra sé per la gran rabbia
81   del pizzicor, che non ha piú soccorso;
e sí traevan giú l'unghie la scabbia,
 come coltel di scardova le scaglie
84   o d'altro pesce che piú larghe l'abbia.
"O tu che con le dita ti dismaglie,"
 cominciò 'l duca mio a l'un di loro,
87   "e che fai d'esse talvolta tanaglie,
dinne s'alcun Latino è tra costoro
 che son quinc' entro, se l'unghia ti basti
90   etternalmente a cotesto lavoro."
"Latin siam noi, che tu vedi sí guasti
 qui ambedue," rispuose l'un piangendo;
93   "ma tu chi se' che di noi dimandasti?"

I do not believe it could have been more grim
  to see all of Aegina in the grip of disease,
    when the air was so full of contamination   *60*
That every living thing, even little worms,
  succumbed, and then the ancient peoples,
    according to what the poets believed,   *63*
Were regenerated from the race of ants—
  than it was to see, through that dark valley,
    the spirits languishing in jumbled heaps.   *66*
One lay on another's belly, one was draped
  over another's shoulders, one crawled on all fours,
    shifting his weight along the sullen path.   *69*
Step by step we went our way in silence,
  watching and listening to the invalids,
    who were unable to lift their bodies up.   *72*

I saw a pair leaning against each other,
  like two pans propped together to dry,
    both spotted with scabs from head to foot.   *75*
A stable-boy who yearns to get back to bed,
  or whose master stands there waiting for him,
    has never worked a currycomb as hard   *78*
As these two scraped themselves with their nails,
  clawing constantly at the raging itch
    that will never give a second's relief.   *81*
Their fingernails would rake over the scabs
  the way a knife cleans scales from a carp
    or trims off the fins from a larger fish.   *84*
"You there," said my master to one of them,
  "rending your chain mail of scabs with your fingers,
    which you sometimes use as pincers too,   *87*
Tell us if there are any Italians here,
  and in return, may your fingernails always
    prove adequate tools for the work you must do."   *90*
"We are both Italians," he replied weeping,
  "both of us that you see ruined like this.
    But who are you to ask about us?"   *93*

E 'l duca disse: "I' son un che discendo
con questo vivo giú di balzo in balzo,
96   e di mostrar lo 'nferno a lui intendo."
Allor si ruppe lo comun rincalzo;
e tremando ciascuno a me si volse
99   con altri che l'udiron di rimbalzo.
Lo buon maestro a me tutto s'accolse,
dicendo: "Dí a lor ciò che tu vuoli";
102   e io incominciai, poscia ch'ei volse:
"Se la vostra memoria non s'imboli
nel primo mondo da l'umane menti,
105   ma s'ella viva sotto molti soli,
ditemi chi voi siete e di che genti;
la vostra sconcia e fastidiosa pena
108   di palesarvi a me non vi spaventi."

"Io fui d'Arezzo, e Albero da Siena,"
rispuose l'un, "mi fé mettere al foco;
111   ma quel per ch'io mori' qui non mi mena.
Vero è ch'i' dissi lui, parlando a gioco:
'I' mi saprei levar per l'aere a volo';
114   e quei, ch'avea vaghezza e senno poco,
volle ch'i' li mostrassi l'arte; e solo
perch' io nol feci Dedalo, mi fece
117   ardere a tal che l'avea per figliuolo.
Ma ne l'ultima bolgia de le diece
me per l'alchímia che nel mondo usai
120   dannò Minòs, a cui fallar non lece."
E io dissi al poeta: "Or fu già mai
gente sí vana come la sanese?
123   Certo non la francesca sí d'assai!"

Onde l'altro lebbroso, che m'intese,
rispuose al detto mio: "Tra'mene Stricca
126   che seppe far le temperate spese,
e Niccolò che la costuma ricca
del garofano prima discoverse
129   ne l'orto dove tal seme s'appicca;

My guide answered, "I am one who descends
  from level to level with this living man,
    and I intend to show him all of Hell."   *96*
At that their mutual support collapsed
  and each of them, trembling, turned toward me,
    along with others who caught what he'd said.   *99*
My good master drew very close to me
  and said, "Say to them whatever you will."
    And just as he wanted, I spoke to them.   *102*
"So that time cannot steal the memory of you
  from the minds of men up in the first world,
    but that it go on living under sun after sun,   *105*
Tell me who you and your people are.
  Do not let your hideous punishment
    make you fear to reveal yourselves to me."   *108*

"I was from Arezzo," one of them answered,
  and Albero of Siena sent me up in flames,
    but what I died for did not bring me here.   *111*
I did say to him, as a kind of joke,
  'I know how to take wing and fly through the air.'
    He had a lot of eagerness but not much sense, *114*
And wanted to be taught the science of flight.
  But when I could not make him a Daedalus,
    I was burned by one who loved him like a son. *117*
But it was for the alchemy I practiced above
  that Minos, whose judgment is infallible,
    condemned me to this last trench of ten."   *120*
And I said to the Poet, "Was there ever
  a people as vain as the Sienese?
    Even the French cannot come close."   *123*

The other leper overheard what I said
  and replied, "Allow me to make an exception
    of Stricca, who was a moderate spendthrift;   *126*
And of Niccolò, too, who invented
  that expensive recipe for cloves
    in the garden where such seeds germinate;   *129*

> e tra'ne la brigata in che disperse
>   Caccia d'Ascian la vigna e la gran fonda,
> 132   e l'Abbagliato suo senno proferse.
> Ma perché sappi chi sí ti seconda
>   contra i Sanesi, aguzza ver' me l'occhio,
> 135   sí che la faccia mia ben ti risponda:
> sí vedrai ch'io son l'ombra di Capocchio,
>   che falsai li metalli con l'alchímia;
> 138   e te dee ricordar, se ben t'adocchio,
> com' io fui di natura buona scimia."

And of Caccia d'Asciano and his companions,
  on whom he squandered vineyards and a vast estate
    and to whom Abbagliato displayed such wit.   *132*
But so that you will know who backs your case
  against the Sienese, take a good look at me
    and see if you can tell who I am by my face.   *135*
I am the shade of Capocchio, who
  falsified metals through alchemy.
    You must recall, if I recognize you,   *138*
How good an ape of nature I could be."

CANTO XXX

INVITING COMPARISON WITH THE PROTAGONISTS *of Ovid's tales of mad grief and violence, two rabid shades rampage through the Tenth Bolgia. One of these Falsifiers of Persons sinks his fangs into Capocchio's neck and drags him across the bolgia's rough floor. Capocchio identifies him as the shade of Gianni Schicchi, who impersonated the dead Buoso Donati and passed off as genuine a spurious will. The other was incestuous Myrrha, who tricked her father into impregnating her. The immobility of Master Adam, who, at the behest of his masters the Conti Guidi, counterfeited of the gold currency of Florence, provides a contrast to their swift and savage depredations. Grotesquely distorted, swollen,*

     Nel tempo che Iunone era crucciata
       per Semelè contra 'l sangue tebano,
3   come mostrò una e altra fïata,
     Atamante divenne tanto insano,
       che veggendo la moglie con due figli
6   andar carcata da ciascuna mano,
     gridò:"Tendiam le reti, sí ch'io pigli
       la leonessa e ' leoncini al varco";
9   e poi distese i dispietati artigli,
     prendendo l'un ch'avea nome Learco,
       e rotollo e percosselo ad un sasso;
12   e quella s'annegò con l'altro carco.
     E quando la fortuna volse in basso
       l'altezza de' Troian che tutto ardiva,
15   sí che 'nsieme col regno il re fu casso,
     Ecuba trista, misera e cattiva,
       poscia che vide Polissena morta,
18   e del suo Polidoro in su la riva
     del mar si fu la dolorosa accorta,
       forsennata latrò sí come cane;
21   tanto il dolor le fé la mente torta.

and parched by hydropsy, he pines for the streams of Romena but is unable to stir an inch to seek revenge on his former employers, who got him into this predicament. Next to him, stinking with fever, lie two Falsifiers of Words, Putiphar's wife and Sinon, the Greek whose lying eloquence deceived the defenders of Troy into opening their gates to the insidious Trojan Horse. With his fist, Sinon strikes the tautly stretched drum of Master Adam's swollen belly, making it resound. Master Adam's response is to elbow Sinon in the face. A vulgar altercation ensues, a plebeian exchange of taunts and insults. Virgil calls a shamefaced Dante away, telling him that listening to such scurrility is reprehensible.

In the season of Juno's furious rage
   against Semele and the race of Thebes—
      a spleen she vented time and again—   *3*
Athamas was so afflicted with madness
   that when he saw his wife cradling their children,
      as she gently walked, one in each arm,   *6*
He cried, "Spread the nets wide so we can catch
   the lioness and her cubs at the pass!"
And then he stretched out his merciless claws,   *9*
Grabbed the one who was called Learchus,
   whirled him around, and smashed his head on a rock;
      his wife leaped into the sea with their other son.   *12*
And when revolving fortune brought to the ground
   the proud heights of Troy and left it in flames,
      breaking the kingdom along with the king,   *15*
Hecuba, wretched, a prisoner of war,
   after she saw her daughter Polyxena die
      and found the corpse of Polydorus, her son,   *18*
As she wandered desolate along the shore,
   was driven to madness and barked like a dog,
      so great was the sorrow that had wrung her soul.   *21*

Ma né di Tebe furie né troiane
  si vider mäi in alcun tanto crude,
24   non punger bestie, nonché membra umane,
quant' io vidi in due ombre smorte e nude,
  che mordendo correvan di quel modo
27   che 'l porco quando del porcil si schiude.
L'una giunse a Capocchio, e in sul nodo
  del collo l'assannò, sí che, tirando,
30   grattar li fece il ventre al fondo sodo.
E l'Aretin che rimase, tremando
  mi disse: "Quel folletto è Gianni Schicchi,
33   e va rabbioso altrui cosí conciando."
"Oh," diss' io lui, "se l'altro non ti ficchi
  li denti a dosso, non ti sia fatica
36   a dir chi è, pria che di qui si spicchi."
Ed elli a me: "Quell' è l'anima antica
  di Mirra scellerata, che divenne
39   al padre, fuor del dritto amore, amica.
Questa a peccar con esso cosí venne,
  falsificando sé in altrui forma,
42   come l'altro che là sen va, sostenne,
per guadagnar la donna de la torma,
  falsificare in sé Buoso Donati,
45   testando e dando al testamento norma."

E poi che i due rabbiosi fuor passati
  sovra cu' io avea l'occhio tenuto,
48   rivolsilo a guardar li altri mal nati.
Io vidi un, fatto a guisa di lëuto,
  pur ch'elli avesse avuta l'anguinaia
51   tronca da l'altro che l'uomo ha forcuto.
La grave idropesí, che sí dispaia
  le membra con l'omor che mal converte,
54   che 'l viso non risponde a la ventraia,
faceva lui tener le labbra aperte
  come l'etico fa, che per la sete
57   l'un verso 'l mento e l'altro in sú rinverte.

But not all of the Furies at Thebes or Troy
  had managed to make anyone so wild
    or so cruel to a beast, much less to a human,   *24*
As two shades I saw, both sallow and naked,
  that bit as they ran, and they ran like pigs
    when the gate of the sty swings open for them.   *27*
One of them went after Capocchio,
  clamped its tusks on his neck, and dragged him along
    so that the hard floor grated his belly.   *30*
And the Aretine, who was left there trembling,
  said, "That savage goblin is Gianni Schicchi;
    he goes rabid and mangles others like this."   *33*
And I responded, "I see—and so may the other
  not sink its teeth into you, kindly tell me
    who that one is before it tears out of here."   *36*
And he told me, "That is the spirit of Myrrha
  ancient and depraved, who exceeded the bounds
    of human passion and made love to her father.   *39*
She entered into sin with her own sire
  by disguising herself as someone else,
    just as that one going off over there,   *42*
In order to win the queen of the herd,
  undertook to impersonate Buoso Donati,
    making a will out in due legal form."   *45*

My eyes were fixed on those two rabid shades,
  until they moved on. Then I turned
    to look at the other ill-born souls,   *48*
And I saw one who was shaped like a lute,
  if only he had been cut off at the groin
    where the legs begin to fork from the trunk.   *51*
Dropsy had so distorted his swollen body
  with a bloated mass of ill-digested humors
    that his face was far too small for his belly,   *54*
And he was forced to keep his lips parted wide
  the way a sick man, feverish with thirst,
    curls one lip down and the other one up.   *57*

"O voi che sanz' alcuna pena siete,
  e non so io perché, nel mondo gramo,"
60   diss' elli a noi, "guardate e attendete
a la miseria del maestro Adamo;
  io ebbi, vivo, assai di quel ch'i' volli,
63   e ora, lasso!, un gocciol d'acqua bramo.
Li ruscelletti che d'i verdi colli
  del Casentin discendon giuso in Arno,
66   faccendo i lor canali freddi e molli,
sempre mi stanno innanzi, e non indarno,
  ché l'imagine lor vie piú m'asciuga
69   che 'l male ond' io nel volto mi discarno.
La rigida giustizia che mi fruga
  tragge cagion del loco ov' io peccai
72   a metter piú li miei sospiri in fuga.
Ivi è Romena, là dov' io falsai
  la lega suggellata del Batista;
75   per ch'io il corpo sú arso lasciai.
Ma s'io vedessi qui l'anima trista
  di Guido o d'Alessandro o di lor frate,
78   per Fonte Branda non darei la vista.
Dentro c'è l'una già, se l'arrabbiate
  ombre che vanno intorno dicon vero;
81   ma che mi val, c'ho le membra legate?
S'io fossi pur di tanto ancor leggero
  ch'i' potessi in cent' anni andare un'oncia,
84   io sarei messo già per lo sentiero,
cercando lui tra questa gente sconcia,
  con tutto ch'ella volge undici miglia,
87   e men d'un mezzo di traverso non ci ha.
Io son per lor tra sí fatta famiglia;
  e' m'indussero a batter li fiorini
90   ch'avevan tre carati di mondiglia."

E io a lui: "Chi son li due tapini
  che fumman come man bagnate 'l verno,
93   giacendo stretti a' tuoi destri confini?"

"You two there, without any punishment
  in this wretched world, and I don't know why,"
    he said to us, "look upon and consider   *60*
The misery of Master Adam.
  When I was alive I had all that I wished,
    and now all I crave is one drop of water!   *63*
The little brooks that run from the green hills
  of Casentino down into the Arno,
    making their waterways cool and lush,   *66*
Are always before me, and to good effect,
  for imagining them parches me far more
    than the disease that wastes the flesh from my face. *69*
The iron justice that devastates me
  draws its logic from the place where I sinned
    and so sends my sighs more quickly in flight.   *72*
Romena is there, where I counterfeited
  the coins that are stamped with John the Baptist,
    for which I left my burned body in the upper world. *75*
But if I could see down here the miserable soul
  of Guido, of Alessandro, or of their brother,
    I wouldn't trade that sight for the springs of Branda. *78*
One of them is down here already,
  if these rabid shades sometimes speak true,
    but what good does it do me if my legs can't move? *81*
If I were only still so free and light
  that I could move an inch in a hundred years
    I would have set out already on the path   *84*
To find him among the disfigured people,
  even though this circle is eleven miles around
    and not less than half a mile across.   *87*
I joined this wretched family on their account:
  they persuaded me to strike those florins
    that each had three carats worth of dross."   *90*

And I asked him then, "Who are those two,
  reeking like a pair of wet hands in winter,
    the ones lying close to your right frontier?"   *93*

"Qui li trovai—e poi volta non dierno—,"
   rispuose, "quando piovvi in questo greppo,
96   e non credo che dieno in sempiterno.
L'una è la falsa ch'accusò Gioseppo;
   l'altr' è 'l falso Sinon greco di Troia:
99   per febbre aguta gittan tanto leppo."
E l'un di lor, che si recò a noia
   forse d'esser nomato sí oscuro,
102   col pugno li percosse l'epa croia.
Quella sonò come fosse un tamburo;
   e mastro Adamo li percosse il volto
105   col braccio suo, che non parve men duro,

dicendo a lui: "Ancor che mi sia tolto
   lo muover per le membra che son gravi,
108   ho io il braccio a tal mestiere sciolto."
Ond' ei rispuose: "Quando tu andavi
   al fuoco, non l'avei tu cosí presto;
111   ma sí e piú l'avei quando coniavi."
E l'idropico: "Tu di' ver di questo:
   ma tu non fosti sí ver testimonio
114   là 've del ver fosti a Troia richesto."
"S'io dissi falso, e tu falsasti il conio,"
   disse Sinon; "e son qui per un fallo,
117   e tu per piú ch'alcun altro demonio!"
"Ricorditi, spergiuro, del cavallo,"
   rispuose quel ch'avëa infiata l'epa;
120   "e sieti reo che tutto il mondo sallo!"
"E te sia rea la sete onde ti crepa,"
   disse 'l Greco, "la lingua, e l'acqua marcia
123   che 'l ventre innanzi a li occhi sí t'assiepa!"
Allora il monetier: "Cosí si squarcia
   la bocca tua per tuo mal come suole;
126   ché, s'i' ho sete e omor mi rinfarcia,
tu hai l'arsura e 'l capo che ti duole,
   e per leccar lo specchio di Narcisso,
129   non vorresti a 'nvitar molte parole."

"When I fell like rain into this trough," he answered,
  "here they were, and since they have never turned,
    I do not think they will for all eternity.   *96*
One is the woman who accused Joseph falsely,
  the other is Sinon, the lying Greek at Troy.
    It's due to their fever they stink as they do."   *99*
One of them, who was perhaps offended
  at being named in so dark a manner,
    hit him with his fist in his rigid belly,   *102*
Which boomed like a drum. Master Adam replied
  by smashing his face with his elbow, which seemed
    no less hard than the other's fist, and said,   *105*

"Though my range of motion is somewhat confined
  by the considerable weight of my body parts,
    I have an arm ready for work of this kind."   *108*
And the other responded, "It wasn't so ready
  on your way to be burned, but it clearly worked
    well enough to counterfeit money."   *111*
And the hydroptic, "True enough, but don't be coy.
  Your testimony was not so reliable
    when they questioned you on the truth at Troy."   *114*
"If I spoke falsely, you falsified florins,"
  Sinon replied. "I am damned for a single offense,
    but your sins outnumber any demon's."   *117*
"Remember, you perjurer, the Wooden Horse,"
  the one with the swollen belly replied,
    "as everyone does. And may that cause you remorse." *120*
"And may the thirst that cracks your tongue plague you,"
  the Greek replied, "like the water, ever so foul,
    that swells your paunch until it blocks your view."   *123*
The counterfeiter rejoined, "Your temperature
  perpetually splits your mouth wide open.
    If I'm parched and bloated with bilious humor,   *126*
Your head pounds and you are burning with fever,
  and it would not take an engraved invitation
    to get you to lick Narcissus' mirror."   *129*

Ad ascoltarli er' io del tutto fisso,
  quando 'l maestro mi disse: "Or pur mira,
132   che per poco che teco non mi risso!"
Quand' io 'l senti' a me parlar con ira,
  volsimi verso lui con tal vergogna,
135   ch'ancor per la memoria mi si gira.
Qual è colui che suo dannaggio sogna,
  che sognando desidera sognare,
138   sí che quel ch'è, come non fosse, agogna,
tal mi fec' io, non possendo parlare,
  che disïava scusarmi, e scusava
141   me tuttavia, e nol mi credea fare.
"Maggior difetto men vergogna lava,"
  disse 'l maestro, "che 'l tuo non è stato;
144   però d'ogne trestizia ti disgrava.
E fa ragion ch'io ti sia sempre allato,
  se piú avvien che fortuna t'accoglia
147   dove sien genti in simigliante piato:
ché voler ciò udire è bassa voglia."

I was standing there intent on listening
  when my master said, "Just keep on looking
    and you will have to answer to me!"   *132*
When I heard him speak to me in anger
  I turned to him with such a sense of shame
    that it spins through my memory even now.   *135*
And like a man who has a bad dream
  and wishes in his dream that he were dreaming,
    longing for what is as if it were not,   *138*
So too I, unable to speak, wished earnestly
  to beg for pardon, and yet all the while
    I was begging for pardon unconsciously.   *141*
"Less shame would wash away a greater crime
  than yours has been," said my gentle guide,
    "so let go of your sadness. But next time   *144*
Imagine that I am still at your side,
  should it happen again that you are in a place
    where people are vying as these have vied,   *147*
For the desire to listen is vulgar and base."

CANTO XXXI

IF VIRGIL'S REPRIMAND WOUNDED DANTE, *his reassurances supply balm for the wound. Leaving behind the last trench of Malebolge, the two pilgrims move silently on. Ahead, through the twilight, they hear a loud horn blast, and Dante sees what looks like a walled city with towers similar to those that surround the town of Monteriggioni. Virgil tells him that what he sees are the*

Una medesma lingua pria mi morse,
sí che mi tinse l'una e l'altra guancia,
3   e poi la medicina mi riporse;
cosí od' io che solea far la lancia
d'Achille e del suo padre esser cagione
6   prima di trista e poi di buona mancia.

Noi demmo il dosso al misero vallone
su per la ripa che 'l cinge dintorno,
9   attraversando sanza alcun sermone.
Quiv' era men che notte e men che giorno,
sí che 'l viso m'andava innanzi poco;
12   ma io senti' sonare un alto corno,
tanto ch'avrebbe ogne tuon fatto fioco,
che, contra sé la sua via seguitando,
15   dirizzò li occhi miei tutti ad un loco.
Dopo la dolorosa rotta, quando
Carlo Magno perdé la santa gesta,
18   non sonò sí terribilmente Orlando.
Poco portäi in là volta la testa,
che me parve veder molte alte torri;
21   ond' io: "Maestro, dí, che terra è questa?"
Ed elli a me: "Però che tu trascorri
per le tenebre troppo da la lungi,
24   avvien che poi nel maginare abborri.

torsos of the fearsome Giants who guard the descent into the Ninth Circle. The
first Giant, the horn blower, is Nimrod, who built the Tower of Babel and who
utters unintelligible words. The next is Ephialtes, who led the assault on Jove.
The third is Antaeus, who was defeated by Hercules in Libya. It is Antaeus who
hands the pilgrims down into the last circle, the frozen lake of Cocytus.

One and the same tongue first wounded me,
   bringing the color to both my cheeks,
      and then supplying the wound's remedy.   3
So, I have heard, the spear of Achilles
   that once was his father's, could bestow
      first a grievous, and then a welcome gift.   6

We turned our backs on the valley of pain,
   going up over the bank that encircles it
      and crossing its width without need for words.   9
It was less than night here and less than day,
   so I could see only a little ahead,
      but I heard a horn blowing so loud   12
It would make any peal of thunder seem faint.
   The sound pulled my eyes along to its source,
      so that all my attention was on that one place.   15
When Charlemagne went down to bitter defeat
   and lost his band of holy knights, not even Roland
      sounded so dread a blast from his horn.   18
I cocked my head in that direction, and soon
   I saw what looked like many high towers
      and asked, "Master, tell me, what city is this?"   21
He answered me, "You are peering through shadows
   from too far away, and so the image you form
      of what you think you see is blurred and false.   24

Tu vedrai ben, se tu là ti congiungi,
quanto 'l senso s'inganna di lontano;
27   però alquanto piú te stesso pungi."
Poi caramente mi prese per mano
e disse: "Pria che noi siam piú avanti,
30   acciò che 'l fatto men ti paia strano,
sappi che non son torri, ma giganti,
e son nel pozzo intorno da la ripa
33   da l'umbilico in giuso tutti quanti."

Come quando la nebbia si dissipa,
lo sguardo a poco a poco raffigura
36   ciò che cela 'l vapor che l'aere stipa,
cosí forando l'aura grossa e scura,
piú e piú appressando ver' la sponda,
39   fuggiemi errore e cresciemi paura;
però che, come su la cerchia tonda
Montereggion di torri si corona,
42   cosí la proda che 'l pozzo circonda
torreggiavan di mezza la persona
li orribili giganti, cui minaccia
45   Giove del cielo ancora quando tuona.
E io scorgeva già d'alcun la faccia,
le spalle e 'l petto e del ventre gran parte,
48   e per le coste giú ambo le braccia.
Natura certo, quando lasciò l'arte
di sí fatti animali, assai fé bene
51   per tòrre tali essecutori a Marte.
E s'ella d'elefanti e di balene
non si pente, chi guarda sottilmente,
54   piú giusta e piú discreta la ne tene;
ché dove l'argomento de la mente
s'aggiugne al mal volere e a la possa,
57   nessun riparo vi può far la gente.
La faccia sua mi parea lunga e grossa
come la pina di San Pietro a Roma,
60   e a sua proporzione eran l'altre ossa;

You will see clearly, when you reach the place,
  how much the sense of sight is deceived
    by distances; just keep pressing ahead."   *27*
Then he took me affectionately by the hand
  and said, "Before we go any farther now,
    so that the reality might seem less uncanny,   *30*
You should know that those are not towers there,
  but Giants, each one lodged in the pit, sunk
    from the navel down in the encircling bank."   *33*

As when a fog melts away, and our sight
  little by little makes out the shapes
    concealed in the haze and dripping mist,   *36*
So too, as I pierced the thick, murky air
  and came closer and closer to the brink,
    my error gave way to a crescendo of fear.   *39*
As above its round wall Monteriggioni
  wears a ring of towers like a granite crown,
    so also here stood the horrible Giants   *42*
Towering above the bank around the pit,
  with half their bodies looming over the rim,
    but still under the threat of the thunder of Jove.   *45*
I could already make out one huge face,
  his shoulders and chest, a great part of his belly,
    and his arms hanging down alongside his ribs.   *48*
Nature most certainly did well to abandon
  the art of making such creatures as these
    and so deprive Mars of such ministers.   *51*
And although she has not repented of whales
  or elephants, a subtle look into this
    shows her to be more just and discreet.   *54*
For if a cunning mind were to be added
  to malevolence and physical strength,
    no place would suffice to harbor mankind.   *57*
His face seemed to me as massive and long
  as the pine cone at Saint Peter's in Rome,
    and the rest of his bones were proportionate,   *60*

sí che la ripa, ch'era perizoma
dal mezzo in giú, ne mostrava ben tanto
63   di sovra, che di giugnere a la chioma
tre Frison s'averien dato mal vanto;
però ch'i' ne vedea trenta gran palmi
66   dal loco in giú dov' omo affibbia 'l manto.
"*Raphèl maí amècche zabí almi,*"
cominciò a gridar la fiera bocca,
69   cui non si convenia piú dolci salmi.
E 'l duca mio ver' lui: "Anima sciocca,
tienti col corno, e con quel ti disfoga
72   quand' ira o altra passïon ti tocca!
Cércati al collo, e troverai la soga
che 'l tien legato, o anima confusa,
75   e vedi lui che 'l gran petto ti doga."
Poi disse a me: "Elli stessi s'accusa;
questi è Nembrotto per lo cui mal coto
78   pur un linguaggio nel mondo non s'usa.
Lasciànlo stare e non parliamo a vòto;
ché cosí è a lui ciascun linguaggio
81   come 'l suo ad altrui, ch'a nullo è noto."

Facemmo adunque piú lungo vïaggio,
vòlti a sinistra; e al trar d'un balestro
84   trovammo l'altro assai piú fero e maggio.
A cigner lui qual che fosse 'l maestro,
non so io dir, ma el tenea soccinto
87   dinanzi l'altro e dietro il braccio destro
d'una catena che 'l tenea avvinto
dal collo in giú, sí che 'n su lo scoperto
90   si ravvolgëa infino al giro quinto.
"Questo superbo volle esser esperto
di sua potenza contra 'l sommo Giove,"
93   disse 'l mio duca, "ond' elli ha cotal merto.
Fïalte ha nome, e fece le gran prove
quando i giganti fer paura a' dèi;
96   le braccia ch'el menò, già mai non move."

So that the bank, which from his waist down
  formed a kind of apron, showed us so much above
    that three Frisians standing on each other's shoulders   *63*
Could not boast that the top one could touch his hair,
  for I counted on him thirty full hand spans
    down to the place where a man buckles his cloak.   *66*
"Raphèl maí amècche zabí almi"
  is what issued from that ferocious mouth,
    which was not fit for sweeter psalms.   *69*
And my guide addressed him: "Stupid soul,
  stick to your horn to vent yourself
    when rage or some other passion strikes.   *72*
Feel around your neck and you will find the cord
  that holds it tied, O confused shade.
    Look how it lies aslant your great chest."   *75*
Then he said to me: "His garbled words
  accuse himself. This is Nimrod, whose fool's plan
    denied the world a single tongue to use.   *78*
Let us leave him alone and not waste our words,
  for every language is to him as his
    to others, and no one understands him."   *81*

We turned to the left and went farther on,
  and at roughly the distance a crossbow shoots
    we found the next one, more savage and huge.   *84*
I do not know, and cannot say, what craftsman
  mastered and bound him so, but his right arm
    was shackled behind him, and his left up in front,   *87*
By a chain that fettered him at the neck
  and spiraled down in five coils around
    the part of his body that was exposed.   *90*
"This one in his pride chose to try his strength
  against Jove on high," my guide explained,
    and this is his reward for that attempt.   *93*
Ephialtes is his name, and he dared great things
  when the Giants put fear into the gods.
    The arms he moved then he cannot move now."   *96*

E io a lui: "S'esser puote, io vorrei
che de lo smisurato Brïareo
99   esperïenza avesser li occhi mei."
Ond' ei rispuose: "Tu vedrai Anteo
presso di qui che parla ed è disciolto,
102   che ne porrà nel fondo d'ogne reo.
Quel che tu vuo' veder, piú là è molto
ed è legato e fatto come questo,
105   salvo che piú feroce par nel volto."
Non fu tremoto già tanto rubesto,
che scotesse una torre cosí forte,
108   come Fïalte a scuotersi fu presto.
Allor temett' io piú che mai la morte,
e non v'era mestier piú che la dotta,
111   s'io non avessi viste le ritorte.

Noi procedemmo piú avante allotta,
e venimmo ad Anteo, che ben cinque alle,
114   sanza la testa, uscia fuor de la grotta.
"O tu che ne la fortunata valle
che fece Scipïon di gloria reda,
117   quand'Anibàl co' suoi diede le spalle,
recasti già mille leon per preda,
e che, se fossi stato a l'alta guerra
120   de' tuoi fratelli, ancor par che si creda
ch'avrebber vinto i figli de la terra:
mettine giú, e non ten vegna schifo,
123   dove Cocito la freddura serra.
Non ci fare ire a Tizio né a Tifo:
questi può dar di quel che qui si brama;
126   però ti china e non torcer lo grifo.
Ancor ti può nel mondo render fama,
ch'el vive, e lunga vita ancor aspetta
129   se 'nnanzi tempo grazia a sé nol chiama."

Cosí disse 'l maestro; e quelli in fretta
le man distese, e prese 'l duca mio,
132   ond' Ercule sentí già grande stretta.

Then I said to him: "If it were possible,
  I would like to be able with my own eyes
  to look upon the mammoth Briareus."   *99*
And he replied: "Close by here you will see
  Antaeus, who speaks and is free from chains,
  and will set us down on the floor of Evil.   *102*
The one you want to see is much farther on,
  and he is bound and built like this one here,
  except that his face looks even more fierce."   *105*
Never has so powerful an earthquake
  made a tower tremble with such violence
  as Ephialtes then made himself shake.   *108*
I have never feared death more than then,
  and the fear itself would have destroyed me
  except that I could see how he was bound.   *111*

We went a little farther on and came
  to Antaeus, who loomed a good five arm spans
  above the pit's bank, not counting his head.   *114*
"You, who once in Zama's fateful valley,
  where Scipio became an heir to glory
  when Hannibal and his hordes turned tail,   *117*
Took a thousand lions as your prey; and who
  (it seems that some believe) had you been
  with your brothers in their war with Heaven   *120*
Would have gained victory for the sons of Earth—
  do not be too proud to set us down below
  where icy Cocytus lies choked with cold.   *123*
Don't make us go to Tityos or Typhon.
  This man can give what is longed for here.
  So bend down, and do not turn up your nose.   *126*
He can make you famous in the world again,
  for he is alive and expects to live long,
  unless grace calls him back before his time."   *129*

So my master spoke, and Antaeus quickly
  stretched out his hands and took my guide
  in the iron palms that once gripped Hercules.   *132*

Virgilio, quando prender si sentio,
   disse a me: "Fatti qua, sí ch'io ti prenda";
135   poi fece sí ch'un fascio era elli e io.
Qual pare a riguardar la Carisenda
   sotto 'l chinato, quando un nuvol vada
138   sovr' essa sí, ched ella incontro penda:
tal parve Antëo a me che stava a bada
   di vederlo chinare, e fu tal ora
141   ch'i' avrei voluto ir per altra strada.
Ma lievemente al fondo che divora
   Lucifero con Giuda, ci sposò;
144   né, sí chinato, lí fece dimora,
e come albero in nave si levò.

As he felt their touch, Virgil said to me,
  "Come here so I can take hold of you,"
    and made a single bundle of himself and me.   *135*
If you stand beneath its leaning wall
  the tower of Garisenda in Bologna seems,
    when a cloud passes behind, about to fall.   *138*
So did Antaeus seem to me when he bowed
  to set us down, and at that moment I wished
    I could have traveled by another road.   *141*
But he set us down gently on the ground below
  that holds Lucifer and Judas in its grip,
    nor did he linger bent over so   *144*
But righted himself like the mast of a ship.

CANTO XXXII

THE POET BALKS *at trying to put into words the horror of the final circle of Hell and invokes the aid of the Muses. The bottom of the pit is a frozen lake of ice in which the final group of sinners, the Traitors—to family, homeland, guests, and benefactors—are immersed up to the neck. Dante is warned to tread carefully lest he step on someone. In the first sector, Caïna, the sinners' heads are bent down, allowing their tears to fall and freeze on their faces. Dante observes two heads jammed close facing one another. He calls out to them, asking who they are, and they look up but do not answer. When they look back down, they butt heads like goats. Another shade, Camiscion dei Pazzi, reveals that*

S'ïo avessi le rime aspre e chiocce,
   come si converrebbe al tristo buco
3   sovra 'l qual pontan tutte l'altre rocce,
io premerei di mio concetto il suco
   piú pienamente; ma perch' io non l'abbo,
6   non sanza tema a dicer mi conduco;
ché non è impresa da pigliare a gabbo
   discriver fondo a tutto l'universo,
9   né da lingua che chiami mamma o babbo.
Ma quelle donne aiutino il mio verso
   ch'aiutaro Anfïone a chiuder Tebe,
12   sí che dal fatto il dir non sia diverso.
Oh sovra tutte mal creata plebe
   che stai nel loco onde parlare è duro,
15   mei foste state qui pecore o zebe!

Come noi fummo giú nel pozzo scuro
   sotto i piè del gigante assai piú bassi,
18   e io mirava ancora a l'alto muro,
dicere udi'mi: "Guarda come passi:
   va sí, che tu non calchi con le piante
21   le teste de' fratei miseri lassi."

they are the fratricidal Alberti brothers from the Bisenzio valley and names several others who betrayed their relatives. The pilgrim and his guide move on to the next sector, Antenora, where Traitors to their homeland are punished. Somehow, Dante kicks one of them in the face. He refuses to tell Dante his name, despite a promise of fame. Bocca degli Abati, whose treachery cost the Guelphs the victory at Montaperti, is betrayed by Buoso da Duera, true to treacherous form; but in reply Bocca outs him too and several other traitors. The canto ends with two more shades eternally—but still more brutally—on top of one another. One of them is gnawing on the other's head. Dante asks why.

If I could write the harsh and grating rhymes
   appropriate to that mouth of sorrow
      upon which rests the bedrock of the world,   3
I would press out more fully all the juice
   of my poem's concept, but since I cannot,
      I begin to speak with some trepidation.   6
This is not something to be treated lightly—
   to describe the bottom of the universe—
      nor for a tongue that cries Mama and Papa.   9
But may those same Ladies aid my verse
   who helped Amphion raise the wall of Thebes,
      so that the telling does not diverge from the fact.   12
And you, O misbegotten souls beyond the rest,
   crowded in this place too hard for words,
      better had you been born as sheep or goats!   15

We were much farther down now, on the floor
   of the dark pit, well below the Giant's feet,
      and I was still staring up at the high wall   18
When I heard a voice say to me, "Watch out
   where you walk so you don't step on the heads
      of the broken, worn out brothers down here!"   21

Per ch'io mi volsi, e vidimi davante
 e sotto i piedi un lago che per gelo
24 avea di vetro e non d'acqua sembiante.
Non fece al corso suo sí grosso velo
 di verno la Danoia in Osterlicchi,
27 né Tanaï là sotto 'l freddo cielo,
com' era quivi; che se Tambernicchi
 vi fosse sú caduto, o Pietrapana,
30 non avria pur da l'orlo fatto cricchi.
E come a gracidar si sta la rana
 col muso fuor de l'acqua, quando sogna
33 di spigolar sovente la villana,
livide, insin là dove appar vergogna
 eran l'ombre dolenti ne la ghiaccia,
36 mettendo i denti in nota di cicogna.
Ognuna in giú tenea volta la faccia;
 da bocca il freddo, e da li occhi il cor tristo
39 tra lor testimonianza si procaccia.
Quand' io m'ebbi dintorno alquanto visto,
 volsimi a' piedi, e vidi due sí stretti,
42 che 'l pel del capo avieno insieme misto.

"Ditemi, voi che sí strignete i petti,"
 diss' io, "chi siete?" E quei piegaro i colli;
45 e poi ch'ebber li visi a me eretti,
li occhi lor, ch'eran pria pur dentro molli,
 gocciar su per le labbra, e 'l gelo strinse
48 le lagrime tra essi e riserrolli.
Con legno legno spranga mai non cinse
 forte cosí; ond' ei come due becchi
51 cozzaro insieme, tanta ira li vinse.
E un ch'avea perduti ambo li orecchi
 per la freddura, pur col viso in giúe,
54 disse: "Perché cotanto in noi ti specchi?
Se vuoi saper chi son cotesti due,
 la valle onde Bisenzo si dichina
57 del padre loro Alberto e di lor fue.

I turned around and saw stretched out,
  beneath my feet, a lake frozen hard
    with a surface more like glass than water.   *24*
Never did the Danube in Austria
  or the Don under its cold and distant sky
    freeze with a sheet of winter ice as thick   *27*
As there was here, for if the Alp Tambura
  had fallen on it, or Pietrapana,
    it would not have creaked, even at the edge.   *30*
And as frogs lie in a pond and croak
  with just their muzzles out of the water
    when the peasant girl has dreams of gleaning,   *33*
So the sorrowful shades were up to their necks in ice,
  their cheeks blue that should have blushed with shame,
    and their teeth clacking like the beak of a stork.   *36*
Their faces were turned downward; their mouths
  gave testimony to the cold they felt,
    and their eyes to the grief in their broken hearts.   *39*
For a moment I looked in every direction,
  then I glanced down and saw two heads
    so close to each other that their hair was tangled.   *42*

"Tell me, you two who are chest to chest,"
  I said, "Who are you?" They bent their necks back,
    and when they had lifted their faces toward me,   *45*
Their eyes, until now moist only within,
  welled up with tears that flowed over their lips
    and froze, locking their faces in an icy grip   *48*
More tightly than a clamp has ever bound boards.
  This enraged them so much that like two goats
    they started to butt their foreheads together.   *51*
Another, who had lost both his frostbitten ears,
  said to me, with his face still cast down,
    "Why are you staring so hard at us?   *54*
If you want to put names to these two heads,
  the valley the Bisenzio runs through belonged
    to their father Alberto, and to them.   *57*

D'un corpo usciro; e tutta la Caina
   potrai cercare, e non troverai ombra
60   degna piú d'esser fitta in gelatina:
non quelli a cui fu rotto il petto e l'ombra
   con esso un colpo per la man d'Artù;
63   non Focaccia; non questi che m'ingombra
col capo sí, ch'i' non veggio oltre piú,
   e fu nomato Sassol Mascheroni;
66   se tosco se', ben sai omai chi fu.
E perché non mi metti in piú sermoni,
   sappi ch'i' fu' il Camiscion de' Pazzi;
69   e aspetto Carlin che mi scagioni."

Poscia vid' io mille visi cagnazzi
   fatti per freddo; onde mi vien riprezzo,
72   e verrà sempre, de' gelati guazzi.
E mentre ch'andavamo inver' lo mezzo
   al quale ogne gravezza si rauna,
75   e io tremava ne l'etterno rezzo;
se voler fu o destino o fortuna,
   non so; ma, passeggiando tra le teste,
78   forte percossi 'l piè nel viso ad una.
Piangendo mi sgridò: "Perché mi peste?
   se tu non vieni a crescer la vendetta
81   di Montaperti, perché mi moleste?"
E io: "Maestro mio, or qui m'aspetta,
   sí ch'io esca d'un dubbio per costui;
84   poi mi farai, quantunque vorrai, fretta."
Lo duca stette, e io dissi a colui
   che bestemmiava duramente ancora:
87   "Qual se' tu che cosí rampogni altrui?"
"Or tu chi se' che vai per l'Antenora,
   percotendo," rispuose, "altrui le gote,
90   sí che, se fossi vivo, troppo fora?"
"Vivo son io, e caro esser ti puote,"
   fu mia risposta, "se dimandi fama,
93   ch'io metta il nome tuo tra l'altre note."

They were born from one body. You may search
  all of Caïna and not find a shade
    worthier than these to be glazed in aspic;   *60*
Not the one whose chest and shadow were pierced
  with one hard thrust from Arthur's hand; not Focaccia;
    not this one here, my perpetual shadow,   *63*
Whose head completely encumbers my view.
  His name was Sassol Mascheroni,
    and if you are Tuscan you know who he was.   *66*
And so you won't make me talk any more,
  know that I was Camiscion dei Pazzi.
    I wait for Carlino to exonerate me."   *69*

After that I saw a thousand faces
  purple and shivering like dogs. It still makes me
    shudder at frozen fords, as I always will.   *72*
And while we were on our way to the center
  where all gravity pools, and I was
    trembling and shivering in the timeless cold,   *75*
Whether it was willed, fated, or mere chance
  I do not know, but picking my way among the heads,
    I happened to kick one of them in the face.   *78*
He moaned and cried out, "Why are you
  grinding me with your heel? If you didn't come here
    to better avenge Montaperti, why give me grief?" *81*
And I said to my master, "Wait here for me.
  I want to clear up a doubt about this one,
    and then we can hurry as much as you wish."   *84*
My leader stopped, and I said to the shade,
  who was still cursing and swearing at me,
    "Who are you to be bawling out others?"   *87*
"No, who are you," he answered, "going through
  Antenora kicking others in the face,
    which would be too much to bear if you were alive?" *90*
"I am alive," was my reply, "and if fame
  has any appeal, it might be worth it to you
    if I put your name in my notes somewhere."   *93*

Ed elli a me: "Del contrario ho io brama.
Lèvati quinci e non mi dar piú lagna,
96   ché mal sai lusingar per questa lama!"
Allor lo presi per la cuticagna
e dissi: "El converrà che tu ti nomi,
99   o che capel qui sú non ti rimagna."
Ond' elli a me: "Perché tu mi dischiomi,
né ti dirò ch'io sia, né mosterrolti
102   se mille fiate in sul capo mi tomi."

Io avea già i capelli in mano avvolti,
e tratti glien' avea piú d'una ciocca,
105   latrando lui con li occhi in giú raccolti,
quando un altro gridò: "Che hai tu, Bocca?
non ti basta sonar con le mascelle,
108   se tu non latri? qual diavol ti tocca?"
"Omai," diss' io, "non vo' che piú favelle,
malvagio traditor; ch'a la tua onta
111   io porterò di te vere novelle."
"Va via," rispuose, "e ciò che tu vuoi conta;
ma non tacer, se tu di qua entro eschi,
114   di quel ch'ebbe or cosí la lingua pronta.
El piange qui l'argento de' Franceschi:
'Io vidi,' potrai dir, 'quel da Duera
117   là dove i peccatori stanno freschi.'
Se fossi domandato 'Altri chi v'era?'
tu hai dallato quel di Beccheria
120   di cui segò Fiorenza la gorgiera.
Gianni de' Soldanier credo che sia
piú là con Ganellone e Tebaldello,
123   ch'aprì Faenza quando si dormia."

Noi eravam partiti già da ello,
ch'io vidi due ghiacciati in una buca,
126   sí che l'un capo a l'altro era cappello;
e come 'l pan per fame si manduca,
cosí 'l sovran li denti a l'altro pose
129   là 've 'l cervel s'aggiugne con la nuca:

And he said, "What I crave is just the reverse.
　Get out of here and stop bothering me.
　　Down in this pit your flattery falls flat."   *96*
I took him by the hair at the nape of his neck
　and said, "Either you tell me your name
　　or you're not going to have any hair left here."   *99*
He said to me, "You can pull out every last hair
　and I still won't let you know who I am,
　　even if you bash my head a thousand times."   *102*

I had already twisted his hair in my hand
　and yanked out more than one or two clumps
　　while he howled and kept his eyes turned down,   *105*
When someone cried, "What's with you, Bocca?
　Don't you make enough noise clattering your teeth
　　without howling too? What devil has got you?"   *108*
"Now," I said, "I don't care if you speak any more,
　you damned traitor. To your eternal shame,
　　I will tell the world the truth about you."   *111*
"Go away," he answered, "and say what you want,
　but if you do get out of here, don't hold back
　　about the one with the ready tongue just now.   *114*
He's bemoaning here the silver of the French.
　'I saw,' you can say, 'the one from Duera
　　down where the sinners stay fresh on the ice.'   *117*
And if you are asked who else was there,
　right by your side is the Beccheria
　　whose throat was slit by the Florentines.   *120*
Gianni de' Soldanieri is a little farther on,
　I think, with Ganelon and Tebaldello,
　　who opened Faenza while it slumbered in dreams."   *123*

We had already taken our leave of that shade
　When I saw in one hole a pair frozen so close
　　that the head of one was the other's hood.   *126*
As a hungry man works on a crust of bread,
　the upper one's teeth were in the lower one's skull
　　where the brain meets the nape at the back of the head.   *129*

non altrimenti Tidëo si rose
 le tempie a Menalippo per disdegno,
132   che quei faceva il teschio e l'altre cose.
"O tu che mostri per sí bestial segno
 odio sovra colui che tu ti mangi,
135   dimmi 'l perché," diss' io, "per tal convegno,
che se tu a ragion di lui ti piangi,
 sappiendo chi voi siete e la sua pecca,
138   nel mondo suso ancora io te ne cangi,
se quella con ch'io parlo non si secca."

And like Tydeus, who was driven by spite
  to gnaw on Melanippus' severed head,
    this one chewed on the bone and the stuff inside.   *132*
"O you who show in so bestial a way
  your hatred for him whom you devour,
    tell me why," I said, "and if what you say   *135*
Shows that your grievance is just and right,
  then, knowing you and his sin, I will try
    to pay you back in the world of light,   *138*
If the tongue I speak with does not go dry."

Canto XXXIII

THE SHADE ON TOP, *a fellow Tuscan, turns from his cannibalistic meal to respond to Dante. It will not be easy for him to retell his grief, but he will steel himself to do so, as long as it brings opprobrium upon his former victimizer, now his victim. He is Count Ugolino; his hated rival, the Archbishop Ruggieri. While it is common knowledge that Ugolino died in Ruggieri's prison, now Dante will hear the cruel details of his death. Confined in the Tower of Hunger with his children, they each dreamed a dream foreshadowing their fates. The next day the door of the tower was nailed shut, and they were left to starve. His sons died first, leaving him, blinded by denutrition, to grope over their dead bodies. Finally famine proved more powerful than grief. The author adds Pisa, the new Thebes, to his anathemas. Leaving Antenora for Ptolomaea, where the Traitors*

La bocca sollevò dal fiero pasto
   quel peccator, forbendola a' capelli
3   del capo ch'elli avea di retro guasto.
Poi cominciò: "Tu vuo' ch'io rinovelli
   disperato dolor che 'l cor mi preme
6   già pur pensando, pria ch'io ne favelli.
Ma se le mie parole esser dien seme
   che frutti infamia al traditor ch'i' rodo,
9   parlare e lagrimar vedrai insieme.
Io non so chi tu se' né per che modo
   venuto se' qua giú; ma fiorentino
12   mi sembri veramente quand' io t'odo.
Tu dei saper ch'i' fui conte Ugolino,
   e questi è l'arcivescovo Ruggieri:
15   or ti dirò perché i son tal vicino.
Che per l'effetto de' suo' mai pensieri,
   fidandomi di lui, io fossi preso
18   e poscia morto, dir non è mestieri;

who violated the laws of hospitality are punished, they find them with their heads bent back, so that their tears freeze over their eyes, denying grief its expression. An icy wind blows, burning Dante's face. A sinner begs the passersby to prize the frozen tears from his eyes. Asking him who he is, Dante makes an ambiguous promise. The traitor is Fra Alberigo, who treacherously slew his guests, causing his soul to be carried off to Hell before his body died, a "privilege" granted to the shades in Ptolomaea. Next to him is the soul of the Genoese traitor Branca Doria. His body too remains up on earth, occupied by a demon who eats and drinks and sleeps and puts on clothes. Dante does not liberate his eyes; and betraying the betrayer he considers to be an act of courtesy.

Lifting his mouth from his savage meal,
   the sinner wiped it on the hair of the head
      he had just been chewing on from behind,   *3*
And he began, "You want me to renew
   a desperate sorrow, the very thought of which
      wrings my soul before I even begin to speak.   *6*
But if my words prove to be the seeds
   whose harvest is infamy for the traitor I gnaw,
      you will see me weep and speak though my tears.   *9*
Who you are I do not know, nor how
   you have come down here, but you seem,
      when I hear your voice, to be a Florentine.   *12*
You need to know I was Count Ugolino,
   and this is the Archbishop Ruggieri.
      Now I will tell you why we are such close neighbors.   *15*
The details of how my trust was betrayed
   by his dark conspiracies, how I was taken
      and put to death, there is no need to recount,   *18*

però quel che non puoi avere inteso,
  cioè come la morte mia fu cruda,
21   udirai, e saprai s'e' m'ha offeso.
Breve pertugio dentro da la Muda,
  la qual per me ha 'l titol de la fame,
24   e che conviene ancor ch'altrui si chiuda,
m'avea mostrato per lo suo forame
  piú lune già, quand' io feci 'l mal sonno
27   che del futuro mi squarciò 'l velame.
Questi pareva a me maestro e donno,
  cacciando il lupo e ' lupicini al monte
30   per che i Pisan veder Lucca non ponno.
Con cagne magre, studïose e conte
  Gualandi con Sismondi e con Lanfranchi
33   s'avea messi dinanzi da la fronte.
In picciol corso mi parieno stanchi
  lo padre e ' figli, e con l'agute scane
36   mi parea lor veder fender li fianchi.
Quando fui desto innanzi la dimane,
  pianger senti' fra 'l sonno i miei figliuoli
39   ch'eran con meco, e dimandar del pane.
Ben se' crudel, se tu già non ti duoli
  pensando ciò che 'l mio cor s'annunziava;
42   e se non piangi, di che pianger suoli?
Già eran desti, e l'ora s'appressava
  che 'l cibo ne solëa essere addotto,
45   e per suo sogno ciascun dubitava;
e io senti' chiavar l'uscio di sotto
  a l'orribile torre; ond' io guardai
48   nel viso a' mie' figliuoi sanza far motto.
Io non piangëa, sí dentro impetrai:
  piangevan elli; e Anselmuccio mio
51   disse: 'Tu guardi sí, padre! chè hai?'
Perciò non lagrimai né rispuos' io
  tutto quel giorno né la notte appresso,
54   infin che l'altro sol nel mondo uscío.

But what you cannot possibly know—
  how cruel my death was—that you will hear,
    and judge for yourself if he has wronged me.   *21*
The mew for hawks that because of me
  has come to be known as the Tower of Hunger,
    and in which others are yet to be imprisoned,   *24*
Had already shown me through its narrow slit
  several waxing moons, when a terrible dream
    tore aside the veil that shrouded the future.   *27*
This man, in my dream, was a master of the hunt,
  tracking a wolf and its cubs across the mountain
    that blocks Lucca from the Pisans' view.   *30*
Driving trained bitches that were lean and eager,
  he had Gualandi out in front of him,
    along with Sismondi and Lanfranchi,   *33*
And after a mere sprint both father and sons
  bore the look of exhaustion, and how real
    the fangs seemed that made shreds of their flanks.   *36*
When I awoke, a little before dawn,
  I heard my children, who were imprisoned with me,
    crying in their sleep and asking for bread.   *39*
You are cruelty incarnate if you are not
  grieving now at what my heart told me,
    and if this does not make you weep, what does?   *42*
They were awake now, and the hour approached
  when our food was usually brought to us,
    and we each were anxious because of our dreams.   *45*
Then I listened as the nails were driven into the door
  of that horrible tower, and I looked upon
    the faces of my children without a word.   *48*
I did not weep; I had turned to stone inside.
  They wept, and my poor little Anselm said,
    'What a look you have, Father. What is the matter?'   *51*
I shed no tear at that, nor spoke a word
  all that day or the following night,
    until the sun next came out into the world.   *54*

Come un poco di raggio si fu messo
  nel doloroso carcere, e io scorsi
57   per quattro visi il mio aspetto stesso,
ambo le man per lo dolor mi morsi;
  ed ei, pensando ch'io 'l fessi per voglia
60   di manicar, di súbito levorsi
e disser:'Padre, assai ci fia men doglia
  se tu mangi di noi: tu ne vestisti
63   queste misere carni, e tu le spoglia.'
Queta'mi allor per non farli piú tristi;
  lo dí e l'altro stemmo tutti muti;
66   ahi dura terra, perché non t'apristi?
Poscia che fummo al quarto dí venuti,
  Gaddo mi si gittò disteso a' piedi,
69   dicendo:'Padre mio, ché non m'aiuti?'
Quivi morí; e come tu mi vedi,
  vid' io cascar li tre ad uno ad uno
72   tra 'l quinto dí e 'l sesto; ond' io mi diedi,
già cieco, a brancolar sovra ciascuno,
  e due dí li chiamai, poi che fur morti.
75   Poscia, piú che 'l dolor, poté 'l digiuno."

Quand' ebbe detto ciò, con li occhi torti
  riprese 'l teschio misero co' denti,
78   che furo a l'osso, come d'un can, forti.

Ahi Pisa, vituperio de le genti
  del bel paese là dove 'l sí suona,
81   poi che i vicini a te punir son lenti,
muovasi la Capraia e la Gorgona,
  e faccian siepe ad Arno in su la foce,
84   sí ch'elli annieghi in te ogne persona!
Che se 'l conte Ugolino aveva voce
  d'aver tradita te de le castella,
87   non dovei tu i figliuoi porre a tal croce.
Innocenti facea l'età novella,
  novella Tebe, Uguiccione e 'l Brigata
90   e li altri due che 'l canto suso appella.

As soon as a slender ray of light streamed
  into that dismal stone cell, I could see
    in their four faces the reflection of my own,   57
And bit both my hands for grief. My children,
  thinking I did this driven by hunger,
    rose up in an instant and cried out to me,   60
'Father, it would give us much less pain
  if you fed on us. It was you who clothed us
    in this pitiable flesh, and you should strip it away!'   63
Then I calmed myself, to spare them more grief.
  That day and all the next we stayed silent.
    Ah, hard Earth, could you not have swallowed us?   66
After we had come to the fourth day, Gaddo
  threw himself down outstretched at my feet,
    saying, 'Father, Father, why don't you help me?'   69
There he died, and as sure as you see me,
  I saw the other three drop, one by one,
    between the fifth and sixth day. Then I began,   72
Blind by now, to grope over their corpses,
  and for two days called them when they were dead.
    Then starvation finished what sorrow could not."   75

When he had said this, his eyes looking away,
  he seized the wretched skull again in his teeth,
    and like a dog ground away at the bone.   78

Ah, Pisa! Disgrace of all the fair lands
  where *sì* is heard, since your neighbors
    won't take your punishment into their hands,   81
Let Capraia and Gorgona shift themselves around
  into the Arno's mouth and make a dam
    so that every last one of your citizens is drowned!   84
Even if you thought that Count Ugolino
  betrayed you along with your walls and castles,
    you should not have tortured his children too,   87
Like a modern Thebes. Their youthful years
  made Uguiccione and Brigata innocent,
    and the other of whom my reader hears.   90

Noi passammo oltre, là 've la gelata
 ruvidamente un'altra gente fascia,
93 non volta in giú, ma tutta riversata.
Lo pianto stesso lí pianger non lascia,
 e 'l duol che truova in su li occhi rintoppo,
96 si volge in entro a far crescer l'ambascia;
ché le lagrime prime fanno groppo,
 e sí come visiere di cristallo,
99 rïempion sotto 'l ciglio tutto il coppo.
E avvegna che, sí come d'un callo,
 per la freddura ciascun sentimento
102 cessato avesse del mio viso stallo,
già mi parea sentire alquanto vento;
 per ch'io: "Maestro mio, questo chi move?
105 non è qua giú ogne vapore spento?"
Ond' elli a me: "Avaccio sarai dove
 di ciò ti farà l'occhio la risposta,
108 veggendo la cagion che 'l fiato piove."

E un de' tristi de la fredda crosta
 gridò a noi: "O anime crudeli
111 tanto che data v'è l'ultima posta,
levatemi dal viso i duri veli,
 sí ch'ïo sfoghi 'l duol che 'l cor m'impregna,
114 un poco, pria che 'l pianto si raggeli."
Per ch'io a lui: "Se vuo' ch'i' ti sovvegna,
 dimmi chi se', e s'io non ti disbrigo,
117 al fondo de la ghiaccia ir mi convegna."
Rispuose adunque: "I' son frate Alberigo;
 i' son quel da le frutta del mal orto,
120 che qui riprendo dattero per figo."
"Oh," diss' io lui, "or se' tu ancor morto?"
 Ed elli a me: "Come 'l mio corpo stea
123 nel mondo sú, nulla scïenza porto.
Cotal vantaggio ha questa Tolomea,
 che spesse volte l'anima ci cade
126 innanzi ch'Atropòs mossa le dea.

We walked on farther, to where the glacier
  wraps another group in its rough sheet,
    their faces not bent downward, but all upturned.   *93*
Their very weeping prevents their weeping,
  and their grief, which cannot escape their eyes,
    turns inward to increase their suffering,   *96*
For the first tears congeal into a knot
  and then, like an eyeglass made of crystal, they fill
    all of the socket beneath the brow.   *99*
And now, although my face was numb
  with the bitter cold and had no more feeling
    than if it had become a hard callus,   *102*
It seemed to me as if I felt a wind,
  and I asked, "Master, who makes this wind blow?
    Has not every vapor here been laid to rest?"   *105*
He answered me, "You will soon be where
  your eye itself will answer the question
    as to the cause of these gusts of wind."   *108*

Then one of the damned in the crust of ice
  cried out to us, "O souls so cruel
    that you are condemned to the last station,   *111*
Lift from my eyes these frozen veils, so that
  I may vent a little the pain that cramps
    my heart, before my tears freeze solid again."   *114*
And so I told him, "If you want my help,
  tell me who you are, and if I do not ease your pain,
    may I be sent down to the bottom of the ice."   *117*
He answered then, "I am Fra Alberigo,
  the one with the fruit from the garden of Evil,
    and here I am more than repaid, date for fig."   *120*
"Oh," I said to him, "are you already dead?"
  He answered, "Of my body's condition
    in the world above I have no idea.   *123*
This circle Ptolomaea has the privilege
  that many times a soul falls into its depth
    before Atropos has severed its thread,   *126*

E perché tu piú volontier mi rade
le 'nvetrïate lagrime dal volto,
129 sappie che, tosto che l'anima trade
come fec' ïo, il corpo suo l' è tolto
da un demonio, che poscia il governa
132 mentre che 'l tempo suo tutto sia vòlto.
Ella ruina in sí fatta cisterna;
e forse pare ancor lo corpo suso
135 de l'ombra che di qua dietro mi verna.
Tu 'l dei saper, se tu vien pur mo giuso:
elli è ser Branca Doria, e son piú anni
138 poscia passati ch'el fu sí racchiuso."
Io credo," diss' io lui, "che tu m'inganni;
ché Branca Doria non morí unquanche,
141 e mangia e bee e dorme e veste panni."
"Nel fosso sú," diss' el, "de' Malebranche,
là dove bolle la tenace pece,
144 non era ancora giunto Michel Zanche,
che questi lasciò il diavolo in sua vece
nel corpo suo, ed un suo prossimano
147 che 'l tradimento insieme con lui fece.
Ma distendi oggimai in qua la mano;
aprimi li occhi." E io non gliel' apersi;
150 e cortesia fu lui esser villano.

Ahi Genovesi, uomini diversi
d'ogne costume e pien d'ogne magagna,
153 perché non siete voi del mondo spersi?
Ché col peggiore spirto di Romagna
trovai di voi un tal, che per sua opra
156 in anima in Cocito già si bagna,
e in corpo par vivo ancor di sopra.

And, so that you may be all the more willing
    to scrape the icy tears from my face,
        know this: the instant a soul has made a betrayal,   *129*
As I did, its body becomes the possession
    of a demon, who inhabits and governs it
        until its allotted time comes around.   *132*
The soul plunges down into this arctic cistern.
    Perhaps the body of the shade wintering
        here behind me still appears above on Earth.   *135*
You ought to know, if you have just come down.
    He is Ser Branca Doria, and many years have passed
        since he was locked up in cold storage like this."   *138*
"I think you are lying to me," I said.
    Branca Doria is far from dead. He eats
        and drinks and sleeps and puts on clothes."   *141*
"In the Malebranche's ditch above," he said,
    "where the sticky tar is boiling hot
        Michel Zanche had not yet arrived   *144*
When this one here left a devil in charge
    of his own body, as did a kinsman
        who joined him in that treacherous murder.   *147*
Now reach out and open my eyes for me."
    But I was content to leave them frozen shut,
        for to be rude to him was courtesy.   *150*

Ah, men of Genoa, of so little worth!
    Indecent, foul, and full of corruption,
        why have you not yet been driven from Earth?   *153*
For with a shade from Romagna, none more vile,
    I saw one of you who has plunged his soul
        into Cocytus' ice, and all the while   *156*
On Earth he seems to be alive and whole.

Canto XXXIV

THE PILGRIMS REACH THE FOURTH AND FINAL ZONE *of Cocytus, Judecca, where Virgil warns Dante that they are at last about to see Dis, king of Hell and embodiment of evil. In fact, squinting ahead, Dante perceives something that looks like a giant sail-driven windmill, towering above the ice, in which the last sinners can be seen to be totally immersed. Half dead with fear, Dante views the three-faced monster, whose arms alone dwarf the mythical Giants Nimrod, Ephialtes, and Antaeus, the last of whom handed them down into the Ninth Circle in Canto XXXI. In each of his three mouths, this rebel against God mangles one of Christian and Roman history's greatest traitors, Judas,*

"*Vexilla regis prodeunt inferni*
　　　verso di noi; però dinanzi mira,"
3　　　　disse 'l maestro mio, "se tu 'l discerni."
Come quando una grossa nebbia spira,
　　　o quando l'emisperio nostro annotta,
6　　　　par di lungi un molin che 'l vento gira,
veder mi parve un tal dificio allotta;
　　　poi per lo vento mi ristrinsi retro
9　　　　al duca mio, ché non lí era altra grotta.
Già era, e con paura il metto in metro,
　　　là dove l'ombre tutte eran coperte,
12　　　　e trasparien come festuca in vetro.
Altre sono a giacere; altre stanno erte,
　　　quella col capo e quella con le piante;
15　　　　altra, com' arco, il volto a' piè rinverte.
Quando noi fummo fatti tanto avante,
　　　ch'al mio maestro piacque di mostrarmi
18　　　　la creatura ch'ebbe il bel sembiante,
d'innanzi mi si tolse e fé restarmi,
　　　"Ecco Dite," dicendo, "ed ecco il loco
21　　　　ove convien che di fortezza t'armi."

Brutus, and Cassius. Now that they have seen everything Hell has to show, Virgil tells Dante to hang onto him tightly and begins to clamber down the gruesome Dis' hairy sides. When he reaches the leviathan's haunches, he inverts his position and begins to ascend, leading Dante to believe that they are going back up. Eventually, however, they scramble down onto solid ground and Virgil explains that they have passed through the center of the Earth. Following a cave hollowed out by an underground stream, they now make their way to the surface and emerge from the darkness of Hell to see the stars.

"*Vexilla regis prodeunt inferni*
   toward us," my master said. "Look straight ahead
     and see if you can make him out."   *3*
Like a windmill turning on the horizon
   when a thick fog drifts and settles in
     or when our hemisphere turns toward night,   *6*
Such a structure I now seemed to see;
   then I took shelter behind my leader's back,
     for there was no other way to block the wind.   *9*
I was now (and I shudder to put this into verse)
   where the shades hung completely engulfed,
     showing through the ice like straw through glass.   *12*
Some are lying sideways, some stand upright,
   one with his head, another with feet on top,
     and another bent over double like a bow.   *15*
And when we had made our way forward far enough
   that it pleased my master to reveal to me
     the creature who had been so beautiful once,   *18*
He stepped to one side and had me stop,
   saying, "Behold Dis. And there is the place
     where you must steel your soul to the utmost."   *21*

Com' io divenni allor gelato e fioco,
     nol dimandar, lettor, ch'i' non lo scrivo,
24   però ch'ogne parlar sarebbe poco.
Io non mori' e non rimasi vivo;
     pensa oggimai per te, s'hai fior d'ingegno,
27   qual io divenni, d'uno e d'altro privo.

Lo 'mperador del doloroso regno
     da mezzo 'l petto uscia fuor de la ghiaccia;
30   e piú con un gigante io mi convegno,
che i giganti non fan con le sue braccia:
     vedi oggimai quant' esser dee quel tutto
33   ch'a cosí fatta parte si confaccia.
S'el fu sí bel com' elli è ora brutto,
     e contra 'l suo fattore alzò le ciglia,
36   ben dee da lui procedere ogne lutto.
Oh quanto parve a me gran maraviglia
     quand' io vidi tre facce a la sua testa!
39   L'una dinanzi, e quella era vermiglia;
l'altr' eran due, che s'aggiugnieno a questa
     sovresso 'l mezzo di ciascuna spalla,
42   e sé giugnieno al loco de la cresta:
e la destra parea tra bianca e gialla;
     la sinistra a vedere era tal, quali
45   vegnon di là onde 'l Nilo s'avvalla.
Sotto ciascuna uscivan due grand' ali,
     quanto si convenia a tanto uccello:
48   vele di mar non vid' io mai cotali.
Non avean penne, ma di vispistrello
     era lor modo; e quelle svolazzava,
51   sí che tre venti si movean da ello:
quindi Cocito tutto s'aggelava.
     Con sei occhi piangëa, e per tre menti
54   gocciava 'l pianto e sanguinosa bava.
Da ogne bocca dirompea co' denti
     un peccatore, a guisa di maciulla,
57   sí che tre ne facea cosí dolenti.

Do not ask, Reader, how frozen and faint
  I became then, for I cannot write it down;
    every word known to man would not be enough.   *24*
I did not die, and yet I was no longer alive.
  Imagine, if you can, what I became,
    deprived of death and bereft of life.   *27*

The emperor of the world of pain
  stood out of the ice up to his chest,
    and I am bigger standing beside a Giant   *30*
Than a Giant would be beside one of his arms.
  You can see how huge the whole must be
    for a part such as this to fit into place.   *33*
If he was as beautiful once as now he is
  hideous, and arched his brow against his Maker,
    well may he be the source of all woe.   *36*
How great a sense of wonder overcame me
  when I saw three faces arranged on his head.
    One was in the front, as red as cinnabar,   *39*
And the other two were aligned with this one
  just over the middle of each shoulder,
    and all of them fused at the crown of his head.   *42*
The one on the right was a pale yellow,
  while the left one was as dark a color
    as those who live beyond the Nile's cataracts.   *45*
Under each face grew a pair of wings
  of a size that matched this portentous bird.
    I never saw sails so large catch the wind at sea.   *48*
They had no feathers, but were bald like the wings
  of the darkling bat, and he beat them slowly,
    so that three winds blew away from him,   *51*
And this was why all Cocytus was frozen.
  He wept from six eyes, and over three chins
    the tears dripped down with bloody slaver.   *54*
In each mouth he chewed upon a sinner
  with teeth like a harrow that scutches flax,
    and so he kept three in constant agony.   *57*

A quel dinanzi il mordere era nulla
   verso 'l graffiar, che talvolta la schiena
60   rimanea de la pelle tutta brulla.

"Quell' anima là sú c'ha maggior pena,"
   disse 'l maestro, "è Giuda Scarïotto,
63   che 'l capo ha dentro e fuor le gambe mena.
De li altri due c'hanno il capo di sotto,
   quel che pende dal nero ceffo è Bruto:
66   vedi come si storce, e non fa motto!;
e l'altro è Cassio, che par sí membruto.
Ma la notte risurge, e oramai
69   è da partir, ché tutto avem veduto."

Com' a lui piacque, il collo li avvinghiai;
   ed el prese di tempo e loco poste,
72   e quando l'ali fuoro aperte assai,
appigliò sé a le vellute coste;
   di vello in vello giú discese poscia
75   tra 'l folto pelo e le gelate croste.
Quando noi fummo là dove la coscia
   si volge, a punto in sul grosso de l'anche,
78   lo duca, con fatica e con angoscia,
volse la testa ov' elli avea le zanche,
   e aggrappossi al pel com' om che sale,
81   sí che 'n inferno i' credea tornar anche.
"Attienti ben, ché per cotali scale,"
   disse 'l maestro, ansando com' uom lasso,
84   "conviensi dipartir da tanto male."
Poi uscí fuor per lo fóro d'un sasso
   e puose me in su l'orlo a sedere;
87   appresso porse a me l'accorto passo.

Io levai li occhi e credetti vedere
   Lucifero com' io l'avea lasciato,
90   e vidili le gambe in sú tenere;

For the sinner in front to be chewed alive
  was nothing compared to the claws that flayed him,
    so at times his back was utterly stripped of skin.   *60*

"The soul up there who is punished the most,"
  my master said, "is Judas Iscariot,
    who has his head within and flails his legs outside.   *63*
Of the other two, with their heads below,
  the one who hangs from the black snout is Brutus.
    See how he writhes and never says a word.   *66*
The other is Cassius, so powerful in stature.
  But night is coming on again, and it is time
    for us to depart, for we have seen all there is."   *69*

Then, as he wanted, I clasped him around the neck,
  and he, gauging the timing and distance,
    made his move when the wings opened wide,   *72*
And caught hold of the great shaggy flanks.
  From one clump of matted hair to another
    and down through frozen crusts he descended,   *75*
And when we had come to where the thigh
  turns within the socket of the hip, my leader,
    straining with the weight and near exhaustion,   *78*
Brought his head around to where his legs had been,
  and struggled with the hair like someone climbing,
    so that I thought we were going back to Hell.   *81*
"Hold tight, for it is by such stairs as these,"
  my master said to me, gasping for breath,
    "that we must depart from evil so great."   *84*
At last he climbed through a vent in the rock,
  perched me on its edge, and then with a careful stride
    brought himself over to where I sat on the rim.   *87*

I raised my eyes, expecting I would see
  Lucifer as I had left him below, but instead
    I saw him with legs stretched out above,   *90*

e s'io divenni allora travagliato,
   la gente grossa il pensi, che non vede
93   qual è quel punto ch'io avea passato.
"Lèvati sú," disse 'l maestro, "in piede:
   la via è lunga e 'l cammino è malvagio,
96   e già il sole a mezza terza riede."
Non era camminata di palagio
   là 'v' eravam, ma natural burella
99   ch'avea mal suolo e di lume disagio.

"Prima ch'io de l'abisso mi divella,
   maestro mio," diss' io quando fui dritto,
102   "a trarmi d'erro un poco mi favella:
ov' è la ghiaccia? e questi com' è fitto
   sí sottosopra? e come, in sí poc' ora,
105   da sera a mane ha fatto il sol tragitto?"
Ed elli a me: "Tu imagini ancora
   d'esser di là dal centro, ov' io mi presi
108   al pel del vermo reo che 'l mondo fóra.
Di là fosti cotanto quant' io scesi;
   quand' io mi volsi, tu passasti 'l punto
111   al qual si traggon d'ogne parte i pesi.
E se' or sotto l'emisperio giunto
   ch'è contraposto a quel che la gran secca
114   coverchia, e sotto 'l cui colmo consunto
fu l'uom che nacque e visse sanza pecca;
   tu haï i piedi in su picciola spera
117   che l'altra faccia fa de la Giudecca.
Qui è da man, quando di là è sera;
   e questi, che ne fé scala col pelo,
120   fitto è ancora sí come prim' era.
Da questa parte cadde giú dal cielo;
   e la terra, che pria di qua si sporse,
123   per paura di lui fé del mar velo,
e venne a l'emisperio nostro; e forse
   per fuggir lui lasciò qui loco vòto
126   quella ch'appar di qua, e sú ricorse."

And if I became confused, well then,
  let the dull minds out there that fail to see
    the point I had passed be the judge of that.   *93*
"Up on your feet," the master said to me.
  "The way is long and the road not easy,
    and the sun is climbing past the third hour."   *96*
It was no great palatial hall where we were,
  but more of a kind of natural dungeon
    with a rough floor and a lack of light.   *99*

"Before I tear myself away from the abyss,
  O my master," I said when I had risen,
    "talk to me and clear up my confusion.   *102*
Where is the ice? And how did Lucifer there
  get stuck upside down? And how did the sun
    transit so quickly from evening to dawn?"   *105*
And he said, "You imagine that you are still
  on the other side of the center, where I
    caught hold of the hair of the Evil Worm   *108*
Who pierces the world. You remained on that side
  as long as I was descending. But when I pivoted
    you passed the point to which all weights are drawn.   *111*
And now you are beneath the hemisphere
  opposite the one that arches over
    the great land mass, under whose zenith   *114*
The Man was slain who was born and lived without sin;
  and your feet are resting upon a little round
    that forms the other face of Judecca.   *117*
Here it is morning when it is evening there,
  and Lucifer, whose pelt formed a ladder for us,
    is in the same position as he was before.   *120*
He fell down from Heaven on this side of Earth,
  and the land withdrew behind a veil of ocean
    and fled to the north, toward our hemisphere;   *123*
And the Earth that once filled the empty space
  where we are standing, perhaps to escape him,
    rushed upward to form what now looms above us."   *126*

Luogo è là giú da Belzebú remoto
tanto quanto la tomba si distende,
129 che non per vista, ma per suono è noto
d'un ruscelletto che quivi discende
per la buca d'un sasso, ch'elli ha roso,
132 col corso ch'elli avvolge, e poco pende.
Lo duca e io per quel cammino ascoso
intrammo a ritornar nel chiaro mondo;
135 e sanza cura aver d'alcun riposo,
salimmo sú, el primo e io secondo,
tanto ch'i' vidi de le cose belle
138 che porta 'l ciel, per un pertugio tondo.
E quindi uscimmo a riveder le stelle.

There is a region below, stretching underground
  as far from Beelzebub as his tomb is deep,
    not known by sight, but only by the sound   *129*
Of a rivulet winding down through a tunnel
  that it has eroded from the solid rock
    as it flows in its gently sloping channel.   *132*
Up this hidden way my guide and I now went
  to return again to the world of light,
    and without thought of rest we made the ascent,   *135*
He leading the way and I following,
  until the beautiful things that Heaven bears
    appeared above through a round opening,   *138*
And we came out again and saw the stars.

Notes

Canto I

Dante's imagined journey through the three realms of the afterlife encompasses a carefully calculated six days. The poet frequently interrupts his narrative to inform his reader of the passage of time on Earth. Beginning writing after the fact, probably in 1308, when he had been exiled from his native Florence for six years, he sets the events of his fiction at the turn of the century, in 1300, when he was still a citizen of what is for him "the divided city" par excellence. The current pope, Boniface VIII (reigned 1294–1303), had declared the year 1300 a Jubilee year, with generous "indulgences" in the world to come for pilgrims who made the trip to Rome.

The protagonist, a pilgrim who sidesteps the Church's mediation and goes directly to the next world while still alive, comes to his senses in the dark wood of error at daybreak on April 8—Good Friday, the day of Christ's death in the Catholic liturgical calendar—and Virgil leads him through the gates of Hell at sunset on the same day. Their journey through Hell ends a day later, toward sunset on Holy Saturday, when Dante and Virgil reach the core of the Earth, where Hell's impotent monarch Satan, or Lucifer ("Dis" in Virgil's Roman mythology, *Inf.* XXXIV.20), is pinned. Their emergence (resurrection) on the shores of the island mountain of Purgatory—the ascent to the Earthly Paradise, the longest leg of the journey, will take three days and three nights—occurs appropriately at daybreak on Easter Sunday, the feast of Christ's resurrection. Accompanied now by the soul of Beatrice—the woman predestined to save him to whose love he has stayed true since the age of nine—the pilgrim takes off for his upward flight into Paradise at noon on Wednesday, April 13. We leave him at the goal of his journey, the infinite Empyrean heaven where the souls of the blessed contemplate God, on the same day. The title of the first book of the *Comedy*, by the way, despite its modern connotations, has nothing to do with fire. *Inferno* simply means "the lower world."

1 *Midway* Dante (born May 1265) reached age thirty-five—midpoint in the proverbial biblical lifespan of "threescore and ten years" (Ps. 89:10)—in the year 1300. (Dante's emulator John Milton, incidentally, was forty-one when he went blind in 1651 "*ere half [his] days* in this dark world and wide," Milton's "On His Blindness," my italics.) Dante's opening line also contains an implicit reference to Isa. 38:10: "I said: In the midst of my days I shall go to the gates of hell." Moreover, the use of the collective possessive "our life" suggests that the character Dante, though he comes onstage with the author Dante's autobiographical background and concerns for the future, will also at some level be a representative figure, a kind of Everyman.

The first canto of the *Inferno,* one of the most explicitly allegorical in the poem, functions as a prologue to all three "canticles" of the *Comedy.* The *Inferno* in fact has thirty-four cantos (one + thirty-three), whereas the *Purgatorio* (abbreviated *Pg.*) and the *Paradiso* (abbreviated *Pd.*) have thirty-three each, making a perfect one hundred in all. The recurrence of the number three—the sacred number of the Trinity—extends to the metrical scheme.

In Dante's original, the metrical scheme is based on a sequence of three-line units, each unit closed and at the same time linked to the next tercet by the middle rhyme to form a continuous chain within each canto (*aba bcb cdc ded efe,* etc.). This scheme, invented by Dante to make his poem easier for a public reciter to commit to memory, is called *terza rima.* (It permitted Primo Levi, a Jewish internee at Auschwitz, to avoid resignation to his fate by reconstructing the Ulysses canto [*Inf.* XXVI] from his high school memories. See *If This Is a Man,* translated by Stuart Woolf, New York: Orion Press, 1959; Italian title *Se questo è un uomo,* Turin: Da Silva, 1947.) Classical poetry like that of the *Aeneid* (abbreviated *Aen.*) of Virgil, a major influence on Dante, did not rhyme.

Rather than naturalistic, the landscape in which the pilgrim finds himself (the wild wood, the abandoned straight "road that runs true," the dark and narrow valley, the sunlit hill) is abstract and symbolic, burdened with a second moral meaning, as are the three beasts that oppose his progress and the Hound that will come to rout them. Moreover, their secondary or allegorical meaning outweighs whatever illusion of reality the poet is able to give them.

The shade of Virgil is different. Dante's selection of him to be his guide is abstractly hyperdetermined. In Dante's rational universe, he represents philosophy (the full potential of human reason not illuminated by Divine Grace)—the bridle of Stoic morality, the guiding hand of the providentially willed Roman Empire, the predisposition of the late pagan world to accept the coming Savior. (In *Pg.* XXII.73, the Roman poet Statius goes so far as to attribute his conversion to Christianity to Virgil.) He is also a book, a poem the poet Dante has studied and loved. Nevertheless, Virgil has, in Erich Auerbach's terminology, a figural rather than an allegorical reality. (Auerbach's seminal essay, "Figura," appeared in German in *Archivum romanicum* 22 [1938]: 436–89 and was translated into English by Ralph Mannheim in *Scenes from the Drama of European Literature,* New York: Meridian Books, 1959, pp. 11–76.) Virgil is not reducible to an ad hoc personification but is at once a historical figure and a fully imagined literary character. His existence as a character is equal to or outweighs his existence as an allegory or symbol.

In this opening canto, Dante is saying that around the age of thirty-five he became aware of having gone morally and intellectually astray, that he tried to get back on the right track, but that certain aspects of the world and his own human frailty prevented him from doing so. He would have been permanently lost if Heaven had not intervened on his behalf and sent an emissary to save him.

6 *fear* Mortal fear is the keynote of this canto (fear for one's life, but also for one's eternal life). The word (or a synonym) is repeated six times (in lines 6, 15, 20, 44, 53, and 90).

17 *that planet / that leads us straight* The planet is the sun, which in Dante's geocentric Ptolemaic universe was thought to rotate around the Earth. The light of the sun, however, is an allegory of the grace of God. No object of our senses, Dante remarks in his philosophical *Convivio* (*The Banquet*), is a more worthy symbol of God than the sun (III.xii.7–8). In line 60 below, the she-wolf will drive the pilgrim back down the hill "to where the sun is mute."

22–23 *as a man who, gasping for breath, / has escaped the sea and wades to shore* The simile of the shipwreck survivor introduces for the first time, almost subliminally, one of the ruling metaphors of the *Comedy,* that of the narrative as a sea voyage, which shows up most conspicuously in Dante's addresses to the reader at the beginning of each new canticle (*Pg.* I.1–3, *Pd.* II.1–9).

30 *my firmer foot* The literal meaning is clear: in climbing, the lower foot momentarily stands still while the higher foot seeks a new foothold. It is also clear that, in this heavily symbolic context, this almost redundant specification must imply a moral, even theological, allegory. Commentators since Dante's own son Pietro Alighieri have cited Saint Augustine's metaphor of the right and left feet of the soul (standing, respectively, for the soul's understanding and its attachments). John Freccero provides the most satisfactory explanation of its implications here—that Dante limps up the slope because his psychic affections are still bent downward as those of the sinners he will meet in Hell are bent toward the Earth—"Dante's Firm Foot and the Journey without a Guide" (1959, now in Freccero, *Dante: The Poetics of Conversion,* edited by Rachel Jacoff, Cambridge, MA: Harvard University Press, 1986, pp. 29–54).

32 *a leopard* Dante's word *lonza* is etymologically the same as Shakespeare's "ounce" ("Be it ounce, or cat, or bear," *A Midsummer Night's Dream* II.ii.31), the initial "l," interpreted as the Romance definite article, having been lost. It could refer to a lynx or a panther. In the fantastical medieval bestiaries, the lynx was a cruel animal fathered by a lion and always in heat. The precise allegorical meaning of the three beasts (or sinful dispositions) that impede the pilgrim's progress or conversion is moot; but the earliest commentators, basing themselves on Scripture (Jer. 5:6 and 1 John 2:16), identify the leopard with lust, the lion with pride, and the she-wolf with avarice or an insatiable greed for the goods and honors of this world. Many exegetes, however, would link them with Ciacco's identification of the besetting sins of the Florentines: "Pride, envy, and avarice are the three sparks / that have inflamed all of their hearts" (VI.74–75) whereas others see in them an anticipation of "the three dispositions rejected by Heaven:— / incontinence, malice, and bestial rage" (XI.81–82), which figure in Virgil's account of the overall classification of the sins of Hell. Others still have suggested a more specifically political

interpretation, identifying Florence with the leopard, the king of France with the lion, and the papal Curia with the she-wolf.

38 *those very stars* The creation of the world ("when Divine Love / first set those beautiful things in motion," I.39–40) was supposed to have occurred in spring, with the sun in the zodiacal house of Aries.

63 *faint through long silence* The true poetic voice of Virgil (or right reason)—for the apparition will immediately reveal himself to be the shade of the Roman poet, with all that his work symbolized for Dante—has not been heard for centuries. The ghost of Virgil will be Dante's guide through Hell and Purgatory.

65 *Miserere mei* The pilgrim's first word in the poem is pronounced in Latin. The appeal has liturgical and biblical precedents (see the repentant David's outcry in Ps. 51 [Ps. 50 in Dante's Latin Vulgate], the penitential psalm par excellence), but it also recalls, in a typical conflation of the biblical and the classical, Aeneas' plea to the Cumaean Sibyl before his descent to the Underworld, *gnatique patrisque, / alma, precor, miserere* ("Pity father and son, / gracious one," *Aen.* VI.117).

68 *Lombards* In Dante's day, the term was used in a generic sense for anyone from Northern Italy. Virgil was born in the village of Andes (today's Pietole) near Mantua. His speech will be recognized—somewhat anachronistically—as Lombard by false counselor Guido da Montefeltro (XXVII.20). The Lombards or Longobards were a barbarian tribe who invaded Northern Italy long after the death of Virgil, toward the end of the sixth century C.E.

70 *I was born sub Julio* Sub Julio means "under Julius" in Latin, though in fact, in 70 B.C.E., when Virgil was born, Julius Caesar, whom Dante erroneously considers the first Roman emperor—he uses both proper names "Caesar" and "Augustus" as synonyms of "emperor"—had not yet begun his political career. At the time of Caesar's assassination in 44 B.C.E.—an event comparable to the betrayal of Christ Himself for Dante, who in Canto XXXIV will place Caesar's murderers Brutus and Cassius along with the archtraitor Judas Iscariot in the maw of Satan— Virgil would have been twenty-six years old.

71 *noble Augustus* The first emperor of Rome, the brilliant general and administrator who presided over the golden age of Latin literature. Born Caius Octavius in 63 B.C.E., the son of Julius Caesar's niece Atia, he took the name Caius Julius Caesar Octavianus when his great-uncle Julius Caesar adopted him and named him as his heir. The Roman Senate conferred the honorific title of Augustus (the imperial title par excellence) upon Octavian in 27 B.C.E. and in 12 B.C.E. that of Pontifex Maximus. He died at the age of seventy-six in 14 C.E.

72 *the false and lying gods* Virgil died in 19 B.C.E., but in the Middle Ages his Fourth Eclogue was read as a prophecy of Christ's birth. His tragic exclusion from salvation will be one of the leitmotifs that lend a melancholy resonance to his character in Dante's *Comedy.* See, for instance, lines 125–29 of this canto.

73–74   *that just / son of Anchises*   Anchises' son Aeneas ("no one more just / or devoted, no one greater in battle," *Aen.* I.544–45) is the hero of the *Aeneid* and the legendary founder of Rome. Guided by the gods, Aeneas sailed from Troy (*Ilion* in Greek, hence the title of Homer's *Iliad,* which narrates the events that took place at Troy), after its destruction by its Greek besiegers in search of the site where the new Troy was destined to rise. Dante gave the same credence to Virgil's epic account of the founding of Rome as he did to the Bible. Not just an adventure-seeking hero, like Odysseus-Ulysses, Aeneas is a model of moral behavior. Dante's anti-Greek prejudice will be evident in his treatment of Ulysses in Canto XXVI.

79   *Can you be Virgil, then . . . ?*   Dido greeted Aeneas with the same question when he first appeared to her out of the cloud that had shielded him and Achates: *Tunc ille Aeneas . . . ?* ("You, then, are Aeneas . . . ?" *Aen.* I.617).

83   *my long study of your works*   In XX.114, Virgil will remark to Dante, speaking of the *Aeneid:* "you know the poem all the way through." Dante appears to have known it practically by heart, no doubt as a result of his medieval schooling with its strong component of memorization, which sometimes led to a lifelong devotion to the word.

85   *my author*   In the etymological sense of Latin *auctor,* "authority." With this tercet, Dante affirms his singularity as a direct heir of Virgil. His *Comedy* will be, so to speak, a Christian continuation of the *Aeneid.*

91   *another road*   In his sinful state, Dante cannot climb the mountain toward God's illuminating light by the "short path" (II.120). He must first come to know the heinousness of sin and its dreadful consequences by passing through Hell, and then he must purify the sinful tendencies of his flesh by climbing the mountain of Purgatory and sharing in its catharsis of guilt.

101   *until the Veltro comes*   Virgil, and Dante with him, has slipped for the first but by no means the last time into the veiled apocalyptic-prophetic mode. The she-wolf of avarice or rampant materialism will be hunted down by an incorruptible terrible swift Hound. We are still in the realm of allegory. In Chapter XXV of the *Vita nuova* (*New Life*), however, Dante warns that the poet who employs allegories ought to be able to explain them when so requested.

Not so his exegetes. There is no consensus concerning the providential Redeemer and restorer of a righteous order whom Dante has in mind (if indeed he has someone specific in mind). If we choose to exclude the Second Coming of Christ Himself, an interpretation opposed by Giovanni Boccaccio in 1374 (Boccaccio left a commentary on the first seventeen cantos of the *Inferno*), among the lay candidates who have been suggested are Henry VII, Count of Luxembourg (crowned king of Germany in November 1308 and Holy Roman Emperor in 1313), in whom Dante invested much hope and to whom he addressed a number

of his *Epistles,* and Cangrande della Scala (whose first name can be read as mean-
ing "Great Dog," which jibes with "Hound"), the imperial vicar in Italy.

105   *between Feltro and Feltro*   In a deliberately obscure prophecy, this line is
the most mysterious of all. A translator, however, has no choice but to choose, and
the uppercase initials mean that we have chosen to follow those who read the two
Feltros as place-names, standing for Feltre in the Veneto and Montefeltro (Mount
Feltro) in the Romagna. Since Verona and its territories lie between these two ge-
ographical points, this reading comforts those who favor Cangrande della Scala
(who played host to Dante in his exile and to whom the poet dedicates the *Par-
adiso*) as Veltro.

However, Giorgio Petrocchi's critical edition of the text, which we follow, spells
both instances of *feltro* (the word seems to have been suggested by the difficult
rhyme with the rare words *veltro* and *peltro*) with a lowercase letter. In this case, *fel-
tro* (sometimes translated as "felt") could be the name of an inferior grade of cloth
and indicate someone of humble origins born between wretched sheets. (This
would fit Christ, except that Christ has already been born.) Finally, many of the
early scholiasts take the phrase to mean "between one Heaven and another," refer-
ring to the astrological inevitability of the Redeemer's coming. However this may
be, what we are left with is Dante's severe judgment on contemporary Italy and in-
deed of the known world (of which his *Inferno* is a faithful reflection) and his pug-
nacious faith in a coming palingenesis.

107–8   Camilla, Turnus, Nisus, and Euryalus are characters in the *Aeneid* (the
first two were natives of Latium, which was conquered by the Trojans; the second
two were casualties among the Trojan victors), all of whom died in battle to estab-
lish Rome and its divinely ordained empire. The coupling in death of the winners
and the losers is Virgilian (*sunt lacrimae rerum,* "here are the tears of the ages," *Aen.*
I.461) and also typically Dantesque. The concreteness of their names gives weight
to the otherwise vague prophecy.

114–23   *to an eternal place*   The first stage of Dante's journey, covered in the
Inferno, will be through Hell, where the damned are punished for all eternity. The
second stage, where he will see "the souls who are content / to stay in the fire"
will be through the temporal realm of Purgatory, whose souls welcome the pains
of expiation because they know that when they have paid for their aberrations,
they will be saved. The third stage, described in the *Paradiso,* will be among the
saints, where Virgil can no longer guide him.

122   *a soul more worthy than I*   The soul of Beatrice, Dante's guide through
the heavens, whom he will meet again in the Earthly Paradise at the top of the
mountain of Purgatory.

124   *the Emperor who reigns on high*   God is the Emperor of "that Rome of
which Christ is a Roman" (*Pg.* XXXII.102). The designation of God as Emperor

is deliberately chosen to complement the role of the earthly emperor, whom Dante (as he will argue in his *Monarchia*) considers as essential as the papacy for the world's salvation. In a negative parallel, Satan or Dis is defined in XXXIV.28 as "the emperor of the world of pain."

134   *Saint Peter's gate*   The gate of Purgatory, through which Dante will pass in *Pg.* IX.

Canto II

1–6   *Day was departing*   Night is falling. A whole day has passed since the dawn broke in Canto I. The elegiac note of these opening lines and the wakefulness and solitariness of the protagonist echo a number of similar moments in the *Aeneid* (III.147, IV.522–31, VIII.26–30, IX.224–28). It is appropriate that the descent into Hell should commence in darkness. The ascent of the mountain of Purgatory will begin instead at dawn, and the flight to Paradise at high noon.

6   *unerring memory*   The role of memory will become far more problematic in the *Paradiso,* where the vision requires a gradual expansion of the protagonist's human capacities. So great indeed that, when he attempts to describe what he saw and understood, memory and natural language—as he constantly reminds us—fail him.

13   *Silvius' father, Aeneas*   The exiled Trojan hero and founder of Rome who gives his name to Virgil's *Aeneid,* Aeneas was the son of Anchises, and, in Book VI of the *Aeneid,* Virgil describes his journey to the Underworld to consult his dead father's shade regarding his future destiny and that of Rome. Dante incorporates many features of Virgil's imagined Underworld in his own description of Hell. Among the events prophesied by Anchises was the birth of Aeneas' last son Silvius (or Sylvius) Posthumus, king and father of kings, to be born to Aeneas' Italian second wife Lavinia after Aeneas' death.

15   *with all his senses intact*   Like Dante, and unlike Saint Paul, for whom the question is problematic, Aeneas visited the Underworld, including both Tartarus and the Elysian Fields, in the flesh (*Aen.* VI.290–94, 413–14). As he enters the sphere of the Moon in Paradise, Dante will allow himself to wonder if his body is still with him (*Pd.* II.37–42).

16   *evil's constant Adversary*   God. For Dante, Aeneas' journey was sanctioned, not by "the false and lying gods" (I.72), but by the Christian God Himself. In Dante's ideology, the Roman Empire and the *pax romana* (the peace Rome's universal domination brought to the world) were part of God's plan to redeem humankind. Under Augustus' adoptive son Tiberius Julius Caesar, Jesus Christ would be sacrificed for our sins. Furthermore, Rome would subsequently become the holy city of Christianity and the seat of the papacy.

24 *Saint Peter's successor* Christ confided the papal keys to Peter, the first pope. The current wearer of the "mantles of popes," in the year 1300, was Benedetto Caetani, pope under the name of Boniface VIII from 1294 to 1303. Dante, we will learn, distinguishing between *sedem* and *sedentem* ("the seat" and "the sitter"), recognized the institution but questioned the performance of the incumbent.

28 *Paul, the Chosen Vessel* Saul, converted on the road to Damascus, who became Paul, the apostle to the Gentiles and author of the Pauline Epistles, defined in the Acts of the Apostles as a *vas electionis* ("a vessel of election," Acts 9:15). In 2 Cor. 12:2–4, Saint Paul claimed to have been caught up into the third heaven: "I know a man in Christ above fourteen years ago (whether in the body, I know not, or out of the body, I know not; God knoweth), such a one caught up to the third heaven. And I know such a man (whether in the body, or out of the body, I know not: God knoweth) that he was caught up into paradise, and heard secret words, which it is not granted to man to utter."

The apocryphal fifth- or sixth-century Latin *Visio sancti Pauli* has Paul also visiting Hell. Dante's own journey will eventually take him, in the *Paradiso,* through the nine heavens of Paradise and to the all-encompassing Empyrean heaven.

32 *I am not Aeneas, I am not Paul* What at first looks like modesty is in fact an invitation to compare Dante to his illustrious precursors and one of the most extreme statements of the poet's conviction that he, like Aeneas and Paul, has been specially chosen by God for this prophetic visionary mission.

In the *Purgatorio,* in the Earthly Paradise, the refound Beatrice tells Dante that he must set down what he has witnessed "in favor of the world that lives in sin" (*Pg.* XXXII.103); whereas, in the *Paradiso,* his ancestor the imperially knighted Cacciaguida (a stand-in for Aeneas' prophetic father Anchises) will similarly urge the poet to record what he has seen and will see ("Nevertheless, setting aside all falsehood, / make manifest your entire vision," *Pd.* XVII.127–28). The poet, incidentally, as previously noted placed Virgil's *Aeneid* alongside Holy Scripture. The events it related led in the fullness of time to the founding of Rome and to the Roman Empire, destined by God in Dante's view to impose peace upon the world (the *pax romana* again), in preparation for the coming of the Messiah.

35 *I fear it may be madness* In his Italian, Dante uses the adjective *folle,* a key word that will recur whenever Dante refers to overreaching hubris. A prime example will be the "mad run" (*folle volo*) of Ulysses in XXVI.125.

52 *Limbo* Limbo is the First circle of Dante's Hell, described in Canto IV. It is where Virgil is condemned to spend eternity, along with the unbaptized infants and the other pre-Christian worthies who lived just lives but did not have the opportunity to know the true faith. There, they are "neither joyful nor sad" (IV.84), without physical pain but with a gnawing sense of loss for the salvation they never knew ("we live in longing without any hope," IV.42).

52   *a Lady*   The description of the Lady immediately evokes the atmosphere of Dante's earliest narrative work, the *Vita nuova* (*New Life*), and the lyric manner of the poet's youth, which Dante will later characterize as his *dolce stil novo* ("sweet new style," *Pg.* XXIV.57).

58   *O courteous spirit of Mantua*   As we saw in Canto I, the historical Virgil was born near Mantua in Lombardy. Dante's Virgil will discourse on the origins of Mantua in Canto XX.

70   *Beatrice*   This is the first appearance in the poem of the Florentine woman Dante loved as a young man (though she has been referred to obliquely). Dante had already told the story of this epiphanic love in his *Vita nuova*. Dead now for ten years, Beatrice descends to Virgil from her place in Paradise. As Virgil hinted in I.122–23, she will join Dante again on the top of the mountain of Purgatory and be his guide through Paradise, where Dante will finally see her enthroned in glory in the Empyrean heaven.

Beatrice, incidentally, is a meaningful name: "she who brings bliss, she who makes blessed." More than her real name, it may in fact be what the Provençal poets called a *senhal,* a name given her by the poet to mask her contingent identity and reveal her essence. In his autobiographical *Vita nuova,* it is suggested that her role in Dante's life was providential, that she was Dante's personal savior.

78   *the heaven of least circumference*   The heavenly sphere of the Moon. In Dante's geocentric universe, the central Earth is encircled by nine moving heavenly spheres of increasing circumference, and the whole is enclosed within the still and infinite Empyrean heaven. The sphere of the Moon is the innermost and closest to the Earth. Just as Virgil symbolizes the reach and limitations of human reason, Beatrice signifies Divine Revelation, through which humankind may transcend the limits of the sublunar world.

94   *a gracious Lady*   The Virgin Mary, mother of Jesus Christ. Neither Mary nor Christ are directly named anywhere in the *Inferno.*

97   *Lucy*   Saint Lucy, a fourth-century Syracusan martyr. Blinded by her persecutors and with a name that recalls the Latin word for light (*lux, lucis*), she is an object of particular devotion for those who have problems with their eyesight. She will return in person to assist Dante in *Purgatorio* IX.

102   *venerable Rachel*   The biblical Rachel, daughter of Laban and second wife of Jacob. For medieval exegetes, Rachel and her elder sister Leah (who was Jacob's first wife and bore him three times as many children) symbolized, respectively, the contemplative and the active lives. Beatrice's place in Paradise is next to Rachel, who sits in the Heavenly Rose below Mary and Eve among the Hebrews who believed in Christ to come (*Pd.* XXXII).

108   *in the flood that outswells even the sea*   The flood of sin, more insidious to the soul than the sea is to the body. The reader may recall the simile in I.22–24, where the narrator compares his momentary deliverance from the dark wood to

the fearful relief of a survivor who has escaped from a storm at sea and looks back from the shore at the perilous waves.

Canto III

5–6 *DIVINE POWER / SUPREME WISDOM, AND LOVE PRIMOR-DIAL* The attributes of the Holy Trinity: Father, Son, and Holy Spirit (alluded to in I.104, "on wisdom, on love, and on virtue"). Hell was created before the contingent world as a prison for Lucifer and the rebellious angels.

8 *SAVE THOSE ETERNAL* Before He created Hell, God created the incorruptible heavens, the angels, primal matter, and the elements.

14–15 *All fear and doubt* Virgil's words echo those of the Cumaean Sibyl to Aeneas as they prepared to enter the Underworld: "Now / is the time for courage and a heart of iron" (*Aen.* VI.261).

18 *the good of the intellect* The Beatific Vision of God's truth, enjoyed by the blessed in Paradise, but from which the damned are forever excluded.

36 *avoiding infamy but unworthy of praise* We are in the Vestibule, or Anteroom, of Hell. Here the pusillanimous, the despicable inmates who avoided all commitment to either good or evil, are punished with a parody of choice as they race after meaningless banners. This is the first instance of what Dante calls the "counterpass," by which the punishment, by reifying a moral condition, fits the crime. In contemning the uncommitted, Dante probably has in mind the words of Apoc. 3:15–16: "I know thy works, that thou art neither cold, nor hot. I would thou wert cold, or hot. But because thou art lukewarm, and neither cold, nor hot, I will begin to vomit thee out of my mouth."

60 *the Great Refusal* Dante does not consider him worth naming, but most commentators have identified this shade as Pope Celestine V. He was elected in July 1294 and renounced the papacy five months later, leaving the way open for the succession of Dante's bête noire Boniface VIII. The identification is moot, however, as the monk Pietro da Morrone lived an exemplary life of prayer and fasting and was canonized in 1313. In any case, Dante's point is that to identify the Great Refuser he has in mind would be to give him a recognition he does not deserve.

78 *Acheron* The River of Sorrow, which must be crossed in Charon's boat to reach the realm of the dead, was a feature of the Underworld in both the *Odyssey* and the *Aeneid*. Dante's description of Charon, with his "shriveled white hair" (line 83) and his eyes "set in wheels of fire" (line 98), is reminiscent of Virgil's. The dead souls who gather on the shore of the river will be sentenced to their appropriate circles by the judge Minos in Canto V.

91–93 *By another way* This may be the first hint that Dante thinks of himself as one of the Saved. We will learn at the beginning of the *Purgatorio* that the souls who do not go to Hell gather at the estuary of the Tiber River to be ferried over the hemisphere of water to the island mountain of Purgatory (which they must climb in order to reach Paradise) in a "lighter craft," propelled by the wings of an angel.

95   *This is willed*   The memorable formula by which Virgil silences Charon will be repeated identically before Minos (V.23–24), and a variant will be used to confound Plutus (VII.11–12). Interestingly, the formula was quoted in a criminal register compiled in Bologna in 1317 and is the earliest testimony to the rapid diffusion of the text of the *Inferno*.

112   *As leaves in autumn*   The source of the simile is *Aen.* VI.309–10: "As many as leaves that fall in the woods / at autumn's first frost."

127   *No virtuous soul*   See *Aen.* VI.563–64: "No virtuous soul may ever set foot / on this accursed threshold." The implication seems to be that Dante is a "virtuous soul."

131   *quaked so fearfully*   This earthquake is presumably a sign of divine intervention. Dante faints in fact and comes to his senses in the next canto on the other side of the river.

Canto IV

24   *The First Circle*   The first of the nine circles of Hell is Limbo (the term means "fringe, edge, or margin"), where the punishment is not physical but of spiritual privation. This is the circle from which the shade of Virgil has been summoned to be the pilgrim's guide.

52   *I was new to this state*   Virgil, who died in 19 B.C.E., had been in Limbo fifty-two years when Christ died on the cross in 33 C.E., only to rise again from the dead, as Christians believe, three days later.

53   *a powerful being descend*   The reference is to the so-called Harrowing of Hell—the descent of the risen Christ to free the dead who had believed in His future coming, declared an article of faith by the Lateran Council of 1215—as seen from the "naive" viewpoint of a pagan shade who died too soon to choose Christ as his Savior.

55   *our first parent's shade*   the soul of Adam, the father of humankind.

59   *Israel*   Jacob was called Israel ("Struggle with God") after he wrestled with the angel in Peniel (Gen. 32:29). His father was Isaac. Jacob had twelve sons, six by his first wife Leah, two by his second wife Rachel, and the remaining four by the handmaidens Bilhah and Zilpah. From these sons were descended the twelve tribes of Israel.

60   *for whom he did so much*   Jacob served Rachel's father, Laban, for seven years with the promise of her hand in marriage, but Laban substituted his firstborn daughter, Leah, compelling Jacob to serve seven more years to win Rachel.

88   *Homer*   The author of the exemplary Greek epics, the *Iliad* and the *Odyssey*, which may date back to the eighth century B.C.E. Dante, who had no Greek, knew Homer and his reputation only by hearsay, from references in the Latin authors he had studied. Nevertheless, he took on faith the superiority of "that lord of highest poetry" (line 95). In Canto XXVI, Dante will encounter Odysseus, the hero of the *Odyssey*, under his Latin name of Ulysses (*Ulixes*).

89   *Horace, the satirist*   The Latin poet Quintus Horatius Flaccus (65–8 B.C.E.) was known in the Middle Ages above all as a satirist. Dante was also familiar with his *Art of Poetry* but apparently did not know his lyric poetry, the *Odes* and *Epodes*.

90   *Ovid*   Dante draws on the author of the *Metamorphoses*, Publius Ovidius Naso (43 B.C.E.–17/18 C.E.), more frequently than on any other poet. The *Metamorphoses* (hereinafter abbreviated *Meta.*) is a brilliantly narrated compendium of ancient mythology.

90   *Lucan*   Of the vast literary production of Marcus Annaeus Lucanus (39–65 C.E.), only the unfinished epic poem on the civil war between Julius Caesar and Pompey, variously titled *Bellum civile* (*Civil War*), *De bello civili,* and *Pharsalia,* has survived. Lucan was forced to commit suicide by opening his veins at the age of twenty-six, having been part of a failed conspiracy against his former friend Nero. Dante knew Lucan's *Civil War* intimately and frequently refers to it.

102   *So that I was sixth*   Though he is writing in Italian and not in Greek or Latin, Dante has no hesitation in placing himself among the classics. He is echoing a line of Ovid's (*Tristia* IV.x.54, *quartus ab his serie temporis ipse fui,* "I myself was the fourth after them in order of time"). Ovid had placed himself fourth in a line of elegiac poets after Cornelius Gallus, Albius Tibullus, and Sextus Propertius. Another poet much admired by Dante but not mentioned at this juncture is Publius Papinius Statius (45–96 C.E.), author of the *Thebaid,* the *Sylvae,* and the unfinished *Achilleid.* Dante and Virgil will in fact meet him in *Pg.* XXI just as he is completing his 1,204–year sentence. His exchange with Virgil in *Pg.* XXII will add a score of names, some historical, some mythological, to the catalog of Virtuous Pagans.

106–14   *a noble castle*   The oasis of light, the castle, and its noble tenants "with grave and solemn eyes / and great authority in their looks" are Dante's elegiac tribute to pre-Christian and extra-Christian achievement. A Stoic atmosphere prevails, and the fact that Christian and Stoic morality are so close makes their exclusion from grace all the more poignant. It is significant that the ethical writings of at least two of the excluded, Aristotle and Cicero, are so present in Virgil's breakdown of the taxonomy of Hell in Canto XI.

121   *Electra*   Daughter of Atlas, and mother, by Jove (Zeus), of Dardanus, the mythical founder of Troy. The catalog of the exemplary "spirits of the great" that follows mixes mythological, legendary, and historical figures. Furthermore, it is partisan, since no Greek heroes are mentioned, only Trojans and Romans. Following a medieval legend, the great Greek warrior Achilles is somewhat ignominiously

placed among those who died for lust in the following canto, Canto V, whereas Ulysses (Odysseus) will appear among the fraudulent counselors in Canto XXVI.

122   *Aeneas and Hector*   Aeneas, the legendary hero celebrated in the *Aeneid* as the founder of Rome, appeared in the *Iliad* as a defender of doomed Troy. The *Aeneid* narrates his tribulations after Troy's fall. Hector, another Trojan hero, was a cousin of Aeneas. He was killed in a final fated duel with the Greek hero Achilles.

123   *Caesar*   Julius Caesar (103–44 B.C.E.), the conqueror of Gaul, one of Rome's great generals, and the author of literary accounts of his campaigns. He subsequently fought and won the civil war against Pompey, defeating him at Pharsalus in 48 B.C.E. Dante considered Caesar rather than his adopted great-nephew Octavian Augustus the first Roman emperor.

124   *Camilla and Penthesilea*   Camilla, a female warrior in the *Aeneid*, was mentioned in I.107 as having laid down her life for the future Rome. Penthesilea, the queen of the Amazons and allied with the Trojans, was slain beneath the walls of Troy by Achilles. These two warrior women who died in battle were remembered together in *Aen.* XI.661–62, where Penthesilea is referred to as "daughter of Mars."

125   *King Latinus*   King of Latium, the area near the river Tiber, when Aeneas disembarked there. His people, the aboriginal inhabitants of the region, were the Latini (whence the name of the Latin language). After giving his daughter Lavinia in marriage to the widower Aeneas, Latinus allowed his queen Amata and the Rutilian Turnus, Aeneas' adversary and Lavinia's former suitor, to foment war against Aeneas and the Trojans. Latinus survived the Latin defeat and made peace with Aeneas.

126   *Lavinia*   The second wife of Aeneas and mother of his son Silvius, in whom the Latins and the Trojans were united.

127   *that Brutus who drove out Tarquin*   Lucius Junius Brutus, the first consul of the Roman Republic, who, according to tradition, defeated Tarquin (not to be confused with Marcus Junius Brutus, a former rival then an ally of Julius Caesar, who nevertheless joined with Cassius in his assassination. Readers of Shakespeare will recall Caesar's Latin cry of surprise at his betrayal, "*Et tu, Brute?* [You too, Brutus?]," *Julius Caesar* III.i.77; see note to XXXIV.65).

128   *Lucretia, Julia, Marcia, and Cornelia*   Four women who were exemplary of Roman Republican virtues. Lucretia, the wife of Collatinus, committed suicide to escape dishonor after being raped by Sextus, the son of Tarquin the Proud, last of the seven kings of Rome (she is the subject of Shakespeare's poem *The Rape of Lucrece*). Julia was the daughter of Julius Caesar and the wife of Pompey the Great, who would become her father's enemy in the civil war. Marcia was the wife of Cato the Younger of Utica, whose exemplary virtues, sung by Lucan in his *Civil War,* combined with his privileged position in Virgil's Avernus or Underworld, will lead Dante to appoint him guardian of the shores of Purgatory. Cornelia, daugh-

ter of Scipio Africanus, conqueror of the Carthaginians, was the proud mother of the successful but ill-fated Gracchi brothers; however, Dante may be referring to another Cornelia, the second wife of Pompey, mentioned along with Marcia by Lucan (*Civil War* II.344–49).

129 *Saladin* Salah ad-Din (1138–1193 C.E.), the Muslim sultan of Egypt, Syria, and Mesopotamia, was proverbial in the Middle Ages for his courtesy, honor, and valor, chivalric values on which Dante set a high premium (see XVI.67).

131 *the master of those who know* Aristotle (384–322 B.C.E.), Greek philosopher, tutor to Alexander the Great, and founder of the "Peripatetic School" of Athens, revered by Dante and his contemporaries. The entire system of Dante's Hell, expounded by Virgil in Canto XI, is based in large part on Aristotle's *Nicomachean Ethics* (XI.80). Maria Corti has shown that Dante studied the *Ethics* in the Latin translation of English philosopher Robert Grosseteste, with a commentary by Albertus Magnus (Maria Corti, *La felicità mentale. Nuove prospettive per Dante e Cavalcanti,* Turin: Einaudi, 1983, pp. 94–123). The *Summa Theologiae* of Albertus' pupil Saint Thomas Aquinas, and indeed medieval scholastic philosophy in general, aimed at reconciling Aristotelian thought and Christian doctrine.

134 *Socrates, and Plato* The two great Athenian philosophers whose thought, according to the Roman thinker Marcus Tullius Cicero (the "Tully" of line 141), followed by Dante in his *Convivio* (IV.vi.13–15), Aristotle perfected. What we know of Socrates, who left no writings, we know from his disciples, especially Plato. Dante's knowledge of Plato was likewise indirect, though an opinion expressed in his *Timaeus* is refuted in *Pd*. IV.22–24. In *Pg*. III.43, in another melancholy evocation of the fate of those in Limbo, Virgil singles out the names of Plato and Aristotle as representative of all the others.

136–38 *Anaxagoras, etc.* Dante did not have first-hand knowledge of the works of these pre-Socratic thinkers, whom he must have encountered either in the *Metaphysics* of Aristotle (who cites them to rebut their theories) or in Cicero. Dante's characterization of Democritus is a direct quotation from Saint Thomas (*Summa Theologiae* I.q.22, a.2). Anaxagoras, Democritus, Zeno, Orpheus, and Galen are all mentioned in Dante's *Convivio*.

140 *Dioscorides, etc.* Dioscorides was the first-century C.E. author of *De re medica,* a sort of medical, botanical, and pharmaceutical encyclopedia, which discusses the medicinal use of plants. His name belongs with those of the scientists and mathematicians in the next tercet. Orpheus and Linus were mythical poets of ancient Greece, and according to some accounts they were brothers and sons of Apollo. They are remembered together in Virgil's Fourth Eclogue (which was read in the Christian Middle Ages as a prophecy of Christ's birth), as well as by Saint Augustine and Saint Thomas Aquinas as poet–theologians. Orpheus' journey to the Underworld to recover his wife Eurydice is narrated by Ovid in *Meta*. X.1–85.

141   *Cicero, etc.*   In the *Convivio,* Dante tells us that his love for philosophy was sparked by his reading of Cicero's *De amicitia* and Boethius' *De consolatione Philosophiae.* Lucius Annaeus Seneca (5 B.C.E.–65 C.E.) was the tutor of Nero. Suspected of conspiracy against his former pupil, he was compelled, like the poet Lucan, to commit suicide. Seneca was the author of *Dialogues* and moral treatises inspired by the Stoic philosophy but is perhaps more famous for his sanguinary tragedies, which Dante also knew.

142–44   *Euclid, etc.*   Euclid was the third-century B.C.E. founder of geometry. Ptolemy was a second-century C.E. mathematician and astronomer, whose geocentric system, followed by Dante, was later overturned by Copernicus (1473–1543) and Galileo (1564–1642). Hippocrates (460–370 B.C.E.) was the most famous medical doctor of antiquity, for whom the Hippocratic oath is named, and the author of the *Aphorisms,* a widely studied medical textbook. Galen of Pergamum (129–201 C.E.) was the chief authority on medicine in the Middle Ages. Considered to be the founder of experimental medicine, he discovered the circulation of the blood. Avicenna (Ibn-Sina, 980–1037 C.E.) and Averroës (Ibn-Rushd, 1126–1198 C.E.) were also doctors and were the two great Arab commentators of Aristotle. Many of Averroës' positions were condemned by the Catholic Church. Dante places his Christian follower, Paris theologian Siger of Brabant (c. 1225–1283), next to Thomas Aquinas (1225–1274) in Paradise (*Pd.* X.133–38).

Canto V

4   *Minos*   In Greek and Roman mythology, Minos, the son of Jove (Zeus) and Europa, was a wise and severe lawgiver and ancient king of Crete. Accordingly, Homer and Virgil made Minos, along with his brother Rhadamanthus and half brother Aeacus, one of the judges in the Underworld. Dante, who in the wording of his presentation conflates Virgil's Minos with his Rhadamanthus, takes away his human dignity, gives him a tail, and makes him into a grotesque medieval hybrid, half-man, half-beast, like all of the mythological guardians of all of the other circles.

20   *the gate's wide mouth*   The easiness of the way to Hell is proverbial both in classical and biblical literature. We find it in Virgil *(facilis descensus Averno* ["the road down / to Avernus is easy"], *Aen.* VI.126) and in Matt. 7:13 ("wide is the gate, and broad is the way that leadeth to destruction").

31   *an infernal wind that never rests*   The "counterpass," or punishment that fits the crime, is in this case a concretization of the common metaphor of the winds of passion. Just as the sinners gave in too readily, submitting their reason to their impetuous desires, so now they are borne willy-nilly on the hellish whirlwind.

34   *the shattered precipice*   Dante does not elaborate on this topographical indication at this point, but in XII.31–45 Virgil will explain a similar avalanche as having been caused by the earthquake that accompanied Christ's death on the cross

(Matt. 27:51). Charles S. Singleton has suggested that the adulterous lovers may be reacting to this reminder of the supreme sacrifice Christ made, out of disinterested love for humanity, so different from the profane love of Francesca and Paolo.

38–39   *who put rational thought below carnal desire*   In his earliest work, the *Vita nuova,* Dante, speaking of his own love for Beatrice, declared that her image "was of such very noble virtue that at no time did it permit Love to govern me without the faithful counsel of reason" (II.10).

40   *flocks of starlings*   You will never see a dense, intricately wheeling flock of starlings on the wing again without thinking of the flight of these countless shades. The difference is that the starlings are self-propelled, whereas Dante's lustful adulterers (who surrendered themselves morally to the winds of passion) are now carried impotently on the wind.

46   *cranes*   Cranes, on the other hand, fly in single file and cry out plaintively as they fly. The value of this second simile is above all acoustic.

58   *Semiramis*   Wife and successor of Assyrian ruler Ninus, mythical founder of Nineveh and the Babylonian Empire, her name (though Dante could not have known it) means "she who comes from the doves." The poet closely follows fifth-century historian Paulus Orosius in accusing her of passing laws to legitimize her incestuous love for her son Ninyas. Dante appears to confuse Mesopotamian Babylon with another Babylon located in Egypt (possibly Memphis). Boccaccio, too, in his *Decameron* identifies the Mameluke sultan of Egypt as "the Sultan of Babylon."

61–62   *she who cut short her own life / for love*   This refers to Dido or Elissa, queen of Tyre and later, after the death of her husband Sychaeus, of Carthage. She will be mentioned by name in line 85. When Aeneas was shipwrecked near Carthage, Dido offered him hospitality, fell in love with him, and became his lover, breaking her vow to remain true to her husband's ashes ("I have not kept my vow to Sychaeus' ashes," *Aen.* IV.552). Jove commanded Aeneas to leave Carthage and sail for Italy, which, ever respectful of his duty (his dutifulness is epitomized in the standard epithet *pius,* which habitually precedes his name), Aeneas did. Dido had a funeral pyre built on the shore, stabbed herself with a Trojan blade, and immolated her body as Aeneas' ships disappeared on the horizon. Medieval readers read the story as an edifying illustration of the victory of reason (Aeneas) over desire or passion (Dido). Later in the *Aeneid,* Aeneas will meet and address the shade of Phoenician Dido in Avernus, but she will not reply (*Aen.* VI.450–76).

63   *Cleopatra*   The historical queen of Egypt who reigned from 51 to 30 B.C.E., mistress of Caesar and Mark Antony. So as not to be captured by Octavian, she committed suicide, allowing herself to be bitten by a poisonous asp after Antony's death in the battle of Actium.

64   *Helen*   The legendary wife of Menelaus, king of Sparta, and "the face that launched a thousand ships / And burnt the topless towers of Ilium" (Christopher

Marlowe, *Doctor Faustus* V.i.97–98). Her abduction by Paris, son of King Priam, was the occasion for the ten-year Trojan War.

65   *Achilles*   According to an independent legend, reported in Servius' fourth-century commentary on the *Aeneid* and given wide diffusion by the medieval French *Roman de Troie* by Benoît de Saint-Maure, Achilles fell in love with Polyxena, a daughter of Priam not mentioned in the *Iliad,* and agreed for her sake to betray the Greek cause. He was, however, killed in an ambush by Polyxena's brother Paris. In his *Achilleid,* the late Roman poet Statius (45–96 C.E.), whom Dante makes a Christian (converted indeed by his reading of Virgil) and places in Purgatory, narrates how Achilles, whose death at Troy had been foretold, took refuge disguised as a girl at the court of Lycomedes, king of Scyros, where he fell in love with and married the king's daughter Deidamia. Dante refers explicitly to this second legend in XXVI.62.

67   *Tristan*   A hero of medieval romance, the best known of King Arthur's knights after Lancelot (whose written history will be instrumental in the downfall of Francesca and Paolo; see note to line 74). The nephew of King Mark of Cornwall, Tristan fell in love with his uncle's wife, Iseult, after they had unknowingly drunk a love potion together. In addition to being adulterous, their love also betrayed Tristan's faith as Mark's kinsman and vassal. From Dante's point of view, all of these, rather than great love stories, are tales of incest, adultery, and betrayal.

74   *those two*   The two spirits, inseparable in death, to whom the pilgrim is especially attracted are two of his contemporaries, whose story he immediately recognizes (in line 116, he addresses Francesca by name without her having given it). They are Paolo, brother of Gianciotto Malatesta, lord of Rimini, and the latter's wife, Francesca, daughter of Guido da Polenta, lord of Ravenna. Paolo was Captain of the People in Florence between 1282 and 1283, and Dante, who was eighteen at the time, may have known him. The exemplary story Francesca will tell is not recorded in any of the contemporary chronicles. We only have Francesca's (and Dante's) word for it. Boccaccio, in his commentary on this canto, seems to embroider on Dante's account, adding a number of melodramatic details he could easily have made up.

82–87   *As doves summoned by their own desire*   With the affecting simile of the doves, birds sacred to Venus (the third ornithological simile in the canto, reminiscent this time of one of Virgil's extended similes, *Aen.* V.213–17), Dante appears to be stacking the deck in the lovers' favor.

92   *peace*   The word will occur again in line 99. Peace is precisely what these storm-tossed souls, carried on the infernal blast, "without hope of comfort or even lesser pain / without hope of repose forevermore" (44–45), hopelessly long for.

100   *Love, which kindles quickly in the gentle heart*   Francesca is quoting the Bolognese poet Guido Guinizzelli, hailed by Dante in *Pg.* XXVI.97–99 as the founder of the *dolce stil novo* and "my / father and of others better than me who

ever / used sweet and delightful rhymes of love." Guinizzelli is the author of an important doctrinal poem or *canzone* that begins almost with these exact words, asserting that love repairs to the gentle heart as naturally as the bird repairs to the green wood. Dante himself wrote and included in Chapter XX of his *Vita nuova* a sonnet that begins "Love and the gentle heart are one and the same thing." The medieval Provençal theory of Courtly Love (expounded in detail in Andreas Cappellanus' *De Amore*), to which the young Dante and the other poets of the *dolce stil novo* school subscribed, presented itself as a virtuous circle. True nobility of soul is demonstrated by the ability to love truly, and the ability to love truly is the source of true nobility of soul. We may note, in Francesca's peroration, the rhetorical figure of anaphora or symmetrical repetition, by which each of the three successive tercets of her speech (itself a rhetorical syllogism) begin with the word "Love." Furthermore, each time it appears (including in line 119, where the pilgrim himself, playing along or accepting Francesca's elegant literary exculpation, uses it), "Love" is personified—an agent. Love is from the start the one in charge. Francesca and Paolo, she is saying, are simply *carried away*. There is an irony in the Italian text that the translation cannot render—in line 106, the apparently beneficent agent *Amor* ("Love") leads Francesca and Paolo to *unA MORte* ("one death," a phrase that in Italian contains the two syllables of the word *amor*). "If you wish to know what kind of love it is, see where it leads," said Saint Augustine.

107   *Caina*   The first of the four divisions of the frozen lake of Cocytus, the lowest circle of Hell, where the traitors are punished (see Canto XXXII). Named after Cain, who slew his brother Abel (Gen. 4:1–16), it is reserved for traitors to their own kin. Francesca's husband, Gianciotto, who murdered the adulterous couple, is destined to end up there.

121–23   *There is no greater sorrow / than to recall a time of happiness*   Francesca is quoting again. The source of this reflection is Severinus Boethius' *Consolation of Philosophy* (II.4.2): "In moments of adversity, having been happy is the most excruciating form of pain."

124–26   *But if you have so great a desire / to learn*   These lines echo the opening lines of Book II of the *Aeneid*, in which Aeneas, at the request of Dido, steels himself to recount the tragic tale of the fall of Troy: "But if you are so passionate to learn / of our misfortunes, to hear a brief account / of Troy's last struggle— although my mind / shudders to remember and recoils in pain, I will begin" (*Aen.* II.3–6). Francesca is preparing to narrate another fall. This same Virgilian subtext will be invoked in the penultimate canto of the *Inferno* by the only speaker in another memorable couple, Count Ugolino, who is inseparably bound to his partner the Archbishop Ruggieri, not by love, as Francesca is to Paolo, but by hate (XXXIII.7–9).

127   *reading for pleasure*   Paolo and Francesca awoke to the fact that their desires were reciprocated while reading a *story*. (They were no doubt reading it aloud,

as was the custom.) No wonder we encountered so many literary characters in the first half of the canto!

128   *Love's mastery over Lancelot*   Love is in charge again. Like Tristan's love for Iseult, the love of Lancelot of the Lake for Guinevere, the wife of his feudal lord King Arthur, violated two taboos—that of marriage (a Christian sacrament) and that of vassalage. The version of the story they were reading was one of the continental sources for Sir Thomas Malory's *Le Morte d'Arthur,* published by William Caxton in 1485 two hundred years after their deaths.

133–36   *how the longed-for smile was kissed . . . / placed his lips on mine*   Francesca has depicted herself and Paolo as passive victims of Love. In these lines, her argument is, so to speak, unmasked. Note how the *passive* literary circumlocution, "how the longed-for smile was kissed" (where the attenuating "smile," which alludes to what Dante, using the technical language of scholastic philosophy, would have dubbed an "accident in a substance"), is transformed into a violently realistic *action:* "Trembling all over, placed his lips on mine" (emphasized in the original by alliteration, *la bocca mi basciò tutto tremante*).

137   *our Galahalt*   Galahalt or Galahault was the go-between who arranged for Lancelot and Guinevere to meet and urged Guinevere to take the initiative. In Paolo and Francesca's case, the book and its author were the panderers. Once again Francesca is shifting the blame, but this time she's right. Dante is an author too, and being an author brings with it a tremendous responsibility. "*Madame Bovary, c'est moi,*" said Gustave Flaubert (regarding another case of a woman who lived to regret confusing literature and life). Francesca's sin could be my fault, reflects Dante, as he faints away.

Canto VI

13   *Cerberus*   In Virgil and Ovid the monster Cerberus was a huge three-headed dog who guarded the entrance to Avernus. Dante recruits him to watch over the souls of the gluttonous, who are punished in this circle. The poet mixes human attributes with his bestial nature to make him more ghoulish and demonic. (In the case of Minos, he had done the opposite, giving animal characteristics to someone who in ancient mythology had a human form.) In the *Aeneid,* to quiet Cerberus, the Sibyl, who was Aeneas' guide, threw him a cake of honey and drugged flour. Here Virgil simply throws fistfuls of dirt into his maw, and the personification of gluttony—no gourmet he—indiscriminately chomps on it.

The canto of the gluttonous is the first in which Dante uses what Italian critics call the "comic" style, choosing a coarse, "cackling" (VII.2), "harsh and grating" (XXXII.1) vocabulary (especially in the rhyme endings) appropriate to the crude subject matter. The poet had developed this register in his experimental poems known as the *rime petrose* ("stony rhymes"), studied by Robert M. Durling and

Ronald L. Martinez (*Time and the Crystal: Studies in Dante's "Rime petrose,"* Berkeley: University of California Press, 1990). The original poems and their English translations can be read in *Dante's Lyric Poetry* (edited and translated by Kenelm Foster and Patrick Boyde, Oxford: Clarendon Press, 1967, vol. 1, pp. 158–75). One thing no translator has yet succeeded in doing is bringing out the three quite different stylistic levels of *Inferno, Purgatorio,* and *Paradiso,* what Gianfranco Contini called Dante's *plurilinguismo* (plurilingualism), which he contrasts with the "*monolinguismo*" (monolingualism) of the fourteenth-century Italian poet Francesco Petrarca (known in English as Francis Petrarch), whose unfailing mellifluousness he contrasts with Dante's omnivorous linguistic span, which ranges from the cacophonously grotesque diction we find in the *Inferno* to the ineffable sublime of the *Paradiso* ("*Saggio di un commento alle correzioni del Petrarca volgare,*" in Gianfranco Contini, *Varianti e altra linguistica,* Turin: Einaudi, 1970, pp. 5–32).

37   *all but one*   This shade will identify himself in line 52 as a certain Ciacco from Florence. He was presumably a real historical personage, and he appears to recognize Dante; but all we know about him is derived from his appearance in this canto. Ciacco is an unusual first name (maybe connected with the French Jacques, maybe, as line 52 suggests, a nickname denoting a swinish nature), but Dante scholars have failed to provide him with a historical last name. Canto VI introduces the political theme, so important in the poem—it will return again, incidentally, with ever widening scope, from Florence to Italy to the Holy Roman Empire, in the sixth cantos of *Purgatorio* and *Paradiso*—for now confined to the politics of Dante's native city.

60   *tell me, if you know*   This is the second shade, not counting his guide Virgil, whom Dante has had the chance to question. In Francesca's case, he had asked about her sin. Here his inquiries, as is customary with visitors to the Underworld, concern the deeper causes of present predicaments, as well as the future. Ciacco will answer Dante's three questions punctually in the order in which they were posed.

61   *the divided town*   Florence, like the other free communes of Tuscany, had a history of political division, first between the rival factions of the Guelphs and the Ghibellines, then, after the *Parte Guelfa* won out, between the White and Black Guelphs (partisans, respectively, of the merchant–industrialist Cerchi and the aristocratic landowning Donati clans).

65   *they will come to blood*   The bloody clash will occur within a month from the date of Dante's journey, on May 1, 1300, when Ricoverino dei Cerchi will have his nose cut off by one of the Donati, bringing to the fore the open rivalry between the two factions. The "rustic party" is the White party led by the Cerchi, who had moved into Florence from the Val di Sieve in the *contado* or surrounding countryside. It was with this faction that Dante was identified. In June 1300, the chief exponents of the Donati clan were exiled and heavy fines imposed.

68   *the other prevail*   The Black Guelphs would prevail at the beginning of 1302, within three solar years from the spring of 1300. Dante would be one of the first to be exiled.

69   *one who now is biding his time*   This is Pope Boniface VIII, who for the time being is playing for time and not taking sides with either of the two "Guelph" (i.e., pro-papal) factions. He will come down on the side of the Blacks in 1301 sending Charles of Valois, the brother of the king of France, to Florence to "restore the peace" by supporting the Donati party. Dante will return to these issues, which are decisive for his biographical future, in a broader historical perspective with Farinata degli Uberti in Canto X and again when he encounters Brunetto Latini in Canto XV.

73   *Two men are just*   Rather than referring to two individuals (Dante and who else?), this statement is generally taken to mean that there are very few just men (impartial men above the fray) in Florence. In Gen. 18:32, God concedes to Abraham that the presence of ten just men would save the corrupt cities of Sodom and Gomorra from destruction, while, in Jer. 5:1, God declares he would pardon Jerusalem for the sake of one man "that executeth judgment and seeketh faith." And see Ezek. 14:13–20, where the Lord declares that of the house of Israel he would spare only three just men, Noah, Daniel, and Job.

74   *Pride, envy, and avarice*   Brunetto Latini will also describe the Florentines as "a people given to envy, greed, and pride" (XV.68). Francesco Mazzoni suggests ("Il canto VI dell'*Inferno*," in *Nuove letture dantesche,* Florence: Le Monnier, 1966, vol. 1, pp. 169–73) that these vices are in fact the opposites of the civic virtues— reverence, justice, and love—championed by Brunetto in his *Li livres dou Tresor* (III.79). Guglielmo Gorni (for whom the leopard stands for envy) is among those who identify these three failings with the three beasts of Canto I (*Dante nella selva,* Parma: Pratiche, 1995).

79–80   *Farinata and Tegghiaio . . . Jacopo Rusticucci, Arrigo, and Mosca*   Except for Arrigo, of whom we hear nothing further, Dante will meet each of these "worthies" in the circles below: Farinata degli Uberti among the heretics in Canto X, Jacopo Rusticucci and Tegghiaio Aldobrandi among the sodomites in Canto XVI, and Mosca dei Lamberti among the sowers of discord in Canto XXVIII. The ingenuous question (which receives an unequivocal answer from Ciacco) indicates that the pilgrim still has a lot to learn.

95   *the sound of the angel's trumpet*   The trumpet that announces the Day of the Last Judgment, when the souls of the dead will be reunited with their resurrected dead bodies to suffer more in Hell and to enjoy greater bliss in Heaven.

106   *your philosophy*   The source of the concept is Saint Thomas Aquinas' commentary on the *De anima* of Aristotle (*lectio* XIV.I.i): "The more perfect the soul is, the greater the perfection it exercises in its different operations." Virgil will use the same possessive adjective in Canto XI when referring Dante to other works by Aristotle, the *Ethics* (XI.80) and the *Physics* (XI.101).

115   *Plutus*   The guardian of the coming circle, the Fourth, in which the avaricious and the prodigal are punished, is Plutus, son of Ceres (Demeter) and Iasion, the personification of wealth. He was depicted as blind, since wealth visits (and quits) good and evil people without distinction.

Canto VII

1   Pape Satàn, pape Satàn aleppe!   "O Satan, O Satan, woe is me!" is how the consensus of commentators interpret this near gibberish. The one recognizable word is the name of Satan, which occurs only here. In XXXI.67, the Giant Nimrod, would-be architect of the Tower of Babel, utters a similarly baffling sequence of syllables, *Raphèl maí amècche zabí almi*. The exhibition of difficult and dissonant double-consonantal rhymes, observed in the note to VI.13, continues in the Italian text of this canto.

8   *hellish wolf*   The guardian of the circle where the complementary sins of avarice and prodigality are punished, Plutus is evidently imagined not with a human but with a wolf's form (see also, in line 15, "cruel beast"), which may recall the ravening she-wolf of cupidity in Canto I. On the fifth terrace of Purgatory, where the Avaricious and the Prodigal are punished, the narrator will exclaim: "Cursed are you, ancient wolf, / who more than all the other beasts find fodder / for your dark hunger without end" (*Pg.* XX.10–12). Dante deplores these two abuses of property in the *Convivio* too: avarice in the canzone *Doglia mi reca ne lo core ardire* and its commentary (*Conv.* IV.xi–xiii), prodigality in *Conv.* IV.xxvii.12–15.

12   *Michael*   The archangel Michael commanded the loyal angels, who thrust down to Hell Lucifer and his rebellious followers (Apoc. 12:7–9).

22   *Charybdis*   The clash of the Tyrrhenian and Ionian seas in the treacherous Strait of Messina off Scylla produced the whirlpool personified by the ancients as the marine monster Charybdis. The dangerous passage is described, for instance, in *Aen.* III.420–23.

27   *rolling along weights that they pushed with their chests*   The punishment is inspired by the myth of Sisyphus, though the scene is infinitely more crowded and confused. Dante's sardonically superior detachment from the twin throngs of the incontinently avid and the incontinently profligate is evidenced by the detailed way he lets his gaze follow their futile "dance" (as well as by the poet's calculated stylistic choice of raucous words already mentioned). He also deliberately refuses to dignify any of these sinners by naming names.

39   *were they all clergy?*   The tonsured are so many that it hardly seems credible to Dante that they should all be ecclesiastics. But there can be no mistake. The rampant venality of the Church's ministers is a theme Dante will return to over and over again.

73–96   *That One whose wisdom transcends all . . . she too turns her sphere and exults in bliss*   With this, the poem's first didactic doctrinal digression, which owes more than a little to Boethius, on a topic Elizabethan poet Edmund Spenser (c.1552–1599) would treat in the "Mutabilitie Cantos" of his *Faerie Queene,* the whole tone and language of the canto change. For the classical world, the goddess Fortune was the cruel, blind, indifferent, and arbitrary dispenser of desirable material possessions. Here there is method in Fortune's madness. On a par with the other angelic intelligences appointed to guide the heavenly spheres and filter down upon the Earth their astrological influences, Fortune is a minister of God, obedient to Divine Providence. Fortune giveth and taketh away, inscrutably, yes, but with a propaedeutic purpose: to educate Christians, as individuals and as nations, to scorn material wealth and to invest instead in virtue.

97   *Now we descend to even greater grief*   The third, narrative panel of the canto's triptych, so to speak, after the description of the punishment of the avaricious and the theological reflection on Fortune, begins here. The stars that were rising when Virgil and Dante set out are sinking: it is midnight, and they must not linger.

101   *a boiling spring*   The spring that forms the Stygian marsh does not rise independently here. We will learn in Canto XIV that the three rivers of Hell—classically designated Acheron, Styx, and Phlegethon—and eventually the frozen lake of Cocytus in the pit of Hell all come from the same source. In the swampy waters of the Styx the wrathful are immersed.

119–125   *make the water at the surface bubble . . . This chant they gurgle deep in their throats*   So far we have encountered lust, gluttony, and avarice, three of the Seven Deadly Sins. Wrath makes four. Since this will prove to be the last circle before we enter the gates of the City of Dis, where the taxonomy changes radically, a number of very respectable commentators, among them some of the earliest and closest to Dante (e.g., the poet's son Pietro Alighieri, Benvenuto da Imola, Giovanni di Serravalle, and Guido da Pisa), would like to slip in the other three—accidia or sloth, envy, and pride—claiming that the proud and the wrathful are both on the surface, while the envious and the slothful are both underwater. At best, I could go along with the sluggish or the slothful, who are complementary to the headlong irascible. A number of modern expositors, however, basing themselves on Aristotle's *Nicomachean Ethics,* are of the opinion that the ones on top are those who were subject to explosive uncontrollable rages and the ones below those whose anger was repressed and smoldering.

Canto VIII

1   *To continue, I would say that well before*   On the strength of this line, Boccaccio, with his fiction writer's taste for complication, hypothesized an interruption in the *Inferno's* composition. According to him, Dante composed the first seven

cantos before his exile and the rest at a later date, after fellow poet Dino Frescobaldi sent him the manuscript of the early cantos, and his current patron Moroello Malaspina insisted that it was worth continuing. This would imply, somewhat improbably, that these initial cantos, in which the broad outlines of the *Comedy* are already evident, were composed before the incomplete *Convivio*, generally considered a philosophical, theological, and political preparation for the poet's magnum opus and written between 1304 and 1307. Boccaccio's *fabula interrupta* theory has been rejected by modern interpreters. That Dante had ambitions for a great work honoring Beatrice is evident from the final chapter (XLII) of the *Vita nuova*, composed around 1294, in which he speaks of a marvelous vision that made him decide not to write any more about her until he could do so more worthily, vowing to devote himself to massive preparation to that end.

8   *What does this signal mean?*   Evidently the tower, a defensive outpost of the Infernal City, is staffed by demons who signal the approach of Dante and Virgil to the city's main garrison.

19   *Phlegyas*   In classical mythology, Phlegyas was the son of Mars and Chryse, condemned to Tartarus for setting fire to the temple of Apollo, who had seduced his daughter Coronis. Phlegyas was glimpsed by Aeneas in the Underworld crying out a warning to study justice and not to scorn the gods, but he had no official demonic role to play as he does here (*Aen.* VI.618–20).

26–27   *only when I stepped in*   Confirmation that Dante travels in bodily form, not just in spirit. Charon's boat also groaned and took in water with the weight of Aeneas (*Aen.* VI.412–14).

32   *a mud-daubed figure*   Filippo Argenti will be identified by name in line 61. Giovanni Boccaccio, who makes him a character in the Seventh Story of the Ninth Day of his *Decameron,* informs us that ungovernable anger was not his only vice and that the name Argenti was a nickname that came from his flamboyant practice of shoeing his horse in silver (*argento*). Because of the staccato animosity of the brief exchange of retorts between Dante and Filippo, commentators have suspected a personal enmity going beyond the fact that Filippo was a Black Guelph and Dante a White. The pilgrim will engage in verbal duels such as this, which seem to owe something to the thrust and parry of the medieval literary tradition of the *tenzone* (from Provençal *tenso*), with a series of characters—Farinata degli Uberti in Canto X, Pope Nicholas III in Canto XIX, and Mosca dei Lamberti in Canto XXVIII. He will also incur Virgil's censure for listening too closely to the squabble between Master Adam and Sinon the Greek in Canto XXX. The back-and-forth of the insulting *tenzone* genre usually involved two participants and challenged the authors' compositional skills in the scurrilous "comical–realistic" register. A *tenzone* in the form of an ongoing exchange of sonnets is extant between Dante and another Florentine, Forese Donati, though its authenticity has sometimes been challenged. The pilgrim's meeting with Forese in *Pg.* XXIII, however, makes much more sense when seen as a palinode or repudiation of that reprehensible exchange.

43–45   *Then he put his arms around my neck . . . blessed is she, the mother who bore you*   Virgil seems to praise Dante for the righteous anger urged by Saint Paul: "Be angry, and sin not. Let not the sun go down upon your anger" (Eph. 4:26). His words are an echo of those of the woman in the Gospels who greeted Christ: "Blessed is the womb that bore thee, and the paps that gave thee suck" (Luke 11:27).

68   *The city called Dis*   In the *Aeneid*, Aeneas and the Sibyl skirt the walls of the City of Dis as they make their way toward Elysium. They do not enter because no virtuous soul may do so (*Aen.* VI.541 et seq.).

69   *great garrison*   These are the rebellious angels. See below: "the angels who fell like rain from Heaven" (line 83).

91   *his own foolish way*   The adjective *folle* occurs again here. We commented on its significance in our note to II.35. The demons consider the pilgrim's journey presumptuous and foolhardy, but the poet has already made sure that we know it has divine approval.

94   *Imagine, Reader*   This is the first of Dante's many direct appeals to his readers, dramatizing the already dramatic situation and involving us in his inner discomfiture. There are seven such apostrophes in the *Inferno* and nineteen in the *Comedy* as a whole. This unexpected opposition, and Virgil's apparent confusion, though he puts a good face on it, seem to take things back to the impasse of Canto I. In fact, just as Virgil providentially appeared to save Dante then, so another more martial deliverer will make his triumphal entrance in the following canto. The atmosphere of foreboding and of a mysterious ritual being enacted will be heightened in IX. 61–63 by yet another metatextual address. Dante's interruptions of the narrative have been studied by Erich Auerbach ("Dante's Addresses to the Reader," *Romance Philology* 7 [1954]: 268–78).

97   *Seven times or more*   There is no call to go back and count the times. Seven is used, as it often is in the Bible, to signify a considerable but indefinite number (see Prov. 24:16, Matt. 18:21, Mark 16:9, and Luke 8:2, 11:26).

124   *There is nothing new in their insolence*   A reference to Christ's Harrowing of Hell when the rebel angels attempted to block the Gate of Hell ("a gate less secret") that the pilgrim and his guide passed through at the opening of Canto III. Mark Musa would see this episode as a figural reenactment of this opposition and a celebration of Christ's victory (*Advent at the Gates: Dante's "Comedy,"* Bloomington: Indiana University Press, 1974).

Canto IX

8   *unless—but so great a Lady*   Virgil is thinking aloud and trying to look more confident than he really feels. The great (i.e., powerful) Lady is presumably Beatrice, whose appeal to Virgil in Limbo was described in II.52–117, though she her-

self was prompted to intervene by Saint Lucy, in her turn alerted by the Virgin Mary. The translation here is slightly interpretive, since the subject of the Italian sentence (*Tal*), rendered as "a Lady," is not in fact gender specific. It could even refer to God Himself, the ultimate sanctioner of Dante's mission. Most commentators are in agreement, however, that Virgil is referring to Beatrice.

16   *Does anyone*   Dante's question, couched in the most general terms, is actually designed to find out if Virgil has been here before and really knows the way. In a moment that foreshadows this one, the Sibyl of Cumae explains to Aeneas that, at the start of her mandate, she was initiated into the mysteries of the Underworld by the goddess Hecate (*Aen.* VI.564–65). Despite the fact that in the Middle Ages magical powers were attributed to Virgil himself (see Domenico Comparetti, *Virgil in the Middle Ages,* translated by E. F. M. Benecke, Princeton, NJ: Princeton University Press, 1997/1895), the association of the poet with the Thessalian witch Erichtho is not found in any classic or medieval source and is apparently Dante's own invention. The second half of Book VI of Lucan's *Civil War* (lines 507 et seq.) describes in gruesome horror-film detail her resuscitation of a mangled soldier's corpse and her conjuring of his soul from the Underworld in order to prophesy the outcome of the battle of Pharsalus.

27   *the circle of Judas*   The fourth and last zone of the lowest circle of Hell, the frozen lake of Cocytus, which houses the souls of the traitors, is named Judecca (in Italian *Giudecca*) after Judas Iscariot, the betrayer of Jesus Christ.

38   *Three hellish Furies*   Daughters of Acheron and Night, the three Furies (Allecto the Unresting, Megaera the Jealous, and Tisiphone the Avenger) are the Latin mythological version of the Greek Erinyes. In the Middle Ages they were interpreted to represent the three modalities of evil: thought, word, and deed (*prava cogitatio, prava elocutio,* and *prava operatio*). They are then the emanation of the world of sin that lies below, inside the walls of the City of Dis. Dante's physical description of them incorporates elements from Virgil, Ovid, and Statius.

44   *queen of eternal lamentation*   Proserpina (Persephone in Greek), daughter of Jove (Zeus) and Ceres (Demeter), was the wife of Dis (Hades), who made her queen of the Underworld. According to the myth, she was abducted while gathering spring flowers on the high plain of Enna in Sicily. In *Pg.* XXVIII, Dante compares Matelda, whom he first sees making a garland in the Earthly Paradise, to the figure of Proserpina before her abduction as described by Ovid in *Meta.* V.391 et seq. As she was queen of the Underworld, the three Furies were in her service.

52   *Medusa*   One of the three Gorgons, daughters, among other strange offspring, of Phorcys and his sister Ceto. Anyone who met their gaze was turned into stone. Though her sisters Sthenno and Euryale were immortal, Medusa, the youngest sister, was mortal and was slain by Perseus who approached her using his shield as a mirror (another version says that the three had only one eye [and one tooth] among them and that Perseus cut off Medusa's head when they were

exchanging it). Perseus subsequently used the head to turn his enemies to stone. Boccaccio interprets Medusa as an allegory of the obstinate persistence in evil that makes the soul indifferent to good and impermeable to Divine Grace.

54   *Theseus*   A legendary king of Athens, one of the great Greek heroes, whose adventures and exploits are too numerous to mention. He is the protagonist of two novels by Mary Renault, *The King Must Die* and *The Bull from the Sea*. Theseus and his friend Pirithous, king of the Lapiths, unsuccessfully invaded the Underworld to rescue Proserpina. Pirithous was devoured by Cerberus, and Theseus was held prisoner until his liberation by Hercules (Heracles).

62   *look well at the teaching*   This is the second of Dante's asides to the reader. It invites us to pay attention to the allegorical meaning (the doctrine beneath the literal veil) of the strange series of events described ("these strange verses").

80   *one who strode along / with dry soles over the swamp*   As we learn in line 85, the deliverer is an angel sent from Heaven. His walking over the waters of the Styx recalls Christ's walking on the waters of the Sea of Galilee.

98   *Your Cerberus*   The twelfth and most dangerous labor of Hercules was to chain the monstrous three-headed dog who guarded the entrance to the Underworld, preventing the living from entering, and drag him out from there (peeling his chin and gullet) onto the Earth. According to another version, followed by Statius in his *Thebaid,* it was Theseus who chained Cerberus. It has been suggested that Dante had in mind Statius' account. In any case, in the Middle Ages, both Hercules and Theseus were seen as *figurae Christi* ("types or figurines of Christ") triumphing over sin.

112–13   *Arles / Pola*   Arles, in Provence, and Pola (present-day Pula), in Croatia, across the Adriatic from Venice, were both renowned as sites of extensive Roman necropolises.

132   *He took a turn to the right*   This, as Dante and Virgil enter the graveyard of the souls of the heretics, is one of the only two instances in the *Inferno*—the other is at XVII.31, where they turn right to mount Geryon, the personification of fraud—when the pilgrim and his guide turn to the right rather than the left, the "sinister" direction symbolic of evil and error. (In Purgatory, they will always keep to the right.) Giovanni Andrea Scartazzini suggests that the allegorical significance of the exception is the need for truth and rectitude in combating the twin falsehoods of heresy and fraud. In his essay "Pilgrim in a Gyre," John Freccero (*Dante: The Poetics of Conversion,* edited and with an introduction by Rachel Jacoff, Cambridge, MA: Harvard University Press, 1986) writes,

> This apparent exception to Dante's rule will help in reality to prove it. Heresy, unlike all other sins in hell, attacks the True, and not the Good; which is to say, in the words of St. Thomas, that its *subiectum* is not *voluntas* but rather *intellectus.* Here is the only instance in Dante's moral system where an error of the speculative intellect is punished in hell, a fact which no pagan, nei-

ther Cicero, nor Aristotle, nor Virgil, would have been able to understand. It is for this reason that the pilgrim must perform his retrograde movement to the right, in order to deal with an aberration of the intellect in the realm of perverted will. (87)

Canto X

11   *Jehoshaphat*   A valley near Jerusalem where, according to the Scriptures (Joel 3:2), at the end of time, on Doomsday, all of humanity will gather for God's Last Judgment, when all souls will be reunited with their resurrected bodies, bringing those in Paradise greater bliss and those in Hell more suffering.

14   *Epicurus*   A Greek philosopher (341–270 B.C.E.), only fragments of whose vast literary output remain. From Diogenes Laertius' *Lives of Eminent Philosophers,* we know that he was a follower of the atomistic materialism of fifth-century B.C.E. thinkers Leucippus and Democritus. The best summary of his ideas is in *De Rerum Natura* by the Roman poet Lucretius (c. 99–55 B.C.E.), a text Dante did not know. What Dante knew of Epicurus he knew through the works of the Roman statesman and orator Cicero. In his philosophical treatise *Convivio* (*The Banquet*), Dante is less judgmental than he is here and cites Epicurus as the leading thinker of one of the three philosophical schools of antiquity (the Epicureans, the Stoics, and the Academics or followers of Plato), all of which were crowned by the thought of the definitive philosopher Aristotle ("the Master of those who know," IV.131). There he states that the Epicureans made the avoidance of pain the supreme goal of life. Here Epicurus is condemned as the inspirer of the Christian heretics "who make the soul die along with the body." The phrase, incidentally, is a direct quotation from Servius' influential fourth-century commentary on the *Aeneid,* which Dante studied. When Anna, endeavoring to quiet her sister Dido's misgivings about her new love for Aeneas, asks her rhetorically "Do you think / any of this matters to ghosts in the grave?" (*Aen.* IV.34), Servius remarks that she is speaking "according to the Epicureans, *who say that the soul dies with the body*" (my italics). The "counterpass," by which the punishment fits the crime, condemns these shades to have their conviction literally enacted: they believed the soul died with the body, so their souls (and, after the Last Judgment, their resurrected bodies too) are entombed for all eternity.

18   *the wish that you withhold*   Virgil, who reads Dante's thoughts, has divined his particular desire to see a famous Florentine worthy who died under suspicion of heresy. Dante had in fact previously questioned Ciacco about his whereabouts in Hell (VI.79).

22   *O Tuscan*   The speaker who interrupts Dante's exchange with Virgil is Florentine aristocrat Farinata degli Uberti, who died in 1264, the year before Dante's birth. Farinata was head of the Ghibelline faction (allies of the emperor)

whereas Dante's ancestors belonged to the rival Guelphs (allies of the pope). Farinata, who did not believe in the soul's immortality and put his faith instead in the permanent ascendency of his party, continues to be obsessed with war and politics. He successfully lures the pilgrim Dante (still not free from contingent earthly attachments) to reenact old rivalries. This episode is discussed as exemplary of Dante's innovative narrative technique in Erich Auerbach's classic *Mimesis: The Representation of Reality in Western Literature* (translated by W. R. Trask from the German, Princeton, NJ: Princeton University Press, 1968/1953, pp. 174–202).

47   *twice I scattered them*   The Guelphs were driven out of Florence for the first time in February 1248, but they returned in January 1251 when they proceeded to drive Farinata and his followers into exile in Siena. In 1260, however, the Ghibelline victory in the battle fought at Montaperti, between Siena and Monte San Savino, led to the second ousting of the Guelphs. What Farinata does not know is that the Ghibellines were expelled once again after his death in 1264. Furthermore, the victory of papal champion Charles of Anjou over the emperor Frederick II's illegitimate son Manfred, who died in the battle of Benevento in 1266, and the subsequent defeat of the Sienese Ghibellines at Colle Val d'Elsa, led to their definitive expulsion from Florence, never to return, in 1267. Before the turn of the century, the Guelphs themselves had split into two factions, the Black Guelphs (partisans of the Donati family) and the White Guelphs (partisans of the Cerchi). As mentioned in the note to VIII.32, Dante sympathized with the latter group.

51   *an art your people have hardly learned*   As we will see, the second (and definitive) expulsion of the Ghibellines is news to Farinata. On this and other occasions, the pilgrim Dante brings information from the world above, unwittingly adding to the affliction of the shades.

52   *another shade*   This second unnamed "Epicurean," who shares Farinata's tomb, is Cavalcante dei Cavalcanti, father of the poet Guido Cavalcanti (a hobbyhorse of Ezra Pound's), whom Dante referred to as his "first friend" in the *Vita nuova*. The tentative appearance and impulsive behavior of the pusillanimous ("weak-souled") elder Cavalcanti provide a powerful contrast to the stoically impassive self-possession of the magnanimous" ("great-souled") Farinata. Whereas the latter's concern is wholly dominated by public political issues, Cavalcanti's mind is ruled by a private fixation—the fate of his son, in whom he had placed his hopes for biological immortality.

58–59   *If it is your genius / by which you journey through this blind prison*   Lacking a supernatural perspective, Cavalcanti assumes that Dante, magus-like, has penetrated the secrets of nature and discovered a way into the world of the dead by himself.

61   *I do not come on my own*   In Canto II, Dante was at pains to stress his reluctance to undertake the journey without a guarantee that it was divinely sanctioned. John Freccero acutely points out that Cavalcanti's is a pagan question, mindful of Ulysses' and Aeneas' journeys to the Underworld, whereas Dante's is a

Christian answer. In terms of a Platonic concept, reinterpreted by the Church Fathers, Cavalcanti sees with the eye of the body, Dante with the eye of the soul ("Ancora sul 'disdegno' di Guido," *Letture classensi* 18 [1989]: 90–91).

68 *Did you say 'held'?* Cavalcanti's violent reaction turns on a casually used past tense. From it he jumps to the conclusion that his son Guido is dead, and, without waiting for Dante's clarification, collapses in despair. Dante brings bad news to both shades. In the case of Farinata (who at this point in the canto has not yet reacted to the news of his party's defeat), it is true bad news. In the case of Cavalcanti, whose flustered appearance interrupts Dante's exchange with Farinata, it is falsely inferred bad news. Moreover, our interpretation of the episode is further complicated by our knowledge (from external sources) that Cavalcanti's son Guido would in fact die in exile a few months after the date of Dante's imaginary journey (several years, that is, before the composition of the poem) and that Dante, as one of the six elected priors who exiled him, would have an involuntary hand in his death. (Guido was exiled with other political troublemakers from both factions to an isolated region in northern Tuscany, where he succumbed to malaria.) Gianfranco Contini suggested, on the basis of sonnets exchanged between Dante and Guido after the period of the *Vita nuova*, which point to a crisis in their relationship, that Dante used the past tense here precisely because the two poets were no longer on familiar terms ("Cavalcanti in Dante," in *Varianti e altra linguistica,* Turin: Einaudi, 1970, p. 440).

76 *Picking up his speech where he had left off* Farinata has been pondering the implications of the pilgrim Dante's last rejoinder so deeply that he has apparently not noticed Cavalcanti's interruption.

78 *that torments me more* The news Dante has brought destroys the only consolation Farinata had left—that all was not lost, as long as the Ghibellines continued to dominate.

79 *that Lady* Hecate or Selene, also identified with Diana (Artemis) and Proserpina (Persephone). In the heavens, she is worshiped as the moon goddess; on Earth, as the chaste goddess of the hunt and the woods; and in the beyond, as ruler of the Underworld. Farinata repays Dante in kind by prophesying the poet's own exile from Florence before fifty lunar months have passed. Dante was exiled in 1302 and died in exile in 1321.

83–84 *why is that city so merciless / against my kindred* Whereas other Ghibelline families were pardoned and allowed to return, the Uberti family, to which Farinata belonged, were permanently banned under pain of decapitation.

85–86 *the slaughter / that dyed the waters of the Arbia red* The bloody battle on the fields of Montaperti, in which the massed Tuscan Ghibellines routed the Florentine Guelphs.

87 *cause such prayers to be said in our temple* This line is usually interpreted metaphorically.

93   *I alone, stood forth*   At the council of Empoli, hard on the heels of the rout of Montaperti, Farinata, who shared Dante's "love for the place of [his] birth" (XIV.1), stood alone against the razing of the city to the ground, a measure championed by all the other Ghibelline leaders.

100   *"We see best," he said, "like one in dim light . . ."*   It is not clear whether this chronological hyperopia that prevents them from seeing recent events applies only to the heretics or whether it is true of the damned in general.

113–14   *I labored under / the misunderstanding you cleared up for me*   Dante explains the surprised hesitation that stopped him from answering Cavalcanti's question about his son's destiny. Because of Ciacco's prophecy in Canto VI, he had inferred that the damned were aware of events happening on Earth. He did not yet know that that awareness was limited to events in the fairly distant future.

119   *The second Frederick*   Frederick II (1194–1250), son of Henry VI of Hohenstaufen and Constance of Hauteville, heiress to the Norman crown of Sicily. He was elected Holy Roman Emperor in 1215. He was known to his contemporaries as *Stupor mundi* ("The Wonder of the World") and was a poet and author himself. His court in Palermo (the *Magna Curia*) was one of the great international cultural centers of the thirteenth century. Dante, who believed that Church and Empire were complementary and that they were both providentially appointed for our salvation, spoke highly of his accomplishments both in the *Convivio* (IV.iii.6), where he is called "the last emperor of the Romans," as well as in the treatise on vernacular composition titled *De vulgari eloquentia* (I.xii.4). As head of the Ghibelline cause and a patron of Moorish scholars, Frederick was cast in the role of Antichrist by papal propaganda. The classic biography is by German historian Ernst H. Kantorowicz (*Frederick the Second, 1194–1250,* trans E. O. Lorimer, London: Constable, 1931/Berlin: Bondi, 1927–1931).

120   *the Cardinal*   Ottaviano degli Ubaldini, created bishop of Bologna in 1240 and cardinal in 1244, died in 1273. A supporter of the anti-papal Ghibelline cause, he is reported by Francesco da Buti, a late fourteenth-century commentator, to have declared: "If there is a soul, I have lost it a thousand times over for the Ghibellines." (See *Commento di Francesco da Buti sopra la Divina Comedia,* per cura di Crescentino Giannini, Pisa: Nistri, 1858–1860.)

131   *her whose beautiful eyes see all*   Beatrice, whose paradisiacal vision is not conditioned like that of the damned, will clarify all of the prophecies concerning Dante's future that he hears along the way. Dante appears to have changed his mind on this point, since it is his great-great-grandfather Cacciaguida who will tie it all together (*Pd.* XVII.37–93).

Canto XI

8   POPE ANASTASIUS   Dante's sources, the ninth-century *Liber episcopalis* and the twelfth-century *Decretum Gratiani,* led him to believe that Anastasius II (pope

from 496 to 498, during the schism of Acacius, patriarch of Constantinople, which divided the Byzantine church from the church of Rome) had been converted by Acacius' emissary Photinus, deacon of Thessalonia, to the Monophysite heresy (from the Greek *mono-* "one" + *physis* "nature"). The Monophysites held that, after the incarnation of the Word, the human nature of Jesus Christ was swallowed up by his divine nature like a drop of rain in the ocean. Recent scholarship has proven that this allegation against Anastasius was false and that the pope's Christology was orthodox.

14   *some profitable way to pass the time*   With this somewhat contrived occasion, this entire canto will constitute a didactic pause devoted to a detailed description and justification of the principles underlying the system of Dante's Hell, a kind of a map of what is to come and a recap of what we have already seen. It is worth pointing out that we are still in the Sixth Circle, about to descend, in Canto XII, into the Seventh. So far we have become accustomed to one circle, more or less, per canto. Since there are nine circles altogether, this means that the remaining three out of the nine circles—each divided, however, into smaller subzones—occupy twenty-two of the thirty-four cantos that make up the *Inferno*. The Eighth Circle alone, with its ten *bolgias,* occupies thirteen cantos, from XVIII to XXX.

24   *Whether by force or by fraud*   The notion is derived from Roman law. Dante probably has in mind a passage from Cicero's *De officiis* (I.13): "Injustice can be committed in one of two ways: either by force or by fraud; fraud appears to characterize the fox, violence the lion; the one and the other are alien to man, but fraud deserves greater hatred." In XXVII.74–75, evil counselor Guido da Montefeltro will declare: "my actions were not / like those of the lion, but of the fox."

25   *fraud is an evil peculiar to man*   Whereas violence may be a spontaneous unthinking reaction, deception implies malice aforethought and the use of reason, the divine gift that distinguishes human beings from brute beasts. The violent are punished in the Seventh Circle, the "fraudulent" in the Eighth and Ninth.

30   *three concentric rings*   The rings are distinguished according to the intended object of the violence—one's neighbor, oneself, or God—all of whom, according to the first two of the Ten Commandments, we ought instead to love. In each of the first two rings, the sinners are further divided into two subcategories according to whether the act of violence was done to a person or to that person's property. Thus we find murderers and robbers in the First Ring, immersed in the River of Blood (XII), and suicides, who did violence to themselves, and profligates, who dilapidated their property, in the Second—the former transformed into an unnatural forest of thorn trees, the latter harried by dogs, their flesh torn by the thorns of the forest they run through (XIII). In the Third Ring, on the burning sands, the would-be violent against God are divided into three subcategories: the blasphemous, the sodomites, and the usurers (XIV–XVII).

50 *Sodom and Cahors*   The names of the two cities stand for the sinful prac-
tices associated with the places: the biblical city of Sodom, destroyed by fire and
brimstone, for sodomy, the modern French city for the usury for which it was fa-
mous. The pilgrim Dante is puzzled about why these two practices are considered
violence against God and will ask for clarification toward the end of the canto
(94–111).

51 *in their hearts*   "The fool hath said in his heart: There is no God" (Ps. 13:1).

55–66 *The latter seems to sever only the bond . . . every traitor is consumed forever-
more*   The final two circles are reserved for the fraudulent, of whom there are ten
taxonomies, and the traitors. Fraud is indiscriminate in its malice. Treachery or be-
trayal is more heinous because it involves the violation of a special trust. The final
circle, Cocytus, is divided into four zones according to the special relationship vi-
olated: Caïna (traitors to kin), Antenora (traitors to the homeland), Ptolomaea (trai-
tors to guests), and Judecca (traitors to benefactors). Much the same categories
would still be invoked by Shakespeare's Macbeth, in a play written three hundred
years after the *Comedy,* against the murder of Duncan: "He's here in double trust: /
First, as I am his kinsman and his subject, / Strong both against the deed; then, as
his host, / Who should against his murderer shut the door, / Not bear the knife
myself" (*Macbeth* I.vii.12–16).

79 *Aristotle*   The Greek Aristotle (384–322 B.C.E.) was, it is worth repeat-
ing, the philosopher par excellence, "the Master of those who know" whom Dante
saw in Limbo (IV.131), along with his medieval Arab commentators Avicenna
(Ibn-Sina, 980–1037) and Averroës (Ibn-Rushd, 1126–1198). Medieval scholastic
philosophy, which flourished in the century before Dante's birth, aimed to demon-
strate the tenets of theology using Aristotelian principles. Aristotle's *Nicomachean
Ethics* was translated into Latin, a language accessible to Dante, by English theolo-
gian Robert Grosseteste (1175–1253). Dante no doubt studied it with the com-
mentary by Albertus Magnus. He would also have been familiar with the detailed
exposition by Albertus' pupil Thomas Aquinas (see *Commentary on the Nicomachean
Ethics,* 2 vols., translated by C. I. Litzinger, O. P., Chicago: Henry Regnery, 1964).

82 *incontinence*   The sins against the Golden Mean, of unrestraint, of failure
to control one's excessive appetites. Aristotle considered the moral failing of *akra-
sia* ("weakness of the will") less grave than *kakia* ("malice") or *theriotes* ("brutish-
ness"). The sins of incontinence, punished outside the walls of Dis, bring harm to
the individual soul; the sins punished within the walls involve others and are so-
cially and politically destructive.

101 *your* Physics   Another of Aristotle's many works, in which he affirms that
"art imitates nature" (*Physics* II.11.194). In theological terms, Dante is saying that
God's art creates nature, while human art ought to follow nature. "Art" for Dante
is not an aesthetic concept but involves all varieties of human activities, ways of life,
and kinds of work.

107 *Genesis* The first book of the biblical Pentateuch has God say to dis-
obedient Adam: "with labour and toil shalt thou eat thereof [i.e., of the tree of
knowledge] all the days of thy life" and "in the sweat of thy face shalt thou eat bread
till thou return to the earth, out of which thou wast taken" (Gen. 3:17–20). Thomas
Aquinas, echoing Aristotle's condemnation in *Politics* (I.iii.23) of the unnaturalness
of money begetting money through interest, says, "Thus, a kind of birth takes place
when money grows from money. For this reason the acquisition of money is espe-
cially contrary to Nature, because it is in accordance with Nature that money should
increase from natural goods and not from money itself" (*In libros Politicorum Aris-
totelis Expositio* I, lectio 8. et seq. *A* 134—cited in Charles S. Singleton's *Commentary
on Dante's Inferno,* Princeton, NJ: Princeton University Press, 1970, p. 182).

113 *in the northwest the Wagon swings low* From the vantage point of Jerusalem,
the constellation of Ursa Major (Charles' Wain or Wagon, also known as the Great
Bear or Big Dipper) is about to set on the western horizon, while that of Pisces is
rising in the east. It is four o'clock in the morning on Saturday, April 9, and the
second day of Dante's journey is about to begin.

Canto XII

4 *the huge landslide* The Slavini di Marco near Rovereto, between Trento and
Verona. Dante's source may be Albertus Magnus' *De Meteoris* (III.6), which offers
the same two possible explanations of how the landslide occurred. The poet, how-
ever, spent several years in Verona at the court of the Della Scala family and prob-
ably saw the scree for himself.

12 *Minotaur* The monstrous offspring, part man, part bull, born to Pasiphae,
King Minos' wife. Pasiphae had asked Daedalus to build a model cow she could
hide in so she could mate with a bull sent to Crete by the sea god Neptune (Po-
seidon in Greek). Minos had Daedalus build the Cretan labyrinth to conceal the
Minotaur and his infamy. Greek iconography pictured the Minotaur with a man's
body and a bull's head, whereas Dante seems to reverse the combination. The
Minotaur, who fed on the flesh of seven boys and seven maidens sent as an annual
tribute from Athens, is an appropriate guardian for the Circle of the Violent.

17 *Theseus* The great Athenian hero, one of whose exploits was the slaying
of the Minotaur. In *Meta.* VIII, Ovid tells how the virgin Ariadne, a daughter of
Minos and Pasiphae (and in some sense the Minotaur's sister), gave Theseus a thread
to guide him through the labyrinth.

38 *shortly before He harrowed Hell* The landslide was apparently caused by the
earthquake that accompanied Christ's death on the cross. Christ's descent into Hell
to free from Limbo the Hebrew patriarchs who put their faith in the Messiah ("The
great plunder of the topmost circle") was already alluded to in IV.52–63. They were

snatched from Dis, the ruler of the Underworld, a name Dante applies to Satan (though he extends the term to the city he governs).

41–42   *I thought the universe was in the grip / of the love*   The Greek philosopher Empedocles (493–432 B.C.E.), whom Dante knew through Aristotle and his medieval commentators, taught that the cosmos is the scene of a cyclical and unending struggle between the forces of integration and those of disintegration. The separation of the four elements creates order, their fusion chaos. From this point of view, the earthquake that occurred at the death of Christ is interpreted, in Virgil's pagan worldview, as a momentary return to chaos, driven by love.

47   *the River of Blood*   In XIV.134, we will learn that the river of boiling blood is named Phlegethon. It was one of the five rivers of the Underworld mentioned by Virgil in the *Aeneid,* where it is described as a river of fire (*Aen.* VI.550–51).

56–72   *Centaurs*   The Minotaur is the guardian of the Seventh Circle, but in addition each of the three subdivisions has hybrid guardians of its own. The warders of the Violent against Their Neighbors, more or less deeply immersed in the River of Blood, are the Centaurs, famously violent creatures with the heads and upper bodies of men and the lower bodies of horses. The frequently depicted battle of the Lapiths and the Centaurs (see, for example, the Elgin Marbles in the British Museum) was interpreted allegorically as a struggle between reason and unreason.

The Centaurs invaded the wedding of the king of the Lapiths, Pirithous, in an attempt to carry off his bride, Hippodamia, and the other female guests. Pholon in particular distinguished himself for violence in that encounter. He and the impulsive Nessus are kept in check in the present instance by Chiron, their head, the wisest of the Centaurs and tutor of Achilles and Aesculapius, the god of medicine. According to Ovid (*Meta.* IX.101 et seq.), Nessus tried to kidnap Hercules' wife Deianira while carrying her on his back across the swollen river Evenus, but Hercules shot him from the bank with a poisoned arrow. The dying Nessus gave his tunic soaked in his tainted blood to Deianira, saying it was a talisman against infidelity. Later, when Deianira heard of her husband's love for Iole, she sent him the shirt. When Hercules put it on, he went mad with the excruciating pain and immolated himself on a funeral pyre.

88   *She who gave me this new duty*   Beatrice, whose name is never pronounced in the *Inferno,* left her place in the heavenly choir to descend into Limbo and urge Virgil to go to Dante's aid (see II.52–54).

107   *Alexander is here*   The Alexander referred to may be Alexander the Great (356–323 B.C.E.), son of Philip of Macedon, as some of the early commentators suggest, although Dante speaks positively of him in his *Convivio* and *Monarchia.* A more likely candidate is Alexander, the proverbial tyrant of Pherae, a city in Thessaly, who came to the throne in 369 B.C.E. by murdering his uncle Polyphron and reigned until his own violent death at the hands of his wife's brothers in 358 B.C.E. His name is associated, as it is here, with that of Dionysius the Elder (432–367

b.c.e.), tyrant of Syracuse in Sicily, by Cicero (*De officiis* II.7), by Valerius Maximus (*Memorabilia* IX.13), and by Dante's mentor Brunetto Latini (*Li Livres dou Tresor* II.119.6).

110   *Ezzelino*   Ezzelino III da Romano (1194–1259), ruler of Verona, Vicenza, Padua, and Treviso, was married to Selvaggia, the illegitimate daughter of the emperor Frederick II, and reputed (especially by anti-imperial propagandists) to be one of the cruelest tyrants of the Middle Ages. His legend was the subject of the Latin tragedy *Ecerinis* by Albertino Mussato (1261–1329), a contemporary of Dante. In the *Paradiso,* Dante will meet Ezzelino's sister Cunizza da Romano in the heaven of Venus.

111   *Obizzo of Este*   Obizzo II of Este, Guelph lord of Ferrara from 1264 to 1293, was rumored to have been murdered by his son, Azzo VIII. Murder seems to have run in the family, as Obizzo himself was accused of drowning his mother because he found her origins as a commoner embarrassing. According to Jacopo della Lana, an early commentator from Bologna, Obizzo, who had a roving eye, may well have been the "marquis" who benefited from Bolognese Venedico Caccianemico's pimping of his sister Ghisolabella. Dante will encounter Venedico among the Panderers and Seducers of the Eighth Circle (XVIII.55–57).

118   *a spirit alone on one side*   The solitary shade is that of Guy de Montfort, Charles of Anjou's vicar in Tuscany, who, to repay the death and humiliation of his rebel father Simon, duke of Leicester, in the battle of Evesham, stabbed to death Henry of Cornwall, cousin of Plantagenet king Edward I of England, during mass in the cathedral of Viterbo ("in the bosom of God") in 1272. Charles of Anjou and Philip III of France were both present and suspected of complicity. The heart, laid to rest in Westminster Abbey, is said to still drip blood because the assassination has never been avenged.

133   *Attila*   Attila, king of the Huns from 445 to 453, after murdering his brother and co-ruler. His reputation for violence earned him the nickname of *Flagellum Dei* ("Scourge of God"). He appears as Etzel in the *Nibelungenlied.* Dante did not question the legend that made Attila responsible for the destruction of Florence (XIII.149).

135   *Pyrrhus and Sextus*   It is not certain which Pyrrhus Dante has in mind. Is it the legendary son of Achilles, Pyrrhus Neoptolemus, the sacrilegious killer of Priam at the altar of Jove (Zeus), who threw Astyanax, the son of Hector, from the walls of Troy to make sure he would never avenge Troy's fall? Or is it Pyrrhus (318–272 b.c.e.), the Molossian king of Epirus and enemy of Rome, whose massive losses in the successful battle of Ausculum gave his name to a "Pyrrhic victory" ("One more such victory and I am lost")?

The second Pyrrhus was killed by an angry street mob. Sextus Pompeius was the second son of Pompey the Great, whose murder, done by Cleopatra's brother (and husband) Ptolemy XIII of Egypt to ingratiate himself with Caesar, he vowed to avenge. Sextus did not ally himself with Caesar's assassins Brutus and Cassius. Still, Dante, who was on Caesar's side (the side of the providential Roman Empire), follows Lucan in condemning Sextus, "the unworthy son of Magnus [i.e., Pompey]" (*Civil War* VI.420).

137   *Rinier of Corneto and Rinier Pazzo*   These men were notorious Tuscan highwaymen in Dante's day. The former operated in the wilds of Maremma on the border between Tuscany and Latium (Corneto—today's Tarquinia—is mentioned again in the next canto as situated in a paradigmatic wilderness); the latter's band ravaged the roads of Valdarno, as far south as Arezzo.

Canto XIII

4–6   *No leaves of green there, but rather of dusk; . . . no fruits clustered there, rather poisonous thorns*   These symmetrical lines have an additional symmetry in the original. Through the rhetorical figure of anaphora, each of the first lines of the first three tercets begins with the negative particle *non,* stressing the nonnaturalness of the wood as well as the importance rhetoric (and the separation between words and things that rhetoric implies) will have in this canto. The canto, which describes the second *girone* (subcircle) of the Violent (the Violent against Self), is the subject of a memorable essay by Leo Spitzer, "Speech and Language in *Inferno* XIII," *Italica* 19.3 (1942): 81–104.

9   *in the lowlands between Cecina and Corneto*   The Cecina River (with the village of the same name) and the town of Corneto (see XII.137) mark the northern and southern confines, respectively, of what were in Dante's day the impenetrable thickets of the Maremma.

10   *Here the Harpies nest*   The Harpies, the monstrous guardians of the wood, were hybrids with a woman's head and neck and the body of a large bird. In *Aen.* III.209–66, Virgil tells how, on their voyage from Troy, Aeneas and his crew were driven from the Strophades by repeated attacks from the foul and repugnant Harpies, whose cattle the Trojans had slaughtered for food, and how the Harpy Celaeno prophesied that, after their arrival in Italy and before they could build their new city, they would suffer hunger so terrible that they would eat their very tables.

19   *the agonizing sand*   The sands on which we will find the blasphemers, sodomites, and usurers (the Violent against God) in Cantos XIV–XVII.

20–21   *you shall see things / you would not believe*   Aeneas himself hesitated before recounting the incredible episode of the discovery of the grave of Polydorus (the youngest son of Priam and Hecuba) beneath a bush that shed drops of black blood, interrupting himself to ask: *eloquar an sileam?* ("should I speak or be silent?" *Aen.* III.39). Dante does not conceal the fact that the Polydorus episode is his inspiration in this canto. In 47–49, Virgil apologizes to the wounded spirit locked in the thornbush: "If he had been able to believe beforehand / what he had never seen except in my verse, / he would never have lifted his hand against you." Though a dead man speaks, the episode in Virgil is more "naturalistic." Polydorus is buried under the bush and the blood in the branches comes up through the roots from his body. Moreover, his words come from underground; they do not ooze out together with the blood from the stub of the broken twig. Dante's reimagining has perfected the scene's *Unheimlichkeit* (uncanniness).

33 *"Why do you break me?"* The shade of Polydorus too had cried out, "Why are you rending my flesh, Aeneas?" (*Aen.* III.41).

37 *We were men once and have now become brush.* Note that his soul is not trapped inside the tree, it *is* the tree. Having rejected its human form by suicide (in line 95 the gesture is already described as an uprooting), it has become a plant, a lower life-form, in the Afterlife. At the Last Judgment, as the speaker explains in 103–8, the suicides too will reclaim their resurrected bodies; but, differently from the other shades, the body and soul they violently divided will remain forever separate, and their bodies will hang from the branches of the trees the souls have become.

40–44 *A green firebrand with flames at one end . . . So too from that broken twig* Another of Dante's brilliantly observed similes.

53 *refresh your fame* We recall Ciacco's request in VI.88–89: "But when you are in the sweet world again / I beg you to recall my memory to others." All of the sinners still set great store by their worldly reputations.

55 *Your sweet words bait me* The speaker of this tour de force of persuasive exculpation, never identified by name, is Piero (the Tuscan form of Pietro or Peter) della Vigna or delle Vigne (1190–1249), jurist, poet, master rhetorician, and secretary to the emperor Frederick II. Of humble origins, he rose to be protonotary and logothete (spokesperson for the emperor), the highest offices in the imperial bureaucracy or Magna Curia. He was the chief compiler of the 1231 *Constitutiones Regni Siciliae,* still viewed as the most important secular legislative document of the Middle Ages (not unworthy of comparison with Byzantine emperor Justinian I's *Corpus Iuris Civilis*).

Piero was sent on delicate diplomatic missions to France and England. Falsely accused of papal sympathies, he was arrested for treason, blinded, and imprisoned. To flee dishonor, he committed suicide by dashing his head against the wall of his cell. A consummate rhetorician (his official letters circulated as models of epistolary style), his response to Virgil's request is a tissue of figures of speech: metaphor (the baited trap and his ensnarement, the biblical metaphor of the keys to Frederick's heart), suspenseful personification (envy as the whore of courts), etymological wordplay, and antithesis (the play on the word "inflamed" [three different verb parts in the Italian], the "scornful" gesture made to escape "scorn," the subject at once "unjust" and "just," the "glad honors" that turn to "mournful grief").

Dante had been falsely accused like Piero and had known banishment, but he nevertheless finds suicide hard to fathom. Piero's speech resembles the contortions of his twisted trunk and the convoluted train of thought that could lead him to such an unnatural act. Piero's name, incidentally, means "Peter of the Vine," and it has been suggested that Dante himself, mindful of Christ's declaration at the Last Supper—"I am the vine and you are the branches"—is alluding in this episode to the contrast between the fruitful vine and the fruitless thornbush, to Christ's just sacrifice for love and Piero's unjust sacrifice for "scorn."

The *Comedy* is an extraordinary network of intratextual allusions, and in *Pd.* XXIV.109–11, the pilgrim Dante addresses Piero's homonym, Saint Peter (to whom Christ entrusted the *keys* of His kingdom, as Frederick did to Piero): "For you entered poor and hungry / into the field to sow the good plant / that was once a vine and has now become a thornbush."

66   *the common downfall of courts*   Life at Frederick's court was probably no less hazardous than life at the court of Henry VIII described by David Starkey in *The Reign of Henry VIII: Personalities and Politics* (London: George Philip, 1985). After enjoying the king's complete confidence for decades, Lord Chancellor Thomas Wolsey died, like Piero della Vigna, in disgrace, in his late fifties. At least Wolsey avoided suicide and execution. His successor as Lord Chancellor, Thomas More (charged, like Piero and Wolsey, with high treason), was executed.

102   *giving it both pain and the means to express it*   The sounds of wailing Dante heard in line 22, which led him to believe there were people hidden in the wood, are explained. The guardian Harpies too break off leaves and twigs, causing pain and opening a channel for lamentation.

115   *Two naked and torn figures*   One of the two gashed and bloody human figures running through the thorny wood of vegetable souls has been identified as the Sienese Lano di Ricolfo Maconi. He is reputed to have dilapidated his considerable inheritance and to have invited death by throwing himself among the assailants from the rival city of Arezzo at the ambush of Pieve al Toppo in 1288. The other spendthrift, Jacopo da Santo Andrea, named by the anonymous Florentine suicide in line 133, was from a small town near Padua. Jacopo was a camp follower of Frederick II murdered in 1239 at the instigation of Ezzelino da Romano (see XII.110).

The two are examples of the wasteful dissipation that is paired with suicide in this circle. The justification for the pairing is found in Aristotle's *Nicomachean Ethics* IV.1: "ruining one's own property seems to be a sort of self-destruction, on the assumption that our living depends upon our property" (translated by Terence Irwin, Indianapolis: Hackett Publishing Company, 1985, p. 86). Unlike Piero della Vigna, these wastrels are minor historical figures who would be unknown but for Dante.

125   *Jet-black bitches*   The ferocious black hounds are the demons that torment these souls, as the Harpies torment the suicides by eating their leaves. In this

symbiosis of pain, however, both dogs and profligates, as they crash through the wood, bring further suffering to the suicides.

143   *the city that changed her first patron*   The legendary patron of pre-Christian Florence was Mars, the god of war. His temple was built on the site of today's Baptistery in the Field of Mars, today's Piazza del Duomo. His anger at being repudiated in favor of Saint John the Baptist, whose image appeared on one side of the gold Florentine florin, is offered here as an explanation for the lack of peace in the city.

In Dante's day, the remains of an equestrian statue, thought to be of Mars, still stood at the end of the Ponte Vecchio. It was reputed by some to retain a protective function. Dante appears skeptical, however, as if the sinner were recounting an old wife's tale. This Florentine suicide is not named by Dante, deliberately according to Boccaccio, who suggests that Dante wished to pillory Florentine violence by leaving him anonymous.

At the start of Canto XIV, Dante will pay the suicide citizenly homage, performing the ritualistic gesture of gathering the twigs and leaves shattered by the spendthrift fugitives and placing them beneath the bush he has been turned into.

Canto XIV

1   *Wrung by love*   Dante's loyalty to Florence, his native city, is greater than his condemnation of its depraved inhabitants.

15   *Cato*   Cato the Younger "Uticensis" (named for Utica, in modern Tunisia, where he chose to fall upon his sword rather than submit to the absolute rule of Julius Caesar). In Book IX of Lucan's unfinished epic poem, *Pharsalia* or *Civil War,* after Caesar's victory at Pharsalus in northern Greece (48 B.C.E.) and the death of Pompey the Great, Caesar's rival, the Stoic Marcus Porcius Cato, arguably the hero of the poem, led his republican troops, on foot like them, on a march across the Libyan desert in a last vain effort to join forces with the Numidian king Juba. Cato was married twice to Marcia, whom we met in Limbo among the Virtuous Pagans (IV.128). So impressed was Dante by the figure of Cato (who also appears in Virgil's Elysian Fields) that he makes him—a republican enemy of Caesar, a pagan, and a suicide!—the guardian of the shores of the island mountain of Purgatory and protector of the Saved (*Pg.* I–II).

22–24   *Some were lying supine*   The Third Ring of the Violent, that of the Violent against God, extends over several cantos. Those lying supine are the blasphemers, and we will see them in this canto; those who move about continually are the sodomites, and we will see them in Cantos XV and XVI; those crouched or squatting are the usurers, and we will see them in Canto XVII just before we go down into the Eighth Circle, where Fraud is punished. The usurers (or loan sharks) are on the very edge of the Seventh Circle, because their practice, condemned by Dante as violence against God's goodness (see XI.94–111), borders on fraud.

28 *huge flakes of fire*   The punishment in this circle, which includes the so-called sodomites, is based on the rain of fire and brimstone visited by God on the corrupt Cities of the Plain, Sodom and Gomorrah (Gen. 19).

30 *Like snow that falls*   The line, which in the Italian reads *come di neve in alpe sanza vento,* seems to be an involuntary reminiscence of a line from a sonnet by Guido Cavalcanti (*Biltà di donna e di saccente core*), *e bianca neve scender senza venti* ("and white snow falling without winds"), remembered also by Petrarch in his *Triumphus Cupidinis* (*come neve bianca / che senza vento in un bel colle fiocchi* "like white snow / that falls without wind on a lovely hill").

31–36 *like the flames*   The source of this narrative comparison is a letter describing the wonders of India, alleged to have been written by Alexander the Great to his tutor Aristotle, which circulated in the Middle Ages under the title *De situ Indiae et itinerum in ea vastitate* ("Concerning the site of India and a guide to its vastness"). The letter is cited by Dominican saint and *Doctor universalis* Albertus Magnus (c. 1193/1206–1280) in his *De Meteoris* (a work referred to in XII.4–6, as well as in Book IV of the *Convivio*), which is where Dante presumably read it.

46–48 *that great one*   The blasphemous shade spread-eagled on the burning sand and fully exposed to the rain of fire and brimstone (who will not be named until line 63) is the young Giant Capaneus, one of the mythological Seven against Thebes whose story is told by ancient Greek tragedian Aeschylus (525–456 B.C.E.) in *Seven against Thebes* and Roman epic poet Publius Papinius Statius (45–96 C.E.) in his *Thebaid*. Dante greatly admired Statius, whom he places in Purgatory, claiming that he was converted to Christianity by studying Virgil. Like Farinata degli Uberti in Canto X, Capaneus "seems so unconcerned / about the fire."

51 *What I was living, that I am dead.*   As Capaneus scaled the walls of the besieged Thebes, boasting that not even Jove could stop him, he was struck down by a thunderbolt. Not even death, however, has tempered his defiance. In XXV.15, in the *bolgia* of the thieves, the blasphemous arrogance of Capaneus (referred to by a circumlocution as "he who fell from the walls of Thebes") will be declared to be outdone by that of Vanni Fucci.

52 *the blacksmith*   Jove or Jupiter (in Greek Zeus) was the most powerful of the ancient gods and the ruler of heaven and Earth. The "blacksmith," who fabricates his thunderbolts, is Vulcan (in Greek Hephaestus), god of fire and metalworking, whose forge was reputed to be located under volcanic Mount Aetna in Sicily. Mount Aetna here is given its medieval name of *Mongibello,* composed of the Latin word *mons* and the Arabic word *jebel,* both of which mean "mountain."

58 *the fight at Phlegra*   The Phlegraean Fields in Macedonia, where the race of Giants attempted unsuccessfully to scale the heavens by piling Mount Pelion on Mount Ossa and Mount Olympus on top of that. The Gigantomachy or Struggle between the Gods and the Giants was one of the most popular of Greek myths and a favorite theme in classical art. Dante would find allusions to it in Virgil's *Georgics*

and Ovid's *Metamorphoses,* as well as Statius' *Thebaid* (II.595), his source for the figure of Capaneus.

In striking down Capaneus, in the closing lines of *Thebaid* X, Jove speaks of his defeat of the Giants at Phlegra. The most dramatic early modern representation of the Gigantomachia are the "comic book" trompe l'oeil frescos by Giulio Romano (c. 1499–1546) in Mantua's Palazzo Te. In Canto XXXI, Dante will encounter the Giants Ephialtes, Briareus, and Antaeus. The last of these will set Virgil and Dante down in the final circle.

79 *Bulicame* The name of a steaming hot sulfur spring just north of Viterbo. The early commentators explain that the prostitutes who lived close by and were forbidden the use of the public baths deviated its course to provide hot water for their private ablutions.

94 *In the middle of the sea* The description of the island of Crete is inspired by *Aen.* III.104 et seq.: *Creta Iovis magni medio iacet insula ponto . . .* ("Crete, the island of great Jupiter, lies / in the middle of the sea . . .")

96 *under whose king* The king was Saturn (Cronus in Greek), who ushered in the Golden Age, the first age of humankind, the age of perpetual spring, when the earth produced its fruits without labor and primitive humankind was innocent and free from sickness, described by Ovid in *Meta.* I.89–112 and Virgil in *Aen.* VIII.324–25. The pagan myth corresponds to the biblical Garden of Eden or Earthly Paradise prior to the Fall. When it was prophesied that one of his sons would dethrone him, Saturn resolved to eat his children. His wife Rhea or Cybele, the Great Mother, hid their youngest son Jove (Zeus) in the caves of Mount Ida, ordering her priests, the Curetes or Corybantes, to cover his infant cries with their shouts and cymbals. Virgil refers to the episode in *Georgics* IV.150–52, Ovid in *Fasti* IV.197–214.

104 *an Old Man* The syncretic myth of the Old Man of Crete with the foot of clay, Dante's invention, conflates the Old Testament dream of Nebuchadnezzar (Dan. 2.31–35) with Ovid's account, in *Meta.* I, of the progressive decadence of humanity through the successive ages of gold, silver, bronze, and iron. The details of Dante's allegory have been variously interpreted. Damietta is a city on the Nile Delta in Egypt. If the statue is facing Rome with its back to Damietta, its gaze follows the daily trajectory of the sun from east to west.

116 *Acheron, Styx, and Phlegethon* The five rivers of Virgil's Avernus were Acheron, Styx, Phlegethon, Cocytus, and Lethe. Dante has already introduced Acheron and Styx. The river of boiling blood first met with in Canto XII and again here is Phlegethon. We do not encounter Lethe, the River of Forgetfulness, in Dante's *Inferno* but at the top of the mountain of Purgatory ("where the souls go to wash themselves— / their sins repented—and to be purified," 137–38).

119 *Cocytus* The frozen lake at the bottom of Hell in which the Traitors are variously immersed (see Cantos XXXII–XXXIV).

Canto XV

4   *the Flemings*   Inhabitants of the county of Flanders in northwest Europe
(the name Flanders means "flooded lands"), created during the ninth century. It in-
cluded parts of northern France, western Belgium, and the southwest Netherlands.
The county enjoyed virtual independence for centuries and considerable prosper-
ity as a center, like Florence, of the cloth industry. Today, Wissant is in French ter-
ritory, southwest of Calais toward Cap Gris-Nez on the Strait of Dover; Bruges,
on the other hand, is a well-preserved medieval city in Belgium.

8   *the Brenta*   In the Middle Ages, Venice and Padua fought for control of
the Brenta River, which flowed into the Venetian lagoon. Like the Flemings who
built dikes to contain the North Sea, the Paduans raised high levees to prevent
spring flooding from the Carnic Alps. Carentana is another name for modern
Carinthia, the southernmost province of Austria, bordering on Italy's Friuli re-
gion and Slovenia.

30   *Ser Brunetto*   The title *ser* (the second element in *messer,* cf. French *mon-
sieur*) placed before Brunetto Latini's first name is a sign of respect, as is the use in
the Italian text of the formal pronoun *voi,* otherwise used only with Farinata and
Cavalcante dei Cavalcanti in Canto X. The whole canto, despite its ultimate con-
demnation of the master's limits (which go considerably beyond "sodomy"), is a
recognition of Dante's debt to Brunetto (c. 1220–1294), the most prominent au-
thor and intellectual in Florence of the generation preceding his own.

A militant Guelph, Brunetto was a notary and an ambassador of the republic, a
poet, a teacher of rhetoric, and a didactic encyclopedist like Dante himself. (The
latter's unfinished *Convivio* had encyclopedic ambitions, and the same is certainly
true of the *Comedy.*) Brunetto's chief intellectual legacy, *Li Livres dou Tresor* (*The
Books of the Treasure* or *Thesaurus*), written in French during a protracted self-
imposed exile from 1260 to 1266, is an encyclopedic work designed to provide its
readers with a basis for active political involvement. The second book adapts and
incorporates Aristotle's *Nicomachean Ethics,* which, as we saw in Canto XI, plays
such a large role in the moral system of Dante's *Inferno.*

Contemporary chroniclers like Giovanni Villani (c. 1280–1348) emphasize
Brunetto's fundamental role in bringing civilization to the Florentines. He may be
absent from the list of worthies whom Dante asked Ciacco about (VI.79–81) be-
cause he was an intellectual, not a man of action. Commentaries on this canto note
that there is no evidence outside Dante's poem for Brunetto's homosexuality
(though D'Arco Silvio Avalle has pointed to an exchange of love poems between
Brunetto and another male Florentine poet, Bondie Dietaiuti). Moreover, Dante's
exact contemporary, Giordano da Pisa, a Dominican preaching in Florence,
claimed—perhaps with understandable professional exaggeration—that the ma-
jority of Florentine males were sodomites.

31 *My son* It has been hypothesized that in Brunetto, Dante is meeting a former teacher, though this cannot be known for certain. There is irony in the fact that their conversation insists so much on the paternal-filial relationship. As a "sodomite," Brunetto is condemned for a sexual practice that cannot lead to the physiological adventure of conception, gestation, and birth, described with such wonder by the character Statius in *Pg.* XXV.

46 *What fortune or what destiny* Like Cavalcanti in Canto X, Brunetto speaks the limited language of paganism. See below, in line 55, "If you follow your star . . ." and, in line 70, "Your fortune."

56 *a glorious port* There is another dramatic irony here. Dante is indeed sailing toward the port of glory—the heavenly glory of Christian salvation—but what Brunetto means is the port of earthly fame.

59 *seeing the heavens favor you so* There is a further ambiguity in the Italian text here. The Italian word translated as "heavens" is singular and could mean either "the heavens" or "Heaven." The deterministic Brunetto means the *stars* in heaven, not "Heaven" as a metonymy for God. The reader learned in Canto II, however, that Dante's journey was in fact willed in God's Heaven.

62 *Fiesole* A settlement of Etruscan origin situated on a hill overlooking Florence. Legend had it that Florence was founded by the Romans after they had destroyed rebellious Fiesole. From the twelfth century onward, Fiesole was subject to Florence. With rustic metaphors, Brunetto contrasts the seed of the noble Romans (from whom Dante claims implicitly to be descended) with that of the uncouth Fiesolans.

85 *How man may make himself eternal* This is another good example of dramatic irony and the need to deconstruct. One way that a man may make himself "eternal" in time is through biological reproduction. Alternatively, for Christians at least, he can secure eternal happiness in the next world by observing God's commandments. Neither of these is Brunetto's case. The as yet unregenerate pilgrim is speaking here from Brunetto's perspective and ascribing eternality, as Brunetto does, to literary fame.

90 *an enlightening lady* Beatrice, to whom Virgil is leading Dante, is the enlightening lady. As the story unfolds, it will not be Beatrice, whom Dante meets in the Earthly Paradise atop Mount Purgatory, but Dante's great-great-grandfather Cacciaguida, whom he meets in Paradise itself (Cantos XV–XVIII), who will tie together the various prophecies Dante hears along the way about his earthly future.

96 *and the peasant his hoe* In other words, I care as much for the illiterate peasant's labors as I do for the caprices of Fortune's wheel. Dante was not a populist.

109 *Priscian* The grammarian Priscian of Caesarea in Mauretania who taught in Constantinople in the early sixth century C.E. His *Institutiones Grammaticae* in eighteen books is the most voluminous work of the Latin grammarians. There is no reference to Priscian's homosexuality anywhere in the literature.

110   *Francesco d'Accorso*   Born in Bologna in 1225, the son of another famous jurist, D'Accorso taught civil law at the university before being invited by Edward I to teach at Oxford University. He died in Bologna, seven years before Dante's journey, in 1293. His condemnation here presumably reflects his contemporary reputation.

112   *The one moved*   This is another of the poet's contemporaries. Andrea dei Mozzi became bishop of Florence (which lies on the Arno River) in 1287 and was transferred for misconduct by Pope Boniface VIII to Vicenza (on the Bacchiglione River). The designation of the pope by his title of *servus servorum* ("Servant of the Servants" [of God]) must be ironic, given Dante's opinion of Boniface's corrupt and presumptuous stewardship (see Canto XIX).

119   *my* Treasure   Brunetto's most important work was written in French during his exile. With it, he is confident that he has ensured himself eternal life. The narrator's description of his exit, however, exposes the fallaciousness of this fond hope. Brunetto is a loser, though he may act and look like a winner. It is worth mentioning that French critic André Pézard devoted an erudite and brilliantly ingenious volume, *Dante sous la pluie de feu* ([Dante under the Rain of Fire] Paris: Librarie Philosophique de J. Vrin, 1950), to his conviction that Brunetto is condemned not for sodomy, but for the unnatural act of writing in French and scorning his God-given natural language.

122   *the green cloth*   A bolt of green cloth was the prize offered to the winner of an annual footrace run the first Sunday of Lent in Verona.

Canto XVI

37   *Guido Guerra*   The only "worthy" of this trio not named by Dante in his query to Ciacco in Canto VI. The absence from the *Inferno* of anyone answering to the name of Arrigo (VI.80) has led at least one critic (Michelangelo Picone) to speculate, not altogether unconvincingly, that "Arrigo" may in fact be a misreading of the manuscript's "Guido" ("Canto XVI," in *Lectura Dantis Turicensis: Inferno,* edited by Georges Güntert and Michelangelo Picone, Florence: Cesati, 2000, p. 224). Guelph leader Count Guido VI of Dovadola (c. 1220–1272), nicknamed Guerra ("War") for his military prowess, was the grandson of Gualdrada, daughter of Bellincione Berti dei Ravignani (praised for his old-time integrity by Dante's ancestor Cacciaguida in *Pd.* XV.112). Cacciaguida's son, Alighieri I, Dante's great-grandfather, married a daughter of Bellincione Berti.

Guido was a hero to proponents of the Guelph cause comparable to Farinata degli Uberti for the Ghibellines. He drove the Ghibellines from Arezzo in 1255 and, banished after the rout of Montaperti (1260), led his fellow Florentine exiles into battle alongside Charles of Anjou at Benevento in Campania against the emperor Frederick II's bastard son Manfred. Manfred, whom the reader meets as a character in *Pg.* III, died of the wounds received in that battle, practically sealing the fate of the Ghibelline cause.

39   *with counsel and sword*   These are metonymies corresponding to the "courtesy and valor"—the aristocratic arts of peace and war—of line 67.

41   *Tegghiaio Aldobrandi*   Another famous Florentine Guelph leader. He was appointed *podestà* or chief magistrate of Arezzo after the 1255 expulsion of the Ghibellines and was a Guelph commander at Montaperti, despite his (unheeded) opinion that the Florentine Guelphs were making a mistake in facing the Sienese Ghibellines on the battlefield. He died in exile in Lucca in 1262, three years before Dante was born.

44   *Jacopo Rusticucci*   Yet another prominent figure in Florentine political life. His dates are uncertain, though he is mentioned as an associate of Aldobrandi in documents dating back to the 1230s, and he was still alive in 1269. The reference to his "wife's ferocity" and the harm she did him has led to considerable speculation, but the allusion remains opaque.

67   *courtesy and valor*   The noncommercial values of the old aristocracy, in Dante's eyes corrupted by early capitalist "progress."

70   *Guiglielmo Borsiere*   External sources do not permit us to better identify this Florentine courtier who died, we learn from the context, shortly before 1300, the year of Dante's journey. Boccaccio makes him a character in one of the tales in the *Decameron* and describes him in his commentary (*Esposizione*) to the first seventeen cantos of the *Inferno*.

73   *The newcomers*   It is generally accepted that pilgrim Dante expresses author Dante's considered repugnance for commerce. This judgment on the decline of customs will be confirmed in the encounter with Dante's ancestor Cacciaguida in the *Paradiso*.

94   *There is a river, the first to hold its course*   The Montone is the first river to flow all the way down from Mount Viso (or Monviso) in the Apennines to the east, passing by the town of Forlì, and debouch directly into the Adriatic, south of Ravenna and the ancient port of Classe, without becoming a tributary of the Po. As a nomadic exile from Florence, Dante acquired a detailed first person singular familiarity with the geography of Italy.

97   *Acquacheta*   The name means "still water." An Italian proverb, not altogether relevant here, warns that *Acqua cheta rovina i ponti* ("Still water ruins bridges").

101   *a single cataract*   The roar of the water is so deafening because it falls from a great height in a single cascade. Its bed might have sloped more gradually and produced a number of lesser and less resounding falls.

106   *a cord*   The knotted and coiled cord Dante hands to Virgil for him to throw down into the abyss as a signal is clearly symbolic, though no commentator has been able to explain it satisfactorily.

131   *a figure swimming upward*   At XVII.97 we will learn that this monstrous hybrid guardian of the Eighth Circle is named Geryon.

Canto XVII

1   *Behold the beast*   The solemn opening marks a canto of transition, from the Seventh Circle to the Eighth, from the sins of Violence to the sins of Fraud, which will occupy thirteen whole cantos, from Canto XVIII to Canto XXX, more than a third of the *Inferno*. In line 7, the beast Geryon will be called "the loathsome image of treachery." He is the guardian of the circle of Fraud, the second lowest circle. Below it lies only the circle of the Traitors, among them Judas Iscariot who betrayed Jesus Christ, Brutus and Cassius who betrayed Caesar, and Lucifer (also called Dis, after the classical ruler of the Underworld), who betrayed (or attempted to betray) God Himself.

As Virgil explained in Canto XI, these last two circles have deceit in common: in the Eighth Circle the victims are, so to speak, random, not bound to the defrauder by any special bond of trust, except the biblical injunction to love our neighbor as ourselves (II.52–56), whereas in the Ninth Circle a closer tie, of kinship, of political loyalty, of hospitality, or of gratitude has been violated.

2   *breaches mountains, etc.*   All defenses are useless against this beast.

10   *the face of a righteous man*   The allegorical personification of Fraud is easily parsed. If all you saw was his face, you would buy a used car from this man. "Beware of false prophets, who come to you in the clothing of sheep, but inwardly they are ravening wolves" (Matt. 7:15). In classical mythology Geryon was a Giant with three bodies from the waist up, six arms, and three heads. Hercules' tenth labor was to steal his cattle.

The references to Geryon in Virgil and Ovid speak of his being somehow threefold, but they do not permit his visualization. Dante's interpretation of his hybrid form—human head, serpent's body, and scorpion's tail—is strongly influenced by the description of the locusts of the Apocalypse, which had faces like men's, hair like women's, teeth like lions', breastplates of iron, and tails like scorpions with poisonous stings (Apoc. 9:3–11).

18   *Arachne* was famous for her intricate weaving, so much so that in her pride she challenged the goddess Minerva (in Greek Athena) to a contest. Minerva's tapestry depicted the gods in a positive light whereas Arachne's depicted their loves, deceits, and misdeeds. In a rage, Minerva tore Arachne's work to shreds and, when Arachne tried to hang herself from a tree, transformed her dangling form into a spider, which, like the deceiver, spins webs to entrap its victims (see Ovid, *Meta.* VI.5–145).

21   *among the guzzling Germans*   In Germany, along the Rhine or the Danube River. To sophisticated Florentine eyes, the Germans had bad table manners and drank too much.

22   *A beaver backs into water*   It was thought that the beaver lured fish by moving its tail in the water, then seized them in its paws.

43   *all by myself*   This is only the second time Dante has found himself alone since the journey began. The first was outside the City of Dis in Canto VIII, when Virgil left him to parlay with the demons guarding the gate.

49   *Dogs in the summer*   The graphic simile of the flea-bitten dogs obliquely downgrades the humanity of this group of sinners. They are the Usurers, who lent money at exorbitant interest rates, identified in Canto XI with the town of Cahors in France, though those Dante meets here are all Florentine except for one, usually identified as Reginaldo degli Scrovegni, who hailed from Padua, near Venice. They were the bankers (*banchieri*) who sat at their stalls or benches (*banchi;* the origin of English "bank") with their emblazoned money bags in front of them, waiting for customers.

The coats of arms on their pouches (whose rampant animals continue the bestial theme) are those of the noble families (whom Dante regarded as his peers) whose descendants had catastrophically substituted the vice of greed for the virtue of disinterested largesse (the aristocratic duty incumbent on the wealthy to be generous, which we call "noblesse oblige"). This munificence is an important component of "courtesy and valor," whose eclipse by nascent capitalism was decried in the previous canto (XVI.67 et seq.). The usurers, as befits their vice, could be said to be "on the cusp," the last category of the Violent, but on the edge of the pit that houses the Fraudulent. Dante meets them in fact after he has already encountered Geryon, "the loathsome image of treachery" and guardian of the next circle.

59   *a yellow purse*   The blue lion on a field of gold was the heraldic device of the Gianfigliazzi family, who sided with the Black Guelphs, some of whose members had practiced usury in France.

63   *with a goose*   The white goose on a field of gules or red was the emblem of the Ghibelline Obriachi family.

65   *a pregnant sow*   A blue sow on a white field constituted the coat of arms of the Scrovegni family from Padua (the name Scrovegni recalls the Italian name for "sow," *scrofa*): Commentators identify this Paduan usurer as Reginaldo degli Scrovegni, tithe collector of the bishop of Padua, who died between 1288 and 1290 leaving a considerable fortune. The breathtaking Scrovegni chapel, whose frescos narrating the life of Christ (restored in 2002) were completed by Giotto and his school in 1305, was commissioned by his son Arrigo or Enrico supposedly in atonement for Reginaldo's sins—using, one supposes, for the purpose a portion of his father's ill-gotten gains. The fame of Giotto, born in 1267 and therefore Dante's exact contemporary, is mentioned in *Pg.* XI. It is a serendipitous possibility that Giotto was painting the chapel at the same time that Dante was writing this canto.

68   *Vitaliano*   Vitaliano del Dente was *podestà* or chief magistrate of Padua in 1307. He married into the Scrovegni family.

73   *three goats*   Three black goats on a gold field was the crest of the Becchi family (the noun *becco* means "billy goat"). The "sovereign knight" has been identified as Gianni Buiamonte dei Becchi, who was knighted in 1297 or 1298. He bankrupted himself by gambling, took the money and ran, was arrested and condemned in 1308, and died in 1310.

75   *just like an ox*   Another bestial simile for a bestial gesture.

82   *stairs*   The "stairs" they will use to descend from now on, due to the unscalability of the walls that enclose the final circles, are provided by their monstrous guardians: the scaly back of Geryon, the powerful hands of the Giant Antaeus (XXXI.131–45), and the shaggy hair of Satan's side and legs (XXXIV.72 et seq.).

86   *quartan fever*   A malarial ague or fever whose paroxysms return every fourth day.

106   *Phaethon*   The son of Helios (Apollo) the sun god and the nymph Clymene, Phaethon asked to be allowed to drive his father's chariot for a day. Scared by the sight of the poisonous tail of the constellation of Scorpio (as Dante is of Geryon's), he let go of the reins, causing the chariot of the sun to swerve off course, first scorching the heavens and leaving the scar of the Milky Way, then flying so close to the Earth as to create the Libyan desert. Jove struck him with a thunderbolt to limit the damage, and he fell into the Eridanus or Po River. Dante will cite the myth, which he read in Ovid (*Meta.* II.47–324), again in *Pd.* XVII.1–3.

109   *Icarus*   The son of Daedalus the inventor, who fashioned him a pair of wings with which to escape from the Cretan labyrinth. Icarus ignored his father's instructions and flew too close to the sun. The sun melted the wax that held his wings together, and he plummeted into the Aegean Sea. Once again, Dante's source is Ovid (*Meta.* VIII.183–235). W. H. Auden's "*Musée des Beaux Arts*" is a reading of Flemish painter Pieter Breughel the Elder's take on the myth.

118–19   *I heard the torrent / thunder*   This is the roar that the river Phlegethon makes as it falls down the sheer drop into the circle below.

127   *As a falcon*   Another closely observed simile that lends credibility to the fantastic by comparing it with what was an everyday sight for Dante's medieval readers—the behavior of a thwarted hunting bird which has lost sight of both its prey and the falconer's lure (a leather pouch containing a piece of meat, sometimes fitted with wings to simulate another bird, attached to a string that the falconer whirls overhead to train the bird to "stoop" to, or swoop down on, a prey in flight). The unheeding falcon would become a symbol of even more radical disorientation for W. B. Yeats: "Turning and turning in the widening gyre / the falcon cannot hear the falconer. / Things fall apart; the center cannot hold; / mere anarchy is loosed upon the world" ("The Second Coming").

Canto XVIII

1 *Malebolge* The Eighth Circle, walled in by the cliff Dante and Virgil have just descended, slopes down toward the central pit and is interrupted by ten concentric trenches or moats (it is also customary to use the Anglicized Italian term "bolgias"), crossed by stone bridges. (*Male-bolge* is a meaningful compound noun meaning "evil pouches" or "pouches for the evil.") Each of the ten categories of the Fraudulent, watched over by demon tormentors, is punished in one of these ditches in the following order: Panderers and Seducers, Parasites and Flatterers, Simoniacs, Sorcerers, Grafters, Hypocrites, Thieves, Fraudulent Counselors, Sowers of Discord, and Counterfeiters. Of these the Fraudulent Counselors and the Sowers of Discord are the only taxonomies not specifically mentioned in XI.58–60, where they are subsumed under "other such filth."

Dante and Virgil (and we with them) will visit all of them, but we should bear in mind that, after confessing to the judge Minos (see Canto V), the sinners are dispatched directly to their particular place of eternal punishment, which is the only part of Hell each sinner knows. With Canto XVIII, incidentally, the second part of the canticle of the *Inferno,* which has thirty-four cantos, begins. In a single canto, with one example of each, Dante briskly liquidates two bolgias and three categories of sinners: the Panderers, the Seducers, and the Parasites or Flatterers. Other sins and sinners will interest him more.

26 *On our side* Dante and Virgil are at the foot of the encircling wall and on the outside edge of the bolgia. The sinners coming toward them on their side are the Panderers; those walking more briskly in the opposite direction on the other side are the Seducers.

30 *the bridge* The Ponte Sant'Angelo, narrow by modern standards, still crosses the Tiber from Castel Sant'Angelo on the right bank to the Monte Giordano, a smallish hill, today hardly perceptible as such, on the left bank. The castle was originally built as the Emperor Hadrian's mausoleum and was the site of a miracle attributed to Saint Michael the archangel. It was transformed into a fortress in 1277 by Pope Nicholas III. In the Jubilee year 1300, when they could earn a "plenary indulgence," or general pardon for their sins by fulfilling certain requirements, the pilgrims thronging the holy city were obliged to observe two-way foot traffic crossing the bridge to and from Saint Peter's. Saint Peter's was one of the four basilicas they were expected to visit and is on the same side of the river as the castle.

50 *Venedico Caccianemico* This polysyllabic name practically fills the line (the effect is even more invasive in the original Italian *Venedico sei tu Caccianemico,* where it begins and ends the metrical unit). And the name's bearer was hoping he could get by unnoticed! He was a prominent aristocratic figure in the Guelph-Ghibelline factional struggles in Bologna and drove out the Ghibellines in 1274. He was born in 1228 and died in 1304 (though Dante believed him dead by the year 1300).

Twice exiled from Bologna for favoring the expansionist ambitions of the Este lords of nearby Ferrara to take over Bologna, Venedico nevertheless served as *podestà* or chief magistrate of the cities of Imola, Pistoia, and Milan and as Consul of the People in Modena. His son married Costanza, daughter of Azzo VIII of Este, marquis of Ferrara. Dante has Venedico confess to pandering his sister Ghisolabella to Azzo's father, Obizzo II of Este, whom Azzo was suspected of murdering in 1293.

51   *pungent sauces*   Near Gaibola, on a hill overlooking Bologna were the *Salse,* a common grave where the bodies of executed criminals, suicides, and the excommunicated were buried. The common noun *salse* means "sauces," so Dante may be punning sardonically on the mordant "spice" of the demon's whip.

61   *'Sipa' for 'sì'*   *Sipa* or *sepa* is the Bolognese dialect form of standard Italian *sia,* the present subjunctive of the verb "to be" (*essere*). It was used as a term of acquiescence meaning "So be it." The two rivers Sàvena and Reno bracket the city to the east and west, respectively. The sense then is that there are more Bolognese Panderers in Hell than there are Bolognese in Bologna. Dante often suggests that the individuals he meets are representative of the vicious propensities of their cities of origin.

69   *a ridge*   This is the start of the bridge that crosses the First Bolgia. From it, Dante and Virgil will be able to look down and see the procession of sinners going in the opposite direction.

86   *Jason*   Jason, the mythological leader of the Argonauts, was raised by the centaur Chiron and sailed to Colchis in quest of the Golden Fleece, which was guarded by a dragon. Even as a representative sinner in Hell, like Capaneus he still retains a heroic aura, especially in contrast to the poet's scornful treatment of the Panderer from Bologna. Dante, who refers positively to the expedition of the *Argo* three times in the *Paradiso* (II.16–18; XXV.7; and, during his final vision, XXXIII.94–96), knew of Jason's exploits from Ovid (*Meta.* VII.1–424) and Statius (*Thebaid* V.403–85). Here Jason is presented as the seducer of both Hypsipyle, daughter of Thoas, king of Lemnos, and Medea, daughter of Aeëtes, king of Colchis. When Jason abandoned her for Creusa, queen of Corinth, Medea killed his new bride and their own two sons as Jason watched in horror.

88   *Lemnos*   Jason and his followers arrived at the Aegean island of Lemnos after the women, shunned by their husbands after being cursed by Venus (in Greek Aphrodite), had put all the men (except for Hypsipyle's father, whom she falsely claimed to have killed herself) to death.

122   *Alessio Interminei*   Not much is known about this member of the noble Interminelli (Interminei is an alternative form) family of Lucca. The early commentators elaborate vaguely on Dante's text, saying he was a notorious flatterer, without providing concrete examples. As was the case with Venedico Caccianemico, his name and place of provenance occupy almost the entire line (see note to line 50). Dante seems to relish outing these two despicable characters.

133 *Thais the whore* The courtesan Thais was not a historical personage but a character in the play *The Eunuch* by the Roman comic author Terence. Since the exaggeratedly adulatory phrase quoted is not spoken directly to Thais' lover Gnatho, it appears that Dante's source was not the play itself but a passage in Cicero's *De amicitia,* where the line is ambiguously quoted as an instance of adulation.

The final lines of the canto describing the repugnant punishment of the Flatterers are a good example in Dante's original Italian of the poet's "grotesque" style. The language used, and in particular the rhyme words, are a tour de force of verbal scurrility. The technical virtuosity displayed is a sure sign of the poet's ability to cast the cold eye of the calculating creative artist, of his nonidentification with his characters, underlining the clinical distance that separates him from them. This is a technique that Dante has employed in previous cantos and that will become more and more common in the last two circles. It will be described (and illustrated once again) in the opening lines of Canto XXXII.

Canto XIX

1 *O Simon Magus* In Acts 8:9–24, Simon, the Samaritan sorcerer (or magus), was baptized by the disciple Philip. When Simon saw the apostles Peter and John lay hands upon the converted and pray that they might receive the Holy Ghost, he offered them money to give him the same power. They naturally refused, saying that the gifts of God cannot be purchased with money. The sin of Simony and the category of the Simoniacs derive their names from Simon.

It is these unworthy pastors and traffickers in the sacred who are punished in this Third Bolgia. Dante and Virgil will first get a bird's-eye view of the bolgia and its inmates from the vantage point of the third bridge and then go down among them. Dante's sympathies, by the way, are with Spiritual Franciscans and their ideal of evangelical poverty. He will eulogize Saint Francis in *Pd.* XI, and he will continue to attack ecclesiastical corruption on every possible occasion throughout the *Comedy.*

4 *That should be of righteousness the brides* If the phrase sounds biblical, it is. The ministers of the Catholic Church frequently referred to the community of the faithful as the Bride of Christ (see line 57).

5 *the trumpet* Another biblical allusion, this time to the trumpet that the angels will sound on the final Day of Judgment (Matt. 24:31).

16–21 *baptismal fonts / in San Giovanni* The interpretation of this comparison is controversial. For one thing, the old baptistery of the church of San Giovanni (Saint John), where Dante himself was baptized, was destroyed in 1576. Some of the early commentators explain that the holes were designed for the officiating priests to stand in to protect them from the milling crowds—baptism was performed once a year at Easter—interpreting the ambiguous word *battezzatori* (here translated as "baptismal fonts") to mean "those doing the baptizing." Others read the word as it is interpreted here.

This second interpretation seems more convincing, not least because the cavity would in this case be filled with holy water for the full immersion baptism then practiced, and hence someone could conceivably drown in it, and because it has the authority of the important *Ottimo Commento* (literally, "Best Commentary"), a commentary on the *Comedy* written between 1330 and 1340 (shortly after Dante's death) by an anonymous Florentine contemporary of Dante. In *Pd.* XXV.8–9, Dante expresses the fond hope that one day he may be crowned with the poet's laurels at the same font in San Giovanni where he was baptized.

25   *the soles of both feet*   The tongues of flame that play on the protruding feet of those trapped upside down in the various holes appear to parody the tongues of flame that descended on the apostles on Pentecost to fill them with the Holy Ghost and give them the power to speak divers tongues (Acts 2:3–4). The difference here is that these flames actually burn the sinners' feet, especially the redder one that attracts Dante's attention. The flame is redder because the sinner was at the top of the church's hierarchy and his rapacity was consequently greater and more deadly.

35   *that gentler slope*   The inner bank of the bolgia is gentler because the whole circle slopes down to the central pit and the final circle is lower than the outside bank and easier to descend.

49   *like a friar*   In this bolgia where all the sinners are clerics, there is irony in the fact that Dante, a lay person, is compared, as he bends to hear the sinner's answer, to a monk hearing the confession of a condemned man. The irony will be heightened when we discover that this particular hole is set aside for popes.

49–50   *confession / from an assassin*   Those who killed for money were punished by being placed headfirst in a hole in the ground and smothered by the dirt thrown on top of them. A contract killer could earn a last-minute reprieve by revealing the name of the contractor.

53   *Boniface*   The sinner in the hole reveals his rank and his identity as Nicholas III (pope from 1277 to 1280) by mistaking Dante for his successor Boniface VIII (pope from 1294 to 1303). Nicholas is in fact surprised that Boniface has arrived so early, since Holy Writ ("the Writ," line 54), the book of the future, to which now that he is dead he has (limited) access, had told him (truthfully) that Boniface would not arrive for another three years. Nicholas' error allows Dante, in terms of the fictional journey, set in 1300, to condemn the current pope to Hell for simony while he was still very much alive. (Though by the time the *Inferno* was written, of course, Boniface was already dead.)

Benedetto Caetani was born at Anagni near Rome in 1235. Elected cardinal in 1281, he became pope in 1294, according to some, after ousting Celestine V (see III.60). The powerful Roman family of the Colonnas were inveterate rivals of the Caetanis, but Boniface's principal enemy was Philip IV of France (see line 87). For

Dante, Boniface was a personal enemy, considered responsible for detaining the poet when he was an ambassador of Florence in Rome and conspiring to have the White Guelphs (including Dante in absentia) expelled from Florence—in other words, the chief author of Dante's twenty-year exile.

In Canto XXVII, Boniface will appear again as the manipulator of the manipulator Guido da Montefeltro, who will dub him "the Prince of the Latter-Day Pharisees" (XXVII.85). As a corollary to the plethora of popes in Hell, critic Joan Ferrante has noted: "The absence of popes as popes is one of the most striking features of Dante's Paradise" (*The Political Vision of the Divine Comedy,* Princeton, NJ: Princeton University Press, 1984, p. 256).

56   *emboldened you to seduce that virgin*   The allegorical virgin whom Boniface seduced was the Church, the Bride of Christ, whose husband he became when he was elected pope—the vicar (or representative) of Christ on earth. For the same vicarious marriage, see also line 111.

69   *the great mantle*   The liturgical robe that was a symbol of the papacy ("the mantles of popes" of II.27).

70   *Orsini*   Pope Nicholas III's family name, Orsini, can be read as "little bears" or "bear cubs." Giovanni Gaetano Orsini was born in Rome between 1210 and 1220. He was elected cardinal in 1244 and became pope, as we saw, in 1277. He was notorious for his nepotism and for shamelessly enriching his family. Politically, he attempted to limit the power of the king of Naples Charles of Anjou, who was also a Roman senator and papal vicar in Tuscany. Dante resented the pope's interference in Florentine politics.

72   *I lined pockets*   A pun on the ill-gotten gains with which he filled his pockets during his lifetime and the hole or "pocket" he himself fills here.

79   *cooked my feet longer*   Nicholas has been uppermost in the hole set aside for the popes for twenty years, since 1280. He will stay on top until Boniface dies in 1303. Then Boniface VIII will succeed him, only to be displaced eleven years later by the French pope Clement V (Bertrand de Got, pope from 1305 to 1314). It was the "lawless shepherd" Clement, "even more loathsome" than Boniface, who took the papacy into its so-called Babylonian Captivity in Avignon in France, where it remained from 1309 to 1377.

Between Nicholas and Boniface, there were four popes not condemned for simony by Dante: Martin IV (1281–1285), Honorius IV (1285–1287), Nicholas IV (1288–1292), and Celestine V (who was pope from August to December 1294 and is generally believed to be "that man / who through cowardice made the Great Refusal"; III.59–60). Between Boniface VIII and Clement V, there was one pope spared by Dante, Benedict XI (1303–1304).

85   *a new Jason*   This is not the mythological hero we met in the previous canto but the biblical Jason who purchased the high priesthood from King Antiochus the Illustrious (2 Macc. 4:8–9).

87   *the French king*   The Capetian Philip IV "the Fair" (1268–1314), who fa-
vored the accession of Bertrand de Got to the papacy, supposedly because Bertrand
promised him a cut of his tithes. Reacting to Boniface's papal bull or edict *Unam
Sanctam* (1302), which affirmed papal supremacy and excommunicated the French
monarch, in September 1303 Philip's constable Guillaume de Nogaret took the
pope prisoner in his summer palace at Anagni, where Boniface's personal enemy
Sciarra Colonna is alleged to have slapped the pontiff in the face. Boniface did not
long survive this sacrilegious humiliation.

95   *Matthias*   The eleven apostles remaining after the betrayal and suicide of
Judas Iscariot (Acts 1:18) drew lots for his succession and the lot fell upon Matthias.

99   *Charles*   Nicholas was alleged to have plotted against papal champion
Charles of Anjou and to have supported—in return for a substantial bribe from
John of Procida—the rebellion against the Angevin rulers, known as the Sicilian
Vespers, which broke out in Palermo on Easter Monday 1282. On this score at
least, subsequent historians have exonerated Nicholas.

101   *the Great Keys*   The Great Keys are the symbolic keys given by Jesus
Christ to Simon Peter (see lines 90–92), the emblems of papal authority. There can
be no doubt about Dante's reverence for the institution of the papacy. It has, how-
ever, been pointed out more than once that the poet places five popes (three here,
Celestine V—probably—in III.59–60, and Anastasius in XI.8) in Hell, two (Adrian
V and Martin IV) in Purgatory, and two (Saint Peter and John XXI) in Paradise.
Given that Dante died in 1321, shortly after completing the *Comedy,* during the
reign of John XXII, that leaves 188 popes unaccounted for.

106   *the Evangelist*   The author of the Apocalypse or Book of Revelation was
John of Patmos. In Dante's day he was assumed to be the same person as John the
Apostle and John the author of the fourth Gospel. "The great harlot, who sitteth
upon many waters, with whom the kings of the earth have committed fornica-
tion" (Apoc. 17:1–3) represents for Dante the corrupt hierarchy of the Church, her
seven heads are the seven sacraments, her ten horns the ten commandments, but
she has lost her virtue. Dante will return to the figure of the harlot in the elabo-
rate allegories of *Pg.* XXXII.

113   *an idolater*   An idolater worships the image of a false god; the simoniac
worships, as it were, the images on the coins he amasses. The figure of a hundred
is naturally a litotes or understatement.

115   *Constantine*   According to an apocryphal medieval tradition, the first
Christian emperor Constantine the Great (288–337) was cured of leprosy by can-
onized pope Saint Sylvester I and out of gratitude donated to him and his succes-
sors the city of Rome. The legal document corroborating the so-called "Donation
of Constantine" was proven to be a later forgery by humanist philologist Lorenzo
Valla in 1440. Dante and his contemporaries, however, still believed in its authen-
ticity, though Dante speaks out against its injustice on several occasions.

Canto XX

9   *the solemn pace*   What is meant are religious processions that move at a slow and solemn pace because the processioners are reciting prayers or singing hymns and often bearing a heavy statue on their shoulders. The Soothsayers tread slowly because they are walking backward, the way their heads are facing.

16   *a palsy*   A paralysis of some part of the body, sometimes accompanied by involuntary twitches and contortions.

22   *our human form*   According to Gen. 1:26, human beings were created in the image and likeness of God.

28   *pity survives here*   True pity (which respects God's judgment upon those who have offended him—in Italian "pity" and "piety" are rendered by the same word, *pietà*) survives where false pity (inspired by unreflective compassion for another's well-merited punishment) is absent.

34   *Amphiaraus*   This king of Argos was persuaded by his wife Eriphyle to join the expedition of the Seven against Thebes, even though he had foreseen his own death and the defeat of the besiegers. He acquitted himself valiantly, but, as he spurred on his chariot, pursued by Periclymenus, son of Neptune (in Greek Poseidon), Jove (in Greek Zeus) opened up a crater before him with his thunderbolt and Amphiaraus plunged down to Avernus. Dante's source is Statius' *Thebaid*.

36   *Minos*   The snarling judge, part man, part beast, we met at the beginning of Canto V, Minos wordlessly indicates to the sinners the circle to which they belong by the number of times he coils his tail.

38–39   *Because he wanted to see too far ahead / he faces behind*   Virgil neatly spells out the principle of what will be called, in the last line of Canto XXVIII, the *contrapasso* (a word transliterated into Italian from the Latin *contrapassum* by Dante, and rendered in this translation by "retribution"), by which the punishment is ironically made to fit the crime. Thomas Aquinas uses the term to explain the biblical *lex talionis* or law of retaliation ("an eye for an eye and a tooth for a tooth," Matt. 5:38). In devising this particular punishment, by the way, Dante may have been influenced by the wording of Isa. 44:25: "[I am the Lord] That make void the tokens of diviners, and make the soothsayers mad. That turn the wise backward, and that make their knowledge foolish."

40   *Tiresias*   T. S. Eliot's "old man with wrinkled female breasts" (*The Waste Land* 219), Tiresias was a blind Theban seer who accompanied the Achaean fleet to the siege of Troy. Ovid (*Meta.* III.316–38) describes how he struck two coupling snakes with his staff and was changed into a woman. Seven years later, he came upon and struck them once again, this time regaining his male gender.

47   *Arruns*   An Etruscan augur who, at the time of the dispute between Caesar and Pompey, was called from his cavern above Carrara in the marble-bearing

Apuan Alps of Lunigiana in northern Tuscany to Rome, where he foretold the coming civil war and Caesar's eventual victory. His gruesome conjurings are described in Lucan's *Civil War* (I.584–638).

55   *Manto*   The daughter of Tiresias who assisted him in his conjurings, according to Statius' *Thebaid*. After the death of her father, Manto quit Thebes (whose protector was Bacchus, and which, after the deaths of the rival brothers Eteocles and Polynices, had fallen into the hands of the tyrant Creon) and wandered through many lands before settling on the marshy island that would become the site of the future Mantua.

59   *Bacchus' city*   Bacchus (Dionysus) was supposed to have been born in Thebes.

62   *the mountains*   The Retic Alps that lie between Italy and Austria (in Dante's day, Austria—he calls it *Osterlicchi* in XXXII.26, from the German *Österreich*—was a small duchy on the Danube, considered by the poet as part of the German Empire). In Dante's day, the Tyrol was a separate political entity ruled by a count.

63   *Benaco*   The Latin name of what is now Lake Garda (*Lago di Garda*) is *Benacus,* transliterated into Italian as *Benaco.* Italy's largest lake, it lies today between the modern regions of Lombardy and the Veneto. Apart from a number of minor torrents on its western, Lombard side, the lake's main affluent, winding a tortuous course down from the Presanella massif, is the Sarca, torrentially swollen in the spring and early summer by the melting snows and glaciers upstream. The exiled Dante already shows an intimate knowledge of the region and may have been a guest of the lord of Verona Bartolomeo della Scala as early as 1303–1304. Bartolomeo's son Cangrande della Scala became one of Dante's most important patrons and the dedicatee of the *Paradiso.*

65–66   *Garda, Val Camonica, / and Pennino*   The town of Garda is on the eastern shore of the lake; the Val Camonica valley lies instead to the northwest. What Dante meant by Pennino is uncertain, but most commentators opt for the Alps in general (though the Pennine Alps are considerably farther off to the west) or the lesser mountain chain that lies between the Val Camonica and the lake.

67   *an island*   This is Friars' Island (known today as Isola Lechi), whose Franciscan convent and church of Santa Margherita fell under the ecclesiastical jurisdiction of three bishoprics. In the Middle Ages, bishops enjoyed temporal as well as spiritual powers. Trent, Verona, and Brescia are three major urban centers to the north, east, and west of Lake Garda, respectively. Trent, which today lends its name to the Trentino-Alto Adige region, and Verona are both on the Adige River.

70   *Peschiera*   In Dante's time, the city stronghold of Peschiera di Garda at the southeastern end of the lake was an outpost fortified against attacks from Bergamo or Brescia by the Della Scala family of Verona.

77   *Mincio*   The Mincio flows out of the southernmost tip of Lake Garda near Peschiera and debouches near Governolo, forty or so miles to the south, into the

Po, Italy's longest and widest river. In its course, the Mincio forms three small lakes in the vicinity of Mantua. The Sarca and the Mincio are considered by geographers to be two parts, almost equally long, of the same river, and the twenty-three miles from end to end of Lake Garda are part of its course.

82 *the ungentled virgin* Virgil is at odds with himself in this account. In the *Aeneid,* as we will see, Manto has a son. See note to line 98.

89 *a strong location* The settling of Venice on a group of islands in the marshy lagoon occurred for similar defensive purposes.

92 *without further augury* In a canto in which soothsayers and augurs are condemned, this apparent aside assumes a polemical value.

95 *Casalodi* Casalodi was a fortress town near Brescia that gave its name to the Guelph Casalodi family, who became early lords of Mantua. The Ghibelline Pinamonte de' Bonacolsi persuaded the credulous Alberto di Casalodi to banish the heads of the powerful noble families of Mantua to placate the party of the people. Subsequently in 1272, finding himself without allies, Casalodi was compelled by a popular revolt to hand the city over to Pinamonte. It was not until 1328, after Dante was dead, that the Bonacolsi were overthrown by the more famous Gonzaga family, with whom Mantua became identified during the Renaissance.

98 *any other account* Paradoxically Virgil himself had given a different version of the founding of Mantua in *Aen.* X.199–200, where he attributed the founding and naming of the city to Manto's son Ocnus. In his fundamental fifth-century commentary on Virgil's epic (which Dante undoubtedly knew), Servius claimed that it was founded instead by the Etruscan Tarcone, whereas for Isidore of Seville in his *Etmologiae* the founder was Manto herself.

It has been suggested that Dante is giving his guide the opportunity to dissociate himself as well as his native city from any suspicion of necromancy. For Virgil as magus, Domenico Camparetti's *Virgil in the Middle Ages* (Princeton, NJ: Princeton University Press, 1997/1895) was already cited in the note to IX.16. See also John Webster Spargo, *Virgil the Necromancer,* Cambridge, MA: Harvard University Press, 1934.

111 *he augured* Augurs claimed to foretell the future by studying the flight of birds. Eurypylus is a Greek hero in Homer's *Iliad,* where there is no suggestion that he was an augur. Like all of his contemporaries, who did not know Greek and had no firsthand knowledge of Homer, Dante is here interpreting the mention of Eurypylus in Sinon's devious account in *Aen.* II.114, as well as Servius' fourth-century gloss of that mention, which seem to suggest that he was an associate of the augur Calchas. The lying Sinon himself is punished in the Tenth Bolgia of the Eighth Circle (XXX.98).

111 *Aulis* The port in Boeotia from which, cutting the cables that anchored their ships, the Greek fleet set sail for Troy, leaving Greece without men and boys

because they were all away fighting. It was Calchas who decided that the time was ripe to appease the ire of Diana (in Greek Artemis) by sacrificing Iphigenia, daughter of Agamemnon and Clytemnestra.

113   *my high tragedy* According to the medieval theory of styles, Virgil's *Aeneid,* on account of its noble subject matter and sustained elevated style, was a paradigm of the "tragic" mode. It is probably not coincidental, especially given the grotesque and often scurrilous style of the *Inferno,* that, only twenty lines further on, in XXI.2, Dante will refer to his own work as his "Comedy."

116   *Michael Scot* Perhaps the most famous of thirteenth-century astrologers, this Scottish philosopher and occult scientist, who lived between c. 1175 and 1235 and whose fame is mentioned by Dante's contemporary, the Florentine chronicler Giovanni Villani, as well as by Boccaccio, became the official astrologer of Emperor Frederick II in 1227. The author of important treatises on astrology and alchemy, Michael Scot was active as a translator of Aristotle, Avicenna, and Averroës from Arabic into Latin.

118   *Guido Bonatti and Asdente* Bonatti was a celebrated stargazer from Forlì in the Romagna and author of a treatise on astronomy in ten books. He was employed by the emperor Frederick II, by Ezzelino da Romano (whom Dante puts among the Violent against Their Neighbors in XII.110, though he will place Ezzelino's sister Cunizza in the heaven of Venus in *Paradiso* IX), by Ghibelline leader Guido Novello before the battle of Montaperti (see the exchange with Farinata degli Uberti in Canto X), and by Guido da Montefeltro, the protagonist of Canto XVII.

Maestro Benvenuto was a toothless cobbler—hence the name *Asdente* ("without teeth")—from Parma who did not stick, as the proverb warns, to his cobbler's last, but took instead to prophecy. He is mentioned scornfully by Dante in his *Convivio* (IV.xvi.6) too. He is treated with respect, however, by his fellow townsman Franciscan friar Salimbene de Adam, in Salimbene's thirteenth-century *Chronicle* (translated by Joseph L. Baird, Giuseppe Baglivi, and John Robert Kane, Binghamton, NY: Center for Medieval and Early Renaissance Studies, 1986).

124   *Cain with his thorns* The Man in the Moon was popularly identified as the biblical husbandman Cain, compelled to wander as a fugitive and a vagabond for all eternity carrying a bundle of thorns on his back as punishment for having offered to God merely the fruits of the earth, a sacrifice inferior to that of his brother Abel the shepherd, who offered the firstlings of his flock. Seeing God favor Abel, Cain slew him (Gen. 4:1–16). The circumlocution, then, indicates the moon, though there was no mention of the moon, favorable or otherwise, in Dante's description of his attempts to escape from the dark wood in Canto I.

126   *the hemispheres' horns* The moon is setting south of the Spanish city of Seville (a reference point also for Ulysses' last voyage at XXVI.110), which lies on the western horizon with respect to Jerusalem, at the point where the northern

hemisphere (that of land) and the southern hemisphere (that of water) meet. As these astronomical indications would inform an educated medieval audience accustomed to interpreting them, it is 6:00 a.m. on Holy Saturday, April 9.

Canto XXI

2   *my Comedy*   The appellation is clearly intended to be compared with Virgil's reference to his *Aeneid* as "high tragedy" at the end of the previous canto. The distinction at this point is primarily stylistic. In the medieval classification of styles, the "tragic" was the highest register and the "comic" the lowest. As has already been pointed out (though translations typically obscure the fact, making all three linguistically similar), the three canticles of Dante's *Comedy* are actually composed in three very different registers, ranging from the *Inferno's* extremes of grotesque realism, through the elegiac *mediocritas* of the *Purgatorio,* to the sustained sublimity of the *Paradiso,* always on the outer edge, with its triumphant syllogistic tercets, expressing the inexpressible via protestations of ineffability, making the unintelligible intelligible through bright obscurity.

It is worth noting that this canto and the next (with a coda at the beginning of Canto XXIII) are the most overtly "comic" in the *Inferno.* The humor is broad, black, and cruel, raucous and raunchy, burlesque, not far removed at times from Marilyn Manson's "Grotesk Burlesk." Dante incorporates into his plot the topos of "the biter bit," typical of medieval farce. Even Virgil, Dante's trusted guide, often simplistically glossed as an allegory of Reason, will reveal his limitations as he allows himself to be duped by the pitch-black devils that throng the stage.

The sin punished in the Fifth Bolgia is Barratry (i.e., graft or political corruption), the secular equivalent of Simony. Dante was sentenced to be burned alive and thus forced into exile on trumped-up charges of barratry. This may explain the superior stylistic distance and the derisory scorn with which he treats tormented and tormentors alike (mingled, of course, with terror of the latter).

7   *their Arsenal*   The extended "epic" simile seems to be based on eyewitness observation of the bustling winter maintenance activity in the Venetian shipyard. For the moment, the only thing in common between the scene the pilgrim peers down on and the remembered scene the poet evokes is the presence of quantities of black and acrid molten pitch. However, soon the banks of the new bolgia, for the moment deserted, will bustle like the busy Venetian Arsenal with hyperactive (and sardonically malevolent) demons—though the boiling pitch with which the bolgia brims will turn out to have a punitive rather than a reparative use.

29   *a black devil*   The hybrid guardians we have seen so far had their origins for the most part in classical mythology. This devil without a name represents the first appearance of the kind of malicious demon we are accustomed to associate with a medieval Hell. There will soon be more of them, and we will get to know

them by name. Their job, which they perform with relish, is to keep the grafters immersed without respite in the hot pitch. Putting together the scattered descriptive clues, they are black with wings and tails, claws, fangs, and, at least in one case (Ciriatto), boarlike tusks. Likewise, at least one (Barbariccia) is bearded. In addition, they tear and torment their victims with long, sharp hooks that appear to resemble gaffs or boat hooks.

37   *Malebranche*   The *Malebranche* (Evil-claws), led by *Malacoda* (Evil-tail), are the guardians of this particular trench of the *Malebolge* (Evil-bolgias). The names of the demons cited later in the canto continue to be grotesquely meaningful and are invented by the poet on similarly allusive principles.

38   *Saint Zita*   The citizens of Lucca, about thirty miles as the crow flies northwest of Florence and eleven miles north of Pisa, are identified by their devotion to the memory of Zita da Monsagrati, a serving woman who died in 1272 with the reputation of being a saint (though she would not be officially canonized until the late seventeenth century). This anonymous "elder," or member of the ruling magistracy, is identified by the commentators as one Martino Bottaio, who died in fact on April 9, 1300, as Dante was making his imaginary journey. The "elders" of Black Guelph Lucca were the equivalent of the "priors" of Florence, the highest office held by White Guelph Dante.

41   *Bonturo*   The reference is sarcastically ironic. Bonturo Dati, who survived Dante and died in 1325, was the most notoriously corrupt politician in a town stigmatized by Dante for its corruption. As was the case with the current pope Bonifice VIII, condemned explicitly to Hell in Canto XIX, the naming of Bonturo here seems an implicit promise that he too will get his just deserts.

48   *the Holy Face*   The *Santo Volto* or Holy Face, a Byzantine image of the crucified Christ carved in black wood, is still on display in Lucca's church of San Martino. The pitch-daubed sinner appears on the surface in an attitude that recalls that of a worshiper on his knees bowing before a sacred image. The Serchio mentioned in the next line is a river that flows by Lucca. The sinner is being told with a vengeance that he can forget about ever again seeing the sights and places he was familiar with.

65   *the sixth embankment*   Virgil has crossed the bridge over the pitch-filled bolgia containing the grafters and is on the levee separating the Fifth Bolgia from the Sixth (where, in Canto XXIII, we will encounter the hypocrites).

94   *Caprona*   In the battle of Campaldino, near Arezzo, fought on June 11, 1289, the Guelph league of Tuscany, made up of combatants from Florence, Siena, and Pistoia, defeated the assembled Ghibellines. Buonconte da Montefeltro, son of the famous *condottiere* or mercenary captain Guido da Montefeltro, was one of the Ghibelline leaders and a fatal casualty of the battle. His body was never found. (For Buonconte's father Guido, see Canto XXVII.) The Ghibellines lost 1,700 men; the Guelphs, 300. A thousand Ghibelline prisoners were marched back to Florence and

either ransomed or left to die. Subsequently, the victorious Guelphs laid siege to Guido da Montefeltro himself, holed up with his men in the castle of Caprona. The stronghold capitulated in August, and its occupants emerged warily, fearful lest their besiegers not keep their promise to guarantee them safe passage. This is an interesting autobiographical reference, as we have no external record of Dante's participation in the siege.

105   *Scarmiglione*   As mentioned in the note to line 37, the names of the demons are intended to be meaningful (though their precise meaning is at times controversial and certainly more connotative than denotative) and suited to their natures. "Scarmiglione" evidently derives from the verb *scarmigliare,* which means—though the verb sounds euphemistic—"to dishevel." (It will be Graffiacane, however, who, in the next canto, hooks the sinner from Navarre by the hair and lifts him out of the pitch so that the other demons can get at him.) The reader may recall the fanciful names of the demons, derived from Samuel Harsnett's *Declaration of Egregious Popish Impostures* (1603), in Shakespeare's *King Lear:* Obidicut, Hoppedance or Hobbididence, Mahu, Modo, Flibbertigibbet, Frateretto, Smulkin, Purr the cat, and possibly Pillicock (see Dante's *Libicocco*).

111   *Another arch close by*   Malacoda is lying. There is in fact no arch or bridge over the Sixth Bolgia left standing. All were ruined by the same earthquake he is about to allude to.

112   *Five hours, etc.*   To buttress his credibility, Malacoda precisely documents the exact time of the earthquake that caused the bridge to collapse. He is alluding to the earth tremor described in the Gospel of Matthew that accompanied Christ's giving up the ghost: "And behold the veil of the temple was rent in two from the top even to the bottom, and the earth quaked, and the rocks were rent. And the graves were opened: and many bodies of the saints that had slept arose" (Matt. 27:51–52). As he states in his *Convivio* (IV.xxiii.10–11), Dante believed that Christ died at the age of thirty-four. So, adding Christ's age to 1266 takes us to 1300 C.E., the year of the poet's imaginary journey.

118–23   *Alichino, etc.*   Commentators agree that *Alichino* is derived from the French *Hellequin,* the leader of a gang of devils (*la mesnie hellequin*) according to popular legend. It has been suggested that the name anticipates that of the *commedia dell'arte* mask of Harlequin (*Arlecchino*). *Calcabrina* is a compound that can be glossed as "hoarfrost-treader" and presumably refers to the speed with which the demon moves, which is comparable with that of the first anonymous devil who brought the grafter from Lucca. *Cagnazzo* is an augmentative-pejorative of *cane* ("dog")—therefore, "big bad dog." *Barbariccia* means "curly beard." *Libicocco* is usually seen as a combination of syllables from the names of two winds, *Libeccio* (from the southwest) and *Scirocco* (from the southeast), alluding once more to rapidity of movement.

Draghignazzo, with the same augmentative-pejorative suffix -*azzo* as *Cagnazzo,* may mean "big bad dragon," though it also contains the word *ghigno* ("sneer").

Ciriatto comes from the Greek word for "pig, swine." *Graffiacane* is made up of a verb and a noun, *graffiare* ("to scratch") and *cane* ("dog"). *Farfarello* suggests lightness but is hard to parse. The consensus of opinion connects the name to the Provençal French *farfadet* ("sprite, hobgoblin, imp"). The name is borrowed by Romantic poet and satirist Giacomo Leopardi for his whimsical *Dialogo di Malambruno e Farfarello,* one of his imaginary dialogues (see Giacomo Leopardi, *Operette morali: Essays and Dialogues,* translated with introduction and notes by Giovanni Cecchetti, Berkeley: University of California Press, 1982, pp. 96–103). Finally, *Rubicante* derives from the Latin *rubor* ("redness") and suggests an irascible hair-trigger temperament, ready to flush with rage at any (or no) provocation.

139   *a trumpeting burst*   This mock-heroic flatulence, highlighted by its echoing through the canto break, provides a memorable moment in the farcical spirit of the medieval comic theater, though Barbariccia's exploit would still have delighted the Parisian audiences of versatile *pétomane* Joseph Pujol (1857–1945), "the Paganini of the fart." Few poets manage to reconcile scatology and eschatology as deftly as Shakespeare and Dante.

Canto XXII

5   *men of Arezzo*   The battle of Campaldino, in which Dante fought with the victorious Guelph cavalry, and the subsequent assault on the castle of Caprona, mentioned in the previous canto (XXI.94), both occurred near Arezzo in southern Tuscany.

15   *in church with saints*   This is a popular proverb counseling adaptation to the lowest common denominator, in keeping with the programmatic "comic" plebeian rhetoric of Cantos XXI–XXII. It could also be read, however, as a piece of stylistic advice.

19   *As dolphins breach*   These behaviors in dolphins were reputed to presage a coming storm.

48   *Navarre*   The kingdom of Navarre, straddling the Pyrenees between Castille and Aragon in northern Spain, fell under French influence in 1234 and was governed in Dante's day by the counts of Champagne. The anonymous speaker was identified by the early commentators as a certain Ciampolo, perhaps an Italianization of the French Jean-Paul, but nothing more concrete than what Dante has him say is known of his career.

52   *good King Thibault*   Thibault II was count of Champagne and king of Navarre from 1253 to 1270.

81   *Fra Gomita*   A member, like the hypocrites Catalano and Loderingo in Canto XXIII of the lay order of the Knights of the Glorious Virgin Mary or Jovial Friars, he governed Gallura on behalf of Dante's friend Nino Visconti of Pisa. For

one thing, he apparently accepted a substantial bribe to free a number of prisoners, claiming to have released them legally. The early commentators have little to add to the cryptic allusions contained in the text, though the Anonymous Florentine claims that Visconti had him hanged when he discovered Fra Gomita's double dealings.

82 *Gallura* One of the four administrative *giudicati* ("judgeships"), each ruled by a so-called "judge," into which Sardinia was divided by its Pisan and Genoese occupiers. The others were Arborea, Logudoro (or Logodoro), and Cagliari. Gallura lay to the northeast of the island.

88 *Don Michel Zanche* Again, not much is known about this character beyond what Dante says. The early commentators claim that he ruled the northwestern "judgeship" of Logudoro on behalf of Enzo or Heinz, the son of the emperor Frederick II, and that he usurped both Enzo's fiefdom and his wife, the Sardinian noblewoman Adelasia de Torres. He was treacherously murdered by his son-in-law Genoese Ghibelline Branca Doria, whose soul Dante condemns precociously to the lowest circle of Hell (XXXIII.137), among those who betrayed the sacred trust of hospitality, though his body continues to go through the motions of living on earth.

Canto XXIII

1 *Silent, alone, without company* A considerable change from the bustle and confusion of the preceding canto.

5 *Aesop* The fable, which had a wide circulation during the Middle Ages, is not in fact one of Aesop's. A mouse asks a frog to ferry him across a stream. The frog, whose intentions are not charitable, persuades the mouse that they must tie themselves together. Halfway across the frog tries to pull the mouse under, but a sparrow hawk, attracted by the struggle, swoops down and picks up the mouse in his beak, still tied to the frog.

13 *because of us* The Navarrese grafter had been released by the Malebranche so that he could call up some of his Tuscan and Lombard companions for Dante to question.

63 *the monks of Cluny* In 1119 Saint Bernard of Clairvaux (Dante's final intercessor in the last canto of the *Paradiso*) wrote a letter criticizing the hypocrisy and laxness of the monks of the tenth-century abbey of Cluny in Bourgogne, France, exemplified in their luxurious robes.

64 *The outside of the cloaks* In his thirteenth-century *Magnae derivationes,* Uguccione da Pisa gives a fanciful etymology for the word "hypocrite," deriving it from *hyper* ("above") and *crisis* ("gold"), meaning "gilded over," though Jesus Christ too compared the hypocritical scribes and Pharisees to "whited sepulchres, which outwardly appear to men beautiful, but within are full of dead men's bones, and of all filthiness" (Matt. 23:27).

66 *the ones Frederick used* The emperor Frederick II, admired by Dante, who nevertheless places him among the heretical Epicureans in the Sixth Circle (X.119), was tendentiously accused of cruelty by Guelph partisans. There is no historical evidence that he actually forced those guilty of lèse-majesté to strip and don a heavy cowl of lead, proceeding to put them into a furnace where the lead would melt and scald them to death.

104 *Catalano and . . . Loderingo* Catalano dei Malvolti, a Bolognese Guelph born around 1210, and his Ghibelline associate Loderingo degli Andalò, also from Bologna, were among the founders in 1261 and earliest adherents of the lay order of the *Cavalieri della Milizia della Beata Vergine Maria* ("Knights of the Militia of the Blessed Virgin Mary"), subsequently known as the *Frati Gaudenti* or Jovial Friars. In May 1266, the year after Dante was born, the two Bolognese were appointed by Pope Boniface VIII as peacemaking chief magistrates of faction-torn Florence. Together they shared the role of *podestà,* usually occupied by a single individual who was not a native of the city and could therefore be expected to be above and aloof from the fray. In point of fact, at the pope's behest, they secretly favored the pro-papal Guelph faction, a policy that exacerbated existing tensions and led to an open clash, resulting in the banishment and persecution of the Uberti family of Ghibelline leaders (we met Farinata in Canto X) and the confiscation and destruction of their property.

108 *Gardingo* Florence's Palazzo della Signoria, which was begun in 1299, now stands in the neighborhood previously associated with a watchtower called the Gardingo going back to early medieval Lombard times. The houses of the Uberti, razed to the ground as a consequence of Catalano and Loderingo's hypocrisy, were built in the Gardingo district.

115 *The one transfixed here* This is the high priest Caiphas (as the Douay Bible calls him), who persuaded the council of the Pharisees that it was fitting that one man, Jesus Christ, die as a scapegoat for the Jewish nation: "Neither do you consider that it is expedient for you that one man should die for the people, and that the whole nation perish not" (John 11:50).

121 *His father-in-law* The father-in-law of Caiphas was Annas (John 18:13), who was also a high priest, before whom Christ was led after his betrayal by Judas.

123 *that council* The council is the Sanhedrin, all of whose members are guilty of hypocrisy, as it were, to the second power. They are crucified, like Caiphas and Annas, at different points along the floor of the bolgia, to be crushed beneath the painfully slow-moving feet of those burdened with the leaden habits. Their eternal punishment, modeled on that inflicted upon Christ on Calvary, is greater than that of the common Hypocrites because their offense was committed directly against the Christian God.

134 *a ridge* This is another radius of the Eighth Circle similar to the viaduct of bridges on which Virgil and Dante had crossed the earlier bolgias, only to find

the bridge over the Sixth Bolgia in ruins. Malacoda had sent them around the circumference of the Sixth Bolgia to find another bridge that was supposedly intact. Instead, all of the bridges over the Sixth Bolgia were destroyed by the earthquake that accompanied Christ's death on the cross (XXI.112–14).

144 *he is a liar* The sinner appears to be savoring Virgil's discomfiture, as he enunciates with solemn irony this biblical truism: "When he [the devil] speaketh a lie, he speaketh of his own: for he is a liar, and the father thereof" (John 8:44).

Canto XXIV

2 *Aquarius* The sun is in the zodiacal sign of Aquarius between January 21 and February 20. The worst of the Italian winter can be said to be over, the sun's rays (Apollo's locks) are becoming steadily, if as yet imperceptibly, warmer. The nights are getting shorter as the spring equinox (March 21) approaches. This is the season described in the extended rural simile with which the canto opens (lines 1–15).

5 *her wintry sister* The twin sister, so to speak, of the winter frost, specifically of the white hoarfrost formed on the grass and branches by frozen dew and fog, is snow, more of a problem for the farmer who needs to graze his sheep.

6 *the quill she draws with* The metaphor (within the simile) of frost as a scribe whose quill pen, quick to lose its point, does not last (though some interpret Dante's Italian to refer to watercolors that dry on the painter's brush) stresses the fact that, unlike snow, which takes time to melt, the hoarfrost disappears quickly, dissolving in the sun's first rays. This is how the face of the world changes its expression (lines 13–14). The initial dejection of the peasant in the simile and his subsequent taking heart, Dante reads in the face of his guide Virgil.

85 *Libya* This reference to the Libyan desert is more literary than geographical. Dante's authorities for the cornucopia of serpents of North Africa are Latin poets Ovid and Lucan, whose metamorphoses he will vow to outdo in the next canto (XXV.94–102). The Italian names in this menacing list of exotic species of snakes (inventively Anglicized in this translation) are in fact not the names of snakes Dante has ever seen but direct calques of the Latin names used by Lucan in his *Civil War* (IX.711–21). As will become more apparent in the next canto, the snakes as well as the people are all sinners, punished for theft by having their human identity constantly threatened and stolen. The two categories, human and serpentine, are condemned to steal each other's forms in these two cantos of Ovid-inspired metamorphoses.

93 *no magic stone* Dante specifically mentions the heliotrope, a stone that, according to the medieval lapidaries, provided protection against poison. It was also supposed to make people invisible.

100   *An o or an* i   It should be noted that the pronoun "I" in Italian is *io,* a combination of these two letters. Moreover, the pronoun is used as a noun meaning "ego" or "self," precisely what is most vulnerable in this disturbingly *unheimlich* or eerie bolgia. The instantaneous disintegration of the thief has a precedent, overtly alluded to in the next canto (XXV.95), in Lucan's account of the equally immediate liquefaction of the Roman soldier Sabellus when bitten while crossing the Libyan desert by a small but extremely venomous reptile called a *seps* (*Civil War* IX.762–88).

107   *the Phoenix*   This fabulous bird supposedly lived for five hundred years and rose again from the ashes of its aromatic funeral pyre. Nard (spikenard) and myrrh, like amomum, are precious ointments made from the extracts of rare plants. Dante's source is once more Ovid (*Meta.* XV.392–407). Since Christian exegetes interpreted the myth in terms of Christ's death and resurrection, the disintegration and recomposition of the thief can be seen as a parody of these events.

114   *seized with paralysis*   An epileptic fit, for example; however, the scientific clinical analysis is placed on the same level of probability as demonic possession.

124   *A bestial life*   By insisting on terms belonging to the animal world ("bestial," "mule," "beast," "lair"), the speaker, Vanni Fucci, a Black Guelph from Pistoia (about twenty-one miles northwest of Florence) is eager to present himself exclusively as a man of Violence—in Dante's system a lesser offense than Fraud. The author, however, has put him in the Seventh Bolgia of the Eighth Circle, along with the other fraudulent Thieves, and not immersed along with the Violent in Phlegethon, the River of Blood in the Seventh Circle, a good twelve cantos back.

125   *mule*   The word was a cant or slang term for "bastard."

132   *blushed with bitter shame*   Despite his swaggering, Vanni's ignominious crime has been exposed, and he has no choice but to confess.

142   *open your ears*   Vanni is about to add—with vindictive relish—to the prognostications Dante has so far heard—from Ciacco, Farinata, Brunetto Latini— concerning coming political events in Tuscany and his own future. Vanni's apocalyptic forecast is couched in the typically allusive metaphorical language of prophecy. In the ongoing struggle between the White and Black Guelphs that, since the definitive eclipse of the Ghibellines in 1267, had taken the place of the rivalry between Guelphs and Ghibellines, the Whites (Dante's party) will at first be victorious. In May 1301, in fact, the local Blacks (Vanni's party) would be dispossessed and driven from Pistoia with the help of the dominant Florentine Whites. In the following year, 1302, however, with the descent into Italy of Charles of Valois, the Blacks would once more return to power in Florence, driving the Whites, including Dante, into exile. The situation of the Whites will deteriorate still further when Mars, the god of war, brings a lightning bolt—Morello Malaspina, marquis of Lunigiana—out of the Val di Magra to lead the Blacks of Lucca and Florence against what has become

by now the last White stronghold of Pistoia. The victory of the Blacks in a decisive battle near Pistoia will put a definitive end to White hopes of returning to Florence. The historical Campo Piceno (*ager Picenus*), referred to by Roman historians, was located between Ancona and the Sangro River in the Marche. Dante and his medieval commentators, however, mistakenly located it near Pistoia.

Canto XXV

2   *made figs with both fists*   The "fig" sign, equivalent to giving someone the finger, was made by pointing a clenched fist at the receiver with the thumb protruding between the index and middle finger. It is illustrated in Desmond Morris et al., *Gestures: Their Origins and Distribution,* New York: Stein and Day, 1979, p. 148. I analyzed Canto XXV in some detail in the essay "The Perverse Image," in Allen Mandelbaum, Anthony Oldcorn, and Charles Ross, *Lectura Dantis: Inferno. A Canto-by-Canto Commentary* (Berkeley: University of California Press, 1998, pp. 328–47). Surprisingly, giving the fig to God was a gesture common enough to be expressly forbidden, for example, by the bylaws of the city of Prato. We are told that two huge marble arms aimed at Florence and brandishing the figs were placed atop a tower in Carmignano at the boundary between their two territories by Vanni Fucci's city of Pistoia.

6   *"You will speak no more"*   This is the first (or second, if we interpret Vanni's figs as a silencing gesture) of several acts of silencing in this canto: Hercules' silencing of Cacus, the three Florentines' interruption of Virgil's and Dante's conversation, pilgrim Dante's silencing of Virgil (line 45), poet Dante's silencing of Lucan and Ovid, the silencing of the voice of humanity in the transformed sinners. This is a canto of uncanny, eerie silence, in which speech (except for Virgil's account of Cacus) is staccato, inarticulate, and minimal.

12   *your founders*   The legendary founders of Pistoia were the followers of the Roman demagogue Lucius Sergius Catilina (c. 108–62 B.C.E.), known as Catiline, a rival of the great Roman orator and consul Marcus Tullius Cicero. Catiline treasonably conspired against Cicero and the Roman state, only to be defeated and killed in 62 B.C.E. by propraetor Marcus Petreius near Pistoria (modern Pistoia). The main sources for the history of the Catilinarian Conspiracy are Cicero's four orations against Catiline and the account by frustrated politician turned historian Gaius Sallustius Crispus, known as Sallust, in his *Bellum Catilinae.*

15   *he who fell from the walls of Thebes*   The blasphemer Capaneus, punished among the Violent against God in the Seventh Circle (see note to XIV.46).

19   *Maremma's swamps*   There was a previous reference to the no-man's-land of the Maremma region in southern Tuscany, "the lowlands between Cecina and Corneto," a byword for untamed wildness, in XIII.9. Its insalubriousness will be cited again in XXIX.47.

25   *Cacus*   This mythological son of Vulcan, half-man, half-beast, is alluded to by Virgil in *Aen.* VIII.194 as *semihominis Caci* ("half-human Cacus"). Dante envisioned him not as a fire-breathing ogre, as Virgil did, but as a Centaur. From his lair in a cave under Rome's Aventine Hill, Cacus preyed upon the local population. When Hercules arrived, driving the cattle he had seized from Geryon, Cacus rustled four of his bulls and four heifers, dragging them backward to his cave to confuse their tracks. One of the heifers, however, lowed, tipping off Hercules to their whereabouts. In the *Aeneid*'s account, Hercules strangled Cacus; according to Ovid in his *Fasti* (I.575–78), however, Hercules clubbed him to death.

43   *Cianfa*   The first of the five thieves whose first names only are mentioned. Another will be tagged in the course of the canto as an Agnello (line 68), a third as a certain Buoso, and a fourth as Puccio Sciancato or "Lame Puccio" (line 149). The fifth thief is not given a name but is identified by a circumlocution in the canto's last line. Though the opening lines of Canto XXVI make it clear all five are Florentines, we are not told what families they belonged to. This makes identifying them all but impossible. According to several early commentators, Cianfa was a member of the Donati clan, though Pietro Alighieri, the poet's son, identifies him as Cianfa degli Abati. Since Dante's point is that their very identity as the souls of human beings is in constant peril—continually stolen from them and restored while they remain impotent to resist—any attempt at identification therefore goes counter to the poet's intentions. In this canto it also becomes apparent that not only the human figures Dante perceives but the snakes too are damned souls.

58   *Ivy*   The ivy simile is borrowed from Ovid's description of the way the nymph Salmacis clung to Hermaphroditus (*Meta.* IV.365), an important subtext for this second metamorphosis. Ovid will be named as a competitor in line 97. The similes of the melting wax and the splendidly observed burning paper are Dante's own.

68   *Agnello*   Identified as one Agnello dei Brunelleschi, though nothing is known of his activities.

80   *under the Dog Star's terrible scourge*   In the so-called "dog days," the hottest and most sultry months of the year, July and August. The Dog Star, Sirius, is the brightest star in the constellation of Canis Major.

94   *Let Lucan fall silent*   This, and the challenge to Ovid below, is an example of the "outdoing" (*Überbietung*) or *Nunc sileat* or *Nunc taceat* topos (from the Latin for "let him now be silent"), popularized by the Latin poet Statius (though Lucan used it too) and exemplified by Ernst Robert Curtius in his *European Literature and the Latin Middle Ages* (*Europäische Literatur und lateinisches Mittelalter* [1948], translated by Willard Trask, New York: Pantheon, 1953, pp. 162–65). Like the opposite topos of stylistic inadequacy that we will encounter, for example, in the opening lines of Cantos XXVIII and XXXII—though it is also invoked, as it were in passing, in 143–44 of the present canto—this metatextual "boast" underlines the poet's artistic

detachment. A curious scientific observer and precise chronicler of a "reality" engineered, according to his fiction, by God, he invites us to attend to how well he is describing the horrors he "saw," putting aside any misplaced pity for the victims.

95   *Nasidius*   Bitten by a serpent while crossing the Libyan desert, his body inflated until it ruptured his armor and spilled out formlessly onto the ground (Lucan, *Civil War* XI.789–804). For Sabellus, another soldier who met a similarly horrible fate, see note to XXIV.100.

98   *Cadmus*   In a passage that will form a less detailed subtext for the last of Dante's climactic metamorphoses (104–38), Ovid describes how Cadmus, the founder of the city of Thebes, and his wife Harmonia were both changed into serpents (*Meta.* IV.576–601).

99   *Arethusa*   The tale of the lovely nymph Arethusa, who, chased by the enamored river god Alpheus, was transformed into a stream to escape his clutches (*Meta.* V.577–641), bears no direct relationship to any of the metamorphoses described by Dante. However, the erotically charged story of the nymph Salmacis (who also gave her name to a fountain) and her fusion with the beautiful Hermaphroditus (*Meta.* IV.285–388) is clearly the inspiration for the metamorphosis described in lines 49–78.

102   *interchanged their substances*   Ovid's metamorphoses involve a before and after: one nature, usually human, is transformed into another, animate or inanimate. What Ovid never described was a reciprocal "telemorphic" metamorphosis like the one Dante is about to describe, in which two natures, remaining at a distance from each other, steal each other's substance or matter—a trans-*material*-ization rather than a trans-*form*-ation.

140   *Buoso*   Some early commentators identify the shade who scuttles off in reptilian form as Buoso degli Abati, about whom nothing historical is known, others as Buoso dei Donati, a nephew and namesake of the Buoso Donati who was impersonated after he died—we will learn in Canto XXX—by Gianni Schicchi. Modern Dante scholarship seems to have opted for the latter. The speaker here (the shade who was changed from serpent to man) has been identified as Francesco (or Guelfo or Guccio) Cavalcanti, the one for whom the village of Gaville still groans (line 151). He was apparently killed by the inhabitants of Gaville, about four miles south of Figline, in the Arno valley upstream from Florence. In retaliation, members of his clan decimated the population of the village.

144   *my quill*   The earlier topos of outdoing is balanced here by the topos of modesty and inadequacy (though the fact that the description may fall short of the reality implies at the same time that the poet really saw what he tried to describe).

149   *Puccio Sciancato*   Puccio Galigai, known by his nickname of Lame Puccio (*sciancato* = "lame"). He is mentioned in several contemporary documents but not as a thief. The bemused pilgrim presumably recognizes him by his limp.

150   *The other was he*   This is the Francesco Cavalcanti referred to in the note to line 140 (though Dante, as previously remarked, studiously avoids naming him).

Canto XXVI

1   *Rejoice, O Florence*   This opening apostrophe recalls the invective against the followers of Simon Magus with which Canto XIX began, or the condemnation of Pistoia in Canto XXV (10–12). Indictments of Pisa (XXXIII.79–90) and Genoa (XXXIII.151–52) are still to come. It has been pointed out that Dante's spelling "Fiorenza" is an anagram, if we remove the *z*, of the name of the Inferno.

9   *Prato*   Florence's closest Tuscan neighbor (ten miles away) and a commercial rival, on the Bisenzio River, about halfway between Florence and Pistoia. Prato was forced into an unwelcome alliance with more powerful Florence to counter the expansionist threat from Pistoia. The exiled Dante, speaking in his own voice as author, identifies with Florence's enemies in their desire for her comeuppance.

21–24   *I rein in my native genius*   Dante, still speaking in the authorial voice, stresses the need for self-control and self-discipline and the metaphorical reins of virtue.

23   *a kind star*   It was Brunetto Latini who referred to the favor of the heavens toward Dante (XV.55–60).

25   *In the season*   Summer is the season in which the sun hides his face least. The fly yields to the mosquito after sunset.

34   *the prophet who was avenged by bears*   After witnessing Elias (Elijah) carried up to heaven in a whirlwind by a fiery chariot drawn by fiery horses, Eliseus (Elisha) was mocked for his baldness by the children of Bethel. He cursed them in the name of the Lord, and two bears came out of the forest and mauled forty-two of them (4 Kings 2).

45   *I would have fallen below*   Again, the author's comment dramatizes the pilgrim's eagerness for knowledge "of men's vices and their valor" (line 99) and its inherent dangers.

54   *Eteocles*   Son of Oedipus and Oedipus' mother Jocasta, elder brother of Polynices, Ismene, and Antigone. When Oedipus banished himself from Thebes, the two brothers, though cursed by their father, agreed to rule in alternate years. Eteocles, however, reneged on the deal and refused to give up the throne. Thereupon Polynices returned with the Seven against Thebes, and the two brothers met in single combat and killed one another. Their mutual hatred was such that, when their bodies were cremated together, the flame from the pyre separated and its two tongues continued to vie with each other for supremacy. The episode is recounted in Book XII of Statius' *Thebaid*.

55 *Ulysses and Diomedes* Two of the most famous Greek heroes of the war against Troy. Ulysses is the Roman name of the wily Greek Odysseus, son of Laertes, husband of Penelope, and king of Ithaca, one of the heroes of Homer's *Iliad* and the central figure in his *Odyssey* (neither of which Dante knew firsthand). As a warrior, Diomedes, son of Tydeus and king of Aetolia, was second only to Achilles. Diomedes inflicted a wound on the Trojan Aeneas, who was healed by his mother Venus (in Greek Aphrodite). Ulysses and Diomedes performed several cunning deeds together, including the stratagem of the Trojan Horse and the theft of the Palladium (a statue of the goddess Pallas Athena that protected the city of Troy). According to the only surviving book of Statius' unfinished epic *Achilleid,* the pair discovered Achilles disguised as a girl on the island of Scyros, where his mother Thetis had hidden him in hope of keeping him away from Troy and his prophesied death. While in Scyros, he had seduced Deidamia, the king's daughter, by whom he had a son, Neoptolemus or Pyrrhus. See note to V.65.

60 *the noble seed of Rome* In Virgil's *Aeneid,* dutiful Aeneas, destined to become the founder of Rome, describes to Dido how he carried his father Anchises on his shoulders out through the gates of burning Troy, leading his son Ascanius by the hand, followed, as he thought, by his faithful wife Creüsa. When he no longer saw her, he returned to look for her, only to encounter her shade, who took leave of him, prophesying his long exile and his destiny to be crowned at long last with "happy times, kingship, and a royal wife" (*Aen.* II.924–25).

69 *how strongly desire inclines me toward it* Multiplying his prayer a thousand times, the pilgrim leans like a flame toward the flame. A moment later, before the *tongue* of flame, Virgil will tell Dante to restrain his *tongue* (line 72), providing more clues to Dante's vital involvement in this encounter.

74 *because they were Greeks* In a controversial poem in four languages (Provençal, French, Latin, and Italian), *Aï faus ris, pour quoi traï aves* ("Alas, false smile, why have you betrayed") attributed by some authorities to Dante, line 4, *Iam audivissent verba mea Greci!* ("Even Greeks might have listened to my words"), seems to refer to the proverbial arrogance and aloofness of the Greeks. The Latin-Lombard Virgil will be the intermediary between Dante and these ancient Greeks, with whose language Dante is not familiar. In his address to the classical heroes (79–84), Virgil will deploy his most persuasive rhetoric in a *captatio benevolentiae,* or flattering appeal meant to capture the favor of his audience, a ploy that is still used by the skilled public speaker.

90–91 *When I left / Circe* The speaker is Ulysses. During his adventurous return from Troy to his native Ithaca, narrated by Homer in the *Odyssey* but known to Dante in a fragmentary manner from later Roman and medieval sources, Ulysses and his men were guests of the enchantress Circe (who at first cast a spell on his followers, changing them into swine, and was later prevailed upon to change them back).

92   *Gaeta*   The modern name of ancient *Caieta,* a promontory and a port on the Tyrrhenian Sea, four miles from Formia in southern Latium. Virgil (*Aen.* VII.1–7) says that the locality was named after Aeneas' wet nurse Caieta, who died and was interred there. Aeneas' honoring her is yet another instance of his filial piety. The mention of Aeneas here is a clue to the fact that Ulysses' behavior is being judged (and found wanting) by the standards of *pietas* (defined in P. G. W. Glare's *Oxford Latin Dictionary* as "an attitude of dutiful respect toward those to whom one is bound by ties of religion, consanguinity, etc.") set by the Trojan hero.

94–96   *my son . . . Penelope*   Ulysses' son by his wife Penelope was Telemachus, and Ulysses' father was Laertes. By the adventurer's own admission, his loving duty to his family was overcome by his gratuitous curiosity and his burning desire for experience. In this he forms a marked contrast to "pious" Aeneas, who undertook his journey from Troy to Rome out of necessity, accompanied by the surviving members of his family and guided at every stage by the gods.

103–104   *Spain, / as far as Morocco*   These are the countries that lie on either side of the Strait of Gibraltar, where the western Mediterranean meets the Atlantic Ocean.

106   *old and slow*   They had arrived, in other words, "at that stage of life when it befits a man / to lower his sails and coil up his ropes" (XXVII.80–81), as Guido da Montefeltro, condemned to this same bolgia, will point out in the next canto.

108   *Hercules*   The actual Pillars of Hercules were two stone columns that stood outside the famous temple of Hercules on the island of Santi Petri, ten miles south of Gades (modern Cadiz). Legend had it, however, that the two facing promontories of Abyla in North Africa and Calpe (the modern Gibraltar—a name of Arabic origin) in Europe, on opposite sides of the *Fretum Gaditanum* (the ancient name of the strait derives from that of Gades), at the outlet from the relatively familiar Mediterranean Sea into the unknown Atlantic Ocean, marked the place where Hercules set up two huge columns with the warning inscription *Non plus ultra* ("Go no farther"). Beyond, for Dante, stretched the undiscovered and uninhabited hemisphere of water, the "unpeopled world" (line 116) from whose bourn no traveler returns.

111   *Ceuta*   Ceuta is on Morocco's Mediterranean coast. Seville in Spain is an inland city actually closer to the Atlantic than to the Mediterranean, as Dante seems to think. It was thought of as the farthest western limit of civilization, as *ultima Thule* was the farthest point north.

112   *Brothers*   Not only Ulysses' companions but also many post-Romantic critics have been swayed by the hero's appeal to what appear to be their noblest impulses. In the *Odyssey,* Ulysses closed his crew members' ears with wax and had them tie him to the mast so as not to let the Sirens' song lure them into shipwreck; in this canto, Dante casts Ulysses himself in the role of Siren.

119–20 *You were not made* Ulysses' persuasive discourse is manipulative. No one can argue with the syllogism's premise—that we should follow reason in order to live a fully human life. But is his conclusion—that we should follow our curiosity wherever it leads—as unquestionably true? And let us not forget that the Fraudulent (and the Traitorous) are in the lower circles of Hell precisely because they used their God-given reason for evil ends. As if to confirm the validity of the general principle, however, in his treatise *De vulgari eloquentia* (*On Eloquence in the Vernacular*), Dante himself described "those illustrious heroes," the Hohenstaufen emperor Frederick II and "his worthy son Manfred," saying "they knew how to reveal the nobility and integrity that were in their hearts; and, as long as fortune allowed, they lived in a manner befitting men, despising the bestial life" (Dante, *De vulgari eloquentia,* edited and translated by Steven Botterill, New York: Cambridge University Press, 1996, I.ii.4).

125 *our last, mad run* In Italian "mad run" is *folle volo.* Light is thrown on Dante's attitude to Ulysses' fatal voyage when we remember that the pilgrim himself, at the outset of his journey, sought confirmation from Virgil that his expedition had divine sanction and was not hubristic and presumptuous. There, in II.35, he had used this very adjective, *folle,* to describe what he feared: "I fear it may be madness" (*temo che la venuta non sia folle*).

130 *Five times* The moon has waxed and waned five times since the "mad run" (line 125) began. Five long lunar months have passed.

133 *a mountain* At the beginning of the *Purgatorio,* it will dawn upon the reader that what Ulysses and his crew caught sight of was the island mountain of Purgatory, where the traces of sin are purged in preparation for Heaven. But Purgatory is a supernatural realm, and the only ones who have access to it are the souls of the redeemed dead, ferried there on a boat propelled by an angel's wings without need of oars (see the previous reference at III.93). Whereas Ulysses and his crew made wings of their oars, the angel helmsman makes oars of his wings.

Canto XXVII

7 *the Sicilian bull* Phalaris, the infamous sixth-century B.C.E. Greek tyrant of Acragas in Sicily (modern Agrigento), a paradigm of cruelty, is reputed to have ordered an Athenian artist named Perillus to construct a hollow brass bull into which he would place his victims, light a fire beneath it, and roast them to death. The bull was designed in such a way that the victims' screams, channeled through resonating chambers, imitated the bellowing of a real wounded bull. When it was finished, Perillus was the first to be put inside to see if it worked. Dante's source for the story is probably Ovid, who remarks in his *Ars amatoria* (I.655–56) that Perillus got what was coming to him.

19 *You, to whom I direct / my voice* Guido da Montefeltro (c. 1220–1298), the soul trapped within the flame, speaks to Virgil, whose leave-taking of Ulysses, which Guido quotes, is elided in Dante's narrative. Guido's recognition of Virgil's "Lombard" speech recalls Farinata's recognition of Dante's Florentine accent in Canto X. In Dante's day the term "Lombardy" included most of Italy north of the Apennines, including Romagna and the March of Ancona, where the speaker is from. There appears to be a small inconsistency here, since Virgil, after his preamble silencing Dante and offering to speak for him to the Greek heroes, is unlikely to have addressed Ulysses in Italian. Not being able to see them, Guido assumes that they are two sinners condemned like him to inhabit tongues of flame in this bolgia.

28 *tell me if Romagna is at peace or war* Renowned military strategist Guido further resembles Farinata in his sincere political concern for his native region, as well as in having fought for the Ghibelline cause most of his life, only to become reconciled with the pope and take vows as a Franciscan friar in 1296. It was from Farinata, incidentally, that the pilgrim learned of the shades' ignorance of the events of recent and contemporary history.

29 *between Urbino / and the ridge from which the Tiber springs* The county of Montefeltro, conferred upon Guido's family by the emperor Frederick II, lay in the mountainous region between the city of Urbino and the eastern slopes of Mount Fumaiolo in the Apennines where the river Tiber rises.

40 *Ravenna* The catalog of the cities of Romagna begins with Ravenna, from the sixth to the eighth century the outpost of the Byzantine empire in Italy. The remaining cities—Forlì ("the land that endured the long ordeal"), Rimini (where "Verrucchio's mastiffs" hold sway), Faenza and Imola ("the cities on the Lamone and the Santerno"), and finally Cesena ("whose side the Savio bathes")— are not named but identified by oblique periphrases, referring either to the rivers they are built on, to memorable events that recently occurred there, or, as was previously the case with the usurers of Canto XVII (lines 55–75), to the heraldic animals displayed in the coats of arms of their ruling families.

41 *The eagle of Polenta* A red eagle on a gold field was the heraldic device of the family of Guido da Polenta, who seized Ravenna in 1275 with the support of the Malatesta clan of Rimini (see line 46). The alliance between these two Guelph families was intended to be further cemented by the marriage of Guido da Polenta's daughter Francesca, whom we met among the Lustful in Canto V, to one of Malatesta's sons.

44 *a bloody heap* In May 1282 Guido da Montefeltro was defending Forlì, traditionally a Ghibelline stronghold, against a two-year siege by a Guelph army, made up of the French and papal troops. At one point, Guido, known for his cunning, is supposed to have tricked the French knights into entering the city, where they found themselves in a trap and were summarily slaughtered.

45   *the green claws*   Forlì is now ruled by the Ordelaffi family, whose arms feature a green lion rampant.

46   *Verucchio's mastiffs*   Malatesta the Elder (c. 1226–1312) from Verucchio was first *podestà* and then lord of Rimini. His firstborn son Malatestino—the Italian word for mastiff, *mastino,* is Dante's punning shortening of his name—succeeded him in 1312 and ruled until his own death in 1317. The stronghold of Verucchio, where the family had its origins, lay inland from Rimini and the Adriatic, north of San Marino. Malatesta's other two sons were Gianciotto, the husband of Francesca, condemned by Dante among the Traitors of the Ninth Circle, and Paolo, her brother-in-law and lover, who was silently with her in the Second Circle. The Sigismundo of Ezra Pound's *Cantos* (8–11) was a fifteenth-century descendant.

47   *dealt so harshly*   Montagna dei Parcitadi, a leader of the Ghibelline faction in Rimini, was deceived, imprisoned, and cruelly put to death by Malatesta in 1295.

50   *the Lamone and the Santerno*   Two small rivers near the cities of Faenza and Imola, respectively. They were currently ruled by Maghinardo (or Mainardo) Pagani da Susinana, who died in 1302, called a "demon" by Guido del Duca, another lord of Romagna, who delivers an invective similar to this one, deploring the factiousness and decadence of the region, in *Pg.* XIV. The family crest was an azure lion on a white field. Despite his espousal of the Ghibelline cause in Romagna, the opportunistic Maghinardo fought alongside the Florentine Guelphs at the battle of Campaldino (1289). In the Florentine crisis of 1301, foretold by Ciacco in VI.67–69, he came in on the side of the pope's champion Charles of Valois and the Black Guelphs.

52   The de facto tyrant of Cesena, on the Savio River, was Galasso da Montefeltro, Guido's cousin, who, however, managed to maintain the illusion of communal "freedom" by keeping the titles of *podestà* and "captain of the people."

61–66   *If I believed*   The wily Guido is deceived (or self-deceived). Unable to see Dante from inside his tongue of flame and to recognize that the pilgrim is still living, he concludes that he is a shade destined for punishment in this circle who can never reveal his secret. (The situation recalls Canto XIX, in which Pope Nicholas III not only mistakes Dante for another sinner but actually takes him for the reigning pope.) Had he not made this mistake, Guido would have been unwilling to confess, since his situation in the afterlife is quite different (and more shameful) from the impression left by the external circumstances of his life. Lines 61–66 are quoted in Italian, without attribution, by T. S. Eliot as the epigraph to "The Love Song of J. Alfred Prufrock."

68   *a Franciscan*   Guido's exemplary conversion in 1296—he was by that time in his seventies—and his retirement to the Franciscan community in Assisi were all people knew of his final years. Unwittingly, he is about to admit Dante, and the poet's readers, into his private space.

70   *the Great Priest*   The pope, vicar of Christ upon earth, the ultimate authority in the Catholic church. The reigning pope, as we have seen, was Boniface VIII (1294–1303) of the powerful Caetani family, a symbol, for Dante, of all that was corrupt, whom the poet has already condemned to Hell in Canto XIX.

74–75   *my actions were not / like those of the lion, but of the fox*   The distinction between force, typical of the lion, and fraud, typical of the fox, goes back at least to the ancient Roman orator Cicero. The same distinction underlay the macroscopic allotment of the circles of Lower Hell to the various groups of the Violent and the Fraudulent (including the Treacherous) explained in XI.24 et seq.

80   *that stage of life*   Guido's definition of old age as the time when the seafarer should finally decommission his vessel and come ashore throws retrospective light on Ulysses' defiance of the rule by undertaking his final adventure when he and his crew were "old and slow" (XXVI.106), another aspect of his "folly."

85   *the Prince*   Another singularly unflattering characterization of Boniface. Like the Pharisees of the New Testament, he is a master of hypocrisy and duplicity.

86   *the Lateran*   The imperial palace assigned by the first Christian emperor Constantine to be the residence of the Pope and Roman Curia. Its abandonment in favor of the Vatican, after the death of Boniface and the so-called Babylonian Captivity of the popes at Avignon, signals the end of the imperial papacy. Boniface's rivals, the Colonna family, lived close by. It was against them that he declared a crusade, not on the Jews and Saracens who were occupying the Holy Land. No member of the Colonna family had engaged in forbidden commerce in the Near East or fought in the ranks of the Mameluke sultan of Egypt when he conquered Acre in 1291. Not only were the Colonna Christians; both Giacomo and Pietro Colonna were cardinals of the Church.

94   *Constantine*   A legend recounted that the emperor Constantine (reigned 312–337) became a Christian after being cured of leprosy by Pope Sylvester (314–335), who lived, in an age when Christians were still persecuted, in a cave on Mount Soracte near Rome. Out of gratitude, Constantine was supposed to have made his notorious donation (XIX.115–17).

102   *Penestrino*   An archaic variant of the name of Palestrina, where the Colonnas had their stronghold. In December 1297 Boniface launched a crusade against his enemies; in September 1298 the defenders of besieged Palestrina, offered good terms, capitulated; and in June 1299, ignoring his promises, Boniface razed the city, leaving only the cathedral intact.

104   *two keys*   Boniface, a wilier trickster than our wily trickster, buttresses his spurious case by citing chapter and verse of Christ's gift of the keys to Peter, the first pope: "I will give to thee the keys of the kingdom of heaven. And whatsoever thou shalt bind upon earth, it shall be bound also in heaven: and whatsoever thou shalt loose upon earth, it shall be loosed also in heaven" (Matt. 16:19).

105   *my predecessor*   An ironical allusion to Pope Celestine V, who resigned from the papacy in December 1294, five months after his election—under pressure, it was rumored, from Boniface, who became his successor. The anonymous man, "who through cowardice made the Great Refusal" (III.60), and whom Dante saw among the uncommitted spirits in the Vestibule of Hell, is usually identified as Celestine.

111   *your High Seat*   The papal throne.

112   *Francis*   Saint Francis of Assisi, founder of the Franciscan order, which Guido had joined.

123   *a logician*   The devil, in giving a doctrinal lesson to a saint (and indirectly to a pope), has in fact demonstrated his command of scholastic syllogistic logic. Sin is a choice, an act of the will. For it to be forgiven, a conversion or change of will is needed. Repentance for what one is about to do cannot take place in advance. Ironically, this is one of the few overtly theological moments in the entire *Inferno*. Meanwhile, "hoist with his own petard" (Shakespeare, *Hamlet* III.iv.207), the wily Guido has met his match in the insidious Boniface—and in Dante, who is broadcasting his secret history.

Canto XXVIII

1–6   *Who could ever tell*   Dante protests that even a writer of prose, not constrained by the necessity to follow meter and a complex rhyme scheme, would be at a loss to describe the horrendous mutilations he now sees. The topos of ineffability, used here for the first time (and repeated with variations at the beginning of Canto XXXII) for the unspeakable horrors of lower Hell, will be a prominent rhetorical figure in presenting the opposite difficulty of speaking adequately about the sublimely indescribable delights of the *Paradiso*. Dante is echoing similar protestations in Virgil (*Aen.* VI.625–27) and Ovid (*Meta.* VIII.533–35).

7   *If all the people*   One hears an echo of the first lines of a *planh* or lament for the English king Henry III, *Si tuit li dol e il plor e il marrimen* ("If all the pain, the tears, and the suffering"), attributed to Occitan poet Bertran de Born, whose headless shade will address Dante at the end of this canto.

9   *the Trojans*   This refers to Aeneas and his Trojan followers, whose wars against the tribes of southern Latium are narrated by Virgil in the *Aeneid*. Some interpreters believe that "Trojans" is an anachronistic metomymy for "Romans," who are mentioned two lines later. But, since Dante's simile is meant to emphasize sheer numbers, it seems better not to subtract a people from his accumulation.

10   *the long campaign*   The high point of the Second Punic War, from the Carthaginian point of view, was the battle of Cannae near Barletta in Apulia in 216 B.C.E., at which the Roman army "perhaps suffered higher casualties in a single day's fighting than any other western army before or since" (John F. Lazenby,

"Cannae," *Oxford Classical Dictionary,* Third Edition, New York: Oxford University Press, 1996, p. 286). The dead have been estimated at between 40,000 and 45,000. According to proverbially infallible Roman historian Livy (Titus Livius, 59 B.C.E.–17 C.E.), the gold rings taken from the corpses as booty filled a bushel basket (fifth-century Christian historian Paulus Orosius, followed by Dante in the *Convivio,* says three bushel baskets). How well Dante actually knew Livy is a moot point.

14   *Robert Guiscard*   The Norman knight Robert of Hauteville (1015–1085), nicknamed Guiscard ("the Wily"), conquered Southern Italy from the Byzantines and the Lombards and was recognized as Duke of Apulia, Calabria, and Sicily by Pope Nicholas II in 1059. In 1084 Robert rescued Pope Gregory VII, who had been taken prisoner in Rome by Emperor Henry IV. Robert died the following year laying siege to the island of Cephalonia near Ithaca. Dante puts his soul among the militant spirits in the heaven of Mars (*Pd.* XVIII.48).

16   *Ceperano*   The descent of papal ally Charles of Anjou into Southern Italy through the pass of Ceperano was facilitated by the betrayal of Manfred's defending barons, who deserted their posts. Manfred, Hohenstaufen emperor Frederick II's bastard son, would himself die in the ensuing battle of Benevento (1266), which all but put paid to the Ghibelline cause.

17   *Tagliacozzo*   Conradin (1251–1268), the last in the Hohenstaufen line, was defeated at Tagliacozzo in August 1268 by the army of Charles of Anjou. Charles' military adviser Érard de Valéry ("old Alardo") outmaneuvered the imperial army by holding a part of his cavalry in reserve and having them attack just when Conradin's strategists, thinking they had won, broke ranks to pursue their apparently routed opponents. The sixteen-year-old Conradin was subsequently captured, tried, and executed in Naples by Charles of Anjou.

31   *Mohamed*   The wounds of Mohamed (570–632) and his cousin and son-in-law Ali ibn Abu Talib (597–660), described with a gruesome relish worthy of Lucan, are complementary. Dante makes Mohamed, the founder of Islam, the spokesman of the Sowers of Discord or schismatics. Dante's Christian sources claimed that, before his apostasy, Mohamed had been a Nestorian Christian (Nestorians believed in the separateness of Christ's human and divine natures). This made him, in their eyes, a divider of the Universal Church from within. Ali, the second convert to Islam, after Mohamed's wife Khadijah, was elected fourth caliph of the Muslim community in 656. Disputes after his assassination led to the schism, so to speak, and within the schism, the separation of Muslims into Sunni and Shia. The Shia reject the first three caliphates and regard Ali, the fourth caliph, as the only legitimate successor to Mohamed. The period of the Christian Crusades in the Near East, which began in 1095, was over before Dante was born.

56   *Fra Dolcino*   Dolcino Tornielli was the successor of Gerardo Segarelli as head of the Apostolic Brotherhood—a contemporary heretical sect that preached a return to the religious origins and refused to recognize the authority of the

hierarchy—founded by Segarelli in 1260 and subsequently condemned by the Roman Inquisition, founded in 1233. Segarelli was executed in 1300, Dolcino in 1307. When Pope Clement V declared a crusade against them, Dolcino and his brethren took refuge in a stronghold on Mount Zebello in Val Sesia, where they held out against their Novarese besiegers, led by the bishop of Vercelli, throughout the winter of 1306, but were forced to surrender for lack of food in the spring of 1307. Since the sinners can see into the future (in line 78, Pier da Medicina will refer to their "foresight"), Mohamed's warning would appear to be ironic; he knows Dolcino will inevitably be a fellow inmate of this bolgia before very long.

73   *Pier da Medicina*   The only early commentator who appears to speak with authority about this character is Benvenuto da Imola, who claims that he was from Medicina between Bologna and Ravenna and sowed discord between Guido da Polenta, lord of Ravenna, and Malatesta da Verrucchio, lord of Rimini. The two families were depicted as heraldic predators in the previous canto (XXVII.40–48).

75   *Vercelli to Marcabò*   This area spans the whole rich Po valley, from Vercelli in the far west to Marcabò in the far east. The latter was a castle, destroyed in 1309, built near the delta of the Po River from which the Venetians controlled river traffic.

76   *two best men of Fano*   Guido del Cassero, head of the Guelph faction, and the Ghibelline Angiolello da Carignano, two of the most prominent citizens of Fano, in the March of Ancona. We have no external account of the plot to drown them, which Dante describes so circumstantially, though we know that Malatestino Malatesta of Rimini (the "evil tyrant"), son of Malatesta da Verrucchio and half brother of Gianciotto and Paolo (Francesca's husband and lover, respectively—see note to V.74), had expansionist designs on Fano, which lay to his south.

79   *Cattolica*   A port town between Rimini and Pesaro, north of Fano.

82–83   *Cyprus and Majorca / Neptune never witnessed*   The two islands, situated, like Vercelli and Marcabò in line 75, at the farthest western and the farthest eastern points, this time of the Mediterranean Sea (identified with the sea god Neptune), stand for the extreme points of the known world. The expression, in other words, is the equivalent of "nowhere on earth."

85   *only one eye*   Blind in one eye, the evil tyrant of Rimini was known as Malatestino dell'Occhio (*occhio* is Italian for "eye"). His soul is destined for Cocytus, among the traitors.

90   *Focara*   A mountain promontory near Cattolica, famous among sailors for its stormy winds. The sardonic irony of this passage is clear: there is no use praying for a calm passage off the cape of Focara, because, by the time the ship reaches that point, Guido and Angiolello will already be at the bottom of the sea!

96   *This is the one*   The man who wished he had never set eyes on Rimini (or, in ancient times, Ariminum) was the Roman tribune Gaius Scribonius Curio, a turncoat who first supported Pompey against Caesar and then switched sides.

According to Lucan, "Curio of the reckless heart and venal tongue" (*Civil War* I.269) joined Caesar in Rimini, urging him to cross the Rubicon and march on Rome. Curio is condemned as an instigator of the Roman Civil War.

98–99   *if a man is prepared / he can only suffer injury by delay*   A paraphrase of Lucan's *semper nocuit differre paratis* ("delay is ever fatal to those who are prepared," *Civil War* I.281).

106   *Mosca*   Ghibelline Mosca dei Lamberti—like Farinata degli Uberti in Canto X, a perpetual exile from Florence—is the last of the five Florentine worthies about whose whereabouts Dante had questioned Ciacco in Canto VI. He speaks of himself in the third person. In 1215, the young Buondelmonte dei Buondelmonti broke off his engagement to a daughter of the Amidei clan to marry a Donati. Offended in their honor, the Amidei called a council of war to decide what to do. It was Mosca who uttered the famous phrase *Capo ha cosa fatta* ("What's done is done"), opting for the extreme remedy, death. Buondelmonte's Easter murder was generally taxed with having sparked the factional strife in Florence between Guelphs and Ghibellines.

109   *"And death to your sons"*   Mosca died in Reggio Emilia, where he had been elected *podestà,* in 1243. As he did to Farinata, with the news of the definitive eclipse of the Ghibelline cause, and to Cavalcante dei Cavalcanti, who interpreted Dante's ambiguous words to mean that his son Guido was dead, Dante adds to Mosca's suffering by informing him that by the year 1300 his family has become completely extinguished.

134   *Bertran de Born*   A famous twelfth-century Provençal troubadour, lord of Hautefort in the Périgord, and a vassal of the English king. He is praised as an outstanding poet of arms in Dante's *De vulgari eloquentia* (*On Eloquence in the Vernacular*). According to legend, he had incited Henry III (the "young king" of England) to rebel against his father, Henry II.

138   *Ahitophel*   Counselor to King David, he encouraged David's son Absalom to persist in his usurpation of the throne (2 Sam. 16:15–17:4), a persistence that led to Absalom's death.

Canto XXIX

9   *twenty-two miles*   In the next canto, the counterfeiter Master Adam will say that the next Bolgia, the Tenth, has a circumference of eleven miles, half that of the Ninth.

10   *the moon*   If the waning moon is at its nadir, below the feet of the pilgrims, then the sun must be already past its noontime zenith over Jerusalem in the hemisphere of land. It is between 1:00 and 2:00 p.m. on Saturday, April 9, 1300. In XX.127, when the pilgrims were in the Eighth Bolgia, eight or so hours earlier, Virgil remarked

that the moon had been full the night before, when Dante was lost in the dark wood, before Virgil came to his aid. Time is growing short because the time allotted to visit Hell—twenty-four hours—is running out. Only five or six hours remain.

20   *a spirit of my own blood*   Geri del Bello, who, as the first cousin of Dante's father, was Dante's first cousin once removed, will be named in line 27. One of the Guelphs exiled after the Ghibelline victory at Montaperti in 1260, he returned like them in 1267, after the death of Frederick II's son Manfred. Geri was tried and convicted for assault in Prato in 1280. In their commentaries to the *Inferno* and to the entire *Comedy,* respectively, Dante's sons Jacopo and Pietro both state that Geri was murdered by a Brodaio dei Sacchetti. His death was not avenged for thirty years. The feud between the Alighieri and the Sacchetti clans was settled in 1342 by the Duke of Athens, Walter of Brienne, whose lordship of Florence (1342–1343) would turn out to be a flash in the pan.

29   *Altaforte*   In Provençal *Autafort,* in French *Hautefort,* in Italian *Altaforte*— these were the names of the castle of Bertran de Born in northern Périgord. Ezra Pound's *Exultations* (1909) contains a poem "Sestina: Altaforte" written in the person of Bertran, with Pound's headnote "Dante Alighieri put this man in hell for that he was a stirrer-up of strife."

36   *makes me pity him*   Dante's compassion does not necessarily imply his approval of the aristocratic tradition of honor-based vendetta, according to which exacting adequate revenge on the offending party (or his descendants) for an injury or for the death of a relative was considered not merely a right, but a moral duty, and constituted a valid legal defense. Dante deplored the civil strife to which such customs gave rise. Saint Paul warned that justice is God's prerogative: "Vengeance belongeth to me, and I will repay. And again: The Lord shall judge his people" (Heb. 10.30).

47   *of Valdichiana and of Maremma*   Valdichiana and Maremma, both in southern Tuscany, as well as the island of Sardinia, were notoriously unhealthy and malaria ridden. The course of the river Chiana, originally a tributary of the Tiber, which stagnated in swamps and marshes in Dante's day, was later inverted, in part by nature, in part by hydraulic engineering, and the river was made to flow into the Arno.

57   *every falsifier*   The falsifiers we will meet in the Tenth Bolgia are divided into four categories: Falsifiers of Metals (Griffolino and Capocchio), of Persons (Gianni Schicchi and Myrrha), of Currency (Master Adam), and of Words (Putiphar's wife and Sinon the Greek).

59   *Aegina*   A Greek island in the Saronic Gulf, a bay of the Aegean Sea. When the island's inhabitants were destroyed by a plague sent by jealous Juno, their king Aeacus, son of Juno's wayward husband Jove by the nymph Aegina—for whom the island, previously called Oenopia, was renamed—entreated his divine father to repopulate his kingdom by transforming the colony of ants that lived in an old oak

into people. Thus was born the race of Myrmidons (from the Greek word for "ant"). Dante's source is Book VII of Ovid's *Metamorphoses.*

109   *I was from Arezzo*   The speaker has been identified by the early commentators as Griffolino d'Arezzo, an alchemist who is here because he sought to change base metals into gold (as he says in lines 118–20), though he was burned at the stake, sometime before 1272, for another reason. He foolishly claimed to credulous aristocrat Albero of Siena (who foolishly believed him) that he knew how to fly. When he failed to teach Albero the trick, the latter reported him to his protector and possibly illegitimate father (which would explain why he loved him like a son), the bishop of Siena, as a heretic.

116   *a Daedalus*   Among the many inventions of the ingenious Athenian Daedalus were the wings made of wax and feathers with which his son Icarus flew too close to the burning sun, causing them to melt. The juxtaposition of the name of Daedalus with Griffolino's own burning may be a sardonic joke.

122   *the Sienese*   Siena joins Lucca (XXI.40–42), Pistoia (XXV.10–15), Florence (XXVI.1–12)—and eventually Pisa XXXIII.79–90) and Genoa (XXXIII.151–57)—as the object of Dante's scorn and opprobrium, with the French thrown in for good measure.

126   *Stricca*   Either Stricca dei Salimbeni, who was *podestà* of Bologna in 1276 and 1286, or Stricca dei Tolomei, another Jovial Friar—in either case members of Sienese first families. Salimbeni's brother Niccolò was credited with introducing the exotic oriental spice of cloves—in Dante's view an expensive and sybaritic import—to Sienese cuisine. We have no details of Stricca's and Niccolò's activities, though making them an exception to the rule is clearly ironic, like excepting Bonturo Dati from the venality of Lucca's public servants in XXI.41. Siena is the garden in which such self-indulgent luxuries find fertile soil. The Sienese named by Capocchio are clearly not in this Bolgia. They may not even be dead.

130   *Caccia d'Asciano*   Caccianemico di Trovato degli Scialenghi, whose landed property was in Asciano, is another Sienese who irresponsibly squandered his substance. His companions were a well-known group of wastrels like himself who are said to have dilapidated their family fortunes—amounting all told to some 216,000 florins—in the space of two years. One member of the same "spendthrift band" who definitely is dead is Lano di Ricolfo Maconi, whom Dante saw pursued by black bitches through the wood of the Suicides (XIII.120).

132   *Abbagliato*   The nickname—a possible equivalent might be our slang expression "sucker"—of Bartolomeo dei Folcacchieri, brother of the Sienese comic poet Folcacchieri dei Folcacchieri.

136   *Capocchio*   A Florentine who, judging from what he says, was an acquaintance of Dante's. He was burned at the stake for alchemy in Siena in 1293. The early commentators, short on firsthand information, speculate that he may at some time have been a fellow student of the poet.

Canto XXX

1 *Juno's furious rage* Jealous Juno, wife of Jove, furious with her husband for his seduction of Semele, daughter of Cadmus, founder of Thebes, first arranged for the incineration of her rival. Then, because the couple had adopted Semele's son Bacchus, Juno incited the Fury Tisiphone to drive Athamas, the husband of Semele's sister Ino, mad. The gruesome story is told in Book IV of Ovid's *Metamorphoses.* The climax synthesized by Dante occurs in *Meta.* IV.512–30. The mad Athamas, calling on his comrades to spread their nets to capture the lioness and her cubs, hunted down his wife Ino as if she were a beast of prey. He seized their son Learchus from her arms and dashed out his brains, whereupon Ino fled, shrieking like a possessed bacchant, with their other son Melicertes in her arms, and leaped into the sea. The pit of Hell is no place for happy endings, so the rest of Ovid's story is of no interest to Dante here. Ino's grandmother Venus pleaded with Neptune to receive both mother and son among the sea gods. Neptune granted her prayer, and Ino and Melicertes were born again as, respectively, Leucothoë, the goddess of the spray, and Palaemon or Portunus, the god of ports.

16 *Hecuba* Dante's source is Ovid. In *Meta.* XIII, the Latin poet relates how, after the fall of Troy, Hecuba, Priam's queen, fell to Ulysses' lot as his slave. Priam had previously sent their youngest son Polydorus for safety to Thrace in the care of Polymestor, but he had made the mistake of sending treasure with him. When Polymestor got news of the Greek victory over the Trojans, he murdered Polydorus for his gold, throwing his body into the sea. The ghost of Achilles appeared to the Greeks when they landed in Thrace, demanding that Hecuba's daughter Polyxena, for whose love he would have been willing to desert the Greek cause, be sacrificed upon his tomb. After the sacrifice of Polyxena, Hecuba went down to the seashore to fetch water to wash her bloody corpse, only to find the dead body of her favorite son Polydorus on the beach. Hecuba secured an audience with Polymestor by offering more gold, but instead she put out his eyes. Pursued by the Thracians, who threw spears and stones at her, she ran after the stones, bit them, and barked like a dog. Hecuba was a paradigm of grief for Shakespeare too. Hamlet's remark about the Player's emotional involvement in her bereavement is proverbial: "What's Hecuba to him or he to Hecuba / That he should weep for her?" (*Hamlet* II.ii.559–60).

32 *Gianni Schicchi* Famous in Florentine lore for his talents as an impersonator, this member of the Cavalcanti clan took the place of Buoso Donati, who was already dead, and dictated a will favoring Buoso's nephew Simone, and bequeathing to himself Buoso's finest mare ("the queen of the herd" of line 43). Giacomo Puccini's 1918 one-act opera *Gianni Schicchi* is based on Dante's anecdote.

37 *Myrrha* The daughter of Cinyras, king of Cyprus, Myrrha was possessed by an unnatural passion for her father. With the help of her nurse, Myrrha was introduced into his bed in the dark as another person and became his lover. One night the unsuspecting Cinyras lit a torch and was horrified to discover that he was

sleeping with his daughter. Already pregnant, Myrrha fled his anger, taking refuge in Arabia. Nine months later, weeping, she besought the gods to end her misery, and they turned her into the aromatic resin-dripping myrrh tree that bears her name. Her child Adonis would be born from the tree's bark. This story is told in Book X of Ovid's *Metamorphoses*.

61   *Master Adam*   An expert counterfeiter in the employ of Count Guido I of Romena and his son, Guido II. Recent commentators identify him as Adam de Anglia, from England (or possibly from Brest in Brittany, under the English crown at the time).

65   *Casentino*   A lush enclosed Appenine valley near the source of the Arno River, north of Arezzo and southeast of Florence. The memory of the lush landscape of this *locus amoenus* ("pleasant place") adds to Master Adam's psychological suffering.

74   *John the Baptist*   The Florentine gold florin, first minted in 1252, was imprinted on the reverse with the image of the city's patron saint and on the obverse with the device of the fleur-de-lis. Master Adam was burned at the stake by the Florentines for debasing the currency in 1281.

77   *of Guido, of Alessandro, or of their brother*   The three "miserable" sons of Guido I of Romena were Guido II, Alessandro, and, in all probability, Aghinolfo. A fourth son, Ildebrandino, was bishop of Arezzo. Guido II died in 1281, the same year as Master Adam, and his shade, since Master Adam counterfeited on his orders, is somewhere in this same bolgia.

78   *the springs of Branda*   The early commentators are divided in their identification of this spring. Some take it to refer to a spring near Romena that has since dried up; others take it to allude to a copious public fountain in Siena, the ancient Fonte Branda, first documented in 1081 and rebuilt in its present architectural form in 1246.

86   *eleven miles around*   In the previous canto we learned that the circumference of the Ninth Bolgia measured twenty-two miles, exactly twice this one.

90   *three carats worth of dross*   A genuine florin was supposed to contain twenty-four carats of gold. Master Adam was melting down fine gold florins and adding three carats of base metal to create an alloy, thereby making a profit of 12 percent.

97   *the woman who accused Joseph*   The wife of the Egyptian eunuch Putiphar, the slave Joseph's master, attempted to seduce Joseph and, when she failed, accused him to her husband of trying to seduce her (Gen. 39:6–23). She and Sinon appear here as Falsifiers of Words, or liars.

98   *Sinon, the lying Greek*   Having drawn the Trojan Horse before the gates of the city, the Greeks pretended to abandon their siege of Troy and sailed off to Tenedos, leaving Sinon behind to be captured by the Trojans. The wily prisoner, a consummate liar, convinced the Trojans that the horse was a votive offering made by

the despairing Greeks in reparation for the sacrilegious theft of the Palladium. "And so through Sinon's treacherous art / his story was believed, and we were taken / with cunning, captured with forced tears" (*Aen.* II.195–96).

129   *Narcissus' mirror*   A metonymy for a pool of cool water. The handsome Narcissus, Ovid tells us, fell in love with his own reflection in a stream and pined away, obsessed with looking at himself. Even beyond death, he found in the Styx a pool in which to gaze upon his image (*Meta.* III.504–5).

Canto XXXI

4   *the spear of Achilles*   The spear the Greek hero Achilles inherited from his father Peleus was capable of healing, with a second touch, the wound it had made.

16   *Charlemagne*   King of the Franks (742–814 C.E.) and founder of the Holy Roman Empire. The most famous of the medieval epic *chansons de geste,* the twelfth-century *Song of Roland,* distantly based on a historical event that occurred in 778 C.E., recounts how the rearguard of Charlemagne's army was betrayed by the traitor Ganelon (see XXXII.122) and routed by the Saracens of Spain at Roncesvalles in the Pyrenees. Their commander Count Roland underestimated the danger and, though urged to do so by his comrade-in-arms Olivier, refused to sound the Olifant, his ivory horn, to call for help until it was too late. By the time he blew it, his hopelessly outnumbered army had been slaughtered. Roland died in a last superhuman effort to warn Charlemagne, which split the horn and burst his temples. The pilgrim Dante will be shown the souls of Roland and Charlemagne among the heroically militant spirits in the heaven of Mars in *Pd.* XVIII.43.

40   *Monteriggioni*   A hilltop fortress town eight miles north of Siena, built by the Sienese in the thirteenth century as an outpost against Florentine expansion. The circular walls with their fourteen symmetrically placed towers, whose imposing ruins can still be seen, were added after the Ghibelline victory at the battle of Montaperti in 1260.

45   *thunder of Jove*   The Gigantes or Giants were the sons of Uranus, the god of the heavens, and Gaia, the earth goddess. They attempted to scale Mount Olympus, home of the gods, and were laid low by Jove's thunderbolt in the Gigantomachy or "the fight at Phlegra" (see note to XIV.58).

51   *Mars*   The Roman god of war. At XIII.143 Mars was referred to obliquely as the first pagan patron of Florence, preceding John the Baptist.

55   *a cunning mind*   A human mind, that is—the divine gift that distinguishes us from the brute beasts like the whale and the elephant (and makes Fraud a graver sin than Violence).

59   *the pine cone*   The ancient bronze pine cone, about eleven feet in height, that in Dante's day stood in the square outside Saint Peter's basilica and now stands

in the gardens of the Vatican Museum. It was brought to Saint Peter's, either from Hadrian's Mausoleum or from the Pantheon, by Pope Symmachus (498–514 c.e.).

63   *three Frisians*   The inhabitants of Friesland or Frisia in the northern Netherlands, between the Scheldt and Weser rivers, were proverbially tall.

65   *thirty full hand spans*   Dante's *palmo* ("hand span") measured about 24 centimeters or almost 9.5 inches. Dante gives rough dimensions for the upper part of the Giant's body, from the waist to the neck and from the neck to the top of the head. Altogether, counting the lower part, hidden by the edge of the pit in which he stands, he would be twice as tall.

67   "Raphèl maí amècche zabí almi"   The Giant's words (like those of Plutus, guardian of the Avaricious and Prodigal in VII.1) are, as Virgil points out, incomprehensible, as befits the architect of the Tower of Babel, whose destruction by God resulted in the confusion of tongues. This has not stopped Dante's exegetes from trying to make sense of them. The construction of Babel is seen as the biblical equivalent of the Giant's defiance of the pagan gods.

71   *stick to your horn*   In his essay entitled "Le chant des géants" (*Lectura Dantis Internazionale, Letture dell'Inferno,* a cura di V. Vettori, Milan: Marzorati, 1963, pp. 274–307), French critic André Pézard has pointed to an interesting passage from the epistles of Paul, where he sets prophecy above speaking strange tongues, that brings together garbled trumpet and garbled words: "For if the trumpet give an uncertain sound, who shall prepare himself to the battle? So likewise you, except you utter by the tongue plain speech, how shall it be known what is said? For you shall be speaking into the air" (1 Cor. 14:8–9). The parodic intent behind the Giant's five meaningless words may be further illuminated by another verse from the same context: "But in the church I had rather speak five words with my understanding, that I may instruct others also; than ten thousand words in a tongue" (1 Cor. 14:19).

77   *Nimrod*   In Gen. 10:8, Nimrod was the son of Chus, who was the son of Cham, fathered by Noah. That he was a Giant and the instigator of the Tower of Babel, built in the plain of Senaar, are later traditions based on misunderstanding of the biblical text and on inference. The building of the tower, "the top whereof may reach to heaven" (Gen. 11:4), and its subsequent destruction by God, was read as a parallel to the myth of the overweening Giants' challenge to the pagan gods. Nimrod has a horn because the Bible identifies him as a hunter.

94   *Ephialtes*   With his brother Otus, one of the Aloadae, twin sons of Neptune and Iphimedeia and foster sons of Aloeus, "who tried / to tear open the sky and pull Jupiter down" (*Aen.* VI.582–84). They grew nine inches every month and were nine years old when they undertook to unseat the gods.

99   *mammoth Briareus*   Dante's adjective *smisurato* renders Statius' *immensus* (*Thebaid* II.596)—both mean "immeasurable." Statius devotes several lines to Bri-

areus, comparing his zeal against the gods with that of Tydeus (see XXXII.130) in battle against Eteocles' warriors.

101 *Antaeus* This invincible Giant wrestler, son of Neptune and Gaia, lived in Libya, where he finally met his match in Hercules, who held him suspended in the air in his "iron grip," away from the earth (his mother's element, whence he drew his strength) and strangled him.

115 *in Zama's fateful valley* The traditional North African site of the great Carthaginian general Hannibal's final defeat by Scipio Africanus in 202 B.C.E. The mythical Antaeus was supposed to have frequented the valley of Zama long before the historical meeting there of Hannibal and Scipio.

123 *icy Cocytus* The frozen lake of Cocytus, in which the Traitors are punished in various sectors, comparable to the divisions of the Seventh Circle of the Violent. In the *Aeneid,* Cocytus is one of the rivers of Avernus, but it is not frozen. In Canto XIV, in his description of the Old Man of Crete, whose tears are the source of the rivers of Hell, Virgil had named Cocytus without elaborating further (XIV.119–20). We will eventually learn that it is the chilling blasts produced by the wings of Lucifer or Satan that freeze its waters.

124 *Tityos or Typhon* The body of Tityos, another son of Gaia or Earth, is stretched over nine full acres in Virgil's pit of Tartarus "And a monstrous vulture with a hooked beak / gnaws away at his immortal liver / and tortured entrails" (*Aen.* VI.597–99). Typhon, taller than the tallest mountain, was the most monstrous of Gaia's offspring. He was alleged to have been crushed by Jove under Mount Aetna in Sicily, where his fiery breath was adduced to explain the mountain's volcanic activity—a theory Dante rejects in favor of a scientific explanation in *Pd.* VIII.70.

137 *the tower of Garisenda* The shorter of the two landmark leaning towers— it was built in 1110 by the Garisenda family—that stand in Piazza di Porta Ravegnana in the center of Bologna. The older tower, built by the Asinelli, is more than twice as tall (320 feet) and leans half as far. The 156-foot Garisenda tower in fact, whose construction was quickly abandoned because of a faulty foundation, and whose top had to be dismantled in the 1400s, already leans threateningly over someone standing beneath it. When a cloud passes over it, one has the optical illusion that it is actually falling. Dante shows his familiarity with Bologna, a European center of learning and legal studies in the Middle Ages, on more than one occasion.

143 *Lucifer and Judas* We will encounter them in Canto XXXIV.

Canto XXXII

1 *the harsh and grating rhymes* In a metatextual rhetorical ploy that is the opposite of the "overgoing" boasts of Canto XXV, but which displays the same

calculated clinical detachment, the poet's apparent confession of his inadequacy to describe (to "press out more fully all the juice") the lowest circle of all actually calls attention to his stylistic resourcefulness and mastery. His is certainly not the tongue of an infant crying for his parents. The rhymes of the Italian text could not in fact be more "harsh and grating" (loaded with median consonants), as "stony," material, and grotesquely cacophonous as the subject matter with which they deal. Dante professes a poetic of adequation of style ("the telling") to content ("the fact"), and its effects on the language of the *Inferno* have already been visible at least from Canto VII on (the rhyming word *chiocce,* translated here as "grating," made its first appearance, in the feminine singular *chioccia,* in VII.2, where it is rendered as "cackling").

11 *Amphion* One of the twin sons of Jove and Antiope, daughter of Nycteus, king of Thebes. In a myth that Dante was familiar with from Statius and Ovid (*Ars amatoria* III.394–99), the poet Amphion borrowed Apollo's lyre and, aided by the Muses (the "ladies" of line 10), charmed the stones of the Tyrian mountains to levitate and build the walls of Thebes. The myth is alluded to several times in Statius' *Thebaid,* in particular in X.873–77, where the blasphemer Capaneus (whom we saw spread-eagled in Canto XIV) has scaled the walls of Thebes and boastfully mocks the legend of their construction. Dante invokes the Muses to assist him as a poet the way they assisted Amphion.

15 *better had you been born* A veiled reference to Matt. 26:24: "But woe to that man by whom the Son of man shall be betrayed: it were better for him, if that man had not been born."

19 *a voice* This speaker is never identified.

28–29 Tambura and Pietrapana are two peaks in the marble-bearing Apuan Alps in northern Tuscany.

33 *dreams of gleaning* The peasant girl dreams of gathering the loose ears of wheat left in the fields by the reapers at harvest time, in summer. The season evoked by the simile is in contrast to Cocytus' eternal winter.

52 *Another* The sarcastic volunteer who betrays the identity of the two trapped shades guilty of reciprocal treachery and fratricide will identify himself in line 68 as Camiscion dei Pazzi.

56 *Bisenzio* A tributary that joins the Arno River upstream from Florence, on whose banks stood the castles of Vernio and La Cerbaia, whose possession was one of the bones of contention between the two shades locked chest to chest, Napoleone and Alessandro degli Alberti, the two sons of Alberto, count of Mangona. Their savage enmity in death is reminiscent of that between the Theban brothers Eteocles and Polynices, mentioned in XXVI.54. As we will see, the canto begins and ends with two different pairs of sinners, each locked together in a paroxysm of undying hatred.

59 *Caïna* The first zone of Cocytus, named after the biblical Cain, who betrayed and slew his brother Abel, where those who treacherously procured the deaths of their kinsmen are punished. In Canto V, Francesca da Rimini said that Caïna was awaiting her husband, who had killed his brother Paolo and herself (V.107). As pointed out earlier, in the note to XI.55–66, citing chapter and verse, Dante divides the Traitors into categories that correspond to those still recognized by Shakespeare in his *Macbeth*.

61 *Not the one* Mordred, a character from the Arthurian legend. King Arthur's son or nephew (accounts vary), he attempted to usurp his kingdom. He was slain in battle by Arthur, who struck him so deep a blow that the sun shone through the wound, wounding, so to speak, his shadow on the ground.

63 *Focaccia* Nickname of Vanni dei Cancellieri, a violent White Guelph from Pistoia. The early commentators suggest that he killed his father or his uncle. A Pistoian contemporary chronicle informs us that he murdered his cousin Detto dei Cancellieri, who belonged to the Black Guelph faction. Focaccia and Black Guelph Vanni Fucci (XXIV.122 et seq.) would have been members of rival clans in Pistoia.

65 *Sassol Mascheroni* A notorious Tuscan traitor who murdered his nephew to steal his inheritance. His punishment in the world had been exemplary. He was rolled through the streets in a barrel whose sides were pierced with nails and his mangled body was then decapitated.

68 *Camiscion dei Pazzi* Motivated like most of his fellows by greed or cupidity, Alberto dei Pazzi, known as Camiscion Camiscione, stabbed his kinsman Ubertino dei Pazzi in the back.

69 *I wait for Carlino* The act of treachery that will be committed by Camiscion's kinsman Carlino dei Pazzi two years from now, in 1302, will be worse than his own, since Carlino will betray not merely a family member but his entire party, thereby earning a place in the second, lower and more shameful sector of Cocytus, called Antenora (see line 89). A White Guelph, Carlino sold the castle he was defending to its Black Guelph besiegers for 4,000 gold florins, obtaining immunity for himself but causing the deaths of many of his White allies. With self-serving infernal calculus, Camiscion figures that his own opprobrium will be mitigated by the more heinous crime of his relative.

81 *avenge Montaperti* The speaker's identity will be betrayed by a vindictive companion in the ice, whom he will immediately repay in kind. He is Bocca degli Abati, a Florentine Guelph who at the battle of Montaperti near Siena treacherously severed the hand of the Guelph standard-bearer, whose standard served as a rallying point, thereby causing the confusion that led to the Ghibelline victory. The graphic clash between pilgrim and shade, in which Dante is infected by the savagery all around him, recalls in a far more violent key the relatively civil exchange between Dante and Farinata in Canto X, in which the memory of the battle of

Montaperti ("The great devastation and the slaughter / that dyed the waters of the Arbia red," X.85–86) also played a central role.

89   *Antenora*   Named for the Trojan Antenor, presented positively in Homer's *Iliad* (of which Dante did not have firsthand knowledge) as wise and just in council and in favor of avoiding further conflict by returning Helen to the Greeks. He is mentioned in passing in the *Aeneid,* but an influential note in Servius' fundamental fourth-century commentary on Virgil's epic, based on an independent Greek source, claimed that Antenor was a traitor to Troy, complicit with the Greeks in the theft of the Palladium and the ruse of the Trojan Horse (see XXVI.59–63). The transition from Caïna to Antenora occurred in line 70, before the pilgrim kicked Bocca.

116   *the one from Duera*   Buoso da Duera, the Ghibelline ruler of Cremona, was instructed in 1265 by Manfred, son of the emperor Frederick II, to check the advance of the army of the pope's French ally Charles of Anjou on the Oglio River near Parma. Instead, he offered such feeble resistance that he was accused (an accusation that Dante tacitly endorses) of having accepted a bribe ("the silver of the French") to let them by.

119   *the Beccheria*   In 1258 Tesauro dei Beccheria, a cleric originally from Pavia, who was Pope Alexander IV's legate in Tuscany, was accused by the ruling Guelphs of plotting the return of the Ghibellines and publicly beheaded. The Ghibellines would return two years later in 1260 under Farinata degli Uberti after their bloody victory at Montaperti.

121   *Gianni de' Soldanieri*   A Ghibelline turncoat who, after Manfred's death at Benevento, went over to the Guelphs, leading the people's revolt against the rule, in the role of nonnative *podestà,* of the Jovial Friars Catalano and Loderingo (see XXIII.104–7). He was expelled from the city, as were the rest of the Ghibellines a year later in 1267.

122   *Ganelon and Tebaldello*   Ganelon is a literary figure, the archetypal traitor in the twelfth-century French *Song of Roland,* who betrayed his stepson, the legendary hero Count Roland to the Saracen king Marsile. Ambushed by the Moors in the valley of Roncesvalles, by the time Roland resolved to blow his ivory horn and summon back the main army, his 20,000 soldiers had already been massacred (see XXXI.16–18). Ganelon was found guilty of treason and attached to four horses, which tore him limb from limb. Tebaldello degli Zambrasi, a Ghibelline from Faenza, betrayed his city twice. On the occasion described here, in November 1280, to avenge an alleged affront committed by the Ghibelline Lambertazzi clan in exile from Bologna (about thirty miles north on the ancient Aemilian Way), he opened Faenza's gates in the dawn hours to their Guelph enemies, the rival Geremei family. His death in the "long ordeal" (XXVII.43)—the 1282 siege in which Forlì, fifteen miles south of Faenza, was defended by Guido da Montefeltro—was interpreted as an act of divine justice.

130 *Tydeus* Wounded to death by a spear thrown by Melanippus, Tydeus begged for his mortal enemy's dying body to be brought to him. Capaneus retrieved it from the battlefield and carried it to the dying Tydeus. Whereupon Tydeus commanded that the head be severed and proceeded to gnash and feed upon it, "as if it were some spattered carnal melon" (Seamus Heaney, "Ugolino," in *Field Work,* London: Faber and Faber, 1979).

Canto XXXIII

4 *You want me to renew* The subtext for the sinner's first words (a subtext referred to again below in lines 40–42) is the exordium of Aeneas' account to Dido describing the fall of Troy: "My Queen, you are asking me to relive / unspeakable sorrow. . . . / What Myrmidon / or Dolopian, what brutal soldier of Ulysses / could tell such a tale and refrain from tears? . . . But if you are so passionate to learn / of our misfortunes, to hear a brief account / of Troy's last struggle— although my mind / shudders to remember and recoils in pain, / I will begin" (*Aen.* II.3–16). The same passage was re-echoed by Francesca da Rimini as she prepared to narrate how she and Paolo first discovered their latent desires (*Inf.* V.121–26).

7 *But if my words* Dante's offer to renew their fame has tempted many of the souls. In the case of the present speaker, however, it is not the thought of his own fame that eggs him on so much as that of the infamy he can bring to his enemy. Conspicuously absent is any intention to—in the words of the Lord's Prayer— forgive the trespasser his trespasses.

13 *Count Ugolino* Ugolino della Gherardesca, count of Donoratico and *podestà* of the maritime republic of Pisa, was born in the early decades of the thirteenth century and died in 1289, after nine months of imprisonment with two of his sons and two nephews in the Gualandi tower ("the Tower of Hunger") in Piazza dei Cavalieri in Pisa. Though he belonged to a traditionally Ghibelline family, he changed sides in 1275 and formed an alliance with his son-in-law Giovanni Visconti, leader of the Pisan Guelphs. Ugolino commanded the Pisan fleet in the disastrous war against Genoa and became *podestà* of Pisa in 1284. When the three Guelph cities of Florence, Lucca, and Genoa formed an anti-Pisan league, he ceded several of Pisa's defensive outposts (the "castles" of line 86) to the Florentines and Lucchesi—an unpopular move that led to him being accused as a traitor. To buttress his rule, in 1285 he invited his nephew Nino Visconti (a friend of Dante's, whom the pilgrim will meet in Purgatory) to govern by his side, but in 1288 the Ghibellines led by Archbishop Ruggieri succeeded in seizing power. According to the version of the facts followed by Dante, Ruggieri persuaded Ugolino to return to Pisa from his country stronghold with false promises (a pact that may have included Ugolino's betrayal of his associate Nino Visconti), thereafter proceeding to

imprison and starve him to death along with his children. We should not allow the compassion stirred by his eloquent account to make us forget that he too is condemned by Dante as a traitor.

14   *Archbishop Ruggieri*   Ruggieri degli Ubaldini, nephew of Cardinal Ottaviano Ubaldini (the "Cardinal" of X.120), left Bologna to become archbishop of Pisa in 1278. In 1288, as previously stated, he took advantage of the release of the prominent Ghibellines previously taken prisoner by the Genoese to organize a conspiracy against Ugolino and his co-ruler Nino Visconti, with the horrible consequences described in the text. In the power vacuum that followed Ugolino's captivity and death, Archbishop Ruggieri was able to take over the civil as well as the spiritual government of the city. In 1289, however, Pisa chose Guido da Montefeltro, the protagonist of Canto XXVII, as its *podestà;* and in 1295, Ruggieri, after being stripped of his church rank and condemned to life imprisonment by an ecclesiastical court, ended his days in jail.

29   *a wolf and its cubs*   In Ugolino's dream, which appears—see line 45—to be shared by his children, Ruggieri is master of the hunt, his Ghibelline allies (the Gualandi, Sismondi, and Lanfranchi families) are the hounds, and Ugolino and his children are the quarry. In all likelihood, Dante allows Ugolino to exaggerate their young ages to add to the pathos and the horror.

50   *my poor little Anselm*   The historical Anselmo was the son of Ugolino's son Guelfo II della Gherardesca and therefore Ugolino's grandson. He was indeed the youngest victim (probably about fifteen) and the only true adolescent among them.

67   *Gaddo*   The elder of the two sons of Ugolino who were captured with him. He had come of age and was already a count. Neither he nor the others were in fact nearly as young as the narrative makes them sound. Ugolino's other son was Uguiccione, mentioned below in line 89.

69   *Father, Father, why don't you help me?*   The phrasing of the child's plea echoes the last words of Jesus Christ on the Cross: "*Eli, Eli, lamma sabacthani?* that is, My God, my God, why hast thou forsaken me?" (Matt. 27:46). Another, probably deliberate, reminder of Christ's cross will come in the phrasing of line 87.

75   *Then starvation finished what sorrow could not*   A famously riddling line: *Poscia, piú che 'l dolor, poté 'l digiuno.* Does Ugolino mean that starvation killed him where grief had failed, or that hunger proved more powerful than grief and drove him to cannibalize his children? The suggestion, with its almost parodic Eucharistic overtones ("Take ye, and eat. *This is my body,*" Matt. 26:26), has already been introduced by the children themselves in lines 61–63.

79–80   *the fair lands / where* sì *is heard*   A circumlocution designating Italy. In his treatise on literary language, *De vulgari eloquentia (On Eloquence in the Vernacular,* I.viii.5), Dante distinguishes Italy from Provence and France by the different ways they each say "yes" (respectively, *oc* and *oïl,* as opposed to *sì*).

82 *Capraia and Gorgona* Two small islands that belonged to Pisa in the Tuscan archipelago, off Piombino and Livorno, respectively, north of the larger island of Elba. The Arno River traverses Pisa before debouching into the Tyrrhenian.

88 *a modern Thebes* Ancient Thebes, capital of Boeotia, had a bloody history. Its kings—Laius, Oedipus, Eteocles, and Polynices—were known for their misfortunes. The episode of Ugolino began by comparing his ravaging the head of Ruggieri with the similar cannibalism of Tydeus, who gnawed on the head of Melanippus in Statius' *Thebaid*. A legend attributed the founding of Pisa to Pelops, son of Tantalus, king of Thebes. Tantalus served up his son Pelops to the gods in a stew.

89 *Brigata* Nino della Gherardesca, known as Brigata, was the elder brother of Anselmo, and a grandson of Ugolino. In attributing such childlike innocence to the other members of Ugolino's family who died with him, Dante the narrator is either misinformed or disingenuous.

111 *that you are condemned* Once again, one of the shades assumes that Dante and Virgil have been assigned to this circle along with him.

118 *Fra Alberigo* Though his soul is in Cocytus, Alberigo dei Manfredi, a member of the Guelph oligarchy of Faenza and yet another of the Jovial Friars (like Fra Gomita in Canto XXII and the Bolognese hypocrites Catalano del Malvolti and Loderingo degli Andalò in Canto XXIII), was still apparently alive in 1300, the date of Dante's journey. In 1285 he invited his relatives Manfredo and Alberghetto dei Manfredi to a banquet. When he called for his servants to bring in the fruit, it was the signal for them to rush in and stab his guests to death. "To be served some of Alberigo's fruit" was the thirteenth-century proverbial equivalent of "to buy the farm."

124 *Ptolomaea* The third zone of Cocytus, in which traitors to the laws of hospitality are punished. The name probably derives from that of the biblical figure of Ptolemee, son of Abobus and captain in the plain of Jericho, who invited Simon with Mathathias and Judas his sons to a feast in the fortress of Doch and, when they had drunk plentifully, had his men take their weapons and slay them. "And he committed a great treachery in Israel, and rendered evil for good" (1 Macc. 16:17). A less convincing hypothesis is that it derives from the name of Ptolemy XIII, Cleopatra's brother and husband, whose ministers assassinated his guest Pompey the Great when he fled to Egypt in 48 B.C.E. after the battle of Pharsalus.

126 *Atropos* One of the three Parcae or Fates. Clotho spins the thread of life, Lachesis measures it, and Atropos cuts it off with her shears. The souls of these heinous traitors are not given any more time on earth in which to repent their sins.

138 *Ser Branca Doria* Member of a Ghibelline family prominent in Genoese and Sardinian politics, born in the Ligurian port city c. 1233. After inviting him as a guest, he murdered his father-in-law Don Michel Zanche—whom Dante condemns among the Grafters in the Fifth Bolgia of the Eighth Circle (see note to

XXII.88)—in order to take possession of the judgeship of Logudoro in Sardinia. His shade was immediately whisked off to Hell—so fast that he got there even before his victim. Branca's act of betrayal is not recorded by contemporary historians, with the result that early commentators differ as to the date. For some it happened in 1275, for others in 1290. In the former case he would have been without a soul for a quarter of a century, in the latter for a decade.

154   *a shade from Romagna*   Faenza, where Fra Alberigo was from, is in the Romagna region. The pilgrim's failure to "ease [his] pain," as promised in line 116, is of a piece with his "accidentally" kicking Bocca in the face in the previous canto (XXXII.78).

Canto XXXIV

1   Vexilla regis prodeunt inferni   "*The banners of the king of Hell advance.*" The line is an adaptation to the present circumstances, almost a parody—the last word *inferni* ("of Hell") is Dante's own addition—of the first line of a Latin liturgical hymn to the Holy Cross by the sixth-century bishop of Poitiers Venantius Fortunatus: *Vexilla regis prodeunt, / fulget crucis mysterium, / quo carne carnis conditor / suspensus est patibulo* ("The banners of the king advance, / the mystery of the cross shines forth, / by which the founder of our flesh / hangs by his flesh from the gallows tree"). The banners of the king of Heaven bear the image of the Cross, the Christian image of salvation; the banners of Satan, the Prince of Darkness, are his six wings, which characterized him, before his rebellion against his Creator, as one of the Seraphim, the highest order of angels (Isa. 6:2). Now, unfledged and batlike, flapping mechanically, they produce the icy winds that Dante asked about in the previous canto and that make Lower Hell freeze over. This is a world of silence where, until Dante's request for clarification in lines 100–105, only Virgil speaks.

20   *Dis*   The name is the Latin variant of that of the Greek god of the Underworld, Hades. Dante entered the City of Dis with the help of the Heavenly Messenger in Canto XI. He now finds himself in the presence of its ruler. Interestingly, the more common appellation "Satan" is never used in the *Comedy*, except perhaps in the unintelligible challenge of Dante's Pluto, the warden of the Avaricious and Prodigal in the Fourth Circle: *Pape Satàn, pape Satàn aleppe!* (VII.1). Other names used for Satan are Lucifer (line 103) and Beelzebub (line 128).

34   *If he was as beautiful*   The story of the defeat of the rebellious angels, led by the fairest angel of all, Lucifer (Milton's Satan), which forms the antecedent to *Paradise Lost,* is not found in the Old Testament, though in a passage from Isaiah we read: "How art thou fallen from heaven, O Lucifer, who didst rise in the morning? How art thou fallen to the earth, that didst wound the nations? And thou saidst in thy heart: I will ascend into heaven, I will exalt my throne above the stars of

God. I will sit in the mountain of the covenant, in the sides of the north" (Isa. 14:12–13). Because Christ's words in Luke 10:18 ("I saw Satan like lightning falling from heaven") seemed to echo the prophet's words, the words of Isaiah were referred to Satan by some Church Fathers.

38   *three faces*   The colors of Dis' three hideous faces—red, whitish yellow, and black—are allegorical inventions inspired by the liturgical color symbolism of the Church, but, like the other allegories to which Dante does not provide a key, their precise meaning is moot. Most of the early commentators see "the emperor of the world of pain" (line 28) as the antithesis of "the Emperor who reigns on high" (I.124—Virgil's periphrasis for God) and his three faces as a parody of the attributes of the three Persons of the Trinity, "DIVINE POWER, SUPREME WISDOM, AND LOVE PRIMORDIAL" (III.5–6)—in other words, impotence, ignorance, and hatred.

62   *Judas Iscariot*   Mangled in Dis' central mouth, the apostle who betrayed Jesus Christ to the chief priests (Matt. 26:14–16, Mark 14:10–11, Luke 22:3–6), thereby setting in motion the events that would lead to the Passion and Death of the Messiah, and then proceeded to take his own life, is the sinner of sinners.

65   *Brutus*   Marcus Junius Brutus, the republican murderer of Julius Caesar, who loved Brutus as a son. Brutus and Cassius (Caius Cassius Longinus, mentioned in line 67) were the two leaders of the successful conspiracy to assassinate Caesar in 44 B.C.E., soon after he named himself dictator for life. Dante considered Caesar the first Roman emperor and not, as was in fact the case, Octavian Augustus, Caesar's adopted son. Pursued by the avengers of Caesar, Mark Antony and Octavian, Cassius and Brutus were defeated at Philippi in 42 B.C.E. and committed suicide. The presence of Brutus and Cassius alongside Judas confirms the equal importance Dante accords to the Roman Empire and the Roman Christian Church, both symbiotic elements in God's plan to save the world. All three, then, could be said to have betrayed Divine Providence.

67   *so powerful in stature*   Shakespeare's "lean and hungry look" (*Julius Caesar* I.ii) is closer to Plutarch's description of "spare Cassius," which, since Plutarch wrote in Greek, Dante could not have known.

68   *night is coming on*   On earth, night is falling—it is about 7:00 p.m. on Holy Saturday (April 9, 1300). Twenty-four hours have elapsed since the journey began at dusk on Good Friday (April 8, 1300), as we were told in the opening lines of Canto II. At this point the narrative speeds up and twelve more hours will go by in fewer than thirty lines.

96   *the sun is climbing*   It is now 7:30 a.m. on Easter Sunday, April 10, 1300. Tierce, the third "hour" of the canonical day, began at 6:00 and ended at 9:00 a.m. Dante's Italian specifies that the sun is climbing toward *mezza terza* ("half tierce"). This is, incidentally, Virgil's first reference to the sun when telling the time. Previous references had been to the moon or the stars (XI.113–14, XX.124–26,

XXIX.10). This is fitting because the wayfarers are at last ascending out of Hell toward the light of day.

111   *the point to which all weights are drawn*   The center of gravity, not only of the Earth, but, since the Earth is at the center of Dante's geocentric system, of the entire Universe.

114–15   *under whose zenith / the Man was slain*   Jesus Christ, the only man who was born without Original Sin and lived a sinless life, was condemned to death and crucified at Jerusalem, which, according to Dante's Christian geography, stood at the center of the northern hemisphere of land. At its antipodes, in the center of the southern hemisphere of water, lay the island of Purgatory. As will be explained in the following lines, the convex conical land mass of Purgatory corresponds in fact to the concave conical cavity of Hell. The impact on the Earth of the huge bulk and weight of Satan created the division of the two hemispheres into land and water, as well as the crater of Hell and the mountain of Purgatory.

117   *Judecca*   The fourth and last zone of Cocytus, named after Judas the archtraitor, where Dis and his victims were confined, described earlier in the canto but named here for the first time.

130   *a rivulet*   Most commentators identify this unnamed stream as Lethe, the river of forgetfulness, which carries down into Hell the sins that the penitent souls have purged by climbing Mount Purgatory and whose memory they have washed away in the purification ritual—a kind of second baptism—that they undergo in the Earthly Paradise at the mountain's summit.

139   *stars*   Each of the three canticles ends symmetrically with the word "stars" (*Purgatorio:* "ready and willing to climb up to the stars"; *Paradiso:* "the love that moves the sun and the other stars").

Index of the Damned

Denizens of Hell—human, mythological, and angelic; former, present, and future—according to Dante. Names in roman type denote characters referred to by name in the translation at least once; names in *italics* denote characters referred to in the translation only by locution. Asterisks denote former dwellers in Limbo, saved by their faith in the coming Messiah.